PILGRIMS OF THE ANDES

Smithsonian Series in Ethnographic Inquiry

Other Books in the Series

PILGRIMS
OF THE ANDES

REGIONAL CULTS IN CUSCO

MICHAEL J. SALLNOW

Smithsonian Institution Press

Washington, D.C.   London

Library of Congress Cataloging-in-Publication Data

Sallnow, Michael J., 1949
  Pilgrims of the Andes.

(Smithsonian series in ethnographic inquiry)
Bibliography: p.
1. Pilgrims and pilgrimages—Peru—Cusco (Dept.)
2. Shrines—Peru—Cusco (Dept.)
3. Cults—Peru—Cusco (Dept.)
4. Cusco (Peru : Dept.)—Religious life and customs.
I. Title.   II. Series.
BL2590.P5S25   1987   263'.042'8537   87-43043
ISBN 0-87474-826-7 (alk. paper)

British Cataloging-in-Publication data is available.

To my parents

Contents

CONTENTS

FIGURES

PLATES

CONTENTS

Preface

The ethnographic foundations for this study were laid in the course of eighteen months' fieldwork in the Peruvian Andes, of which twelve months, from March 1973 to March 1974, were spent in the community of Qamawara, in the district of San Salvador, province of Calca, department of Cusco. I accordingly owe my greatest debt to the people of Qamawara, who so generously allowed me to share their lives with them and who have welcomed me again as a *compadre* on my return visits. I hope this book is a vindication of their trust. All names of community members in this account have been changed.

Many other people in Peru helped me in countless ways during my fieldwork. In particular I should like to mention Dr Jorge Flores, who first drew my attention to the district of San Salvador and its unusual configuration of shrines; Sr Manuel Luna, who did so much to ease my entry into Qamawara; and Sra Carmela F. de Sánchez, who always provided a warm welcome and refreshment at her *tienda* in San Salvador whenever I passed through the village. In Cusco, I enjoyed the support and friendship of other researchers and travelers, including Katherine Arnold, Seán Conlin, David Gow, Rosalind Gow, Lois Keith, and George Primov. Of the church officials I encountered, I should especially like to thank Padre Oscar Pantegoso and Monseñor Severo Aparicio, Auxiliary Bishop of Cusco, for their kind assistance and cooperation. As an overseas researcher I was affiliated with the Programa Académico de Ciencias Sociales of the Pontificia Universidad Católica del Perú, and I should like to express my gratitude to the staff there, in particular to Dr Fernando Fuenzalida, Dr Manuel Marzal and Dr Juan Ossio, for both formal and informal help during my stay and since.

Since my original fieldwork, I have pursued the study of regional cults in various historical archives: the Archivo Arzobispal del Cusco, the Archivo Histórico del Cusco, and the Archivo General de Indias in Seville. I extend my thanks to the staff at these institutions, especially to Srta Nieves Ríos Zevallos, for placing their materials at my disposal. I should also like to thank Sra Gladys Becerra de Valencia for transcribing and translating some of my Quechua narratives from Qamawara.

My fieldwork was initially written up as a doctoral thesis at the University of Manchester, where my supervisor was Dr Richard Werbner. Dissimilar though our field locations were, our respective interests in regional cults coincided exactly, and I owe much to his intellectual stimulation, encouragement, and friendship, then and since. Many of the ideas pursued in the following pages are derived from his comments and suggestions, for which this blanket acknowledgment scarcely suffices. I should also like to register an intellectual debt to the late Victor Turner, whom I never met but whose writings on pilgrimage I shall always value for having blazed a trail for the serious anthropological study of the subject. He will be sadly missed.

Earlier drafts of parts of this study were presented to seminars in the departments of anthropology at the universities of Manchester, St Andrews, Sussex, Swansea, and the London School of Economics and at the Centre for Latin American Studies, University of Cambridge. I should like to thank the participants in these seminars for their many helpful comments and criticisms.

Several people kindly undertook to read the first draft of the completed manuscript, in whole or in part, and offered valuable information and guidance for the subsequent revision: Dr Jorge Flores, Dr Ivan Karp, Professor John Rowe, Dr Henrique Urbano, and Dr Richard Werbner. I alone, of course, am responsible for any errors of fact and interpretation that remain.

The maps and diagrams were drawn by Alison Aspden and Gary Llewellyn of the Drawing Office of the London School of Economics. I am most grateful to them and to Jane Pugh for bringing their patience and skill to bear on what at first seemed a formidable task. Thanks also to Gavin Allan-Wood and Kate Sage of the Photographic Unit, who prepared the plates.

The research has been supported by a number of bodies. The original fieldwork was made possible by a Foreign Area Fellowship from the U.S. Social Science Research Council, supplemented by a grant from the Radcliffe-Brown Fund of the Association of Social Anthropologists. Shorter visits to Peru and Spain in 1980 and 1984 were supported by the U.K. Social Science Research Council, the Staff Research Fund of the London School of Economics, and the Nuffield Foundation. I am indebted to all of these organizations and to their officers for their assistance.

Finally, I express my deep gratitude to my wife, Anna, who has endured the long gestation of this study with goodwill and forbearance and who has been throughout a constant source of support and encouragement. To her I give special thanks.

CHAPTER I

Pilgrimage
in Perspective

This is a study of the sacred landscape of an Andean peasantry. In it I shall investigate how and why people and resources are periodically mobilized around certain holy objects and sites and how the religious geography defined by such movements adapts and transforms itself with the passage of time.

My interest in this topic was aroused in the course of fieldwork in the peasant community of Qamawara in the department of Cusco, southern Peru, during the early 1970s, and the religious landscape of the Cusco region is the object of the present study. The spatial perspective shifts, however, from Qamawara and its immediate locality, through the Cusco region itself, to the wider politico-economic and cultural environment in which it lies. The temporal perspective shifts as well, from a general treatment of Andean religious history, through a more circumscribed documentation of the development of central Andean religious geography and of the histories of Cusco's principal shrines, to the present-day ethnography of local and regional cults. As this might suggest, I have drawn liberally on the work of other scholars in a range of different disciplines in order to place my own material in context. But my central concern, the articulation of individuals and communities through the cults of translocal and regional shrines, has been until now a largely neglected area in Andean anthropology, and it is this gap that I seek to fill.

For the people of Qamawara, journeys to distant, reputedly miraculous shrines exert a perennial fascination. Casual conversation will often turn to a discussion of the relative merits of the various shrines in the region, of who is sponsoring which local pilgrimage contingent that year, who the musicians and dancers are, how much is being spent and—if the speaker is old enough—how much better these things were done in the past. Preparations for a pilgrimage are spread over many months, and the memory of it is savored far longer.

Embarking on such a pilgrimage, the Qamawaran peasant leaves behind a compact, close-knit, and enduring world. The community numbers a few hundred native speakers of Quechua, who earn their subsistence from herding and agriculture. They and their neighbors in the communities nearby owe their livelihoods, as did their ancestors, to the bounty of the *apus*, the immanent local nature spirits of the surrounding lakes and hills. Each community has its own Christian patron saint, fêted on its day, while all the communities pay homage to the patron saint of the municipality to which they are subordinate. Enclaved in the landscape by a ring of tutelary nature spirits, the patronal icons of the various communities rigidly graded and ranked, it is a world that is ritually bounded, hierarchical, introverted, and exclusive.

At the shrine, the pilgrim enters a very different realm. Here, clustered around the shrine sanctuary—a simple chapel, perhaps, or a great basilica—is a motley gathering of people from hamlets, villages, and towns across a wide area. They have come in their hundreds, thousands, or tens of thousands to worship, according to their lights, before a statue or painted image of Christ or the Virgin Mary. The shrine has an illustrious past, historically accessible and embellished by myth: it probably sprang spontaneously from the landscape, in a prodigious manifestation of the divine. Though Christian, served by priests and a lay staff, it may well hallow a pagan sacred site, or it may have direct associations with a native, non-Christian cosmology.

The shrine has the power to work miracles, to change the fortunes of its devotees. The peasant has perhaps come to ask for some special, private favor, or to fulfill a vow to make the journey in return for a favor already granted: the recovery of one of the family from illness, the success of a child in a school examination, the favorable outcome of a lawsuit, or whatever. The prayer joins those of the other devotees, some of them also Quechua-speaking peasants, others possibly Spanish-speaking market traders, factory workers, clerks, teachers—the shrine holds out the hope of blessings to all comers.

Many of these Spanish-speaking pilgrims will have attended the fiesta as individuals. Our peasant votary, however, does not travel alone, but as one of a little company of acquaintances from home, who together escort a small portable icon to the shrine in the name of the community. If male, he may be one of the group's ceremonial dancers, whose routines punctuate the journey there and back. Or he may be its sponsor, committed to feeding the pilgrims en route and to meeting the expenses of the dancers and musicians, thereby reaping prestige in the eyes of his fellows.

Throughout the journey the pilgrim group maintains a studied insularity from other similar contingents and submits to an internal régime of strict equality and sharing. The pilgrimage intensifies the bonds of kinship and neighborhood: for the time being, all members of the group are brothers and sisters to one another. At the shrine, the various groups converge to form a single yet internally divided congregation; their movements begin to be ritually orchestrated one with another, and they may be caught up in ceremonial enactments of wider, categorical, geographic-cum-ethnic identifications.

It can be seen from this brief sketch that, in several senses, Andean pilgrimage connects two worlds. First, it leads to a special kind of rendezvous with the deities: it is a bridge between the human and the divine realms. The miraculous shrine that is its goal is a spot on the spiritually animated landscape where divine power has suddenly burst forth. Forces that are usually submerged have here broken the surface, in an epiphany that has become fixed in the perceptual territory of human beings. And not just in space: the shrine marks an irruption into history, the entry of the divine into the temporal as well as the spatial order of reality. By approaching it, pilgrims seek to tap its still active power, to draw this into their lives and thereby to induce existential change.

More than this, Andean pilgrimage mediates between two *types* of divine power. Its focal shrines are nominally Christian, presided over by the clergy, but they are invariably pregnant with pagan associations. In the local setting, the Christian patron saints stand apart and distinct from the apus, the pagan spirits of nature. In contrast, not only are miraculous shrines typically established near important pagan sites, but many are lithic images on rocks or crags. They pertain, in fact, to the same religious topography, the same sacred landscape, as do the apus themselves. In the locations, histories, and cosmologies of miraculous shrines, native and nonnative religious traditions are brought into direct relation.

Third, pilgrimage is a passage from an exclusive cultic domain, bounded and hierarchical, to an inclusive one, unbounded and fluid. The passage is heavily ritualized, being undertaken by rural pilgrims in separate contingents, each self-consciously reconstructing and heightening the closure and homogeneity of its home community. It is a periodic turning outward, an eversion, by which many separate microcosms reorient themselves in a fleeting, macrocosmic setting. Yet here, even as the ritual performances meld the pilgrims into more extensive, categorical groupings, local identities are simultaneously stressed and advertised.

This introductory account is the merest approximation, a prelusory image that I shall later have occasion to refine and nuance. But it will serve for the time being to indicate the broad features of the phenomenon and also to suggest the theoretical angle that could be adopted for the more detailed picture. Partly with this aim in mind, and also with a view to clearing away some unhelpful preconceptions, I shall now turn to a selective review of the literature on Latin American pilgrimage.[1]

Sociological Perspectives

An early attempt to construct a comprehensive model of Latin American pilgrimage was Henry F. Dobyns's study "The Religious Festival," submitted as a doctoral dissertation to Cornell University in 1960. At a time when most anthropological research in the area tended to be concentrated on the "little community," Dobyns addressed himself explicitly to wider concerns. Combing the available ethnography for references to supra-community ritual, he classified the cases he found into four types. First there was the locality festival, involving only participants from neighboring villages; second, the area festival, similar but larger in catchment and congregation; third, the regional cult, in which pilgrims constitute a special cult of devotees of the particular saint or shrine and may be drawn from throughout a department or state; and finally the confusingly labeled communitywide cult, exemplars being Mecca and Jerusalem, where pilgrims are drawn from the entire global membership of a world religion. The last type lay beyond his purview.

Having established a typology of sorts, Dobyns offers a general explanation for these various phenomena by invoking Robert Redfield's ideas on great and little traditions. Pilgrimage, he claims, is "a mechanism for bridging the institutional gap between the contemplative élite of a great religious tradition and the particularized and localized peasants on their farmsteads and the little communities" (Dobyns 1960, 88). Different kinds of festival create functional linkages of varying span between élites and local groups and also between different local groups themselves. Cultural ideas are therefore diffused throughout a given population. The regional cult of Magdalena in Sonora state, Mexico, for example, "helps to bring into functional linkage the ethnically diverse peoples of Sonora, acting as an institution for intensive culture contact for the whole region" (Dobyns 1960, 96). At the other end of the spectrum lie the locality festivals of Chichicastenango and Samachique in Guatemala (Bunzel 1953); both of these are administrative centers whose pilgrimages perform the same function of horizontal and vertical linkage within their respective jurisdictions (Dobyns 1960, 85).

Supracommunity festivals, in other words, do the same as community festivals, only on a grander scale: they integrate individuals and groups into ever more extensive congregations—locality, area, region, world. More than this, they are one of the means by which the great and little traditions keep in touch with each other, thereby maintaining the unity of the religious system as a whole.[2]

4

This essentially Durkheimian model consists of two closely linked elements. The first has to do with levels of *social* organization and the manner in which pilgrimage, along with other supralocal institutions, integrates groups in each successive tier. This type of approach to regional phenomena has more recent advocates. Carol A. Smith, for example, in her preamble to a collection of papers on regional social systems, contends that for maximum integration

[the] patterns of community linkage . . . should reflect but should also restructure the general organization of local institutions at each higher level—local system, regional system, macro-region, nation, world. The levels of organization defined in this view are of special import for understanding societal integration (1976, 17).

On this view, regional relationships and institutions have a necessarily integrative function—denying any possibility of dissonance between relationships in different institutional domains or between different sets of relationships in the same domain.

It is worth noting, though, that while Dobyns treats all festivals, large and small, as elements of a single continuous series, representing successive levels of integration from that of the little community to the level of the entire confessional fellowship, his hybrid typology hints at a more subtle conceptualization. It tacitly distinguishes between locality and area *festivals* on the one hand, and regional and communitywide *cults* on the other. The congregations of festivals are identified geographically, on the basis of residence. Those of cults, in contrast, are identified primarily by their socioreligious status, as devotees of the shrine in question. The implication is that festivals and cults are two distinct kinds of phenomenon, qualitatively differentiated according to the absence or presence of a chosen devotional commitment. I shall return to this point later.

The second element in Dobyns's model of pilgrimage is the idea of levels of *cultural* organization, the notion of great and little traditions. This distinction has secured a place in anthropological discourse largely through the writings of Robert Redfield and has been a frequent resort of anthropologists working in areas under the sway of the so-called historical or world religions. Redfield sets out the model thus:

[In] a civilization there is a great tradition of the reflective few, and there is a little tradition of the largely unreflective many. The great tradition is cultivated in schools and temples; the little tradition works itself out and keeps itself going in the lives of the unlettered in their village communities. The tradition of the philosopher, theologian and literary man is a tradition consciously cultivated and handed down; that of the little people is for the most part taken for granted and not submitted to much scrutiny or considered refinement and improvement (1956, 41–42).

Having established the dichotomy, he goes on to consider how the two halves are related to each other:

The two traditions are interdependent. Great and little traditions have long affected each other and continue to do so. . . . [They] can be thought of as two currents of thought and action, distinguishable, yet ever flowing into and out of each other (1956, 42–43).

Their relationship is hierarchical and is perceived as such:

Great and little traditions are dimensions of one another; those people who carry on the lower layers and those who maintain the high alike recognize the same order of "highness" and "lowness" (1956, 50).

Holism is finally restored at the highest level, that of the civilization:

[A] civilization . . . is a great whole, in space and time, by virtue of the complexity of the organization which maintains and cultivates its traditions and communicates them from the great tradition to the many and varied small local societies within it (1956, 59).

In various obiter dicta (1956, 33, 56–57) he sees pilgrimage as one of the means to this end.

The theoretical problems posed by this formulation are well known. By setting up two artificially constructed systems that are then brought into relation with each other, Redfield fails to account for the systemic qualities of the so-called composite culture as it is practiced (cf. Tambiah 1970). The bipolarity of his formulation forces a straitjacket on the data, inhibiting a looser, more Weberian interpretation of the diverse styles of religiosity that may be encountered among different occupational and status groups (cf. Geertz 1960). Its admitted faithfulness to the hierarchical world view of the people themselves, and perhaps also to that of Western intellectuals, makes it vulnerable to the criticism of raising ideology to the status of analytical tool. And the civilization supposedly sustained by the great tradition is far too general and abstract an entity within which to analyze geographically and historically specific relations and processes.

Nevertheless, Redfield's model need not be jettisoned altogether. Distinctions between the reflective few and the unreflective many, the lettered and the unlettered, systematized and unsystematized, cultivated and taken for granted can be dispensed with and with them the invidious terms *high* and *low, great* and *little*. There are, however, two related distinctions, confounded in Redfield's model but better highlighted and held separate, that I should wish to salvage.

The first—inescapable in a study of Catholicism—is the idea of an opposition, or rather a tension, between official and unofficial religion, between the orthodox and the unorthodox. Official religion is to be seen, not as a static corpus of doctrine and liturgy, but rather as the outcome at any particular moment of a continual process of officialization, of a dialectical interplay between the official and the unofficial (cf. Vrijhof 1979, 237–41). This process of officialization is ostensibly driven by, and in turn sustains, institutional hierarchy. Official religion is the product not so much of theological musings as of institutional dynamics: "orthodoxy . . . is what suits those who wield power in an ecclesiastical institution" (Stirrat 1981, 184).

The second element to be extracted from Redfield's model is a more general one. It is the idea of a compromise or accommodation between two countervailing cultural tendencies, the one particularistic, the other universalistic—an idea pursued by Marriott (1955), though still within the essentialist confines of Redfield's model. I shall return to this notion in a moment, by way of the work of perhaps the best-known anthropological writer on pilgrimage, Victor Turner.

In a series of publications in the 1970s, Turner developed a comprehensive model of the pilgrimage process (Turner 1974a, 1974b; Turner and Turner 1978). His starting point is the pilgrim's *choice*. "Pilgrimages in all historic, large-scale religions," he claims, "rest initially on voluntarism" (Turner 1974a, 198). The optional nature of pilgrimage, the relationship with a saint or deity freely entered into by a devotee, though frequently tinged with obligation, sets it apart from the quotidian order of social existence where status and duty prevail.

In the Mexican *municipio* 'district' of San Bernadino Contla described by Nutini (1968), for example, Turner observes a dichotomy between "a complex religious structure focused on *local* chapels and shrines, offset by a looser, voluntaristic religious *affiliation* focused on distant shrines" (1974a, 191, emphasis in original). Similarly, medieval European pilgrimage, "though generically framed by obligation and institutionalized in a great system of obligation within that frame, represented a higher level of freedom, choice, volition, structurelessness, than did, say, the world of the manor, village or medieval town" (1974a, 177). Pilgrimage displays a "tension and ambiguity between status and contract and an attempt to reconcile them in the notion that it is meritorious to *choose one's duty*" (1974a, 177, emphasis in original).

The journey from a familiar homeland to a far shrine both effects and symbolizes this distance from onus and constraint. Furthermore, the focal shrines of pilgrimage are themselves peripheral, typically located apart from administrative and ecclesiastical centers and sometimes in the wild, away from human habitation altogether.

Turner acknowledges as his inspiration the ideas of Arnold van Gennep. He sees pilgrimage itself as liminal, akin to the central, liminal stage of a tribal rite of passage. As in that transitional phase of status relinquishment, pilgrimage temporarily divests individuals of the roles they play in everyday life and places them in a state of freedom and unmediated fellowship—a state of *communitas*. This idea, proposed in his earlier study of ritual (Turner 1969), is a model of society "as an unstructured or rudimentarily structured and relatively undifferentiated *comitatus*, community, or even communion of equal individuals who submit together to the general authority of the ritual elders" (1969, 96). Pilgrimages can be regarded "both as occasions on which communitas is experienced and as journeys toward a sacred source of communitas" (Turner 1974a, 203).

Communitas, in its pure, existential form, however, must forever elude the pilgrim. The communitas of pilgrimage is normative, ordered, so as to enable the group to persist, its members to be controlled, and its resources to be mobilized. Pilgrimages are "liminoid," quasi-liminal (Turner and Turner 1978): "though [they] strain in the direction of universal communitas, they are still ultimately bounded by the structure of the religious systems within which they are generated and persist" (Turner 1974a, 205–6).

The transcendent dichotomy between structure and communitas subsumes all others—obligation versus voluntarism, centrality versus peripherality, hierarchy versus equality, heterogeneity versus homogeneity, exclusiveness versus inclusiveness, and so on. It also defines the diachronic dimension of the model. Each pilgrimage has an entelechy, "its own immanent force controlling and directing development" (Turner and Turner 1978, 25). Typically, a cult passes through a phased process from haphazard communitas to institutionalized devotion—"from vision to routinization, from antistructure through counterstructure to structure" (1978, 26).

Pilgrimage shrines may thus transform into centers of political and economic power. But equally, they may recover their communitas potential when that power decays or is displaced. Yucatán, where many Christian shrines are established near former Mayan cities, provides an example of this perpetual pendulum. It is a process

by which, under certain conditions, communitas petrifies into politico-economic structure but may be regenerated as a communitas center when a new alternative politico-economic center develops or forcibly replaces the old. The new secular structure enters into a complementary relationship with the old structure, which then becomes sacralized and infused with liminal communitas. Former centrality has become peripherality, but peripherality may then become the setting for new centrality, as waves of pilgrims invade, and many settle near the peripheral shrines (Turner 1974a, 227).

Here, van Gennep's scheme is inscribed into history.

Dobyns's and Turner's approaches to pilgrimage, both of them drawing on Latin American material, offer a useful contrast. In the one, pilgrimage—like any other collective ritual activity—is functionally integrative, linking together the disparate residential and ethnic groups in a society, and these with the religious élites, in successive levels of inclusiveness. In the other, this archetypal inclusiveness of pilgrimage is structurally *dis*integrative, a temporary abeyance of the hierarchical social order in favor of an egalitarian, role-free mode of association.

Turner's paradigm, then, takes us beyond sterile functionalism, suggesting a dialectic of sorts. As an analytical tool, however, it is too inflexible to be of much use in the majority of instances. The inflexibility arises because the relation between each pair of dichotomized variables is seen as zero sum—the more of one, the less of the other. The effect of this is to make most concrete instances into anomalies, assimilable to the model only by reckoning out contrary features into a single measure. Further, the dichotomized variables are determinately harmonized into the grand polarity between structure and communitas. As Werbner has argued, the weakness of Turner's model is that "like other ideal typologies . . . it tends to represent as mutually exclusive alternatives—the halves of parallel dichotomies—what are, in fact, *aspects* which combine in a surprising variety of ways within a range of actual cases" (1977, xiii, emphasis in original). A looser conceptualization giving the full range of variables free play would offer a better means of registering the complexity and contingency of diverse instances.[3]

Werbner broadly identifies the phenomena under consideration as regional cults. They are "cults of the middle range—more far-reaching than any parochial cult of the little community, yet less inclusive in belief and membership than a world religion in its most universal form" (1977, ix). Such cults, he contends, should be accorded full analytic autonomy, to enable us to attend to their proper, internal relations and processes. They have their own central places, shrines that define their own regions and display their own forms of nodal organization. The flows of people, goods, services, and ideas focused upon these central places are part of the internal momentum of the cults themselves, characteristically cutting across and overriding important political, economic, or ethnic boundaries. The relation between cult regions and regions focused in other ways—political, ecological, economic—is therefore not preempted by the model but must always be a matter for empirical investigation (Werbner 1977).[4]

In examining Andean pilgrimage cults from this perspective, the most helpful, preanalytic image to hold in mind is of a tangle of contradictions, a cluster of coincident opposites. To begin with, the phenomena lie at the intersection of particularistic, place-bound religiosity and its generalized, person-bound counterpart (cf. Werbner 1979, 668). To the extent that pilgrimage affords direct access to the sacred to all who choose to avail themselves of it, regardless of provenance, it is person-bound and hence supracultural, potentially transcending all geographical and social frontiers. Given that this sacredness must be tapped at a particular spot in the landscape, at a shrine anchored in physical space, it is place-bound, part of a unique, historically configured cultural topography and having a particular pattern of groups and peoples within its ambit.

The rest flows from this. Exclusiveness may be fully accented in the midst of inclusiveness. The same sets of cultic relations may be the vehicles for both affirming and denying hierarchy and privilege. Cults that over-arch and transcend boundaries simultaneously offer arenas for expressing or exaggerating them, or even for establishing new ones. Regional cults, in other words, provide at once for both universalism and particularism, for both the recession and resurgence of social and cultural differentia-tion. In giving dialectics the rein, synchronically as well as diachronically, we might be taking our cue from Simmel: "Contradiction and conflict not only precede . . . unity but are operative in it *at every moment of its existence*. . . . There probably exists no social unit in which convergent and divergent currents among its members are not inseparably inter-woven" (Simmel 1955, 15, emphasis mine).[5]

Simmel's metaphor is apt. Universalism and particularism are better regarded not as tendencies pulling against each other, but rather as the warp and weft of a seamless cultural fabric—related orthogonally, so to speak, rather than opposed antithetically in the same dimension. An ecumenical cosmology—whether pegged to a world faith or to an indig-enous religious movement[6]—gives special emphasis and impetus to the universal dimension, but it must always consist of an interplay between the two. Regional cults, poised as they are between two modes of relat-edness between human beings and gods, the one mediated by physical location, the other by mental disposition, capture and frame this essential process.[7] In them this perpetual tension is transposed to a cosmic plane, and through them it achieves some form of temporary, unstable resolution.

For this reason, regional cults commonly appear as parties to wider, external social processes. Under their aegis, as they ebb and flow, merge and split, ethnicities may be fused, sharpened, or redrawn; trade networks ramify, flourish, and decay; empires expand, consolidate, and collapse; and new creeds may be propagated, challenged, and subverted. Regional cults enshrine a persistent, fundamental, spatial-religious tension, which underlies and animates many of these critical changes and transforma-tions. Their internal momentum makes them more than mere functional integrators, or structural antitheses, of relations external to them; they can actively redirect and reshape those relations at all levels, from inter-personal to international. The sacred sediment of their central shrines can endure through the rise and fall of chiefdoms, states, and even re-ligions; conversely, new hierophanies might burst forth from the land-scape at any moment, establishing new cults that can act as fresh catalysts for incipient social and historical processes.

Geographical Perspectives

Sometimes a landscape seems to be less a setting for the life of its inhabitants than a curtain behind which their struggles, achievements and accidents take place. For those who, with the inhabitants, are behind the curtains, landmarks are no longer geographic but also biographic and personal (Berger 1976, 15).

Social scientists have approached the relation between peoples and their landscapes from various perspectives. A familiar one in social anthropology is the cognitive or intellectualist perspective, which aims to elicit structural homologies between spatial organization and social organization. In this vein, spatial organization has been regarded essentially as a system of classification, either deriving from (cf. Durkheim and Mauss 1963) or defining (cf. Lévi-Strauss 1966) social groups and classes. Thus, Lévi-Strauss likens ethnogeographical systems to totemic ones: they can serve both to universalize and to particularize. Human groups are identified with their named habitats and vice versa, so social relations become spatial relations and spatial relations social ones.

In this view, the landscape becomes a kind of totemic topography, an inventory of material forms from which a system of classification of social groups is constructed. The mythogeographies of Australian Aborigines, for example, recount the peregrinations of founding ancestors and civilizing heroes, who leave peoples, languages, and cultures in their wake (Berndt and Berndt 1970, 15–29). Such mythogeographies serve to anchor the local group in space but also to expand its horizons to territories and groups farther afield. Geographical systems of classification can also work in the reverse direction, differentiating individuals within the group by reference to specific sites: "space is a society of named places just as people are landmarks within the group" (Lévi-Strauss 1966, 168).

Yet if we are to step "behind the curtains," in Berger's words, we need to go beyond a purely mechanical formulation such as this. We need to pose, in addition, questions concerning the phenomenological or experiential aspects of space, place, and landscape. Recently, in a quest for a new, humanistic geography, a number of writers have taken up these problems, and while we should be alert to the possibility of ethnocentric, Western bias, it is worth briefly considering some of their ideas.

Running through much of this literature is an antipodal contrast between two dimensions of experience. Relph, for example, attempting to sketch the lineaments of the notion of place, writes: "The essence of place lies . . . in the experience of an 'inside' that is distinct from an 'outside.'" The difference between inside and outside is "the difference between safety and danger, cosmos and chaos, enclosure and exposure, or simply here and there" (Relph 1976, 49). Similarly, Tuan postulates a universal counterpoint between bounded place on the one hand and boundless space on the other. "Human beings require both space and place. Human lives are a dialectical movement between shelter and venture, attachment and freedom" (Tuan 1977, 54).

The same antithesis recurs in Appleton's study of the aesthetics of landscape, in art and reality. Appleton analyzes experience of landscape into three clusters of sensations: sensations of prospect, of refuge, and of hazard. *Prospect* refers to symbols of unimpeded vision, openness, space; *refuge* refers to symbols of sanctuary, enclosure, place; while *hazard* refers to symbols of exposure, obstacle, threat (Appleton 1975, 85–106). Here, however, the sensations are interpreted not psychologically or sociologically but ethologically, in terms of a somewhat rickety theory of their origins among the primeval hunters.

Underlying all these analyses is the notion that the spatial experience is somehow directional, vectored. It can be directed *to* places or *from* them. Reversing the direction has critical consequences. The inward vector marks out place from the surrounding environment. Boundaries are established: place is circumscribed, staked out, defined, even defended against the exterior. Place is carved out from space. Images of identification, attachment, and belonging come to the fore, matched by those of separateness, exclusion, and alienation. The outward vector, on the other hand, makes place itself actively define and shape the surrounding environment. In this mode, place creates and sustains a focalized spatial field; the experience of place now hinges, not on being inside or outside, but rather on being either at the center or defined in terms of it. Characteristic images are now of nearness and distance, superiority and inferiority, controlling and controlled, dominance and submission. Place and space ultimately derive their existential qualities from an interplay between these two perceptual possibilities, which respectively generate a dialectic between interiority and exteriority and between center and peripheries.

Landscapes exist in time as well as in space, however. Experience of landscape involves not just immediate perception but also an interior awareness of its "pastness," be that past recent, historic, ancient, primordial, or mythic. Landscape can be a potent medium for materializing time in space, for establishing what Bakhtin, borrowing from the theory of relativity, called a chronotope—in which "time thickens, as it were, takes on flesh, becomes artistically visible; likewise, space becomes charged and responsive to the movements of time, plot and history" (Bakhtin 1981, 84).

The temporal experience of landscape can assume many different forms. For the Apache, for example, the landscape is a repository of past moral transgressions. Named places—rocks, clefts, valleys—are here used as mnemonics to hold errant individuals to the old ways (Basso 1984). Mythical time is commonly encoded in the natural landscape, as in the case of the central Australian desert, littered with the topographic memorials to wandering heroes who strayed from their goals and were stopped short in their tracks (Berndt and Berndt 1970). The modern cult of antiquity has as one of its tenets the preservation, sometimes the wholesale reconstruction, of historic, architectural, and archaeological landscapes, a phenomenon closely related to the rise of nationalism and the need for tangible evidence of unique cultural continuity (Lowenthal

1985, 393). Conversely, temporalization of the landscape can be a cultural strategy for disposing of the historic past altogether, as in America during the years following the Revolution. In this instance, the disdain and revulsion characteristically displayed toward the European historical heritage was matched by what amounted to a deification of the American landscape: primordial nature was substituted for the foibles of history. Man-made landscapes were to be ephemeral, geared to no more than the immediate needs of the living, so that future generations could start anew. "Inherited land and houses epitomized the tyranny of forebears and the burden of the past. . . . The glory of America, thought one observer, was that it was all periodically pulled down" (Lowenthal 1976, 94).

Beyond the specific parameters by which landscape is perceived and experienced, we should be aware that the word *landscape* itself, as Cosgrove points out, carries multiple layers of meaning. In one sense it connotes not so much the world as seen as a way of seeing the world. It suggests a subjective, affectively charged perception of the environment, a synthetic, holistic perception conformed by the particular cultural perspectives and personal dispositions of the human subject. In another sense, however, *landscape* denotes a *social* product, the historical consequence of successive transformations of nature by collective human agency, the accumulated sediment of past human action (cf. Cosgrove 1984, 13–14).[8]

One of the aims of this study is to pursue these two ostensibly antithetical aspects of landscape, the one synchronic and egocentric, the other diachronic and historical, in order to arrive eventually at a convergence and a unification of them. My intention, in other words, is to render the contemporary, subjective experience of the sacred landscape as an integral part of the historical processes that have shaped, and are continuing to shape, the cultural environment of Andean peoples.

The Cusco Region

The vast mountain chain that defines the western profile of South America rises and broadens in its middle latitudes to heights of 7,000 meters and to a width of up to 500 kilometers. This central section, stretching through central and southern Peru, western Bolivia, and northern Chile, bordered on one side by the desert strip of the Pacific seaboard and on the other by the rain forests of the Amazon basin, presents a picture of astonishing climatic and ecological diversity. The section with which we are chiefly concerned lies on the eastern side of the Andean spine, in the southern Peruvian department of Cusco (see appendix 1, maps 1, 2, and 5).

The Cusco region is contoured by rivers that rise in the lakes and glacial meltwaters at altitudes of up to 6,000 meters along the Pacific-

Atlantic watershed. They flow in a roughly northwesterly direction, first across the cold, treeless tundras of the *puna* 'high plateau' ecological zone, then etching deep, fertile valleys and rugged fissures into the folds of sedimentary rock to give rise to the *kishwa* 'temperate valley' zone, then passing between the gentler, tree-clad hills of the subtropical *montaña* 'forested mountain' zone, eventually converging to form the Ucayali River, which flows northward through the lowland tropical forest to its confluence with the Amazon.

One of these river valleys, that of the Vilcanota-Urubamba, forms the principal geographical axis of the Cusco region. Today, the valley carries the main road and rail routes from the region to Puno and the *altiplano* 'tableland' in the southeast, and to Quillabamba and the *selva* 'jungle' in the northwest. On one side it is paralleled by the Mapacho-Paucartambo valley, on the other by that of the Santo Tomás and Apurímac rivers. The high *cordilleras* are crossed by transverse roads through the mountain passes.

Cusco city is situated on a tributary of the river Vilcanota, at an altitude of 3,300 meters. With a population of around 120,000 it is the only town of any size in the area; of the other population centers within a 100-kilometer radius, its closest rival is Sicuani, with about 13,000. Intensive settlement in the region is concentrated in the valleys, where nucleated villages laid out on a grid pattern are the rule; in the mountains, a dispersed pattern of residence prevails. Altogether, the present population of the area shown in map 5 is approximately half a million (see appendix 2, table 1).[9]

Livelihood is based for the most part on herding and agriculture. Many communities practice mixed agropastoral production, but across the area as a whole, herding tends to be concentrated in the high puna zones of Canas, Canchis, and Chumbivilcas in the southeast, while intensive agriculture—especially cereal cultivation—predominates in the temperate intermontane valleys and flood plains to the northwest. The chief crops are potatoes and maize, while the principal livestock are sheep, llamas, and alpacas.

Cusco city has some light industry and during the last few decades has become something of a tourist mecca. As a result it now boasts a modern airport for domestic flights, as well as numerous hotels, restaurants, and souvenir shops. Health, educational, and legal services are all overwhelmingly concentrated in the city. As a departmental capital it houses the regional offices of state bureaucracies, and there is also a military garrison. Urban administration is in the hands of a municipal council, headed by an *alcalde* 'mayor'. The department as a whole is nominally governed by a prefect; it is divided into provinces, each in the charge of a subprefect, which in turn are subdivided into districts, the lowest level of civil administration, each headed by an unsalaried governor.

The population of the area is descended from the aboriginal Amerindian peoples and the postcontact European settlers, most of them Spanish. Despite 450 years of miscegenation, racial terms are still used as metaphors of cultural habitude. There are two dominant ethnic stereotypes.

The first is denoted by the Spanish words *indígena* or—more pejoratively—*indio*, both translated as 'Indian', though other nonracial terms in local usage are approximately congruent: *campesino* 'peasant', the term chosen by the military radicals who seized power in 1968 to replace the racial labels, held to be discriminatory and outmoded;[10] and *runa* (Quechua) 'people', which is finding favor among political campaigners and anthropologists but is not commonly used as a term of self-reference in the Cusco region. The stereotype depicts a country dweller who practices subsistence agriculture or pastoralism in a peasant community or who is employed on an estate or rural cooperative. He or she has had little or no formal education, speaks the native language Quechua with perhaps a smattering of Spanish, and is illiterate—and therefore, until recently, disenfranchised. An Indian, in the stereotypical representation, wears "traditional" Andean dress, in fact made up mostly of elements of colonial Spanish garb—shirt, waistcoat, homespun knee breeches and poncho, knitted cap, and rubber sandals for a man, and blouse, homespun multilayered skirts and shawl, regionally distinctive hat, and rubber sandals for a woman—and chews coca, a mild indigenous narcotic. Racially and culturally, an Indian's roots are regarded as aboriginal.

The counterpart of this stereotype is designated by the Spanish word *mestizo*, meaning literally 'mixed race', frequently contracted to *misti*. *Vecino* 'citizen' or 'neighbor' is in effect a synonym for mestizo in rural areas. These terms denote a rural or urban dweller engaged in commercial farming, shopkeeping, large-scale commerce or some other business enterprise, or salaried employment such as schoolteaching, clerical work, or government service. A "typical" mestizo has had several years of schooling, speaks Spanish and perhaps Quechua as well, and is fully literate. He or she wears store-bought, Western-style clothes and inclines toward the general cultural mores of the city. Physically, Caucasian features are stressed. Mestizos are seen as the contemporary bearers of the Hispanic cultural tradition in the Andes.

In addition to these two polar stereotypes with their various tag terms, there are other folk labels, more or less depreciatory, such as *cholo* and *mozo*, which designate supposedly intermediate categories. *Blanco* 'white' denotes those few individuals with putatively "pure" European ancestry. *Criollo*, meanwhile, literally 'a person born in the Americas of European parents', today connotes the popular classes and life-styles of Lima and the other coastal cities, to which many *serranos* 'highlanders' aspire.

The importance of this racial terminology lies not in its demarcation of objective demographic or sociological groups, which it does imprecisely if at all, but rather in its denotation of the dominant cultural categories by which Andean people themselves understand their own, varied ways of life.[11] The racial idiom of social and cultural diversity serves as a pervasive metaphor of superiority and inferiority, of native and foreign, and of inclusion and exclusion. It casts the complexities of cultural practice into a simplified, ethnohistorical framework in which a Hispanic tradition is seen to be in perpetual confrontation with an Indian one. Perhaps nowhere is this fractured world view more evident than in the field of religion.

Cusco city is the seat of an archdiocese, the oldest bishopric in Peru. Today, the archdiocese itself covers the populous central band of the department from Quillabamba in the north to Acomayo in the south, while the four southernmost provinces are constituted as a subordinate prelature centered in Sicuani. The lowland section of the department north of Quillabamba is incorporated into a separate apostolic vicariate, which also includes the department of Madre de Dios and part of Loreto and which is controlled by the Dominican religious order (Hegy 1971, 58–61).[12]

The archdiocese is divided into fifty-two parishes, their boundaries or those of their constituent vice-parishes for the most part coincident with political districts. As elsewhere in Peru, there is a chronic shortage of clergy. In 1969 the archdiocese had only ninety-eight priests, forty-two diocesan and fifty-six regular; eighteen parishes had no resident priest, a proportion which reflected the national average.[13] In the prelature of Sicuani the situation was even worse, with more than half the parishes vacant (Hegy 1971, 64, 99). Apart from a small Protestant minority, clustered in the larger towns, the population is professed to be Roman Catholic. Yet from personal observation, it is evident that even where masses are regularly held in rural parishes, attendance is nugatory.

There is, however, a religious map of Cusco that exists in counterpoint to the ecclesiastical divisions of parishes and vice-parishes, a map which plots a religious fervor scarcely discernible in the weekly parochial routine. Scattered across the region are shrines of Christ and the Virgin that are proclaimed to be miraculous, and to whose annual festivals pilgrims flock in their thousands. Images of Christian divinities have here bonded with the Andean landscape to become peculiarly potent sources of divine power. And it is the cults of these miraculous shrines that betray strikingly the tensions and contradictions of a culture divided against itself.

To disclose the cultural significance of this enchanted terrain, I shall adopt first a historical perspective, then an ethnographic one. The historical treatment begins 3,000 years ago, with the cult of Chavín; the ethnographic account begins in the district of San Salvador, in the hinterland of Cusco. In these twin perspectives, the mountainous environment from which Andean people wrest their living will be revealed as a vast, complex, ever-changing religious icon.

PART ONE

PART ONE

CHAPTER 2

A Pre-Columbian Panorama

In the evening of 16 November 1532, the Inka emperor Atawalpa, mounted on a sedan and accompanied by a mostly unarmed retinue of thousands of his men, entered the square of Cajamarca for his fateful confrontation with the Spanish invaders. Proffered a breviary by the Dominican friar Vicente de Valverde, Atawalpa cast it disdainfully to the ground. At this, the Spaniards rushed out from their hiding places and in two hours massacred some six thousand bewildered Indians. Atawalpa himself was taken prisoner and obliged to deliver as ransom a roomful of gold, only to be executed by Pizarro some months later.

It was fitting that the Spanish conquest should have been triggered by what to the invaders was a blatant act of sacrilege. Spain had been cleared of Muslims only forty years earlier, in 1492, and in one of those curious historical coincidences Columbus's departure that same year was to open up a whole new continent to conquer in the name of Christ. That the conquistadors were eager to portray their activities as another religious crusade is evident from the dutiful proclamation to the natives at appropriate moments during the campaign of a specious text known as the Requirimiento. Formulated by a royal commission in 1513, the Requirimiento

contained a brief history of the world, with descriptions of the Papacy and Spanish monarchy and of the donation of the Indies by Pope to King. The Indian audience was then required to accept two obligations: it must acknowledge the Church and Pope and accept the King of Spain as ruler on behalf of the Pope; it must also allow the Christian faith to be preached to it. If the natives failed to comply immediately, the Spaniards would launch their attack and "would do all the harm and damage that we can," including the enslavement of wives and children, and robbery of possessions. "And we protest that the deaths and losses which shall result from this are your fault" (Hemming 1972, 130).

With this document, every battle assumed cosmic proportions: no longer between two mere secular armies, but between the beloved of God and the hosts of the Devil.

While this rigid, antagonistic dualism of Christianity was novel to the central Andes, the imperial crusade in itself was not. Until about A.D. 800, the diverse peoples of the area had remained fractionated, political and cultural constituencies tending to follow the natural patterns of valleys, cordilleras, and punas. But around that time, the central sierra produced a social upheaval, which in both its immediate and its long-term effects bears comparison with the rise of the Roman Empire in the Old World. Two dominant powers, which integrated the heterogeneous population into complex, centralized polities, emerged in the region. It was during this period, in fact, that an Andean peasantry came into being for the first time (W. H. Isbell 1977, 54).

One of these powers had its capital at Wari (Huari) near the present-day town of Ayacucho; the other had its center at Tiwanaku (Tiahuanaco), just south of Lake Titicaca (see appendix 1, map 3).[1] The Wari empire was a conquest state. The dominance of Tiwanaku, however, rested on the power and influence of a religious cult and its priesthood. The Wari empire, moreover, drew much of its religious and cultural stimulus from Tiwanaku. At their height, these two centers between them controlled an area that stretched from Cajamarca in the north to Mizque in the south—a span of nearly 2,000 kilometers.

These first pan-Andean federations were short-lived. Their disintegration was followed by another period of political fractionation until the Inkas of the Cusco valley reunified the area, extending their rule still farther before their brief domination was usurped in turn by the Spanish. It is thus possible to date from around twelve hundred years ago the beginning of the ebb and flow of a centralizing state against a background of ethnic and regional diversity, of shifting relations between rural producers, local lords and urban élites, of conflict and symbiosis between domestic, regional, and state-sponsored religious cults—in short, those processes that characterize the dynamic interactions between community, region, and state in complex agrarian societies.

Arguably, though, the foundations of statehood were laid even earlier—two thousand years earlier—with the cult of Chavín. It is here that a historical geography of Andean religion must begin.

Cults and Empires

The Cusco region, along with the rest of the central Andes as far north as the Ayacucho area, was not in fact directly affected by the Chavín cult. The significance of the movement here lies not so much in any substantive continuities that it heralded—though these there undoubtedly were, in the religious iconography of Tiwanaku two thousand years later, for example—as in the precedent that it set for the area as a whole. For the first time, a religious cult was able to expand its influence over the diverse and divided agropastoral peoples of the northern highlands and seaboard, serving as a medium for interregional communication and exchange on a scale that was to rupture forever the previous pattern of cultural isolationism. With the cult of Chavín, pilgrimage religion was born in the Andes.

Archaeological evidence shows that the Chavín cult originated between 1,000 and 800 B.C. in northern Peru, spreading rapidly north and south in a process that was probably completed within a century (Keatinge 1981; Rowe 1967; Willey 1951). The architecture of its temples suggests an oracular religion, perhaps centered on the so-called staff god depicted on a stone monument at the type site of Chavín de Wántar. Despite the clearly recognizable Chavín style, there is a degree of artistic variation between the different regions that fell under the shadow of the cult, indicating a process of syncretism in which local deities selectively acquired attributes derived from Chavín (Keatinge 1981, 177). This local variation, coupled with the virtual absence of secular buildings such as garrisons, storehouses, and fortifications, argues against a sustained military campaign as an accompaniment to religious diffusion. It seems likely that the cult was under the control of a powerful and influential priesthood and was spread by proselytizing missionaries and—once its momentum had been established—by returning pilgrims (Mason 1968, 59; Lumbreras 1974, 70–71).

The Chavín cult, by establishing a common denominator for diverse peoples and cultures, stimulated considerable economic activity. Under its auspices, through the guarantee of safe passage between universally recognized sacred sites, interregional exchange developed and flourished (Keatinge 1981, 184). With the gradual attenuation of Chavín religious influence during the course of the first millenium B.C., long-range trade slowly petered out, but thenceforth interregional exchange was never entirely absent from the Andes (Lanning 1967, 106). This association of a superordinate religious cult and long-distance trade against a background of extreme political fractionation, moreover, was to be crucial in the later development of civilized states (Keatinge 1981, 185–86).[2]

Much of the central sierra remained culturally fragmented throughout this period. Although some settlements in the area developed into
urban centers—Pucará, for example, north of Lake Titicaca, during the
first century B.C.—their influence beyond their own environs was limited.
It was nonetheless in the Titicaca basin that an even more influential cult
eventually dawned.

The site of Tiwanaku, located at an altitude of 3,600 meters, betrays
a long developmental sequence beginning in the first millenium B.C. The
principal ruins, however, date from around the ninth century A.D. (Rowe
1963, 7–15). Their formal, monumental style, together with the presence
of a number of massive monolithic statues, was for long held by ar-
chaeologists to indicate the existence of a ceremonial center only, but it
now seems certain that there was an urban settlement proper, as well as
a number of associated satellite towns scattered around the southern
reaches of the lake (Browman 1978, 328).

Between A.D. 500 and 1000, the dominance of Tiwanaku spread
throughout much of present-day Bolivia, northern Chile, and the southern
extremity of Peru. Despite the evident sophistication of its urban élite
and their ability to mobilize labor on a vast scale, the dominion of
Tiwanaku did not rest on military conquest so much as on the peaceful
diffusion of its prestigious religious ideas coupled with the stimulation
of extensive interregional trade. Its cult, carried outward from the heartlands by merchant missionaries and pilgrims, syncretized with local cults
and traditions to give rise to new religious and artifactual styles (Menzel
1964, 67–69). That trade and proselytization went hand in hand is
apparent from the astonishing variety of raw materials imported into the
urban center, not only from other highland ecological zones but also from
the coastal and tropical forest regions. In particular, evidence of the
frequent use of hallucinogenic plants from the jungle suggests that the
rites of the Tiwanaku priesthood entailed drug-induced states, associated
perhaps with some form of religious mysticism (Browman 1978, 335–
36).

The ruins of Tiwanaku are replete with representations of divinities
hewn from grey andesites transported from Copacabana, sixty-five
kilometers to the north (Browman 1978, 332). Their meaning and significance, however, are largely matters for speculation. Iconological studies indicate a sun god, an earth goddess, and a goddess of water, while
the famous carving on the monolithic gateway suggests a weather god
associated with thunder and lightning—perhaps the antecedent of Tunupa
in sixteenth-century Aymara religion (Rowe 1976, 9). The similarity of
this gateway carving to the Chavín staff god argues for some kind of
continuity across the long hiatus which separated the two cults (Rowe
1971, 117–18). The commonly expressed view that the carving represents a supreme creator god is derived chiefly from the status accorded
to Tiwanaku and Lake Titicaca in the Inka mythology of the fifteenth

century (cf. Bushnell 1963, 94). Whatever the precise content of the religious cult of classical Tiwanaku, an association between the creator god–culture hero generally known as Wiraqocha on the one hand and Lake Titicaca and water symbolism on the other pervaded much central Andean mythology at the time of the Spanish invasion, as will be seen presently.

It was during the period of Tiwanaku cult expansion from the altiplano that the first truly centralized Andean state flowered and died. Its capital was Wari, 700 kilometers northwest of Tiwanaku, in the valley of Ayacucho. The valley had for some time been an area of urban settlement, and around A.D. 800 it became the hub of a vast empire, which at its apogee stretched from Cajamarca in the north to Kacha, near Sicuani, in the south (Menzel 1964, 70).

The Wari empire seems to have developed around a multiethnic core, the dominant components of which were the Wanka and Chanka peoples. In contrast to Tiwanaku, the widespread disruption of local cultures attests to the military nature of its expansion (Bennett 1953, 113). The existence of zonally specialized peasant settlements such as Jarkampata, near the imperial capital, and large storage and redistribution depots such as those at Wiraqochapampa in the northern highlands near Huamachuco and Pikillajta just south of Cusco, suggests that the economy of the empire was founded upon the control and articulation of the diverse ecological zones of the region, rather along the lines of the vertical model of the pre-Columbian Andean economy set out by Murra (Murra 1975; Lumbreras 1974, 151–78; W. H. Isbell 1977). The location of Pikillajta is probably related to the frontier between the Wari and Tiwanaku spheres of influence, since both traffic between the two centers and military movements would have followed the communications artery between Titicaca and Cusco (W. H. Isbell 1977, 53).

The Wari empire in fact drew the greater part of its religious inspiration from Tiwanaku. The religious motifs employed by the Wari élite to decorate their characteristic oversize urns, which were ceremonially destroyed in iconoclastic sacrifices to the imperial gods, were derived directly from the gateway god and his attendants (Menzel 1964, 66–67). As time went on, these motifs began to be used on nonceremonial ceramics in combination with local designs, suggesting a gradual diffusion of the religious ideas of the imperial élite among the subject peoples, accompanied by a secularization of the religious symbols (Rowe 1976, 7).

Ethnohistorical evidence suggests that another component, or aspect, of imperial religion was derived from the shrine of Wariwillka, situated in the Mantaro valley in the original territory of the Wanka people, one of the nuclear tribes of the empire (Duviols 1971, 368–70; 1979). According to Duviols, the principal monolith, or *wanq'a*, of the god Wari at Wariwillka was replicated throughout the empire in subordinate wanq'a shrines, each of which served as an abode for his spirit. Wanq'a cults were quintessentially agricultural, concerned with the conquest, possession, enclosure, fertility, and defense of arable lands. The monolith itself was the material symbol of the enduring charismatic political power of the victorious warlord who had annexed the territory (Duviols 1979, 18–21). During the sixteenth century, more than six hundred years after the Wari empire had collapsed, Christian extirpators of idolatry in the north-central Andes discovered numerous monoliths, some of them "armless stone giants," others with "strange faces . . . horrifying to look at," which were identified by the Indians as manifestations of Wari, "the god of force" (Arriaga [1621, chaps. 2, 10] 1968, 24, 82, 84).[3] For its part, Wariwillka was still functioning as an important oracle at the time of the Inkas.

Besides Tiwanaku in the altiplano and Wariwillka in the sierra, there was during this period a third important ceremonial center, whose cult came to be linked to Wari imperial expansion. This was the coastal shrine of Pachakamaq, situated near the mouth of the Lurín valley just south of modern Lima. The site of Pachakamaq, like that of Tiwanaku, was already occupied during the first half of the first millenium A.D., and during the second it developed into a city with an oracular shrine of immense importance. It probably gained some of its religious impetus indirectly from Tiwanaku, with which it may have had trading links through the intermediacy of the imperial capital of Wari. By the tenth century, however, its own independent sphere of religious influence extended north to Chicama, south to Nazca and inland to Jauja, possibly even to the tropical forest (Rowe 1963, 14–15; Menzel 1964, 70; Rostworowski de Diez Canseco 1977, 202–4).

Despite its widespread reputation as an oracle, Pachakamaq lacked an adequate political foundation of its own. It lay within the territory of the ethnic lords of Ichma but was in effect controlled and protected by whoever controlled them. It remained politically subject to Wari throughout the ascendancy of the latter. There seems to have been a persistent rivalry between the highland shrine of Wariwillka, proper after all to the Wanka component of the Wari multiethnic nucleus, and the "foreign" shrine of Pachakamaq on the coast (Earls 1981, 71–77). Pachakamaq, like Wariwillka, was still fuctioning at the time of the Inkas, who wisely incorporated it into their pantheon. In 1533 it was visited by a party of Spaniards in search of gold for Atawalpa's ransom, who left a detailed eyewitness account.[4]

At the time of the Inkas, central Andean mythology associated Pachakamaq, like Tiwanaku, with the creator god Wiraqocha. *Pachakamaq* is a Quechua word, from *pacha* 'world' and *kamay* 'to create' but the title was not necessarily bestowed by the Inkas, since Quechua linguistic influence in the area may well have predated the Inka conquest (Torero 1972, 82–83). It has been argued, then, that the shrines of Pachakamaq and Tiwanaku were the cardinal loci of a pan-Andean creator god (Pease

1973, 31–38). Rostworowski de Diez Canseco, however, claims that the coastal deity was originally entitled Ichma; he was a chthonic god associated with darkness and the sea, the attribute of creator being an Inka superimposition (1983, 42–43).

Wari dominion was short-lived. By the close of the tenth century the empire had fallen, the disintegration of political power accompanied by depopulation and economic depression around the imperial capital and by the extinction of the imperial religious motifs in the formerly dependent territories (Menzel 1964, 69–72). Tiwanaku, too, declined in importance, and the main site was eventually abandoned.

To the north, the collapse of Wari hegemony led to a revival of earlier Moche cultural elements, culminating in the extensive coastal empire of Chimú. Here, in the cities of Chan-Chan, Chikitoy, and Pakatnamú, indigenous urban development reached its apogee (Lumbreras 1974, 180–90). In the central highlands, however, cities and empires gave way to a more dispersed residential pattern and to loose-knit political federations. But in the two great shrines of Tiwanaku and Pachakamaq, the coordinates had been set for a sacred geography that was to stake out the Andean cosmos for centuries to come.

Regional Autonomy

The respite from state formation in the central highlands lasted for about four centuries, from A.D. 1000 to A.D. 1400. It was in effect an extended interregnum between Wari-Tiwanaku dominion on the one hand and the Inka and Spanish states on the other. Archaeological and ethnohistorical evidence indicates that the period was marked by intense political and cultural regionalism (Lumbreras 1974, 179–215). The site of Tiwanaku itself was abandoned and the lacustrine area was characterized by chiefdoms and petty states divided politically but loosely united by the common denominator of the Aymara language. The site of Wari, too, was abandoned, and the Wanka and Chanka peoples developed their own separate cultural-political identities, the Chanka consolidating into a military federation that was eventually to challenge the Inkas of Cusco to the east. The Wanka shrine of Wariwillka continued to exert a regional dominance throughout this period. Pachakamaq, meanwhile, maintained and perhaps even increased its pilgrim traffic, for the city actually expanded during the twelfth and thirteenth centuries.

One document in particular offers a fascinating glimpse of a regional culture during this era. This is a sequence of oral Quechua narratives from the community of San Damián de Checa, situated in the Huarochirí region of the north-central Andes east of modern Lima, which were collected and recorded by a Catholic priest, Francisco de Ávila, around the year 1600 to assist in the extirpation of idolatry in the area (Ávila [1598?] 1966).[5] The narratives merit special attention here, since they are less contaminated by Inka influence than most other early accounts of pre-Hispanic society, reaching back before the years of Inka domination into the distinctive ethnohistory of the area. They expose certain religious structures and processes that, as I shall argue later, are endemic to central Andean society and have continued to manifest themselves, transformed, to the present day.

The narratives dwell on two preeminent gods or *wak'as:* Pariaqaqa, a male deity, associated with a snow-capped mountain in the area, who had five sons, brothers, or avatars, and his sister or sister-in-law Chaupiñamka, a large crag with five "wings," who also had five sisters or manifestations.[6] A notable feature of the document is the inconsistency between accounts from different *ayllus,* local kin-based communities, with regard to the names, relationships, and divine powers of the various deities, an inconsistency of which Ávila's informants were well aware:

People of different ayllus tell different versions of these stories, including the names of the wak'as; the people of Mama pronounce them differently from those of Checa. Some claim of Chaupiñamka: "She was the sister of Pariaqaqa"; others claim: "She was the daughter of Tamtañamka"; . . . Some say of Tamtañamka: "He was the son of the Sun." But a claim such as this we are unable to believe (Ávila [1598, chap. 13] 1966, 88–89).[7]

The document begins with the creation of the world and of human beings by Kuniraya Wiraqocha (Ávila [1598, chap. 1] 1966, 20–21). Pariaqaqa—according to one story the son of the creator ([chap. 15] 94–95) and to another the son of the Sun ([chap. 13] 64–65)—first enters the narrative in an episode describing his placing five eggs in the mountains, which hatched into five falcons. These in turn changed into men, the "sons" of Pariaqaqa. The five walked through the land, and, seeing the pride and misdeeds of the people, they sent floods that washed all the people, their houses, and their llamas into the sea ([chap. 5] 44–45). Here as elsewhere, Pariaqaqa's power is represented through the image of water—in the bringing of rain and cataclysm, the creation of lakes and irrigation canals, and abstractly in the ocean itself.

Pariaqaqa was the god of the Yauyo people. The Yauyos had for long been subject to the Yunkas, the Wanka colonists of the region, whose god Wallallo Karwinko had defeated all the other wak'as and had demanded human sacrifice from his worshipers (Ávila [1598, chaps. 1, 8] 1966, 20–21, 56–57). Pariaqaqa waged war on Wallallo Karwinko, a mythic portrayal of a Yauyo rebellion against their overlords following the disintegration of the Wari empire (Earls 1981, 74). First, Pariaqaqa attacked from five directions with red and yellow rain and bolts of lightning. But Wallallo Karwinko survived, assuming the form of an immense fire reaching to the sky. Pariaqaqa eventually quenched the flames with an avalanche of water, followed by continuous lightning bolts (Ávila [1598, chap. 8] 1966, 56–61).

The defeated god fled eastward into the mountains to the Wanka heartlands, and Pariaqaqa deputed one of his sons to keep watch lest the god return. Then he dealt with Wallallo Karwinko's wife, casting her into the sea and posting another of his sons to guard against her return. While Pariaqaqa himself is chiefly associated with the center of his domain, his sons or brothers are associated with the periphery, extending and protecting the frontiers and serving as emissaries to foreign peoples. Pariaqaqa's victory over Wallallo Karwinko effected an ecological transformation of the region from hot montaña to temperate sierra.

Pariaqaqa then gave orders for his worship by the victorious Yauyos and the remnants of the vanquished Yunkas. He and his brothers made their home in a precipice (qaqa 'large rock or crag') on the mountain to which he gave his name, saying, "Here people will come to adore us" (Ávila [1598, chap. 17] 1966, 100–101). The annual fiesta to the god, known as Aukisna 'for our grandfather' was apparently scheduled to mark the heliacal set or "disappearance" of the Pleiades on 24 April, which throughout the central Andes signals the close of the annual cycle and the death of the earth (Zuidema n.d., 5–6).

Both the living and the dead participated in the fiesta, each family bringing out the mummies of its ancestors to adore the snow-capped peak. At first, people from all over the region went to Mount Pariaqaqa itself to worship him, but later the inhabitants of each area adopted the practice of gathering on a nearby mountaintop within sight of Pariaqaqa and worshiping him there. Each kin group would annually select a ritual representative known as a waqsa, and the waqsas from all the communities would congregate at the mountain to sing and dance for Pariaqaqa and to offer sacrifices of llamas and coca to him. On their return the people would question them as to the demeanor of the deity—whether he was angry or at peace—and there would follow five days of community festivities. The penalty for failing to honor Pariaqaqa in this fashion was sterility and death (Ávila [1598, chap. 9] 1966, 64–71).

The cult of Pariaqaqa was counterbalanced by that of his sister or sister-in-law Chaupiñamka. She was a goddess of fertility, and her fiesta seems to have coincided with the heliacal rise of the Pleiades on 8 June, which announces the arrival of the new year (Zuidema n.d., 5–6). She had a voracious sexual appetite, and at her fiesta the waqsas performed a special dance in which they exposed their genitals in order to please her; with this dance, nature would begin to mature again (Ávila [1598, chap. 10] 1966, 72–75).

The oracle of Chaupiñamka would reveal to her devotees the misdeeds that were the cause of their sufferings. Some communities, however, preferred local manifestations—"sisters"—of the goddess, claiming that Chaupiñamka herself sometimes lied ([1598, chap. 13] 1966, 84–89).

Not only were all these local manifestations seen as one, but each was also seen as representing the five sister goddesses:

Thus, when the people came before one or other of them, they exclaimed, "Ah, Ñamka, the five," and they told her their troubles, whatever the community that was suffering (Ávila [1598, chap. 13] 1966, 88–89).[8]

The cults of Pariaqaqa and Chaupiñamka were confessional and penitential. After an ecclesiastical visit to the area in 1621 it was reported that

in the province of Huarochirí, and in all its towns, they celebrate a festival and assembly of the population called a Watanchana. During this celebration they describe in order the faults they have committed during the year, such as not obeying their kurakas ['native chiefs'], not doing their assigned work, being lazy, and not appealing to their wak'as. The chief priest holds in his hand a thin strand of yarn, in lieu of a whip. After he has sacrificed to Chaupiñamoq, the sister of the idol Pariaqaqa, both of which are famous in this province, he strikes them with the yarn and they are absolved (Arriaga [1621, chap. 18] 1968, 140).

Several times the Ávila narrative refers to rivalry between Checa and other communities in the region, in particular that of Quinti. Genealogically the people of Checa were "younger brothers" to those of Quinti, and they resented their junior status. With the aid of Tutaykiri, the most powerful of Pariaqaqa's sons, Checa was able to conquer Quinti, and from then on the people of Checa were treated by everyone in the area as equals (Ávila [1598, chap. 11] 1966, 76–79). In another myth, a man from a Yunka ayllu of Checa trapped an animal sent by Wallallo Karwinko to kill Pariaqaqa, but a Quinti man claimed the credit. When Pariaqaqa discovered the truth he cursed the descendants of the Quinti impostor but elevated the ayllu of the man from Checa to the status of yañka 'high priest' of his cult. Thus, the indigenous and subjugated Yunkas came to exercise the crucial intermediary role between the oracle and the people (Ávila [1598, chap. 17] 1966, 100–103). There was also jealousy between Checa and Limca over the tutelage of Makawisa, another of Pariaqaqa's offspring (Ávila [1598, chap. 19] 1966, 108–11).

The coastal shrine of Pachakamaq, situated some seventy kilometers from Checa at the Pacific drainage of Mount Pariaqaqa, is featured prominently in the narrative. It is characterized not so much as a creator god as a powerful tellurian divinity, "he who animates the world." When he turned his head to either side, the earth trembled; if he were to turn his entire body, in that instant the universe would end (Ávila [1598, chap. 22] 1966, 128–29).

When the Inka presence began to be felt in Huarochirí, a woman discovered a stone wak'a in her fields, and took it home to show her parents and kin. Questioned by a divine emissary from the Inka, the wak'a said his name was Lloqllaywanku and that he had been sent by his father Pachakamaq to protect the people of Checa. The woman's small house was converted into a large shrine for the wak'a, and people from many different ayllus came to celebrate his fiesta with dancing and singing, in much the same manner as for Pariaqaqa. To Lloqllaywanku's wrath were attributed illnesses, injuries, earthquakes, and enemy oppression; all could be relieved by appeasing the shrine with offerings. On one occasion when his cult slackened, Lloqllaywanku deserted his people and returned to Pachakamaq, causing much illness; he relented only after a delegation had delivered offerings of llamas, cavies, and cloth to the coastal sanctuary. Afterward, Lloqllaywanku was adored with renewed fervor (Ávila [1598, chap. 20] 1966, 112–15).

The Huarochirí narrative is of course a post-Inka document. From it, nonetheless, it is possible to extrapolate back to the pre-Inka epoch tentatively and to begin building up a picture of social and religious processes during the period of regional autonomy. Clearly, it was a time of great flux, with the shifting political and military fortunes of ethnic groups, communities, and lineages being represented in the victory or defeat of their wak'as and the devotion, neglect, or apostasy of mortals with respect to their divine tutelaries.

These beings, associated with mountains, crags, or other natural features, were capable of successive replication across the landscape through the idioms of siblingship, affinity, and descent, lending a veneer of cultural unity to diverse populations scattered across the region. In all probability these secondary avatars were originally local ancestral wak'as recast in the image of the newly dominant regional divinity. Indeed, local and regional shrines pertained to the same hierarchical order, being assimilated into the same unifying theogonies. Pilgrimage to the central shrine or its local outposts brought together representatives from many different communities seeking the protection, deliverance, or oracular pronouncements of the deity.

While Pariaqaqa and Chaupiñamka were temporarily established as the preponderant wak'as of the Huarochirí region, here as elsewhere along the coast and western cordillera the sanctuary of Pachakamaq continued to exert a focal influence. The mythical drama between Pariaqaqa and Wallallo Karwinko could be seen as a regional resonance of the rivalry between the supercenter of Pachakamaq and the Wanka shrine of Wariwillka, which persisted throughout this period.

A recurrent feature of the myths is conceptualization of the various manifestations of divinities, and also temporal and spatial sequences, as sets of five. The number clearly has special significance. It occurs on some thirty occasions in different contexts in the course of the narrative and also crops up repeatedly in another mythical sequence, that of Poma de Ayala ([1620] 1966; see also Ossio 1973). Pease has suggested that besides having an obvious bodily mnemonic—the five fingers of the hand—the number has a key cosmological meaning in Andean culture. If the number four stands for the totality of space—the four cardinal points—

then five becomes the maximal expression of that totality, the four cardinal points plus the center (Pease 1968, 66; see also Bastien 1978, 195; Silva Santisteban 1978). Five then appears as the numerical epitome of the unresolved tension between diametric and concentric dualisms—the first consisting of a quadratic system of double dichotomies, the second of an opposition between center and peripheries (cf. Lévi-Strauss 1968). I shall take up this point again later.

In spite of the overarching regional cults of Pariaqaqa and Chaupiñamka, the picture which emerges from the Huarochirí narrative is of a loose-knit culture, the people of each community retaining their own, ethnocentric perspective on the regional shrines and their local derivatives. There was no general agreement between communities as to the relationships and rank orders of the various wak'as and their multiple derivations, and their mythologies were skewed so as to incorporate earlier, local traditions and to reflect community pride and chauvinism. Indeed, the cults constituted arenas for the pursuit of intercommunal and interethnic rivalries. The narrative is, of course, heavily "Checa-centric"; it can be assumed that some at least of the stories would have been given a rather different slant elsewhere.

The wak'as of Huarochirí were intimately involved in the destinies of their devotees. They were on the one hand the guarantors of the natural order, their continued veneration ensuring the annual round of seasons and the fertility of human beings, crops, and livestock. Conversely, they were held responsible for breaches in that order, from personal misfortunes such as illness and injury to the cosmic calamities of earthquake and flood. They also intervened actively in the political domain, as the instigators of military campaigns and as champions against external aggression. The last role is well illustrated by the wak'a Lloqllaywanku, the quasi-historical account of whose cult presages the subjection of Huarochirí to the Inka yoke. The apparition of Lloqllaywanku and the subsequent growth of his worship were linked directly to the political uncertainties triggered by Inka activity in the area. The attribution of the new wak'a's parentage was astute, to say the least, for Pachakamaq was greatly respected by the Inkas. Extraordinary circumstances thus called into being new shrines, which yet drew their significance from their placement within the existing grid of sacred sites and symbols.

As already noted, the myths associate Pariaqaqa and his various manifestations with lightning, rain, and flood. This weaponry is mobilized most spectacularly in the battle with Wallallo Karwinko, who retaliates by attacking Pariaqaqa with fire. Defeated, Wallallo Karwinko flees eastward into the mountains while Pariaqaqa establishes his dominion in the western cordillera.

The elemental confrontation between fire and water in this set piece exemplifies a cardinal conceptual opposition in Andean cosmology: that between the sun and fire on the one hand, and the moon—associated with the meteorological phenomena of rain, thunder and lightning—on the other. Zuidema (1962) has shown that, in pre-Hispanic times, the moon-water complex tended to be dominant in the cultures of the coastal regions, while the sun-fire complex assumed primacy in the cultures of the inland mountain valley peoples. It might be added that in altiplano cultures—at least in that of Tiwanaku—the pattern seems to be reversed again, the meteorological powers once more assuming center stage.

Now the Huarochirí region drains into the Pacific, while the Mantaro valley, the heartland of the Wanka, drains into the Amazon basin to the east. Lake Titicaca, although situated on the Pacific side of the Andean watershed, constitutes, along with Lake Poopó farther south, an essentially interior drainage system, a kind of inland sea. The Vilcanota valley to the northwest, meanwhile, the heartland of the Inkas, drains into the Amazon basin. In each instance, then, the continental divide becomes a cosmological axis, marking off those cultures whose hydrographic orientation is toward the tropical lowlands from those oriented toward the "ocean"—either the Pacific or Lake Titicaca. This is in accord with the ecological transformation that followed upon Pariaqaqa's victory over Wallallo Karwinko. It is also in accord with the equivalence established by Inka cosmology between Titicaca and Pachakamaq and with the ritual attention paid by the Inkas to the watershed between Titicaca and Cusco.

This symbolic opposition can be seen to recur continually in the Andean archaeological and ethnohistorical record, its fundamentally diametric nature continually transforming into concentrism. Thus, in coastal and "oceanic" highland cultures the sociopolitical center is frequently represented by lunar and aquatic or meteorological imagery, the subdued or threatening periphery by sun and fire. In "Amazonian" highland cultures the symbols are typically transposed, solar imagery being associated with the center, water, the weather gods, and the moon with the periphery. The people of Huarochirí appropriately summoned up an avatar of the preeminent coastal god of Pachakamaq as a bulwark against the warlike sunworshipers from the mountains inland. On this occasion, however, highland heliolatry prevailed.

What of the Cusco area itself during this period of regional autonomy? Here both the archaeological and the ethnohistorical data are fragmentary. No material comparable to the Huarochirí narrative exists, thanks to the thorough reworking of local traditions by Inka mythopoets. Behind their imperial re-creations, however, a pre-Inka society similarly tribalized and regionalized can be discerned, different ethnic groups vying with one another through their religious insignia.

In the predominantly volatile religious culture of the region, certain important shrines took precedence. The place later accorded to Tiwanaku and Lake Titicaca in Inka cosmology suggests that, though the site of Tiwanaku was for the time being unoccupied, it continued to exert a pervasive religious influence across the central Andes analogous to that of Pachakamaq on the coast. As elsewhere in the sierra, the pattern of shrines in the Cusco region itself followed the orography of the area. The snow-capped Mount Ausankati, at 6,384 meters the highest peak in the region, visible ninety kilometers to the southeast of the Cusco valley, was doubtless an ancient shrine, comparable in regional renown to Mount Pariaqaqa farther north. Poma de Ayala places it first in a list of the most important wak'as in the Inka quarter of Qollasuyu, and notes that the emperor used to offer it much gold and silver ([1620] 1966, 1:196).

Meanwhile, it is possible to deduce from the accounts of both Poma de Ayala (1:185–96) and Cobo ([1653, book 13, chaps. 13–16] 1956, 92:167–186; see also Rowe 1979) that the Cusco landscape was studded with many lesser shrines—not just mountains but also natural features such as crags, caves, lakes, springs, and rivers. These local sources of sacredness, the origin and tutelary shrines of a myriad communities and local groups, gave rise to a patchwork of religious geography that was constantly changing as the cults waxed and waned, depending on their oracular reputations, the wealth and power of their priesthoods, patterns of trade and exchange, and the political and military fortunes of their adherents.

Archaeologically, the diagnostic element of Cusco culture in this period is known as Killki, after the site where the distinctive ceramics were first identified (Rowe 1944, 52, 60). The style is the product of a fusion between Wari and earlier, local elements (Lumbreras 1974, 215). There is evidence that around this time a local or regional kingdom emerged along the Vilcanota valley. The remains of small villages pertaining to this polity have been located, one near the present village of Pisac. A myth recounted in one of the chronicles further suggests that this kingdom had its capital near the present town of Calca, at the foot of the twin snow-capped peaks of Pitusiray and Sarasiray (Murúa [1611, book 1, chaps. 91–92] 1964, 2:17–25).

This incipient state, if such it was, apparently lasted into the early Inka era (Lumbreras 1974, 215). It was eventually eclipsed, however, as the Cusco conquerors rose to their brief but immortalized ascendancy.

The Imperial Inkas

During the fifteenth century the central sierra once again began to feel the stirrings of empire. Competition between ethnic sovereignties and coalitions for the control of Pachakamaq, inspired by what might have been a neo-Wari revivalism, reverberated through the region. The skirmishes culminated in the famous semimythical battle between the powerful Chanka confederacy and the Inkas of the Cusco valley, conventionally placed around the year 1438. The Inka victory unleashed a relentless military drive to subjugate all the nations of the Andes.

As the Inkas expanded their dominion, they gradually assembled myths of origin and dynasty fitting to an empire from the cultural miscellany they encountered. According to the origin myth set down by Molina of Cusco, the creator god destroyed the first race of human beings in a flood because of their disobedience. He then raised up anew all the nations of the world at his abode in Tiwanaku, giving to each a language, dress, songs, and the seeds they were to sow, and ordered them to pass under the earth and to emerge at the places he directed. Each nation made a shrine of its *paqarina,* the place from which it had issued.

Since it was dark, the myth continues, the creator made the sun, moon, and stars and ordered them to go to an island on Lake Titicaca and thence to rise to heaven. While the sun was ascending, it called to the Inkas and to their chief Manko Qhapaq and said, "You and your descendants are to be lords and are to subjugate many nations. Look upon me as your father, and you shall be my children, and shall worship me as your father." With these words he gave Manko Qhapaq a headdress for his insignia and a battle-axe for his arms. At this point the sun, moon, and stars were commanded to fix themselves in the firmament. In the same instant Manko Qhapaq and his brothers and sisters, by command of the creator, descended under the ground and emerged in the cave of Paqaritampo, at the point where the sun rose on the first morning after the creator had divided night from day (Molina of Cusco [1573] 1916, 5–9).

Following the creation sequence the myths split into two cycles, one recounting the travels of the creator god Wiraqocha and his "sons" or manifestations, the others dealing with Manko Qhapaq and his brothers and sisters—the Ayar siblings. The two cycles evince determinate structural parallels and contrasts (cf Urbano 1981).

The Wiraqocha cycle is an amalgam of various local legends of subordinate peoples. In it, Wiraqocha and his avatars fan outward from Lake Titicaca to describe a global space that stretched across the central Andes. They are depicted in the main as civilizing agents, stressing ethics and morality and imparting wisdom, knowledge, and the skills of agriculture and weaving to the various nations. In other words they represented the universal aspects of Andean culture. Their message was frequently spurned, and they would then wreak punishment on the people, but they themselves were sometimes tortured or even murdered.

Wiraqocha's northwesterly journey was made straight, in a direct line from Tiwanaku. Locations mentioned on this journey include the Kanas settlement of Kacha, near Sicuani, where the people attacked him and were punished with fire raining down from the sky and where a temple to him was subsequently established; Urcos, where he was received gladly and where a sumptuous shrine to him was built (Betanzos [1551, chap. 2] 1968, 10–11); and Pucará, which in one account is bracketed with the important shrines of Tiwanaku, Pachakamaq, the Wanka shrine of Wariwillka, and the Konchukos shrine of Katekil, all of them said to have been places at which Wiraqocha had turned the disobedient inhabitants to stone (Molina of Cusco [1573] 1916, 10). When Wiraqocha reached the coast he walked across the sea and disappeared (Sarmiento de Gamboa 1960, 210).

The travels of the Ayar siblings, meanwhile, had a much more restricted, regional radius. Their journeyings mapped out the sites of Cusco, the nearby mountain shrine of Wanakauri, and other surrounding shrines. It is the Ayar siblings who laid the foundations of the Inka dynasty, and the dominant themes in the myths are territoriality, militarism, politico-religious organization and hierarchy (for example, Cieza de León [1554, chaps. 6–8] 1973, 24–35).

The legendary exploits of Manko Qhapaq's early successors need not detain the reader. The story of Yupanki, however, merits attention, for here the symbolic opposition apparent in the myth of origin and in the Wiraqocha-Ayar cycles receives full elaboration and partial resolution.

The Inka chief Wiraqocha Inka had fled in the face of the Chanka attack on Cusco, and it was left to his son Yupanki to defend the town. On the eve of battle, Yupanki was visited by a vision of a figure dressed like the Inka, with golden rays surrounding its face, serpents twined round its arms, and pumas between its legs and around its shoulders, which told him he would conquer many nations. Following his victory Yupanki usurped his father's chieftainship, rebuilt Qorikancha, the temple at Cusco, as a shrine to the apparition, and embarked on his great military crusade (Betanzos [1551, chap. 8] 1968, 21; Molina of Cusco [1573] 1916, 18; Sarmiento de Gamboa [1572] 1960, 232).

The Spanish chroniclers were divided as to whether this crucial vision, the divine inspiration for Inka imperialism, was Wiraqocha or the Sun, and the debate continues among anthropologists and ethnohistorians to this day (Rowe 1960; Zuidema 1962, 1976; Duviols 1976b; Demarest 1981). The iconography of the vision does indeed include attributes of both deities. This should be taken, however, not as evidence that the deities are one and the same, as Demarest (1981, 21–22) has argued, but as signifying the partial subsumption of one by the other—specifically of Wiraqocha by the Sun, the latter being indisputably the object of Yupanki's subsequent devotion (Betanzos [1551, chap. 8] 1968, 21; Molina of Cusco [1573] 1916, 18).

According to this interpretation, the ascendancy of the Sun over the god Wiraqocha symbolized transcendences in a number of other domains: of Yupanki over his father, Wiraqocha's namesake; of Cusco's upper moiety, associated with the chiefs and with the Inka tribe proper, over the lower moiety, associated with the priests and with the original inhabitants of the Cusco valley, who were supposed to have incited the Chanka; and of the Inka people over the Chanka confederacy itself (Zuidema 1964, 156–57, 243–46). Inka Yupanki received the epithet Pachakuti, 'transformer of the world', for his reign ushered in the latter stage of the fifth sun, or age—that of Inka Runa, Inka people (Poma de Ayala [1620] 1966, 1:35–90; Imbelloni 1946; Ossio 1973, 190–91).

Another prodigious occurrence associated with the Inka Pachakuti and his father refers to two mountains in the vicinity of Cusco, Pachatusan and Ausankati, as auguries of the retired chief's impending death. Pachakuti was away from the capital on a military campaign to the north.

> They say that at that time news arrived of how a miracle had occurred in Cuzco, of how a serpent had emerged from the mountain of Pachatusan, half a league long and two and a half fathoms wide, with ears, fangs and whiskers; and it came by Yuncaypampa and Sinca, and from there entered the lake of Quibibay; then there came forth from Asoncata two comets of fire, and one passed to Potina [a volcano] near Arequipa, and the other came near Guamanca where there are three or four high snow-covered mountains, and they say they were animals with wings, ears, a tail and four legs, with many spikes on their backs like fishes; and from a distance they looked like fire. And Pachacuti set out for the city of Cuzco, where he found that his father, Viracocha, was very old and sick (Santacruz Pachacuti Yamqui [1615] 1950, 242, my translation).

This myth is a transformation of the one which saw Pachakuti launched on his imperial mission. On this occasion, the divine signs bring him back to Cusco, not to usurp temporal power from his father but to preside over his death and apotheosis (Santacruz Pachacuti Yamqui 1950, 243). The terrible creatures that are the portents of this crisis issue forth from the two major mountain wak'as of the Cusco region.

Pachatusan also features in another Inka myth, which in view of the importance of the mountain in our later discussion is worth citing in full:

> In that season there came from Opatari three hundred Indians, all loaded with casks of gold dust, for it was new year; and that night it began to hail heavily on all the crops, as far as the roots, and the Ynga, on the advice of the elders, ordered that all three hundred Indians should take their cargos of gold to Pachatusan, a very high mountain, and there he buried all of them with the gold they were carrying, killing them . . . instead of showing gratitude he did the contrary; and the said vast quantity of gold has not been recovered to this day (Santacruz Pachacuti Yamqui [1615] 1950, 254, my translation).

While the Inka kings were wont to portray themselves as omnipotent rulers presiding over a uniform, rigidly centralized bureaucratic kingdom, the reality was different. The *pax Inkaica* was imposed upon an exceptionally heterogeneous population, with indigenous provincial polities ranging from virtually autonomous groups of villages to the mighty Chimú state. These multifarious entities were knit together by astute political pragmatism: mobilizing and manipulating ethnic loyalties and cleavages, veiling dealings with subject groups with traditional notions of reciprocity, assimilating local chiefs into the Inka ruling class, and guarding against rebellion by settling newly conquered territories with loyal *mitimas* 'colonists'. The Inka achievement lay precisely in the extension of local political and economic institutions to embrace an empire (Moore 1958; Rostworowski de Diez Canseco 1976; Murra 1980; Pease 1982; Rowe 1982).

The business of state in the diversified dominion was conducted largely through the idiom of religion, for local and regional shrines continued to serve as the sacred emblems and oracular spokesmen for the various communities and nations. It is in the articulation of the metropolitan and provincial shrine cults, then, that the delicate balance of forces which held the empire intact can be perceived.

Military conquest or—as was often the case—peaceful capitulation was evidence to the Inkas at least of the superiority of their gods over those of their subjects. The Inka solar cult was made universal by establishing in the main provincial capitals a counterpart of Qorikancha, the temple of the Sun. Monthly sacrifices were performed in these provincial temples to match those in Cusco, recreating the local in the image of the center (Bandera [1557] 1965, 161; Cobo [1653, book 12, chap. 35] 1956, 92:136).[9] The export of the state cult to the provinces was matched by the transfer of subsidiary images of provincial wak'as to the metropolis, where they were kept in a special temple, each on its own altar with its insignia and attendants but with a chain around its foot to signify the vassallage of its people (Valera [1589] 1950, 145). By this means the Inkas appropriated and made into a whole the symbolic capital of their subjects. The vast edifice of interlocking cults was supported by the produce of the so-called Sun lands in each community, lands that in reality were dedicated to the whole gamut of local, provincial, and imperial gods (Rowe 1946, 265).

Despite the fiction of Inka religious supremacy, the main provincial shrines were respected, even feared, by the Cusco conquerors. The long-standing Andean tradition of oracular religion was incorporated into their statecraft, and they consulted such famous oracles as Wariwillka, Katekil, and Pachakamaq (Rowe 1946, 302). Such royal patronage, while it added luster to a shrine, was not without risk. Katekil was consulted by Topa Inka as he traveled northward to quell a rebellion, and it correctly foretold his death in battle. As a result the reputation of the shrine spread, and a sumptuous temple was built. Later, however, the emperor Waskar, Topa Inka's son, angry that such wealth had accrued from the prediction of his father's death, ordered that the temple be burned to the ground (Arriaga [1621, chap. 2] 1968, 26–27). Ironically, Topa Inka was something of a religious reformer: he took a close interest in the oracular pronouncements of the various wak'as of the realm, with a view to

establishing their competence and circumscribing their powers (Poma de
Ayala [1620] 1966, 1:185).

The ancient coastal sanctuary of Pachakamaq, for its part, the Inkas
held in the highest reverence. They erected a temple of the Sun within the
shrine precincts but otherwise allowed it to function as before. Topa Inka
was careful, however, to ensure that this powerful wak'a, too, was brought
within the ambit of state control by having one of Pachakamaq's four sons
lodged in the pantheon in Cusco, "so that it might protect him and give
him answers to the questions he asked it" (Santillán [1553] 1950, 59).

As for Tiwanaku-Titicaca, though the main site was in ruins, a shrine
on one of the islands in the southern part of the lake still functioned as
an important pilgrimage site in the region. Topa Inka consolidated his
conquest of Qollao by establishing on this island an important temple
of the Sun. An adjacent island was dedicated to the moon. Copacabana,
situated on a mainland peninsula and the embarcation point for the
islands, also harbored a revered pre-Inka shrine, a figure of blue stone
with a human face and the body of a fish, which was worshiped as the
god of the lake (Calancha [1639, book 1, chap. 3] 1972, 1:139). Here
the Inkas established another shrine and also a hospice for pilgrims. Here,
too, were settled two thousand tax-exempt colonists drawn from forty-
two nations of the empire to service the shrine complex, who were to be
supported by the indigenous population of the village (Ramos Gavilán
[1621, book 1, chap. 12] 1976, 43–44).

As noted, the two aquatic shrines of Pachakamaq and Titicaca were
both associated in Inka mythology with the creator god Wiraqocha, Lake
Titicaca as the cradle of creation and Pachakamaq as the preeminent
shrine on the coast from which he disappeared across the waves. Cos-
mologically, the two sites were rendered directly equivalent, together
defining the outer edges of the Inkas' sun-blessed domain:

The Inka proclaimed: "At the lake below that we call Titicaca, at the place
called Pachakamaq, there the world ends. Beyond, there can be no settlement,
nor any light." . . . And in accordance with this belief, the Inkas were obliged
to adore these two wak'as above all others (Ávila [1598, chap. 22] 1966,
126–27).

The Inka empire was conceptualized spatially as comprising four
suyus 'quarters' in relation to the imperial capital: Chinchasuyu to the
northwest, Antisuyu to the northeast, Qollasuyu to the southeast, and
Kuntisuyu to the southwest. Cusco city itself was organized according
to the diametric dualism characteristic of Andean culture, with the hanan
'upper' moiety associated with the Inka king and the imperial élite and
the hurin 'lower' moiety associated with the original, pre-Inka inhabitants
of the valley.

In addition to this basic dualism, the city formed the hub of a set
of forty-one imaginary lines (ceques or siqis) radiating outward to the

horizon. Located on or near each ceque was a series of shrines, some ancient, others associated with previous Inka rulers, whose upkeep was charged to particular social groups (Cobo [1653, book 13, chaps. 13–16] 1956, 92:167–86; see also Rowe 1979). Ceques had multiple functions in Inka cosmology and social organization. They underlay the formal ordering both of space, orienting the topography of the region toward Cusco, and of time, providing horizon markers for the observation of the rise and set of heavenly bodies from which the state calendar was constructed. They further sustained the hierarchical order of social groups in the capital and joined this hierarchy with the temporal and spatial orders by an elaborate calendrical division of ritual labor between the various groups (Zuidema 1962, 1977).

The chronicles indicate that the Inka calendar was a fusion of an earlier agricultural and sidereal calendar used by the original inhabitants of the Cusco valley with a later political and solar calendar instituted by the Inkas and used for state administration. Given the varied Andean ecology, an agricultural calendar can only ever embrace a limited population; a solar calendar, on the other hand, can provide fixed temporal markers over and above local agricultural cycles. Accordingly, imperial time was organized around the solstices and the equinoxes, with the movements of the moon, planets, and stars coordinated to the solar cycle by means of a complex calculus (cf. Zuidema 1977, 1978, n.d.).

The two months dedicated to the equinoxes, both of them associated with the cults of Wiraqocha and the moon, were, respectively, the month following the March equinox in the Gregorian calendar, when the feast of the king was held, and the month preceding the September equinox, when the feast of the queen was celebrated. For the king's feast, Inka Raymi, the king offered sacrifices to all the wak'as of the realm and invited people of all ranks to eat and drink at his expense; the nobility engaged in competitive sports and games (Poma de Ayala [1620] 1966, 1:169–70). The queen's feast, Qoya Raymi, was a ritual cleansing of the empire of the diseases caused by the onset of the rains (Poma de Ayala 1966, 1:176–77). Each solstice occurred in the middle of a double month. Both double months were dedicated to the state cult of the Sun, with the festival of Inti Raymi, 'Sun Feast', held around the June solstice—announced by the heliacal rise of the Pleiades on 8 June—and that of Qhapaq Inti Raymi, 'Great Sun Feast', around the December solstice (Zuidema 1977, 246–47; see also Urton 1981).[10]

The Inkas' Cuscocentric cosmos was continually reconstructed in a series of annual rituals. One of these was the pilgrimage undertaken by Inka priests on the day of the June solstice, during the Inti Raymi. The priests proceeded in a straight line to the sanctuary of Willkanuta, 150 kilometers away on the continental divide. They returned to Cusco following the river, also known, of course, as Vilcanota. On the outward and return journeys they rested at a series of stations. On the same day, another group of priests celebrated the sunset on Mount Wanakauri, southeast of Cusco city, and the sunset at an unidentified location northwest of the capital (Molina of Cusco [1573] 1916, 28–31).

The purpose of these rituals was to celebrate the birth of the Sun: Willkanuta translates from the Aymara as 'house of the Sun'. The significance of the particular direction derived from the fact that the long-distance ceque that the priests followed, when extended beyond Willkanuta, passes through Pucará and the sacred peninsula of Copacabana to Tiwanaku. Thus Cusco, Wanakauri, Willkanuta, and Tiwanaku were all aligned on a single ceque associated with the birth of the Sun—the same ceque followed by Wiraqocha on his mythical journey northwest from Tiwanaku. It tracked northwest beyond Cusco to reach Ecuador, the northernmost part of the empire (Zuidema 1982, 439–45).[11]

Another important Cuscocentric ceremonial was the sacrifice of Qhapaq Hucha. *Qhapaq* means 'great' or 'royal'; *hucha* had a wide semantic field, including 'sin' or 'fault' and 'dispute' or 'business' (Zuidema 1982, 425–26). A Qhapaq Hucha was held during each solstitial feast, and another was staged on the occasion of a significant event or crisis of the empire—a military victory or defeat, the coronation or demise of the king, and the like (Duviols 1976a, 11–12). The two types of ritual might thus be seen as respectively marking out annual and epochal time, and they perhaps differed in scale and ceremonial grandeur.

A Qhapaq Hucha consisted of a sequence of centripetal and centrifugal movements focused on Cusco. First, sacrificial victims—immaculate children and livestock—were sent to Cusco from all over the empire. Some were slaughtered in the capital in honor of the imperial gods—Wiraqocha, the Sun, the Moon, and Thunder. Others were blessed and sent back, together with apportionments of blood from the metropolitan sacrifice, to be immolated at the principal provincial shrines. A *kipukamayoq*, a specialist in the knotted rope abaci (*kipus*) used by the Inka bureaucracy, kept account of how much was to be sacrificed to each wak'a (Molina of Cusco [1573] 1916, 88–95; Murúa [1611, chap. 29] 1964, 2:109–11). On these return journeys the victims and the parties escorting them did not follow the roads but traveled in straight lines along the ceques radiating outward from Cusco, "without turning off at any place, crossing over the ravines and hills that they encountered before them . . . until each group arrived at the place where they were awaited to receive the said sacrifices" (Molina of Cusco [1573] 1916, 90). Here, then, in a conceptual triumph over the rugged Andean terrain, was the perfect expression of Cusco as the *axis mundi*, its power diffusing radially and uniformly, through the medium of the bodies of sacrificial victims, from the center to the peripheries (see also Zuidema 1982, 429–31).

The final stage of a Qhapaq Hucha involved the convergence on the capital of the statues or busts of the wak'as themselves, accompanied by their priests and retinues (Cieza de León [1554, chap. 29] 1973, 110–

12). This was the occasion for the official revaluation of all the provincial wak'as and the revision of their mutual ranking. As in pre-Inka times, the relative values of local and regional shrines were unstable and subject to reassessment, ostensibly on the basis of oracular success. Now, however, in place of the many inconsistent ethnocentric shrine hierarchies there was but one official league table, revised at each Qhapaq Hucha to take account of shifts in the balance of power among shrines and nations and between them and the center, which was legitimated by the exchange of gifts and the bestowal and withdrawal of royal favors. Now, too, the king and the ethnic lords entered into negotiations concerning diplomatic or military missions and new economic and fiscal contracts, all conducted according to Andean canons of reciprocity (Molina of Cusco [1573] 1916; Cieza de León [1554] 1973).

The Quechua narrative from Huarochirí contains a detailed account of such negotiations, characteristically couched in a religious idiom, during a Qhapaq Hucha convened by Topa Inka during the latter half of the fifteenth century. The account is clearly colored by local perceptions, thus providing a useful corrective to Inka propaganda.

For twelve years, the narrative says, and at a cost of thousands of lives, the imperial army had been attempting without success to subdue three recalcitrant tribes. Much saddened, Topa Inka decided to summon to Cusco all those shrines to which he customarily offered gold and silver. Wak'as from all over the realm were borne on their litters to Haukaypata, the great square of Cusco. Pachakamaq was among them, but Pariaqaqa could not decide whether to attend, eventually sending his son Makawisa, who humbly kept to the edge of the gathering.

The emperor addressed the assembled gods with a mixture of entreaties and threats, imploring them as recipients of his largesse to assist in the military campaign but threatening to burn them all if they declined. Pachakamaq refused, claiming that if he so desired he could destroy the entire world, the Inkas included. But Makawisa nobly offered his services, and the emperor gave him his personal litter to ride into battle. The wak'a and his troops easily defeated the rebels, using Pariaqaqa's customary weapons of lightning and flood. In fear and gratitude, the Inka emperor allocated fifty of his men to the service of Makawisa and offered him anything he wanted. The wak'a asked only that the emperor become his waqsa, devotee. Thus, Topa Inka himself was obliged to pay homage to the shrine in dance and song (Ávila [1598, chap. 23] 1966, 130–35).

Through the use of such strategies of religious reciprocity combined with brute military force, the Inkas built up an empire, which at its apogee stretched 4,000 kilometers from Pasto, southern Colombia, in the north to the Maule River, central Chile, in the south. There are indications, however, that at the time of the Spanish invasion the centrifugal forces of ethnicity and regionalism were beginning to reassert themselves and that these, together with other problems of the Inkas' own making—the unwieldy expansion of the tax-exempt class, for example, and the tendency for succession to be resolved by civil war—were dangerously weakening the integrity of the empire. The Spanish, of course, adeptly exploited these internal divisions and debilities. But had they never arrived, the problems that beset the empire, still less than a century old, might in any event have proved terminal.

Spanish Catholicism

The parties—societies, cultures—to a colonial encounter are not systems, but processes. It is necessary to consider not so much what they were at the time of contact, but what they were becoming and how it was happening. The historical collison between Hapsburg Spain and Inka Peru was a collision between two distinct yet comparable sets of developments unfolding on opposite sides of the globe; in the course of the violent subjugation of the Andean peoples by the European colonizers there emerged a composite set of social and cultural processes, in part contingent upon and in part continuous with what had gone before. My treatment of religion in Spain before the conquest of the New World will be briefer and historically shallower than my treatment of that in the Andes, for reasons of space and because the background and context are better known to a Western audience. My aim, though, is the same: to identify and trace those significant developments and changes, emergent and in train, that were subsequently to guide the course of Andean religion to the present day.[12]

At the same time that Topa Inka was pursuing his religious reforms of the oracles of the empire, the institutional foundations of Spanish Christianity were also undergoing profound changes, which, though inspired by domestic concerns, were to help prime it for its coming role as the religious arm of an even more extensive, global dominion. Ferdinand and Isabella, respectively the heirs to the thrones of Aragon and Castile, whose marriage in 1469 laid the basis for the political unification of Spain, were presiding over the final stages of the long crusade to free the country from Moorish control. The wealth and temporal power of the ecclesiastical establishment, however, posed a serious threat to the extension of the royal prerogative into the newly reclaimed territories. The worldliness and immorality of the clergy must also have offended the deep religious piety of the so-called Catholic monarchs. Furthermore, late medieval Spain was politically divided and culturally regionalized. The imposition from Madrid of firm discipline and orthodoxy on a degenerate Christianity, for long compromised by both Judaism and Islam, could lend the fledgling state an important unifying influence. The religious reforms and realignments introduced by Ferdinand and Isabella thus came to serve both religious and political ends.

In 1478 a radical overhaul of the clergy was inaugurated, to be intensified during the 1490s under the supervision of the Franciscan cardinal Ximénez de Cisneros. The more blatant excesses of both regulars and seculars were curbed, the fulfillment of their pastoral duties enforced, and their overall intellectual caliber raised considerably. All these reforms were to make the Spanish clergy—especially the regulars—a more effective proselytizing force. Additionally, the Christian humanism of the Spanish Renaissance initially encouraged by the reforms was carried to the New World by persons such as Bartolomé de Las Casas, to persist there in dogged counterpoint to the dominant exploitative ethos of the colonial régime.

In 1478, too, the pope authorized the establishment of the Holy Office of the Inquisition in Spain. It was originally intended to purge Spanish Christianity of crypto-Judaism but later widened its brief to include Moorish converts, Illuminist mystics, Erasmians, Protestants, and heretics of all hues. In the New World, however, the Inquisition did not achieve the same notoriety it possessed in the Old. Crypto-Jews were once again its principal target, Indians being technically beyond its jurisdiction. But in general its religious function in the colonies was largely ceded to its political function, and it became another instrument for the regulation of the colonial church by the Spanish monarchy (cf Lea 1964).

Over and above these particular reforms was the steadily tightening grip of the crown on the ecclesiastical establishment. The church under whose auspices Christianity entered the Americas was controlled in all matters save those of doctrine and dogma, not by the pope in Rome, but by the king in Madrid. The royal patronage, *patronato real*, originally granted by Pope Innocent VIII to Ferdinand and Isabella in 1486 to clinch the reconquest of Granada, was gradually extended as Ferdinand wrested more and more concessions from successive popes. Eventually, with the bull *Universalis ecclesiae regimini* of 1508, Julius II granted full rights of patronage for the whole of the Spanish Indies, discovered and undiscovered. Thus, for a period of nearly three hundred years the Spanish crown enjoyed in effect papal vicariate in its overseas dominions. The importance of this singular arrangement in the creation and consolidation of empire is inestimable. Not without reason did a Mexican advocate describe the royal patronage in 1755 as "the most precious pearl in the royal diadem" (Shiels 1961, 1).

Patronage conferred on the Spanish kings the right to exercise a vast range of functions to do with church administration and finance in the colonies. The crown appointed all clergy and guided their policies and movements, sometimes placing clerics in civil offices, sometimes converting lay officials into bishops. It marked and altered diocesan and parish boundaries, fixed all benefices, administered and collected tithes, superintended church councils and synods, and controlled the communication of papal decisions to the colonies (Shiels 1961, 7; Pike 1964, 4–5; Mecham 1934, 27–37).

Papal surrender of these cherished rights, an about-face against the long-established tradition of Roman supremacy, is perhaps to be explained by political instability in Italy coupled with the advance of Turkish forces in the east, which persuaded the popes to throw in their lot with sympathetic monarchs and to devolve the costly responsibility of overseas evangelization on those secular powers willing to shoulder it (Shiels 1961, 17–18; Boxer 1978, 78). The Council of the Indies knew the geography of its territories, moreover; the popes did not (Shiels 1961, 11).

Madrid's control of the colonial church, however, was never total. While secular clergy vowed obedience to the episcopal hierarchy—which was firmly in the monarch's thrall—regulars pledged obedience to a general in Rome and to his provincials overseas. Jesuits took an additional vow of obedience to the pope. The religious orders therefore to some extent fell outside the jurisdiction of the royal patronage, a situation that successive kings attempted to remedy (Pike 1964, 6). There was enduring conflict on the ground as regulars and seculars competed for benefices and stipends and bishops strove to bring regulars under their control (Haring 1947, 187). The conflict was symptomatic of a fundamental contradiction in the colonial church between its function as guardian of a religious nationalism focused directly on Madrid and its function as propagator of a universal faith ultimately centered in Rome.

Nevertheless, for the crown the political advantages of patronage were enormous. For the church, the effects were equivocal. It has been argued that the benefits of a secure institutional foundation were all but outweighed by the concomitant spiritual debilitation—that however diligently the early Hapsburgs may have discharged their religious duties under the grant, the long-term consequence of royal patronage in Hispanic America has been an incapacity on the part of institutional Catholicism to differentiate itself fully from the political sphere and to pursue its spiritual mission wholeheartedly (Vallier 1970, 45–47).

The cultural product exported to the Indies through the royal patronage was a specifically Iberian brand of devotional Catholicism in which were blended a rich diversity of pagan, early Christian, and medieval traits. Some idea of the texture of this religion can be gained from the responses to a questionnaire issued by Philip II to the towns and villages of New Castile between 1575 and 1580, which sought information on miracles and vows, chapels and shrines, relics and indulgences, of which the local people were cognizant. These data, elegantly presented and analyzed by William Christian (1981a), depict a religion anchored in a sacred landscape of holy sites and geared to the preoccupations of a predominantly rural livelihood, but constantly changing in response to developments in the wider political and religious domains. This dia-chronic process is clearly revealed in the successive strata of religious devotions extant in New Castile during the 1570s. Indeed, an exami-nation of these strata affords us a cursory retrospect of Christian de-votional history.

Christian identifies four devotional layers in the responses to the questionnaire. The first was composed of devotions centered on the bodies or relics of saints. Devotion to the saints had its roots in the early days of the church, when the faithful gathered to commemorate a local mar-tyrdom or the death of a confessor or bishop. This gave rise to what is still the commonest type of saint's feast, the *dies natalis*, the anniversary of the person's "birthday" into heaven. In direct transgression of pre-Christian taboos surrounding death and corpses (Brown 1981), the earthly remains of these early saints became cult objects invested with miraculous powers. They were also incorporated into formal worship, for from early in the history of the Church it was required that relics be placed in every altar (Wilson 1983, 5).

In northern Spain, medieval hermits became local saints, and their relics are still revered. In New Castile and the southern provinces, the reconquest came after the golden age of eremitism, and indigenous relics were sparser. While some parish churches in the sixteenth century still boasted miraculous cures from ancient and treasured bodies or bones, most relics were derived from the large—and largely suspect—collections that emanated from Rome and were circulating about Christendom at the time, many bearing papal authentication. Devotion to the latter relics was casual, but possession was still nevertheless a source of civic pride and intervillage competitiveness. Indeed, for the most part relics were divisive and reinforced community chauvinism (Christian 1981a, 111, 126–41).

Indulgences were closely analogous to these "papal" relics. They too issued from Rome and by the end of the sixteenth century were so nu-merous that they had become a debased currency; yet they still enhanced the sanctity of local shrines in relation to their neighbors and competitors (Christian 1981a, 143–46).

Conversely, some of the great pilgrimage centers of medieval Chris-tianity owed their fame to saintly relics and papal indulgences. St Mary of the Portiuncula, the small chapel near Assisi where in 1226 St Francis died, was the first pilgrimage shrine in Europe to owe its success to the skillful advertisement of a probably counterfeit indulgence. Santiago de Compostela, in northern Spain, whose cult quickly came to epitomize the crusade against the Moors—the battle-cry "¡Santiago y cierra Es-paña!" "St James and close in, Spain!" echoed down the centuries—was founded on a dubious claim to the possession of the body of St James the Greater and in the eleventh century was "lifted to the front rank of medieval shrines by a combination of shrewd promotion and excellent communications" (Sumption 1975, 143, 116).

The second layer of religious devotions in sixteenth-century New Castile consisted of those focused on the images, rather than the relics, of saints. Following the wave of iconoclasm instigated by the Byzantine emperor Leo III, the Second Council of Nicaea in 787 set out the official position on the cultus of images: they were to be objects of dulia, veneration, as distinct from latria, the worship due to God alone (Addis and Arnold 1955, 419). In the East, literalness of form was avoided by restricting iconic representations to two dimensions, and they came to occupy a central place in the liturgy. In the West three-dimensional statues, probably derived from the effigies and busts of reliquaries (Wilson 1983, 5), fell within the ambit of a more popular and informal religiosity. Images permitted a greater physical flexibility in devotion than did relics, since they were not necessarily tied to cathedrals, monasteries, or parish churches but could be taken out into the countryside to deal with specific emergencies and to create new loci of sacredness (Christian 1981a, 21).

In sixteenth-century New Castile, images of titular saints of parish churches were—as they are today—the objects of routine fiestas on their days. More important were the images of those saints whose cults had their origins in collective vows made by the villagers in times of crisis, such as epidemics, drought, or other disasters. For each crisis there was a specialist advocate whose aid the villagers could enlist—St Sebastian for pestilence, St Gregory of Nazanzius for vine worm, St Agatha for hail, and so on—but where there was uncertainty, a lottery might be held to choose the intercessor. A vow might entail not working on the saint's day, fasting on its vigil, holding a procession, or constructing an image or chapel. Such votive devotions frequently continued long after their original causes had been forgotten (Christian 1981a, 23–69). They rarely spread beyond their immediate localities, each becoming a part of the distinctive devotional complex of a particular community or village.

The third stratum of religious devotion was attached to shrines of the Virgin Mary. The earliest Marian feast, first recorded in the fifth century, was probably a commemoration of her Assumption, the equivalent of the *dies natalis* (Turner and Turner 1978, 155). The ancient belief that Mary was assumed bodily into heaven, enunciated as dogma only in 1950, would seem to rule out relics, and this perhaps accounts for the slow growth of her cult in the early church. As late as the twelfth century only four Marian feasts were widely celebrated, those of the Purification (2 February), Annunciation (25 March), Assumption (15 August), and Nativity (8 September) (Addis and Arnold 1955, 540). Around that time the clergy, chiefly the mendicant orders, began to propagate her cult in earnest, primarily as a universalizing influence to counteract the religious localism fostered by devotions centered upon saintly relics (Turner and

Turner 1978, 171). Their aims, however, were quickly compromised. As the popularity of the Virgin spread, not only did ingenious "relics," such as tunics, graveclothes, phials of milk, and locks of hair begin to appear and multiply (Warner 1976, 291), but her cult itself was enshrined, becoming focused on particular relics or statue reliquaries many of which, like the girdle of Chartres, gave rise to enduring pilgrimage devotions (Sumption 1975, 49–50).

One of the reasons for the enormous proliferation of Marian shrines in central and southern Spain from the twelfth century on was the vacuum left by Moorish occupation: after the reconquest, there were simply not enough shrines of saintly relics to reconsecrate the territory (Christian 1976, 61). Here, "invention" of Marian relics was secondary to apparitions and discoveries of images. The belief in the Assumption of the Virgin meant that she could reappear to selected mortals less problematically than a devoutly dismembered saint (cf Turner and Turner 1978, 155). As far as the discovery of images was concerned, the common tradition was that these were ancient statues hurriedly hidden as the Moors advanced, then unearthed one by one as the reconquest rolled them back (Foster 1960, 161). There was a grey area, however, between the discovery of statues and the witnessing of apparitions: the preeminent Castilian shrine of the Virgin of Guadalupe, for example, which together with the Virgin of Montserrat was one of the twin poles of Iberian devotion to Mary, rested on a fable in which both themes were incorporated. Seer-discoverers were invariably men, frequently herders, but attested apparitions dated from the period before the Inquisition began examining Catholics. After 1500, religious virtuosity of this kind was a risky business (Christian 1981a, 76; 1981b, 19–20, 92, 111, 150–87).

Marian shrines of New Castile were qualitatively different from those of other saints. They offered general rather than specific relief, not just to a village but to groups of communities and to individuals: they represented a "higher, more permanent level of advocacy" (Christian 1981a, 73). Many miracles were attributed to them. They were typically situated away from human habitation, near caves, springs, or trees or on cliffs or peaks. They may be seen, suggests Christian, as elements in

a paganization (from *pagus*, country), of Christianity—a kind of encoded recapitulation of the process by which rural pre-Christian notions of a sacred landscape reasserted themselves over an initially cathedral- and parish-church–centered religion (Christian 1981b, 20).

The fourth layer of religious devotion in sixteenth-century New Castile was only just beginning to manifest itself at the time of the questionnaire of Philip II but was to assume greater prominence during the succeeding centuries. It was focused on specific shrines of Christ himself, whose worship until then had been mainly of a general nature rather than centered in shrines. The shrines were images of Christ crucified that had been profaned, or had suddenly begun to cure, or had been "discovered" painted on walls, or had displayed some sign such as sweating, bleeding, or weeping, or for some other reason had become fixed as unique loci of sacredness (Christian 1981a, 194–96). As might be expected, these Christ shrines had no particular thaumaturgic specialization, and their divine help could be sought in the face of any misfortune, from individual sickness to war.

The shift toward Christocentric shrine devotions had its roots in the medieval period. From the eleventh century on there was an increasing stress in Western Christianity on the human as well as the divine nature of Christ, the formal, distant figure of an impersonal divinity yielding to a more immediate, accessible, human God. This growing emphasis on Christ's humanity found expression in the art and iconography of the later Middle Ages, which depicted with greater realism than ever before not only the agonies of his Passion and death but also the maternal tenderness he experienced at his mother's breast. There was no theological contradiction between Christ's two natures, between Christ the suffering human being and Christ the omnipotent king and judge; rather, the one led naturally to the other, for "only by imitating Christ the man could one placate Christ the judge" (Sumption 1975, 133).

There was in fact already a Christ shrine in Catalonia, Cristo de Berito, a crucifix from Syria mentioned in the Second Council of Nicaea in 787, which had sweated and bled. It was managed by the Franciscans, and reproductions of the image, known as *majestats*, were common in the Catalan region in the eleventh century. It was not until the fourteenth century, however, that Christ shrines came to be objects of devotion and pilgrimage elsewhere in Spain. One of the first was San Salvador de Oviedo, a statue of the seated Christ on the church's high altar, though its miraculous reputation was fused with that of the more ancient saintly relics beneath. Subsequent Christ shrines, such as those of Burgos, Orense, Valencia, and Seville, were crucifixes; the Burgos and Seville images were among the most famous, both of them managed by the Augustinians. Many of these statues were ancient, having lain dormant for centuries before manifesting some sign, such as sweating blood, which triggered the devotion. Their legends were linked to that of the Syrian crucifix in Catalonia: San Salvador de Valencia, for example, like Cristo de Berito, was said to have been either found at sea or carried miraculously upriver from the sea (Christian 1976, 54–55, 66–67).

The establishment and development of Christ shrines in Spain coincided with the rise of flagellant processions and brotherhoods, means whereby the faithful could emulate Christ's sufferings (Christian 1981a, 185). As a result, images of Christ carrying the cross (Cristo Nazareno) and of Christ being whipped (Cristo de la Columna) joined those of the crucifixion as devotional foci, becoming enshrined in their turn (Christian 1976, 67–70). During the seventeenth and eighteenth centuries, the expiatory imitation of the Passion by exclusive brotherhoods gave way to more widespread, contractual Christocentric devotions based on vows and petitions to a diversity of shrines (Christian 1981a, 201).

This Iberian phenomenon whereby the new Christology crystallized, so to speak, into popular devotions attached to specific miraculous shrines was the result of a combination of historical factors. As with Marian shrines, the cultic vacuum left by Moorish occupation was partly responsible, coupled with competition between religious orders in the newly reclaimed territories: Christocentric devotion of this kind peaked during the years following the reconquest of Granada (Christian 1976, 71). The seventeenth and eighteenth centuries, meanwhile, were a period of state building in the peninsula, with new, internally more heterogeneous political entities being fashioned from the former kingdoms and duchies. The wars, epidemics, and economic depressions that marked this period of political upheaval perhaps led a troubled people to seek the direct source of divine assistance and solace (Christian 1981a, 201). Furthermore, in such an unstable political climate, the enshrinement of Christ lent to the identity of a community or region its highest religious expression. Christian also acknowledges that the advent of Protestantism, with its strictures against hagiolatry, may have provoked a shift to a more tangible form of Christocentric devotion in Spain as a defensive strategy (1981a, 199). In any event, by the end of the eighteenth century these Christ shrines had declined in popularity, and today most are either ignored or forgotten (1981a, 204). In modern Spain, as throughout Catholic Europe, most by far of the important regional, national, and international shrine devotions are Marian.

Of these four kinds of religious devotion in sixteenth-century Castilian Catholicism, only two—those focused on shrines of Mary and Christ—came to assume great importance in the New World. Though saintly relics were exported to the Spanish colonies, they did not become the objects of intensive cult. Quite possibly, the missionaries played down their significance lest they undermine their attempts to extirpate indigenous cults of mummies of the dead. In any event, by the sixteenth century relics had become severely devalued in Spain, those few still highly venerated being jealously guarded by the communities that possessed them.[13] Images of the lesser saints, for their part, were bestowed upon the Christian neophytes of the New World in abundance, as divine patrons of this or that parish, village, or town, and their aid was occasionally invoked by the colonial clergy in times of crisis, but in general they tended not to become the foci of special votive devotions among the laity.

From the outset, however, the figure of Mary was the resort in adversity both of the Spanish colonizers and of the native converts, her presence becoming fixed and enshrined in the physical landscape through signs, visions, and miracles. Meanwhile, the advent of miraculous shrines of the suffering or crucified Christ in the New World coincided with the rise to popularity of their Spanish counterparts, but unlike the latter they have not been abandoned, and their cults have continued, along with the more numerous Marian shrine devotions, to the present day.

The enshrinement of Christ and the Virgin in the Spanish colonies thus faithfully reflected domestic devotional fashions. But arguably these fashions were born of something more fundamental than a quest for ever more powerful and less specialized sources of supernatural aid, as a purely intellectualist interpretation would have it. According to the Hispanicist John MacKay, Christ in Spanish religion has always been the center of a cult of death: Christ crucified is an expiatory victim dying in order to bestow immortality, a continuation of the fleshly life. Mary, assumed body and soul into heaven, symbolizes that bodily immortality. Consequently, Christ tends to appear in only two dramatic roles: as an infant in his mother's arms and as a suffering and bleeding victim. The image of Christ in Spanish religion is in fact a travesty of the idea of the human Christ from which it was derived: "it is a picture of a Christ who was born and died, but who never lived" (MacKay 1932, 98–99, 110). Other observers, such as Richardson, Pardo, and Bode (1971) and Klaiber (1977, 3–4), have noted the central position of the suffering Christ in Spanish-American Catholicism. Even allowing for the author's Presbyterian prejudices, the following is a fair characterization of the theology that Spain exported to the New World:

A Christ known in life as an infant and in death as a corpse, over whose helpless childhood and tragic fate the Virgin Mother presides; a Christ who became man in the interests of eschatology, whose permanent reality resides in a magic wafer bestowing immortality; a Virgin Mother who, by not tasting death, became the Queen of Life—that is the Christ and that the Virgin who came to America! He came as Lord of Death and of the life that is to be; she came as Sovereign Lady of the life that now is (MacKay 1932, 102).

Reflecting on the influence of religion in the formation of the pre-Columbian Andean empires, Rowe (1976) notes that throughout the 2,500 years from Chavín to Inka there was a progressive subordination of religion to politics, a gradual domestication of cults and their priesthoods to serve the interests of secular powers. The Chavín cult achieved its predominance through priestly proselytization and influence. Tiwanaku's power was likewise theocratic rather than military, but the contemporaneous empire of Wari, to which it lent direct religious impetus, was carved out through conquest. The final and most audacious imperial venture, that of the Inkas, had its mythical beginnings in the overthrow of the hierocracy by the warrior chiefs and the ascendance in classic, Weberian fashion of a worldly, unmystical religious ethic (Weber 1958, 282–83).

In the panorama of Andean prehistory, however, states and empires were infrequent and ephemeral, unable to sustain themselves for very long before succumbing to the chronic forces of political and ethnic separatism. Geographically far-flung though these dominions were, chronologically they coruscated only briefly among the shifting constellations of local communities and ethnic chiefdoms. Participation in empire by these smaller political constituencies was occasional and short-lived. Regionalism, not state centralism, was the rule.

In consequence, the enduring features of the cultural environment lay in the religious domain, regional and supraregional shrines providing the coordinates for successive political and economic geographies. The Chavín cult generated an extensive pilgrimage network that laid the foundations for interregional exchange in the Andes. The shrine of Pachakamaq, though probably never an administrative center in its own right, endured two successive empires as one of the holiest sites in all of Peru. Oracular shrines of certain ethnic groups, such as Wariwillka and Katekil, also survived successive bouts of state formation and decay. Meanwhile the influence of Tiwanaku-Titicaca, once the fount of a great theocracy, has persisted to the present day.

As chance would have it, Spain on the eve of its conquest of the New World had taken the process of subordination of religion to politics further than the native Andean states had ever been able to achieve. Institutional Catholicism in the Andes was to become first and foremost a mechanism of political and social control and only secondarily an ethical and spiritual teaching. According to the Peruvian philosopher José Carlos Mariátegui, Inka religion "lacked the spiritual power to resist the Gospel" (1973, 163). Yet despite the power conferred on the Church by landed wealth and royal patronage, the Gospel was to make remarkably little headway. Cult, not creed, was to be Catholicism's principal contribution to Andean religion; and it was primarily with a sacredness inscribed in the landscape itself that the cult would have to come to terms.

CHAPTER 3

The Andes
Reconsecrated

"Everything that is inflammable is burned at once, and the rest is broken into pieces." So ran the blunt instruction in a manual for missionaries extirpating idolatry in early seventeenth-century Peru. The writer's own tally was impressive: on one of his tours, which lasted seventeen months, he and his fellow visitor discovered and destroyed 603 "principal" wak'as, 3,418 *konopas* (household shrines), 189 *wanq'as* (stone field or farmstead shrines), and 617 *malkis* (ancestral mummies) (Arriaga [1621, chap. 2] 1968, 19–20.)[1]

But Father Arriaga was not so naïve as to believe that theatrical desecration of this kind would entirely eliminate pagan religious sentiments. He was well aware that manufactured effigies and cult objects were only one facet of idolatry. Far more significant to the natives was the sacred quality of the landscape itself. Lakes, mountains, springs, rivers, crags—"these are all *wak'as* that they worship as gods, and since they cannot be removed from their sight because they are fixed and immobile, we must try to root them out of their hearts, showing them truth and disabusing them of error" ([1621, chap. 2] 1968, 24).

This the extirpators signally failed to do. The concerted campaigns against idolatry had begun late, more than fifty yea₁s after the conquest, and a habit of religious pluralism had already begun to establish itself. Arriaga notes that a "common error" of the natives "is their tendency to carry water on both shoulders, to have recourse to both religions at once. . . . Most of the Indians have not yet had their *wak'as* and *konopas* taken away from them, their festivals disturbed, nor their abuses and superstitions punished, and so they think their lies compatible with our truth and their idolatry with our faith" ([1621, chap. 8] 1968, 72–73). By the practice of planting crosses on pagan sites and shrines that could not be physically destroyed, moreover ([1621, chap. 16] 1968, 129), Christian missionaries merely confirmed in the eyes of the natives the sacred status of the locales. Animism persisted, continuing to mediate the processes of agropastoral production at the local level, but with its cultic expressions suppressed, marginalized, and eventually reclassified theologically as superstitious and hence tolerable survivals.

Meanwhile, numerous images of Christian saints—the *wak'as* of the Spaniards, as the Indians perceived them (Arriaga [1621, chap. 13] 1968, 110)— peopled the landscape. Until the 1570s, these saints were installed mainly as the emblems and divine patrons of preexisting native groupings and ethnic constituencies, on which the protocolonial economy was based. Following the major reforms of that decade, the cult of the saints bifurcated. With the dismantling of national identities and the resettlement of the native population into nucleated communities, saints' cults were thoroughly insinuated into village life, becoming the principal vehicles through which local power structures were legitimated. But running parallel to this process of cult localization was one of cult regionalization. Shrines of the Virgin—and later of Christ—began to be established on the basis of miraculous occurrences, and these shrines came to command extensive pilgrimage devotions.

In this chapter and the next I shall expand upon this bare summary of the progressive Christian reconsecration of the Andean landscape. First, though, a diagnostic feature of those shrines that rose to regional and in some instances transregional prominence—their alleged miraculous quality—must be clarified.

The Concept of Miracle

The first formal Christian definition of miracle, *miraculum*, is generally credited to St Augustine (A.D. 354–430). Augustine was not at first a great enthusiast of miracles, claiming that while they were important for convincing unbelievers in the early stages of missionary activity, now that the church was well established they were no longer necessary. When orthodoxy came under attack, however, he became firmly committed to their continuing occurrence (Sumption 1975, 57).

Augustine's initial definition casts the net wide: "I call a miracle anything which appears arduous or unusual, beyond the expectation or ability of the one who marvels at it." Here, the miracle is located in subjective perception alone: it is a vehicle of personal revelation. Some years later, he offered a more exact and objective specification: "We give the name 'nature' to the usual and known course of nature; and whatever God does contrary to this, we call 'prodigies' or 'miracles' " (quoted in Hardon 1954, 230, 231).

The Augustinian definition of miracle has been elaborated but not much altered by Christian theologians since. St Thomas Aquinas, writing in the thirteenth century, defined a miracle in Augustinian terms as "an occurrence beyond the order of all created nature." He argued, though, that miracles were not necessarily prodigious; any effect, however insignificant, was miraculous if it surpassed the powers of nature. It might do this in one of three ways: *substantially*—that is, by producing a material effect, such as making the sun turn back; *subjectively*—consisting in the subject rather than the substance, such as raising the dead to life; or *qualitatively*—producing a natural effect in an unnatural manner, such as curing a long-standing illness. St Thomas was also concerned with the question whether demons could work miracles; he concluded that they could not, for although their work might appear miraculous, they in fact operate within the framework of created forces, albeit forces unknown to us (Hardon 1954, 232–34).

St Thomas's codifications reflected the growing concern of the medieval church with the proper authentication of miracles. From around the eleventh century, heaven-sent cures and other unusual incidents attributed to reputable shrines especially were subjected to rigorous investigations by the ecclesiastical authorities. These investigations tended to be more legal than scientific, concentrating on the corroboration of dates and places and on the character and reliability of witnesses (Sumption 1975, 64). Placing judgment on divine intervention at the disposal of church experts was clearly a strategy designed to strengthen the hand of a centralizing institution in the face of phenomena which by their very nature were random and uncontrollable, but which could nevertheless be turned to good account.

During the Counter-Reformation, these investigatory procedures were further tightened and formalized (Kemp 1948). At the same time, the concept of miracle was refined. Pope Benedict XIV, writing in the eighteenth century, added to the element of transcendence of nature that of religious purpose: an effect was a miracle only if it was directed to the confirmation of truth or personal sanctity. God, in other words, does not tamper with nature gratuitously. Here, we can detect an anxiety over and above the issue of legalistic authentication, an attempt in the now pluralist Christian environment to monopolize judgment not merely on the circumstances but also on the religious meaning of miraculous phenomena. The modern theological concept of miracle in the Catholic Church rests essentially on these two elements of Pope Benedict's definition: miracle as a transcendence of natural laws and miracle as a divine sign (Hardon 1954, 242–57).

With the rise of scientific positivism, however, the domain of transcendence was shrinking fast. In 1748, Hume delivered a rationalist attack on the idea of miracle that is still the point of departure for some philosophical discussions of the issue, such as those by Smart (1964) and Swinburne (1970). Miracles now became the residue that remained after scientific explanation had whittled away all that it could. Today at Lourdes, for example, the evidence for an alleged miraculous cure is exhaustively examined by appointed doctors, who strive to disprove the claim that anything has occurred that medical science cannot explain. Such is the caution of the authorities that in recent times the number of authenticated miracles has been reduced to an average of about one a year (Neame 1968, 138).[2] The wonder-working reputation of the shrine among the million or so pilgrims who visit it annually bears little relation to this minimalist approach to the miraculous on the part of the church.

The notion of miracle in the Andean context is a Christian implant, propagated by the clergy. There is no directly equivalent term in Quechua: only the Spanish words, *milagro* and *milagroso*, are used. They are applied only to effects produced by or involving Christian divinities; similar effects ascribed to pagan deities are not classed as miraculous. We are not concerned at this point to distinguish between those occurrences that have been officially designated as miracles and those that have not, but with phenomena that were and are *popularly* deemed miraculous, often by both laity and clergy alike. These phenomena fall roughly into two categories.

The first is that of mystical theophany—an apparition of a divine personage, or the chance discovery of an image, or the first prodigious event attributed to an image, or some other initial divine sign to a human witness. By and large, such occurrences would conform to what Aquinas labeled substantial miracles. The sign permanently marks and makes sacred a particular spot or object, sometimes a manufactured image but often a rock or crag. As already observed, the hallowing of unusually shaped rocks and the petrification of mythical personages are pervasive themes in Andean religion and mythology, and it is chiefly by way of the notion of miraculous theophany that they have been assimilated into the Catholic cult. Whatever their material form, miraculous shrines in this sense, like their nonmiraculous counterparts, are each regarded as a unique locus of sacredness. Thus, each Christ shrine is thought to be the abode of a separate spirit known as a *taytacha* 'little father', each Marian shrine of a *mamacha* 'little mother', though relations of substance and even of identity are imputed in specific cases. A theophanic shrine is anchored in both space and time: it owes its origin to an event or series of events in which the divinity manifested itself to a human witness, and it persists as the sacred locale in which the event occurred.

The second category of miraculous phenomena, partly overlapping the first, comprises those occurrences that stem from the active thaumaturgy of such a theophanic image, the material or spiritual favors it bestows on its devotees or, alternatively, the misfortune it wreaks upon those who have incurred its displeasure. These miracles are usually subjective or qualitative according to Aquinas's schema and are typically more akin to the insignificant effects allowed for in his definition rather than to the arduous marvels of Augustine's. What is regarded by a devotee as a miracle—the eventual recovery from an illness, a good yield of young livestock, success in an examination, or whatever—would not necessarily strike an observer as preternatural or out of the ordinary. Rather, miraculous intervention by a deity might be imputed as a final cause of good or occasionally bad fortune, in much the same way as witchcraft is used to explain misfortune among the Azande of central Africa—as a second spear in an etiology that does not include the notion of chance (Evans-Pritchard 1937).

Whereas the innate thaumaturgic powers of local patronal icons in the Andes are unstressed and implicit, those of miraculous shrines are overtly stressed and proclaimed. A pilgrimage to a miraculous shrine might be undertaken to supplicate the shrine spirit for some special favor or in fulfillment of a vow to make the journey in return for a request already granted. An important shrine might be described as very miraculous, this being given as the reason for the large numbers of pilgrims who frequent it. Again, we encounter the notion of a miraculous shrine as a finite, historical phenomenon. The waxing and waning of a shrine's popularity in the course of time are read as indications of its increasing or declining thaumaturgic powers. A local patronal shrine is not normally subject to such vagaries of fortune: its congregation is territorially and socially fixed, and its cult is observed as a matter of course.

Following the Spanish conquest, half a century was to elapse before attested miracles would make their appearance in the central Andes, leading to the establishment of important centers of pilgrimage according to a superficially European pattern. To understand the emergence and significance of these miraculous phenomena in the Andean setting, it is necessary to sketch the relevant socioreligious developments throughout those first fifty years.

Localization of Cults

Geographically, ecclesiastical and secular political organization in the Spanish viceroyalty of Peru developed hand in hand. The first bishoprics to be founded were those of Cusco in 1536—where the first bishop was Pizarro's chaplain Vicente de Valverde—and Lima, the new capital, in 1539. Initially subject to the archbishop of Seville, Peru became in 1545 a religious province in its own right, centered in Lima (Haring 1947,

184). By the end of the century the province comprised eight dioceses: Lima itself, Huamanga, Cusco, Arequipa, Chuquiabo, La Plata, Santa Cruz, and Quito (Arriaga [1621, chap. 19] 1968, 157).

Cusco's first cathedral was inaugurated in 1538 and was dedicated by Valverde to the Virgin of the Assumption—apparently against the wishes of the conquistadors, who favored the Immaculate Conception (Esquivel y Navia [1749] 1980, 1:90). Within a few years six parishes had been established in the city, each with its own special patron: Santa Ana, San Blas, San Cristóbal, Los Reyes (Belén), San Pedro, and Santiago. In addition, the parishes of San Sebastián and San Jerónimo were founded in the city suburbs. Indians were assigned by ayllu to each parish, in accordance with Inka practice (Vargas Ugarte 1962, 1:129).

In the rural hinterland of the diocese, meanwhile, the division of mission fields immediately after the conquest followed as elsewhere the boundaries of the extensive *encomiendas,* grants by the crown to Spanish settlers of the labor and produce—though not the land—of specified Indian populations. *Encomenderos* were obliged to provide for the spiritual instruction and welfare of their charges by installing resident priests. They themselves, prohibited from living on their encomiendas, had to reside in Cusco city.

There is no doubt that some of the friars to whom proselytization was entrusted during the early years were dedicated men, inspired by the new Christian humanism of early sixteenth-century Spain, according to which the Indian was someone to be not merely converted but civilized, humanized, purified, and reformed, so as to realize his full intellectual and spiritual potential (Gibson 1966, 71–72). But in a religious view, the initial missionary drive was only superficially effective. There were simply too few priests for such an enormous task, and cursory instruction followed by mass baptism left Indians with scant understanding of the new religion. Even by 1569 the total number of priests and friars resident in the viceroyalty of Peru was still only about 350; the estimated need was for 1,500. New Spain, with a smaller population, already had more ministers (Kubler 1946, 403).

The problem was exacerbated in Peru by the generally inferior quality of the clergy, particularly of the seculars who followed in the wake of the regulars to take up the benefices that had been created. Also, Peru had a much briefer experience of initial concerted missionary activity than did New Spain. For by the middle of the sixteenth century, with the virtual extinction of Christian humanism in Spain itself, the missionary ardor in the New World had dimmed, and the energies of the church were being absorbed instead by ecclesiastical politics and the management of its accumulating wealth.

The apparent tolerance of the religious authorities at this time toward pagan practices is evident in contemporary descriptions of the Corpus Christi fiesta, a grand parade of all the saints of the diocese modeled directly on those staged in many Spanish cities (Angles Vargas 1983, 2:579). The timing of this extravaganza was astute, for the feast's novena and octave in late May or June coincided with a period of intensified ritual activity in the pre-Hispanic calendar associated with the heliacal rise of the Pleiades on 8 June and the solstice on the 21st.[3] In its collocation of provincial religious images in the city plaza, the former Inka ceremonial ground, moreover, the festival recalled the final phase of the Qhapaq Hucha that had been staged around the solstice. From Garcilaso's account of the Corpus fiesta of 1555 we can infer the manner in which the cult of the saints was operating in rural areas at the time and in particular the kinds of constituency with which the new divine tutelars were associated.

More than a hundred saints attended, sumptuously dressed and borne on litters around the plaza, followed by the Eucharist in a monstrance of gold, silver, and jewels. The saints were drawn from the city parishes and from the rural encomiendas; in some instances the Indians of an encomienda had one saint and the encomendero another, the object of his personal devotion (Garcilaso de la Vega [1617, part 2, book 8, chap. 1] 1966, 2:1415–19).

Superficially, as Garcilaso remarked, the event did indeed resemble the processions of saints and their confraternities held in towns throughout Spain at this time. But there was an important difference. The Indians accompanying the Christian images in Cusco were organized not according to any Iberian model but on the basis of national affiliation— affiliation, that is, to one or other of the diverse ethnic groups of the region. Each nation paraded in its distinctive ceremonial costume, carrying aloft along with its saints an image of its bird or animal totem, or a picture of its *paqarina*—spring, river, lake, mountain, cave, or whatever. Each had its band of flutes, drums, and tambourines, and they sang not in Quechua but in their native tongues, "so as to differentiate one nation from another." The various nations paid homage to the Blessed Sacrament in order of "antiquity"—that is, according to the sequence of Inka conquest, the most recently conquered passing before the monstrance first, the Inkas last. The remaining Inkas of royal blood were permitted to accompany the cathedral chapter and city council on the dais, "thereby recalling that the empire had once belonged to them and doing them honor" (Garcilaso de la Vega [1617] 1966, 2:1416).

In this celebration of national identities, chauvinism was never far below the surface. On this occasion, an Indian of the Kañari nation provoked a near riot by ostentatiously displaying the head of an Inka captain whom he had decapitated in a duel during the rebellion of Manko Inka in 1536. The Kañaris, having suffered heavily at the hands of the Inkas, had been enthusiastic allies of the Spaniards throughout the conquest. To press the point home, the Kañaris had decorated their litter with scenes of battles in which they had fought alongside the conquistadors against the Inkas. The Spanish licentiate confiscated the offending items and warned against causing such scandals in the future, much to the satisfaction of the Inkas and all the other Indians present (Garcilaso de la Vega [1617] 1966, 2:1417–19).

This account of the Cusco Corpus during the 1550s indicates that the cult of the saints had been but lightly imposed on a native population still deeply divided along ethnic lines. Indeed, ethnic separatism was clearly encouraged within certain limits, so as to provide a framework within which Indians could be gradually weaned from their idolatry and persuaded to transfer allegiances from the native tutelary deities to their Christian successors. Thus, the Corpus fiesta presented the remarkable spectacle of the old religious emblems and the new being carried side by side in public procession, with the full blessing of the church authorities.

This relaxed attitude toward the pagan past, symptomatic of both overconfidence and laxity on the part of the clergy, was to have convulsive consequences. During the 1560s a millenarian movement swept through the central Andes prophesying the imminent overthrow of the white invaders. Known as the Taki Onqoy, literally 'dancing sickness', the movement seems to have had its origins in the province of Huamanga (present-day Ayacucho) and to have spread eastward to encompass the entire diocese of Cusco, southward to Arequipa and La Paz, and northward to Lima (Millones 1973, 87). The florescence of the movement coincided with widespread preparations among the Indians for an armed uprising against the Spaniards, masterminded by the rebel Inka Titu Kusi, who was still holding out against the conquerors in his jungle stronghold at Willkabamba. Titu Kusi doubtless figured that the messianic fervor igniting the Indian masses would help to carry forward his plans for military rebellion. Nevertheless, cult and plot were separate and quite distinct phenomena. The military plans were discovered and quashed in 1565; the Taki Onqoy, on the other hand, had originated several years earlier and was not fully suppressed by the religious authorities until the early 1570s (Wachtel 1973, 119–21).

The central precept of Taki Onqoy was the total separation of the Andean and Spanish worlds. The Christian faith was to be rejected in its entirety and the cults of the old gods were to be resumed in their ancient form. Where their shrines had been destroyed by missionaries, they were raised to life by libations of *chicha* 'maize beer' and offerings of maize to the sacred ruins by the practitioners of the cult. Neophytes had to undergo traditional rites of purification that entailed fasting and sexual abstinence and had to abandon Spanish clothing in favor of traditional Indian dress. All traces of Hispanic culture were to be abjured in preparation for the new age that was about to dawn. An apparent anomaly in this otherwise thoroughgoing nativism was the adoption by two female acolytes of the cult leader Juan Choqni of the Christian titles of Santa María and her namesake María Magdalena, a point to which I shall return later.

In the Taki Onqoy, the cult of the wak'as was transformed from a place-bound to a person-bound religiosity. Whereas formerly they had been worshiped in their various sacred locales—mountains, streams, caves, and other natural features of the landscape, as well as manufactured effigies—now they entered into the bodies of adepts of the cult, inducing trance and ecstasy and stimulating their hosts to dance and sing in their honor. Possessed of the spirits of the wak'as, these adepts went about the land preaching the millenarian prophesy, the forthcoming defeat of the Christian God by the resurrected deities. In fulfillment of this prophecy, all the wak'as would unite and congregate in two batallions, one at Lake Titicaca in the mountains, the other at Pachakamaq on the coast—the two wak'as which together staked out the Andean cosmos. The Spaniards would perish in a great flood, and a new humanity would bloom in the Andes (Wachtel 1973; Millones 1973).

Despite the opportunist association of Taki Onqoy with Titu Kusi's planned uprising, then, the movement was far from being a religious drive planned to restore the Inka empire to its former glory. Neither Cusco nor the defeated and discredited imperial divinities featured in its strategy, but instead the myriad local and regional gods together with the two great supercenters of Titicaca and Pachakamaq. Its cosmic weapon—cataclysm—was consistent with the aquatic symbolism of both these sites, which as in Inka times symbolized the latent power of the periphery in relation to the dominant center. For in the indigenous scheme of things the Spanish had replaced the Inkas as supreme rulers, and opposition to them was accordingly expressed in terms of the geographical coordinates of the Inkas' own concentric cosmology. The wak'as were to forget their old enmities and ally with one another against the common foe, the Christian God. The alliance of these subimperial wak'as signified the goal of overcoming ethnic and ayllu rivalries among the colonized Indians in favor of a pan-Andean unity. It was a unity that expressly was not to be imposed from above by the Inkas or neo-Inkas, but which was to be built up out of the very regional loyalties and ethnic solidarities it sought to transcend.

The movement was vigorously suppressed by the clergy, and its leaders were punished. There were further outbreaks of nativist millenarianism in the central Andes—the Muru Onqoy in Aymaraes in 1590–91, for example, prompted by an epidemic, and a movement in Arequipa in 1600 triggered by an earthquake and a volcanic eruption (Curatola 1978, 69–71). But these were crisis cults confined to specific localities, and they did not achieve the regional spread of the Taki Onqoy.

As Stern has demonstrated (1982, 51–71), the Taki Onqoy was less a response to political and economic oppression than a reaction to cultural compromise, to the insidious interpenetration of things indigenous and things Spanish in a great many areas of life. As such the crisis was pan-Andean, and at its core lay a conflict of religious loyalties. Native ethnic-religious identities, far from having been suppressed by the colonists, were the foundation upon which the encomienda system had been erected and were thus the cultic constituencies for the new religion. Saints and wak'as jostled for attention, and it was this chronic confusion, almost a cultural schizophrenia, that the Taki Onqoy attempted to resolve.[4] It failed, of course; but the malaise that had engendered it still demanded cure.

The colonial authorities rose to the challenge. During the decade that followed, the viceroy Toledo instituted a radical program of resettlement and draft labor that changed the face of Andean society. Later, the church abandoned its pious hope that paganism would simply wither away alongside the newly implanted faith and launched a series of remorseless campaigns against idolatry (Duviols 1971). This opened a new phase in the Christianization of the Andes, when trends that had been incipient during the first decades of colonization were accelerated and consolidated. It was a period during which the cult of the saints passed from being a mere foreign ceremonial adjunct to become firmly embedded both in Andean religious consciousness and in the rural political economy.

Toledo's principal reforms were, first, the resettlement of the dispersed native population in *reducciones,* villages laid out on a grid pattern around a church and plaza, where the Indians could be more effectively policed and converted, and the introduction of the labor draft, *mita.* The draft was primarily for working the silver and mercury mines, but it soon came to be applied to a range of other activities, in agriculture, the textile workshops, and public works.

Furthermore, the newly galvanized viceregal administration, aware that encomenderos might entrench themselves as an obstructive feudal aristocracy, began to take over encomiendas as they fell vacant on the deaths of their holders, redesignating them as administrative units known as *corregimientos* under the direct control of officials of the crown, the *corregidores.* To protect the source of draft labor and tribute, the Laws of the Indies decreed that the lands of Indian communities were inalienable. Communities were also permitted a limited degree of self-government under their kurakas, thereby sparing the state part of the cost of their administration.

The reforms themselves, and the efforts by the natives to evade them—only *originarios,* the original inhabitants of an area, were liable to the mita, *forasteros* 'strangers' being exempt—produced vast population movements that helped to weaken subimperial loyalties and gradually to erase awareness of national ethnic identities. In their place there emerged much narrower sets of attachments to community and locality, attachments that were directly expressed in Christian religious observances. The one-to-one correspondence between encomiendas and mission fields had already been abandoned following the instructions of the First Lima Council of 1551 on the organization of *doctrinas,* the Indian parishes, and the Second Lima Council of 1567 ruled that each doctrina should number 400 heads of household (Vargas Ugarte 1962, 1:129). From the 1570s on, doctrinas came to be centered in the larger reducciones. The overarching, supralocal saints' cults fell away, and each doctrina began to cultivate its own particular repertoire of religious festivals. The Christian cult became local and introverted, signifying corporateness and exclusiveness rather than membership in any wider, episcopally focused communion.

An important factor in this increasing localization of the cult of the saints in the rural areas was the establishment from the 1570s onward of Indian *cofradías,* local confraternities each dedicated to a particular Christian saint or advocation and to the celebration of its annual feast (Kubler 1946, 405). The number of such confraternities increased significantly during the campaigns against idolatry. They undoubtedly served at first as surrogates, or cloaks, for the suppressed cults of the local wak'as and provided the kurakas with an institutional articulation between the rulers and their people (Varón 1982). As time went on, confraternities and their cults became definitively incorporated into local power structures in a process that was more or less complete by the mid seventeenth century. Not just doctrinas and their annexes but also their hinterland communities were invested with patron saints and sodalities, all ranked in direct relation to the politico-religious statuses of the respective settlements (Celestino 1982, 151). The configuration of these "cult territories" came to constitute both the geographical map and the ideological charter for local political authority, conferring a degree of stability on rural colonial society that was to last for nearly a hundred years (Kubler 1946, 347; see also Armas Medina 1953, Marzal 1983).

Meanwhile, a similar process of cultic involution was taking place in Cusco city itself, where the Spanish population had been expanding steadily. Certain religious images came to acquire unique associations with the city and to be held in special affection by clergy and laity alike. The first such urban shrine was the wooden statue of the Virgen de Belén, the Virgin of Bethlehem, sent to the city by the emperor Charles V in the 1550s but alleged to have been lost at sea until discovered by some fishermen off the port of Callao. The city parishes in Cusco cast lots to decide which should receive it, and the winner, Los Reyes, changed its name to that of the Marian advocation. Such was the popularity of the statue that in 1560 the city council ordered that a new road be opened to the sanctuary to accommodate the flow of visitors (Esquivel y Navia [1749] 1980, 1:200–204).

Another focus of civic devotion was a cathedral statue of the Virgin of the Immaculate Conception, whose cult was already well established by the beginning of the seventeenth century. In 1651 La Linda, the Pretty One, as the statue was popularly known, was installed as patroness of the diocese, Santiago from the eponymous parish being named patron of the city (Vargas Ugarte 1956, 2:156; Esquivel y Navia [1749] 1980, 2:99–101).

More directly instrumental was the devotion that sprang up around the Virgen de Soledad, the Virgin of Solitude, whose image was housed in the church attached to the Mercedarian monastery. In 1614, when the city was in the grip of an epidemic of erysipelas, the image was credited with a series of miraculous cures. Thenceforth it was held in special reverence (Esquivel y Navia [1749] 1980, 2:23–25).

In addition to these special civic attachments to imported Marian advocations, an entirely Cusquenean advocation was created toward the end of the sixteenth century on the basis of the alleged miraculous deliverance of a group of Spaniards during Manko Inka's siege of the city in 1536. During the siege the Spaniards had taken refuge in the great hall of Suntur Wasi on the main square. Red-hot slingshot landed on the thatched roof of the building, but the Virgin was said to have descended from heaven to smother the flames with her cloak (Hemming 1972, 193–94). The incident was first recorded only in 1600 and was later subjected to heavy elaboration. The Virgen de la Descensión, as she was called, won a permanent place in the mythology of the city. Though there is no shrine as such, she is commemorated in the altar of El Triunfo church, built on the site of Suntur Wasi.

The fiesta of Corpus Christi in Cusco registered the social and religious changes that were taking place in the region during this period. By 1620, attendance at the festival was so poor that the *corregidor* 'governor' was prompted to issue a decree ordering all communities within ten leagues of the city to attend with their saints and dancers, along with the urban parishes (Esquivel y Navia [1749] 1980, 2:41). The Indians in the rural areas, their former national constituencies dismembered and their pagan religious emblems proscribed, were developing their own community-centered ceremonial cycles around particular, local pantheons of saints and advocations, and as a result enthusiasm for the wider diocesan festival of Corpus Christi began to fall away. At the same time the more Hispanic population of Cusco city was generating its own exclusive civic loci of religious devotions, and the Corpus fiesta was becoming more an urban than a diocesan event in any case.

All this reflected a greater preoccupation in both town and countryside with local hierarchies of power and a correspondingly greater investment of time and capital in their ritual and religious underpinnings. The burghers of Cusco glorified the city and their reputations by pouring wealth into church ornamentation and religious festivities. In the countryside, meanwhile, Indians were induced to do the same, albeit on a smaller scale. National identities gave way to allegiance to community and parish, and social status and political authority came to hinge upon discharging rotational offices, or *cargos,* in local fiesta systems. The Cusco Corpus in fact came to be replicated in miniature in villages and towns throughout the diocese, in annual parades on the appropriate days of the patron saints of parishes and of their dependent chapelries, which mapped out the vectors of ecclesiastical and secular power. The Cusco celebration itself was eventually to be reduced to a purely local event, embracing just the parishes and convents of the city.[5]

Regional ritual articulation was not absent, however. The corollary of this process of cult localization was the florescence of pilgrimage, focused upon miraculous shrines of the Virgin or Christ, and the sites of Pachakamaq and Titicaca, the twin geographical and cosmological coordinates of the Taki Onqoy, were among the first to be favored.

Regionalization of Cults

Around the year 1600, a Lima merchant and his wife erected a small chapel on the road from Lima to Pachakamaq and commissioned a painting of the Virgin of Guadalupe for it. This advocation, as noted earlier, was popular not only in its native Castile but throughout Spain. There was in fact already a sanctuary dedicated to it in Pacasmayo in northern Peru—a "franchise shrine," to use Christian's expression (1981b, 97)—which had become an important pilgrimage site, controlled by the Augustinians.[6]

The Pachakamaq image achieved in turn almost instant renown. Before long more than twelve masses a day were being celebrated to cope with the flood of pilgrims. Sailors in particular sought the protection of the shrine against the perils of the sea. In 1611 the brother of the founder decided to donate both the chapel and the extensive plot of land surrounding it to the Franciscans, so that the shrine could be properly maintained and the religious needs of its devotees adequately cared for. During the mid seventeenth century a new sanctuary and college were built, with a larger copy of the original painting installed on the high altar (Vargas Ugarte 1956, 2:106–9).

The pagan shrine of Pachakamaq had of course been desecrated during the conquest, an early victim of the conquistadors' religious looting. Yet in the ensuing decades, as both Spanish missionaries and acculturated Indians strove to find, or establish, parallels between Andean and Christian belief so as to facilitate conversion, the Pachakamaq deity acquired the reputation among some advocates as the direct counterpart of the Christian God. Garcilaso, writing in the first years of the seventeenth century, claims that for the Inkas, while the Sun was the visible manifestation of God, Pachakamaq was the creator of the universe and the true divine majesty. The Devil had deceived the Indians by claiming, through the mouthpiece of the eponymous coastal shrine, that he, Satan, was Pachakamaq. But now that the Christians had arrived, the true identity of the deity could be restored: missionaries should in future use Pachakamaq as the Quechua term for the Christian God (Garcilaso de la Vega [1617, part 1, book 2, chap. 2] 1966, 1:70–72).

Garcilaso's theological gymnastics were in part an attempt to render Andean belief within a framework intelligible to a Spanish audience (MacCormack 1985, 465). But there is another factor at work. Garcilaso was steeped in Inka court culture, and the emphasis of his entire work is heavily on the Inka. It is thus possible to appreciate his insistence that an Inka belief in an abstract and unknowable Supreme Being had been travestied in the shrine-focused cults of non-Inka peoples and transformed into the devil worship abhorred by the Christians.

Such ideas would have contributed to the popularity of the Guadalupe shrine among native converts, for here—it was alleged—was a diabolic inversion of the authentically Andean idea of the true Godhead, finally reclaimed for Christianity. The advocation, meanwhile, would have had an intrinsic appeal to Spaniards, especially to seamen on shore leave far from their homeland. Location and advocation happily combined to make the shrine one of the great early colonial pilgrimage centers.

Gradually, however, devotion to the Virgin of Guadalupe began to decline. By the time of independence the income from the shrine barely sustained the chaplain. There was an attempt to resuscitate the cult in the mid nineteenth century, but to no avail. In 1928 the sanctuary was demolished, though the original image is preserved elsewhere (Vargas Ugarte 1956, 2:109).

The demise of the Guadalupe shrine must have been caused in part by the rise of others that were being spawned by the expanding metropolis. By the mid-sixteenth century, an image of the Virgin of the Rosary in the Dominican Convent in Lima—by tradition, another of the gifts of Carlos V to the colony—had been adopted as a mascot by the viceregal authorities and was further sanctified during the early 1600s by its associations with the visions of Santa Rosa, who of course became another important focus of devotion in the city after her death in 1617 and her canonization in 1671 (Vargas Ugarte 1956, 2:71–78; Attwater 1965, 300).[7] If these shrines catered to the religious needs of the Spanish segment of the population—Rosa, though her parents were poor, was of impeccable Spanish descent—the shrine of Señor de los Milagros, whose cult originated in the mid-seventeenth century, answered to those of the large African sector. Indeed, it is possible to argue for a continuity between the Guadalupe and Milagros cults, which would make the latter an indirect descendant of the pagan shrine.

Titicaca, Pachakamaq's highland counterpart, found a more direct Christian successor in the famous shrine of the Virgin of Copacabana (see appendix 1, map 4). The official mythohistory of this shrine was set down by an Augustinian friar less than fifty years after its founding. During the early 1580s, the story runs, the Indians of the lakeside village of Copacabana were plagued by bad harvests and other misfortunes. Accordingly they decided to form a confraternity dedicated to a saint other than their patron Santa Ana, to help them in their adversity. The upper moiety favored the Virgin, but the lower moiety wanted San Sebastián. Neither side would give way, so an Indian from the upper moiety named Francisco Tito Yupanki decided to clinch the argument by making a statue of the Virgin for the village. He was inspired to this task after seeing a vision of a beautiful Indian woman and her child at the water's edge.

Unfortunately, the first clay image he produced was considered so rudely fashioned that it was ordered to be removed from the church. Undeterred, Tito Yupanki traveled to the booming mine town of Potosí to learn sculpture and began work on a second image modeled on a statue in the church of Santo Domingo there. Accompanied by one of the governors of his moiety, a kinsman, he then petitioned the bishop of La Plata, in whose diocese Copacabana lay, for permission to form a confraternity, showing him a painting of the statue he was making. The bishop rejected their petition, saying that Francisco was better fitted to painting monkeys than to sculpting statues of the Virgin.

Tito Yupanki returned to Potosí to collect his statue before going on to La Paz. There he encountered a Spanish artist whom he persuaded to retouch the image. Meanwhile the governor, who had remained in La Plata to press their case, finally succeeded in gaining episcopal consent for the confraternity, and he and Tito Yupanki returned to Copacabana to announce the fait accompli. Reluctantly, the lower moiety agreed to the confraternity but not to the image, which they refused to allow into the village.

The hapless Tito Yupanki returned to La Paz to seek a buyer for his work, but he chanced upon a Franciscan monk who was so taken with the image that he recommended it strongly to the parish priest of Copacabana. The statue eventually entered the village in pomp in time for the fiesta of Candlemas, 1583. During the procession, a bronze crucifix fell and struck the corregidor on the head, but he was unharmed. This was hailed as the Virgin's first miracle (Ramos Gavilán [1621, book 2, chaps. 2–6] 1976, 112–16).

Sabine MacCormack offers a revealing analysis of the local political setting for these events. Among the residents of the upper moiety of Copacabana were descendants of the colonists who had been settled there by Topa Inka when the existing cult centers were "solarized," while the lower moiety consisted essentially of the indigenous people whose forebears had been obliged to support the newcomers. The conflict between the moieties thus had deep historical roots. Furthermore, the Inkas of colonial Copacabana belonged to that faction that had supported the Spaniards: the governors of the upper moiety in 1582 were grandsons of the kuraka of the village at the time of the conquest, who had allied with Paullu Topa Inka in assisting the conquistador Almagro on his Chilean campaign. The upper moiety, then, had direct links with the successive colonizers of the area, first the Inkas, then the Spanish; the lower moiety were the colonized (MacCormack 1984).[8]

The Copacabana Virgin quickly gained a reputation for miracles. At first it fulfilled its original brief by bringing rain—albeit selectively— to the fields of its devotees from the upper moiety. Soon it began to cure, to converse with worshipers, and to change its facial expression. As a result it began to attract wider attention, not only from the laity but also from the clergy who were active in the area.

The Titicaca region was being evangelized by the Augustinians and the Dominicans, the latter having been criticized in a secret report of 1573 for their scandalous activities (Documentos sobre Chucuito [1573] 1970, 5–36). The Augustinians, at first weaker in numbers than most of the other orders working in the colony, early recognized the value of Marian pilgrimage centers as ecclesiastical power bases. The order already controlled the important shrine of the Virgin of Guadalupe at Pacasmayo in northern Peru; custodianship of Copacabana would enable them to consolidate their position in the south, and in particular to gain the edge over the Dominicans in the Titicaca region. The Augustinians already possessed a number of doctrinas in the area, among them Pucarani, some sixty kilometers from Copacabana, where they had been in residence since 1567. In 1584 they acquired for their church in Pucarani an image of the Virgin said to have been sculpted by the same Tito Yupanki who had fashioned the Copacabana image, itself installed only the preceding year and already proving a major attraction. The Pucarani image, known as Nuestra Señora de Gracia, was also a Candlemas advocation, and it too became a focus of devotion in the region. Its cult continues today, though on a somewhat limited scale and with participation confined mainly to Aymara-speaking peasants (Vargas Ugarte 1956, 2:286–87).

But the Augustinians clearly coveted Copacabana. In 1585 they petitioned the king, and despite spirited resistance from the incumbent secular priest they persuaded the viceregal authorities of the merits of their case and took control of the shrine in 1589. They immediately began planning a new sanctuary, which was eventually completed in 1669 (Vargas Ugarte 1956, 2:268–71). The order controlled the shrine until 1826, when the disruptions of the wars of independence obliged them to abandon it. In 1842 it was entrusted to the Franciscans, though they did not assume permanent custodianship until 1894 (Santa Cruz 1971, 206–12).

In the twentieth century, Copacabana has assumed the position of Bolivia's principal shrine. It has been patronized by successive archbishops and presidents and has been the scene of various national and international civic-religious ceremonies (Santa Cruz 1971, 214–19). Its cult is as active as ever. A fiesta is now held, not only on 2 February, but also on 6 August; the latter is attended by thousands of pilgrims of varied occupational status—peasants, traders, truckers, and urban workers and professionals—from Bolivia and southern Peru. A notable feature of this fiesta is the sale by local artisans of elaborate models of trucks and houses to the pilgrims, for whom they represent the material favors sought from the Virgin.

Besides the Virgins of Copacabana and Pucarani, both controlled during the early years by the Augustinians, there was yet a third Marian shrine established in the southern Titicaca region, under the auspices of the Dominicans. It was located in the lakeside doctrina of Pomata, only forty kilometers from Copacabana. The order ran the doctrina until 1576 or 1577, when they were obliged by the viceregal authorities to leave, but they resumed control in 1596 (Vargas Ugarte 1956, 2:170–71). The date of origin of the cult of the miraculous Virgin of the Rosary of Pomata is not clear, but its evident popularity during the closing years of the sixteenth century after the Dominicans had regained control seems to have been matched by a slight decline in the fortunes of Copacabana. Later, the publication of an engraving of the icon spread its fame throughout the central Andes, from Cusco to Potosí and beyond (Gisbert 1980, 83). Miraculous shrines were here evidently being used as weapons by the two rival religious orders, battling for dominion over an area whose rich pagan associations promised fertile ground for Christian missionaries.

The cult of the Virgin of Pomata persists today, but it was the Virgin of Copacabana that sank the deepest roots. Its fame is reflected not only in the popularity of its sanctuary as a pilgrimage center, but also in the number of Marian shrines throughout the central Andes that trace their origins directly or indirectly to the Virgin of the Lake.

Perhaps its most famous derivative is the Virgin of Cocharcas, situated some thirty kilometers west of Andahuaylas in the modern Peruvian department of Apurímac. The origin myth of Cocharcas not only elaborates the theme of the neophyte's resolve pitted against ecclesiastical deprecation that runs through the Copacabana story, but also expands the original narrative geographically by incorporating some of the places visited by Tito Yupanki into a more extensive locational set.

The story tells of a youth named Sebastián Kimichi, who, having injured his hand in a game with friends and being unable to help his parents in the fields, traveled to Cusco to find work. While receiving religious instruction from the Jesuits in the city, he heard of Copacabana from a pilgrim and determined to go there to seek a cure. Lodging overnight in Pucará, he dreamt of the Virgin and awoke to find his hand healed.

He continued his journey to Copacabana, where he made thanksgiving to the Virgin and decided to acquire a copy of the image for Cocharcas. He traveled on to La Paz and La Plata, where he sought permission from the bishop to beg alms for his mission, and returned to Copacabana to purchase a copy of the Virgin sculpted by the prolific Tito Yupanki himself. Before he could leave, however, the Augustinians confiscated the statue on the grounds that he had begged alms for it without authorization. Eventually they released it, and Sebastián retraced his steps to Cocharcas, the image exciting much devotion along the route.

His troubles were not over, however. The parish priest of Urcos, just outside Cusco, wary of the neopagan fervor with which the image was greeted, informed the bishop of Cusco, who had Sebastián imprisoned while the matter was investigated. His credentials having been established, he was allowed to continue his journey, arriving home in the year 1598. As the image of the Virgin came in sight of the village, there began a great thunder and tempest, which ceased as soon as she was installed in her chapel. The image immediately began performing miracles for her devotees.

Soon afterward, Sebastián undertook a second pilgrimage to collect funds for a larger sanctuary for the Virgin. Again he headed southeast, carrying with him a portable replica of the image—a *demanda*—and accompanied by a kinsman. In the course of their travels they reached Cochabamba, where their funds were impounded by the priest, who took them for impostors. Sebastián fell ill and died in the town, leaving the portable image in the church there. His companion, having traveled to Cusco, returned to Cochabamba to recover the money and took it home to Cocharcas. The new basilica was completed in 1623 (Vargas Ugarte 1956, 2:128–33).

Originally the Cocharcas image, like that of Copacabana, was a Candlemas advocation, but the first bishop of Ayaucho decreed that its principal fiesta be celebrated on 8 September, the feast of the Nativity of the Virgin, because February was in the middle of the rainy season, when floods and landslides made it difficult for pilgrims to attend (Vargas Ugarte 1956, 2:133).

The annual fiesta is still patronized by thousands of devotees, mainly from the departments of Apurímac and Ayacucho (Pélach y Feliu 1972, 7). There are in fact three images of the Virgin of Cocharcas in the sanctuary: the Patroness, the Reina Chica 'Little Queen' and the Reina Grande 'Great Queen'. During the September fiesta the Reina Chica is carried toward Ayacucho and the Reina Grande toward Cusco, the Patroness remaining on her throne. According to popular tradition this throne is situated over a lake; were the image to be removed, there would be a flood (Morote Best 1953, 97–98).

The shrine of the Virgin of Cocharcas, while at one level linked to its parent shrine in Copacabana, is at another level an element in the circumscribed regional shrine system of Apurímac and Ayacucho. Here, relations between shrines are phrased explicitly in terms of siblingship, with certain Virgins ranked in order of sororal seniority. The composition of such sibling sets and the rank order of their members, however, vary from locality to locality, and in some places the Virgin of Cocharcas herself is allotted a rank subordinate to other, less widely known shrines. The community of Caipe, province of Abancay, for instance, recognizes a trio of sister Virgins: the eldest is in the town of Abancay, the youngest in Cocharcas, while the middle sister is in Caipe itself (Tejado 1943, 2). In addition, the Virgin of Cocharcas now has namesakes in many other parts of Peru (Morote Best 1953).

Another important Copacabana derivative, whose origin, like that of the Virgin of Cocharcas, is approximately contemporaneous with that of the parent shrine, is the Virgin of Characato, situated ten kilometers from the city of Arequipa. The image of this Virgin was apparently brought from Copacabana by an Indian pilgrim in 1590. On arrival it was put to one side because of a defect. The priest commissioned a sculptor to correct it, but when it was brought out the blemish had miraculously disappeared. Controlled by the Mercedarian order until 1786, the sanctuary became a focus of devotion for pilgrims attracted by the many miracles with which the Virgin was credited, among them the miraculous flowing of water in a dried-up stream in 1686, when the crops were suffering from drought (Vargas Ugarte 1956, 2:147–50).

The Virgin of Characato shares the attentions of the Arequipeños with two sister Virgins, Caima and Chapi. All three, like the Copacabana original, are Candlemas advocations. The Virgin of Caima, three kilometers north of the city on the slopes of Mount Chachani, was already an object of cult in 1589, when it was taken to the city to dispel the plague (Vargas Ugarte 1956, 2:144).

Devotion to the Virgin of Chapi, located some forty kilometers southeast of Arequipa, is more recent, dating from the late eighteenth century. Today, it is the most popular of the three. It is said that in 1897, during the construction of a new sanctuary for the image, a miraculous spring burst forth in an area that is otherwise extremely arid. Now the place is a new Lourdes, with sick pilgrims coming to bathe in the miraculous waters in the hope of a cure, not only during the titular fiesta in February but also at the feast of the Nativity of the Virgin on 8 September (Vargas Ugarte 1956, 2:153–54). Once again the recurrent association between miraculous shrines and water is encountered; indeed, the three Virgins serve as ecological markers for the different sources of irrigation and drinking water on which the Arequipa region depends (Poole n.d., 7).

To complete this survey of Copacabana derivatives, the Virgin of the Purification in the village of Torata near Moquegua, in the department of the same name, can be mentioned. This image, too, is supposed to be a copy of the Virgin of Copacabana brought to the village in 1600. Cosme Bueno affirms that it was famous in colonial times, and its popularity continues today (Vargas Ugarte 1956, 2:151–52).

In addition, both Pucará and Urcos, two of the stops on Sebastián Kimichi's legendary journey, boast important Marian shrines. Though there is no evidence of direct mythical association between these shrines and the Copacabana and Cocharcas Virgins, the circumstantial links are strong. The fiestas of both shrines give occasion for important regional fairs, the Virgin of Pucará on 16 July and the Virgin of Kaninkunka, just outside Urcos, on 2 February. Pucará, it will be recalled, was the site of a local culture that predated Wari-Tiwanaku and retained a special ritual significance into the Inka era. The Pucará Virgin is linked in turn to the renowned Virgin of Mount Carmel in Paucartambo, fifty kilometers east of Cusco city on the edge of the montaña, with which it shares the same advocation and which is said in some legends to have been brought directly from Pucará by itinerant traders (Poole n.d., 14). The shrine of Kaninkunka, meanwhile, consisting of an image of the Virgin painted on a rock, is supposed to give especial succor to travelers, as a piece of doggerel inscribed on the façade of the sanctuary advertises. Situated on the shore of a lake, it preserves the association with water that characterizes many of these shrines.

The outstanding features of this initial phase of cult regionalization in the colonial central highlands were, first, that it was based exclusively on Marian images, and second, that Copacabana provided the seminal advocation for a widely ramified system of derivative shrines. The first requires a general explanation, the second a specific one.

The enshrining of Mary in early colonial Peru may be seen at one level as an extension of a process already well under way in Spain, where images of the Virgin had been steadily gaining in devotional popularity since the twelfth century. In the colonial situation, Mariolatry was contagious. The reverence displayed by the Spaniards toward this saint above all others lent her a special prestige in native eyes, for she was clearly one of the most powerful wak'as in the Christian pantheon.

At another level, the syncretic identifications of Christian deities with native deities that established themselves during the first years of proselytization gave a particular cast to the Virgin as a religious figure. The Christian God was initially identified with the celestial divinities of the Inka pantheon, especially the Sun. Mary, on the other hand, just as in Spain, entered into association with the spirits of nature—of mountains, lakes, rivers, and springs. These twin identifications are explicit in early colonial iconography (Gisbert 1980).[9] There is no doubt that they were actively fostered by the clergy, especially by the Augustinians, whose founder had laid the foundations for such a strategy of evangelization (Gisbert 1980, 12).

Despite the universal symbolism of the Virgin in Christian theology, therefore, the syncretic field that she entered in the Andes was the non-imperial, regional stratum of native religion, that attaching to particular landscapes inhabited by specific peoples. Seen in this light, the use of Marian epithets in the nativistic movement of Taki Onqoy is perhaps less puzzling than it first appears to be. Similarly, the ubiquitous enshrining of the Virgin throughout the central Andes during the years immediately following the suppression of the Taki Onqoy becomes readily comprehensible. Mary was the natural successor to the emasculated pagan gods of the Andean landscape, in the eyes both of the natives and of the missionaries who cannily exploited their religious sensibilities.

The Copacabana Virgins illustrate another aspect of this partial appropriation of the Marian cult by Indians. All the images were alleged to have been fashioned by the same sculptor, a native of the village. The religious authorities were clearly uneasy about the possibility that Christian images, which played an important part in the liturgy, would pass out of their aesthetic control: Tito Yupanki's early efforts were ridiculed, and even some of his later ones were criticized as defective in some way.[10] But their eventual acceptance set a precedent. Not only were they produced by an Indian rather than a Spanish artist; they were also identifiably Andean rather than merely imported Iberian advocations. They were not simply franchise shrines of Spanish Virgins, like those of Guadalupe at Pachakamaq and Pacasmayo. Instead, they were unique to the Andes, and while conforming to the iconographic conventions of the respective liturgical advocations—the Virgin of the Purification, or of the Rosary, or whatever—they were nevertheless Andeanized by the addition of small but significant details. The Virgins of both Copacabana and Pomata, for example, sport multicolored plumes of feathers above their heads—a clear mark of indigenous assimilation (Mesa and Gisbert 1982, 1: plates 55 and 56).

The friars who promoted the Marian shrines of southern Titicaca were well aware that the area was steeped in mythical and sacred meanings. It had been an important pilgrimage center in both pre-Inka and Inka times and in the current mythology of the people of the area was the setting for the exploits of Tunupa, the Aymara deity whose myths were merged under Inka auspices into the Wiraqocha cycle. Tunupa was assimilated in turn into Christian mythology: Ramos Gavilán makes him one of the disciples, who had reached America centuries before. Tunupa, he tells us, went preaching at Carabuco, an Aymara village on the eastern shore of the lake. He was attacked by infidels, tied to a cross, whipped, and stabbed to death. His body was placed on a raft on the lake, which was blown by the wind with such force against the bank that it opened up an outlet (*desaguadero*). The raft was carried along the resultant channel to Aullagas, where the waters passed underground, and there the body of the martyred disciple remained (Ramos Gavilán [1621, book 1, chap. 8] 1976, 31–32). The cross on which Tunupa was supposed to have been tortured is still to be seen at Carabuco; it is worshiped as a nominally Christian relic, but its pre-Columbian origins are scarcely in doubt (Bandelier 1904).

The pagan aura that hung over southern Titicaca, however, was only one of the factors that made it the bridgehead of the Marian colonization of the central sierra. In 1545, a rich silver vein was discovered at Potosí, and an enormous mining complex grew up there. Production was boosted dramatically from 1571 onward following the discovery of a process that used mercury as a catalyst for refining inferior ores, and this in turn stimulated the development of the mercury mine at Huancavelica, some distance to the northwest of Cocharcas. Colonial society was transformed. What had initially been a congeries of loosely coordinated local agricultural economies resting upon the decentralized extraction of Indian labor and produce now became a single complex machine geared to the operation of the mines. The Potosí region became the central node in a vast network of migratory and commercial flows, importing mita labor, foodstuffs, coca, and cloth from as far afield as Cusco, and of course mercury from Huancavelica. Different regions became economically more integrated, both internally and with one another. Thus at the same time as native national identities were being eroded and the Indian population fragmented into narrowly based reducciones and doctrinas, new regional and interregional patterns of relations were being established through the traffic of labor and produce generated directly and indirectly by mining.

Christian pilgrimage in the central Andes arose in part as the religious correlate of the continuous, cyclical movements of people and goods across the landscape that were engendered by this concerted mining economy. The locations, mythohistories, and dates of founding of the early shrines all point to such a correlation. The instant popularity of Copacabana and of the other shrines clustered around the southern reaches of Lake Titicaca, as well as the establishment of Copacabana derivatives elsewhere, undoubtedly owed much to the location of the area on the teeming transport route to Potosí. All postdated the advent of the Huancavelica–Potosí axis, and following the establishment of the Copacabana shrine distant satellites, as well as a local competitor, Pomata, were founded in rapid succession. Indeed, it was the Huancavelica–Potosí axis that was traced out time and again in the journeyings of Francisco Tito Yupanki and Sebastián Kimichi. This became the trunk route across the central Andes, trodden every year by tens of thousands of miners, porters, merchants, and administrators. Many of these travelers became pilgrims as well, and their ranks were swelled as the reputations of the Virgins spread. The southern Titicaca zone, through the pilgrimage traffic that its Marian shrines acquired and generated, through the replication of the Copacabana icon elsewhere and through the determinate itineraries of its legendary founder and that of Cocharcas, its most famous scion—in these ways the zone became once again the religious fulcrum of the central Andes, the source and origin of an extensive sacred geography that consolidated the spatial structure of the colonial political economy.

To sum up. Following the demise of the Taki Onqoy, there was set in train a twin process whereby the Christian cult was simultaneously localized and regionalized. While local fiesta complexes were developed that were centered on community patron saints, the Marian colonization of the wider central Andean landscape gave rise to universalistic miracle cults based on long-range pilgrimage. Southern Titicaca, thanks to the deep-rooted and pervasive pagan associations of the area and to its location on an important communications artery, became the node of a far-flung, interregional system of miraculous shrines that quickly ramified throughout the central sierra.

Significantly Cusco, the erstwhile Inka capital and now the diocesan seat, was not part of the system. As noted, the city was already stocked with Marian images enjoying a measure of popular devotion, foremost among them La Linda and Belén. These Virgins did not, however, belong to the Copacabana network—indeed, they predated it—but were civic shrines patronized mainly by the Hispanic urban population, having no syncretic associations with pre-Columbian cults or relational significance in any wider, regional system.

Along with the Virgen de Belén, however, the city of Cusco is supposed to have received from Carlos V another image, a crucifix, which many years later, following the earthquake of 1650, was to be enshrined as Señor de los Temblores, Lord of the Earthquakes. The enshrining of Temblores in Cusco was the cue for the emergence of miraculous Christ shrines throughout the area. Thus the figure of Christ himself joined that of Mary in the progressive reconsecration of the regional landscape. It is to this that I now shall turn.

CHAPTER 4

The Miraculous Landscape of Cusco

On 31 March 1650, at around two o'clock in the afternoon, a violent earth tremor shook Cusco to its foundations. The toll in human life was light—about thirty dead—but the tremor cut great swathes of devastation through the vainglorious city. Then as now (see, for example, Bode 1974), earthquakes were attributed to the wrath of God as punishment for sin and idolatry, and the catastrophe provoked public displays of penance and mortification that amazed even a contemporary observer.

The clergy, this writer tells us, and in particular the religious orders, took the lead. They processed around the plaza stripped to the waist, their bodies covered with ashes, with ropes fastened around their necks, chains about their bodies, and shackles around their ankles, crowns of thorns on their heads and gags in their mouths—save, that is, for a Franciscan novice, who wailed: " 'This is the justice which the Lord our God sends to wicked man, for his grave sins have brought about the ruin of this city.' At this declamation, such was the howling and weeping of the people that it seemed the world had come to an end" (Anonymous 1651).

The religious authorities determined to institute a commemoration of the dreadful event. For this they mobilized a crucifix which had stood unremarked in the cathedral for a century and which they dubbed Señor de los Temblores (Angles Vargas 1983, 2:619–20). The image quickly acquired the reputation of having "miraculously" held the forces of nature at bay and also for having granted the personal petitions of its devotees. Its fame as a miracle worker spread well beyond the Cusco region: painted representations on canvas were soon being traded as far away as Ecuador and Argentina (Gade 1970, 220).

Every year on 31 March the image was brought out and carried alone through the streets, followed by a throng of penitent townspeople. Special processions, often with Temblores accompanied by La Linda and the Virgen de Belén, were held throughout the colonial period whenever disaster threatened or struck, be it earthquake, plague, famine, drought, or even the attempted invasion of the viceroyalty by English privateers in 1740. Invariably, the rogations were deemed successful (Esquivel y Navia [1749] 1980, vol. 2). More recently, following the devastating earthquake of 1950, Temblores was set up in the Plaza de Armas for three days and nights so that the distraught populace could implore his mercy (Vargas B. 1956, 38). The fact that on this occasion two thirds of the city was destroyed and 40,000 people were made homeless, but only seventeen were killed, was taken as further proof of the miraculous power of the image (Gade 1970, 221).

The enshrinement of Christ in Cusco, in part a reflection of Iberian trends of the time, set an iconographic precedent for the area. Thenceforth, new miraculous shrines in the region were more likely to be advocations of Christ than of the Virgin, and this bias has persisted to the present day. In this concluding chapter on the historical geography of Andean religion, I shall trace the development of Cusco's miraculous landscape and examine its spatial, temporal, and cosmological patterning.

An Inventory of Shrines

Map 6, appendix 1, shows the principal regional shrines of the area, together with the dates of their titular fiestas. It also indicates the principal annual fairs, with which many of the shrines are associated. In addition to these regional shrines, there is a further layer of far more numerous interlocal or vicinal pilgrimage sites, whose character and distribution I shall discuss presently. First I shall catalogue the principal regional centers, adducing ethnographic, historical and mythohistorical data where available, though these are inevitably uneven. In part 2 of the book, the cults of two of these shrines will be described and analyzed in detail.

Señor de los Temblores is now the *patrón jurado* 'sworn patron' of Cusco city. Because of its metropolitan location, it is somewhat set apart from the shrines in the rural hinterland of the city. It is in fact one of several seismic crucifixion shrines whose devotions originated in the towns and cities of seventeenth-century Peru. The best known is in Lima, Señor de los Milagros 'Lord of the Miracles', a mural painted by a freed slave on the wall of a meeting house used by an African confraternity. From 1654 onward the wall survived repeated earthquakes, while the image itself defied efforts to cover it with whitewash. Gradually it became an object of widespread devotion; an oratory was built around it, later enlarged into the church of Las Nazarenas. Its procession on 28 October, the feast of Christ the King, lasted all day and was joined by thousands of devotees (Descola 1968, 110). The procession is still a fixture in Lima's religious calendar, and though it is now a civic event, watched by the president of the republic from his balcony, the close association of the image with the blacks of the city has remained (Banchero Castellano 1976; Vargas Ugarte 1949).

Cusco's Señor de los Temblores has likewise come to appeal to the poorer, "Indian" sector of the city's population. Through the years the smoke from the candles of its devotees has darkened the wooden face of the statue, thus making it a Christ in their own image (Barrionuevo 1969, 54). When in 1834 the cathedral authorities retouched the statue by removing the stain of candle smoke there was a near riot, for it was believed that a white taytacha would lack verisimilitude and would no longer work miracles (Aguilar 1922, cited in Uriel García 1973, 129).[1]

There was another incident in 1869, triggered by a rumor that the bishop had sold the images of Temblores and Belén. An angry mob stormed the bishop's palace, smashing the doors and baying for his blood. A barrage of ecclesiastical censures was later unleashed against the participants in the riot.[2]

The shrine of Señor de los Temblores, kept in the cathedral on a side altar, is moved to the high altar on the eve of its fiesta and on other special occasions. Today its fiesta is held in the afternoon of the Monday before Easter, when it is carried on a silver bier, not on a ceremonial circuit of the main square as are the saints at Corpus, but in a three-hour procession through the streets and alleys of the city, stopping for a while at the church of Santa Teresa, which traditionally provides the litter bearers. Red flower petals are thrown in its path, to symbolize the blood of Christ. As many as 50,000 people witness the occasion (Paredes 1969). But despite its connection with the poor and underprivileged of the city, Temblores, like Lima's Señor de los Milagros, is squarely within the civic domain. Its fiesta is presided over by the city's religious, civil, and military leaders—the archbishop, prefect, mayor, chief magistrate, and garrison commander. Indeed, in the case of Temblores it was never really otherwise, its populist appeal having come about as a direct result of heavy promotion by the diocesan hierarchy.

The unusual construction of the Temblores image—layers of cloth wound like a bandage around a straw mannequin, with wooden head, arms, and legs—does in fact enable it to be dated from around the year 1560 (Gisbert 1980, 100). But the technique gives the lie to the widespread tradition that the crucifix was sent from Spain by Carlos V (cf. Barrionuevo 1969, 54), for it is an exclusively Andean method of image-making derived directly from that used to fashion the former pagan idols, the bandaged imperial mummies and the cloth images of Qorikancha (Gisbert 1980, 103). The mythical denial of the Andean origin of Temblores in favor of a royal Spanish pedigree identical to that of the revered

Virgen de Belén would seem to be a strategy designed to give the image an appropriate cachet for its use in episcopal ceremony. Conversely, the importance attached by devotees to the taytacha's smoke-darkened visage reads as a kind of re-Andeanization of the Hispanicized Andean icon.

Two Christ shrines to the west of Cusco city along the road to Lima, Señor de Mollepata and Señor de Inkilpata, are also said to have been sent to Peru by Carlos V along with Temblores. As they were being transported from Lima to Cusco, the myth runs, two of the three crucifixes became excessively heavy at Mollepata and Inkilpata, respectively, signaling their desire to be left at those spots. The porters therefore continued their journey to Cusco with only one image (Morote Best 1953, 89).

The shrines of Mollepata and Inkilpata share the same feast day, 14 September, the Exaltation of the Cross, though the fiesta of Señor de Inkilpata is actually held on the octave. The latter shrine is housed in the chapel of the former hacienda of Inkilpata, expropriated in the agrarian reform of the early 1970s, and associated with its fiesta had been a number of expensive cargos for the provision of dancers and musicians that had been shouldered by hacienda peasants (Guillet 1979, 19). The fiesta is the occasion of a regional agricultural fair, with traders coming from all over the department of Cusco. The fair was said to be a recent phenomenon of only a few decades' standing, its establishment reflecting the postwar importance of the Pampa de Anta area as the breadbasket for the expanding population of Cusco city.

One myth collected in the field from an informant in Maras dates current interest in the Inkilpata shrine from the 1950 earthquake in Cusco. The day before the tremor, a truck driver leaving Cusco for Lima was stopped by an old, bearded man at the roadside, who begged a lift. The driver refused, for the cab was already full, but the man insisted and the driver relented. As they were passing through Inkilpata, the man asked to be set down for a moment to go into the church. He was gone so long that eventually the driver went in to fetch him. The church was empty, though he noticed that the Christ on the crucifix was very similar to the old man. He abandoned the search and continued his journey. Next day he stopped at a police checkpoint and learned of the terrible earthquake that had razed the city. He realized then that his passenger had in fact been a miraculous Señor. As news of this apparition spread, pilgrims began to flock to the shrine, and the regional fair became established.

This myth is clearly a reworking of the relations between Señor de Inkilpata, Señor de los Temblores, and the notion of an earthquake as an awful sign of the hand of God in the affairs of human beings. It also reiterates the notion of these shrines as sacred blazes on the trunk route from Cusco to Lima. Yet paradoxically it suggests that, on this occasion, the taytacha was fleeing the stricken city and seeking sanctuary elsewhere.

The shrines of Inkilpata, Mollepata, and Temblores all consist of statues alleged to have been imported from Spain during the early colonial period. Most other Christ shrines in the region tend instead to be based on later apparitions of Christ in various advocations at particular spots on the landscape, usually to poor peasants in the first instance.

One of the most famous of these apparitional shrines is Señor de Wank'a (Huanca) 'Lord of the Crag', situated in the Vilcanota valley not far from San Salvador on the eastern slope of Mount Pachatusan, of special importance in Inka mythology and cosmology and today a powerful apu, 'hill spirit' (see plate 10). The first apparition is said to have occurred in 1674. The seer was an Indian miner fleeing to escape punishment from his master, and the vision, appropriately enough, was of Christ's scourging. The cult did not really get under way, however, until nearly fifty years later, when the Cusco region was gripped by a terrible epidemic. The Christ figure appeared again in the role of doctor, to cure a Spanish mine owner. The site became an important regional shrine, the focus of devotion being a crag bearing a painting of the original vision. The Mercedarian order has controlled the shrine since its inception, and through the years has propagated its cult assiduously, particularly among the urban and middle-peasant sectors. Nowadays, some 20,000 devotees come to its titular fiesta and accompanying regional fair on 14 September, attending in informal village groups or as individual pilgrims. The event is distinct from the fiesta of San Salvador's patron saint, Christ Savior, which is held on 6 August with local attendance only.

Comparable in importance to Señor de Wank'a is Señor de Qoyllur Rit'i 'Lord of the Snow Star', an isolated mountain shrine eighty kilometers east of Cusco (see plate 7). Like Wank'a it is associated with a sacred mountain, Ausankati, believed to be the most powerful apu in the region. The shrine is said to date from a vision of Christ to an Indian shepherd boy around the year 1780, the time of the unsuccessful rebellion of Tupac Amaru II against the Spanish colonists. Again the focus of devotion is a crag, this time bearing an image of Christ crucified. There are also a number of subsidiary shrines in the immediate vicinity, among them a crucifix in the church of Ocongate village known as Señor de Tayankani, whose origin is linked to that of Señor de Qoyllur Rit'i. The principal shrine, now housed in a large sanctuary, has remained free of direct control by the regular clergy and is today managed by a lay brotherhood drawn from provincial capitals and from Cusco city. Its titular fiesta attracts around 20,000 pilgrims, most of them attending in formal sponsored community-based groups known as *naciones,* each with its complement of musicians and ritual dancers. The commercial activities at the fiesta are chiefly geared to the provision of services to pilgrims. There is also another, much smaller fiesta on 14 September which is exclusive to locals, in particular the villagers of Ocongate.

Wank'a and Qoyllur Rit'i each occupies a special place in the regional shrine system, and they are regarded as the main regional pilgrimage centers for mestizos and Indians, respectively. Their mythohistories and cults will be examined in detail in later chapters.

There are five other important Christ shrines within a hundred-kilometer radius of Cusco city. Two share exactly the same title and advocation. One of the pair, Señor de Pampak'ucho in the village of the same name in the district of Colcha, province of Paruro, dates from colonial times, when an Indian girl is alleged to have discovered a *lienzo* 'canvas' in the fields depicting the Cristo Nazareno, Christ stumbling under the cross. Its principal fiesta is celebrated on 16 August—not a liturgical Christ feast but the day of San Roque, by whose name the shrine is sometimes called. The fiesta is the occasion of a small regional fair, in which pilgrims from the agricultural provinces of Paruro and Acomayo bring maize to exchange for pastoral products brought by those from Chumbivilcas (Poole 1981).

As Poole shows, the shrine of Señor de Pampak'ucho has two complementary aspects. As a pilgrimage shrine it is the patron saint of strangers. The village of Pampak'ucho has as its own patron saint the Virgin of the Assumption, whose fiesta runs concurrently with that of Señor de Pampak'ucho but quite independent of it, each fiesta having its own cargos and dancers. Indeed, the locals say that the miraculous Christ actually leaves the village for its fiesta, going to visit its "older brother," the miraculous Christ shrine in Pampamarca, whence it is supposed to have originated. Señor de Pampak'ucho is also regarded as the local patron of irrigation and agriculture, however, and is celebrated in that aspect by the residents of the village exclusively in another fiesta on 2 January, the feast of the Holy Name of Jesus, this being the original date of the fiesta of Señor de Pampamarca before it was moved to its present fixture of 14 January. According to tradition, the chapel of Señor de Pampak'ucho used to be located on the river that divides Pampak'ucho from the neighboring village of Qochirway, which is said to have coveted the image. The chapel is now situated squarely in the center of Pampak'ucho, on the village plaza, though quite separate from the village church. During its fiesta in August it is "received" into the church by the Virgin of the Assumption, just as the visiting pilgrim traders from the puna are received into the residents' homes to engage in barter (Poole 1981).

The other Señor de Pampak'ucho—the name means "edge of the plain"—is in the town of Sicuani. It is alleged to have its origins in the nineteenth century, when the town was coming into prominence as a bulking center for the wool export trade with Britain. It too is a canvas depicting the Cristo Nazareno advocation, discovered under circumstances similar to those of the discovery of its namesake in Paruro. The canvas inspired such devotion in a townsman that he built a sanctuary where it could be properly venerated (Aguilar Claros 1945, 16–17).

The sanctuary is situated on the outskirts of town, some distance from the main church, which houses the patronal Virgin of the Immaculate Conception and which serves as the cathedral of the Sicuani prelature. It stands on the slopes of Mount Sunto, a pre-Hispanic shrine which was a station on the annual pilgrimage by Inka priests from Cusco to the watershed at Willkanuta (La Raya) at the June solstice. As will be seen, several of the miraculous shrines situated along the axis of the Vilcanota-Huátanay valleys are sited near former stations on this Inka pilgrimage route.

Since 1941, the fiesta of Señor de Pampak'ucho in Sicuani—also held on 16 August—has been accompanied by a small fair of agricultural products and cottage manufactures. Similar fairs were established in other centers in Canas-Canchis around the same time (Orlove 1977, 151), though some have since become defunct—that of Yanaoca, for example, which unlike Sicuani's did not have the benefit of a miraculous shrine as its patron (Valencia Espinoza 1979, 185–86). The fiesta of Señor de Pampak'ucho is sponsored by a *mayordomo* 'steward' from the town, and in the past dance groups are said to have come from as far afield as Juliaca to escort the image on its procession around the plaza before the sanctuary. Nowadays the image excites little enthusiasm, and the impression is of a mainly commercial event rather than of a religious occasion.

Two other important Christ shrines of the region are Señor de Pampamarca and Señor de Tungasuca, situated in villages five kilometers apart in the province of Canas, just off the trunk road between Cusco and Puno. Both date from the colonial era, and both have associated fairs: during the 1780s, Tungasuca attracted people not only from the diocese but also from Huamanga, Arequipa, and La Paz (Oricaín [1790] 1906, 360). Señor de Pampamarca, also known as Señor de la Caña, is an image of Christ as just judge; its fiesta is held on 14 January, not a liturgical Christ feast but the day of San Hilario, and its extensive fair is devoted mainly to livestock. Señor de Tungasuca, meanwhile, also called Señor de Añaypampa, a crucifixion advocation, has its fiesta on 14 September, Exaltación, with a fair dealing chiefly in agricultural produce.

To the northwest of Cusco, in the provincial capital of Urubamba, there is another Christ shrine, in this instance a cross rather than a representational image. Known as Señor de Torrichayoq, after the tower which graced its original chapel (*torre* 'tower'), it had its origin in 1866, when the road between Calca and Lares was widened. First to reach the pass was the team from Urubamba, organized by a group of prominent, civic-minded villagers who called themselves the Mutual Protection Society, and to mark the achievement they planted a cross at the spot. Some years later the cross appeared in a dream to a villager, saying it was cold and wanted to come down from the mountain; but it was left to the man's son, on assuming the presidency of the society, to arrange its removal—much to the distress of the local peasants, who regarded it as their own. Its first miracle was to ensure that the mountain water supply of Urubamba was never again turbid (Roca W. 1979, 116–119).

The fiesta of Señor de Torrichayoq is held on the feast of Pentecost. It is organized by the society, whose traditional devotional dance is that of *sijlla*;[3] professionals and the self-employed, such as taxi drivers and truck drivers, are prominent in the devotion to the shrine. The main event is the procession of the cross, swathed in richly decorated cloths, from its chapel to the parish church. Despite the participation of devotees from elsewhere in Cusco, the fiesta is less a regional pilgrimage than a civic, locality festival, with smaller crosses from nearby communities and sites being brought in to accompany Señor de Torrichayoq on its procession (Roca W. 1979, 119–32).

In addition to these Christ shrines there are a number of important Marian shrines in the region, with many of which commercial activities are associated. The best documented is the Virgen de Tiobamba, situated northwest of Cusco city near the village of Maras, in the province of Urubamba. It consists of a fading image of Mary on an adobe wall, now incorporated into a graceful baroque sanctuary with distinctive campaniles flanking its entrance. The sanctuary stands alone in the middle of a broad plain overlooked by the snow-capped Mount Chikón, at the side of the road which in Inka times carried the heavy traffic between Cusco city and the northwestern montaña. Nowadays traffic takes the metaled route via Pisac and Calca, and the Maras road is little used.

According to local tradition, the Tiobamba Virgin appeared miraculously to a disabled Indian girl many years ago. The image has always been associated with miraculous cures: contemporary murals in the sanctuary depict the Virgin curing victims of the epidemic of 1719–20 (Mesa and Gisbert 1982, 1:191). A glimpse of its history is provided by a document dated 1766, which is preserved in the parish archives of Maras, in which the mayordomo-priest of the sanctuary petitions the bishop of Cusco to upgrade it from a chapelry of the doctrina of Maras to the status of vice-parish.

The document claims that the image was then already a century old. Through the years, its miraculous reputation had attracted increasing numbers of pilgrims, many of them sick and seeking a cure. The original adobe chapel had been replaced by the present sanctuary, lavishly furnished thanks to the offerings of pilgrims. There were visitors all year round, with 6,000 or more from the diocese and beyond attending the annual novena for the titular fiesta of the Assumption, to which a perpetual plenary indulgence attached. The document recounts the various miracles wrought by the Virgin, including one where the parish priest of Maras, jealous of the popularity of the shrine, which to him presaged declining fortunes for the parish itself, tried to scratch the image physically from the wall, only to make it reappear more beautiful than ever.

He tried again, mounting a ladder and striking the Virgin on the face. But when he raised his arm to strike a second blow he was suddenly paralyzed and fell to the ground. Astonished by this miracle, he became one of the Virgin's most ardent devotees. The image thenceforth displayed a scar on its cheek, which had defied all efforts to remove it.

The significance of this myth is readily apparent. The ostensible justification for upgrading Tiobamba to the rank of vice-parish was that this would allow baptisms and burials to take place there, the latter being particularly important, since many of the sick pilgrims died at the shrine and the corpses had at present to be taken to Maras for interment. Also, the two masses a day permitted at the sanctuary by Church regulations were inadequate for the numbers of devotees. It is clear, however, that the Maras priests had been attempting to restrict religious activities at the sanctuary, for the petition expressly requests that priest-pilgrims be permitted to celebrate mass without interference from the parish priest, or from anyone else. The petition was successful: the status of vice-parish was conferred a few years later.

During the novena of Tiobamba's titular fiesta a large colonial fair was held (Oricaín [1790] 1906, 349). Llama and burro trains from the altiplano and the montaña brought produce for barter and sale. The fair is supposed to have been the occasion for the setting of the price of maize for the whole of southern Peru (Valcárcel 1946, 480).

Today, Tiobamba's fiesta on 15 August attracts around 3,000 people, a few still coming from as far afield as Puno and Quillabamba. Nowadays, however, there is no resident cleric, and masses are celebrated by priests from Maras or Urubamba. A statue of the Virgin modeled on the shrine image is carried through the fair, accompanied by a statue of San Rafael and several groups of ceremonial dancers—ukukus, who clear a way through the crowd; ch'unchos extranjeros, who use their long staves to form a "road" for the saints to pass through; and qhapaq qollas, who bring up the rear. The dancers traditionally come from Chinchero and Roqchi, two nearby villages.

As for the fair, spread out across the plain, the traders most in evidence are the pottery manufacturers from Tinta and Pucará. They exchange their wares directly for maize, potatoes and ch'uñu 'freeze-dried tubers' from the various ecological levels of the locality, using the pots themselves as measures (Fioravanti-Molinié 1982, 221). There are also stalls at which industrial manufactures, conspicuously factory-made clothes, are sold. As will be seen, the fair has some competition from a similar event held at exactly the same time only thirty kilometers away in Calca, though without the attraction of a miraculous Virgin.

Just outside the village of Oropesa, close to the main road heading southeast from Cusco city, is the shrine of the Virgen de la Ermita, the Virgin of the Hermitage. Mount Kispikancha, another station on the Inkas' Willkanuta pilgrimage, rises two kilometers distant. The Virgen de la Ermita, like Tiobamba, is an Assumption advocation dating from the seventeenth century. The shrine was already well established in 1656, when its mayordomo petitioned the bishop to remove a tavern that had been set up immediately alongside by the lieutenant corregidor.[4] In 1674, it is described as a place of pilgrimage for devotees from Cusco city and the surrounding area.[5]

The recent history of La Ermita has been rather troubled. During the 1940s the sanctuary was flooded when the Huátanay burst its banks, and it had to be rebuilt on higher ground. Subsequently a drunken sacristan accidentally set fire to the Virgin, which was completely destroyed. The present image is a copy. The cult continues today on a muted scale, with a small fair accompanying its fiesta on 15 August. The occasion is especially favored by people from Langui, Layo, El Descanso, and other high-altitude villages south of Sicuani, who bring kañiwa (Chenopodium pallidicaule) and medicinal plants to exchange for the local maize (Valencia Espinoza 1979, 188–90). Oropesa's local patron, Christ Savior, is fêted separately on the 6th of the same month.

Another important Marian shrine in the region has already been mentioned: the Virgen de Kaninkunka, between the villages of Urcos and Huaro. This consists of a resplendent golden image of Mary on a crag, housed in a sanctuary of unremarkable external appearance but whose interior is covered in baroque murals. The sanctuary itself dates from the late seventeenth or early eighteenth century (Gisbert 1980, 42; Mesa and Gisbert 1982, 1:242). It stands above a lake, at the head of a pass and directly facing Mount Wiraqocha, another station on the annual pilgrimage of Inka priests to the shrine of Willkanuta. As noted earlier, Urcos itself was featured in the foundation myth of the Virgen de Cocharcas as the site of one of Sebastián Kimichi's tribulations on his journey homeward from Copacabana.

The Kaninkunka Virgin is a Candlemas advocation, and her fiesta and fair on 2 February attract several thousand people. The event has been a source of contention between the neighboring villages of Urcos and Huaro. Ever since colonial times the fair used to be held at the sanctuary itself under the jurisdiction of Urcos, but when Huaro became a district it demanded half the income from the levies and taxes. Urcos promptly relocated the fair closer to town and retained full control (Gonzales H. 1957, 18). Huaro, however, provides the lay custodians for the sanctuary, though ecclesiastical control rests with the parish priest in Urcos. The fiesta has a number of local cargos for the organization of dance groups (Marzal 1971, 114). The fiesta is distinct from the patronal fiestas of the two villages, Urcos's on the feast of the Immaculate Conception and Huaro's on the feast of the Virgin of Mount Carmel.[6] For the latter, on 16 July, a small portable Virgin is brought from the Kaninkunka sanctuary to take part in the procession—a ritual statement of Huaro's rights in the shrine cult.

Thirty-five kilometers to the south, on the outskirts of the village of Marcaconga, district of Sangarara, province of Acomayo, there is another important Marian shrine that shares many salient characteristics with the Virgen de Kaninkunka. Known as the Virgen de Alta Gracia, it too is an image of stone, situated just north of Lake Pomakanchi on the edge of the marshy plain of Yanapampa, yet another station on the Willkanuta pilgrimage of the Inkas. From the foundations of the sanctuary there issues a small spring whose water is much valued for curative purposes, especially for heart diseases. The titular fiesta of the shrine, celebrated on 8 September, the feast of the Nativity of the Virgin, prompts a small fair and attracts people from throughout the surrounding provinces. It entails a number of local cargos for dance groups who attend upon the Virgin (Vargas Ugarte 1956, 2:164).

Finally, the Virgen de Carmen in the provincial capital of Paucartambo, fêted on 16 July, should be mentioned. As noted earlier, this shrine is linked with the Virgin of Pucará, and indirectly with that of Copacabana. Its founding myth and contemporary fiesta will be analyzed in detail later, in connection with the Qoyllur Rit'i cycle. Here, it might be observed that although the image is held to be miraculous, its fiesta—like that of Urubamba's Señor de Torrichayoq—is more a civic festival than a regional pilgrimage.

The important shrines of Christ and Mary so far considered constitute only one stratum in the miraculous geography of the Cusco region. Far less conspicuous, having much smaller devotional catchments, are the numerous minor shrines, some of them dating from apparitions within living memory, which operate at the margins of priestly control and which are patronized almost exclusively by Quechua-speaking peasants from upland communities, haciendas, and cooperatives. These interlocal, or vicinal, shrines are usually situated in the mountains, away from the main transport routes, and attract pilgrims in the hundreds rather than the thousands for their annual titular fiestas. The Cusco landscape is literally studded with such minor miraculous shrines, some doubling as patron saints of peasant communities, others situated on the outskirts of settlements, still others standing alone in isolated oratories. An exhaustive mapping of them would be a formidable task. Map 8, appendix 1, shows those in the San Salvador-Pisac area and indicates the ones regularly visited by pilgrims from the fieldwork community of Qamawara. Other communities in the area have different local pilgrimage networks drawn from the same geographical inventory.[7]

Pilgrimages to these interlocal shrines are for religious and recreational purposes only. There are no commercial activities beyond the provision of lodging, food, drink, and other essential services to the visitors. Most of the shrines are controlled by local peasants, who may be obliged periodically to undertake cargos at the fiestas but who may recoup modest sums from the cash offerings of devotees. A priest may be contracted to say mass, but otherwise there is usually little clerical interference. The distinction between regional and interlocal shrines is of course one of degree rather than kind. It has a diachronic dimension, for most regional shrines began as interlocal shrines, while the staffs of minor sanctuaries today often nurse the hope that eventually their shrines, too, will win fame and widespread renown.

Typical of these vicinal shrines is Señor de Wat'a, situated in the hamlet of Wat'a Chico in the district of Caicay, province of Paucartambo. It consists of a crudely painted image of the crucified Christ on a crag, around which has been built a small thatched chapel. Its annual fiesta is held on 31 August and it is accordingly sometimes referred to as Señor de San Ramón, the saint whose feast day this is.

The myth of origin of Señor de Wat'a tells of a boy who was guarding pigs near some rocks when a beggar came up to him and asked for money. He went home to ask his mother for some, but she refused. The boy returned to the beggar and told him that he had no money but would give him all he had—some pieces of bread. The child fumbled in his pockets for the bread, and when he looked up the beggar had become miraculously transfixed to a crag as a taytacha.

The boy in this story is none other than the man who now controls the shrine. In 1973 the titular fiesta attracted about 500 people, divided among a dozen or so sponsored community-based groups or naciones. Each group had its troupe of ceremonial dancers, the principal styles being wayri ch'uncho, qhapaq qolla and ukuku. It was a two-day affair, each group depositing its portable icon, or lámina, in the chapel on the evening of the 30th and collecting it the following day.

Both staff and pilgrims were Quechua-speaking peasants. Yet the "saint" who administered the shrine dealt with devotees in a noticeably high-handed, imperious manner, insisted on speaking in Spanish to the predominantly Quechua monolingual congregation, and was treated in turn much as an ethnic superior might expect to be treated. At least for the duration of the fiesta he raised himself above the status of his fellows, the differentiation being couched in the familiar idiom of ethnicity.

Most interlocal shrines are associated, like Wat'a, with crags or rocks. In the Cusco region most of them are Christological advocations, reflecting the preponderance of Christ figures over Marian ones among the major regional shrines. There are, however, some interlocal Marian shrines as well. One such is the Virgen de Allaq, situated in the puna in the district of Quiquijana, province of Quispicanchis. This is a small image about fifteen centimeters in height, which is alleged to have appeared on a crag, around which a little chapel has been constructed. It is a Nativity advocation, and its titular fiesta on 8 September is attended by pilgrims from several communities, with dancers in the ch'uncho, ukuku and machula styles (García 1983, 41–42).

The apparitional myths of these interlocal shrines tend to use a more restricted range of themes than those of older, better established pilgrimage centers. The most common theme is the enclavement, usually cruciform in the case of Christ shrines, of a mysterious stranger in a rock, or the chance discovery of such an enclavement. The local clergy, however, are characteristically suspicious of such phenomena and may quash attempts to foment a cult around them, as in a case in the 1950s from the Puno region (Escobar 1967, 63).

Occasionally, the parties to such conflicts have carried their cases to the diocesan authorities. In 1889, for example, some children discovered in a field near Sicuani a stone which was alleged to have been imprinted with a miraculous cross. Their parents showed it to the parish priest, who promptly confiscated it. The parents appealed to the bishop, saying that the community wanted to build a chapel where they could render cult to the cross, citing Lourdes as a precedent. The priest protested that the so-called cross was simply the random marking of an ordinary stone and that to venerate it would be idolatrous. But the bishop, after having the stone examined, sided with the petitioners and granted a license for the chapel.[8]

Besides these rural interlocal shrines, there is another class of minor miraculous shrines in the region, which lie beyond the scope of the present study but which it is important to mention here. These are the urban shrines in the city of Cusco and its sprawling poorer suburbs. One of them, a cadaverous image of a child known as El Niño Compadrito, the focus of clandestine cult by certain city residents for many years, is the subject of a recent pioneering study (Valencia Espinoza 1983). Others include Señor de Wimpillay in the suburb of the same name, a eucalyptus tree with branches in the shape of a cross; a shroud bearing Christ's portrait, known as El Soldadito, 'the little soldier', on account of its proximity to a military garrison, worshiped in the suburb of Zarzuela; and Señor de Mollichayoq, a wooden cross worshiped by the residents of a central city neighborhood (Valencia Espinoza 1983, 50–51). All are regarded as intensely miraculous.

The church authorities have not looked kindly on these heterodox urban cults. During the 1970s Archbishop Luis Vallejo Santoni, a prelate respected by many for his progressive views and his sympathies with liberation theology but who was intolerant of what he regarded as superstitious practices, expressly proscribed the cults of Señor de Wimpillay and El Niño Compadrito. His death in an automobile accident in 1982 was seen by devotees as El Niño's revenge (Valencia Espinoza 1983, 70–71).

Meanwhile, in the rural areas, apparitions continue to arouse interest among an avid populace. In 1974, rumors of a manifestation of the Virgin to a peasant woman in the district of San Salvador quickly spread to Lima, where they created a buzz of excitement among the district emigrants there. But nothing came of the vision. I would guess that the miraculous shrines of the region, both existing and defunct, represent but a tiny fraction of the visionary experiences and imaginative self-deceptions that have colored the lives of the people through the centuries. What evidence is there that such shrines are anything other than random fixtures, in time and space, of such pervasive religious susceptibilities?

Pattern and Contingency

The well-worn hypothesis by which novel cults are linked with crises can be applied first. For some shrines, there is indeed evidence—in a few instances direct, in others circumstantial—to link the devotional fervor that launches the cult of the so-called miraculous image with a calamitous event: a natural disaster or epidemic, an actual or threatened social dislocation or upheaval, or the like. In the preceding chapter the cult of the Virgen de Copacabana was shown to have been born at a time of severe famine in the village, caused by a drought. More spectacular, the cult of Señor de los Temblores originated in the aftermath of an earthquake and was one of several seismic Christs in colonial Peru. Señor de Wank'a became a center of cult just as an epidemic was sweeping through the region. The apparition of Señor de Qoyllur Rit'i occurred at the time of the unsuccessful revolt of Tupac Amaru II, the effects of which—as will be seen later—were experienced acutely in that locality.

Even where no shrine is established, the excitement stimulated by a miraculous manifestation may betray a climate of uncertainty and fear. In 1921, with wool prices rising, there were widespread revolts in the Canas-Canchis area as peasants reacted to landowners' attempts to take over their pastures. News of a miraculous apparition of both Christ and the Virgin in some large stones in a suburb of Sicuani spread through the area, and crowds of peasants and costumed dancers gathered at the spot. The authorities became nervous, and the police were sent in to disperse the people (*La Verdad* 3 December 1921, cited in La Lone 1978, 183–84).

It may be recalled that there is an analogous instance in the ethnohistorical record of Huarochirí. The apparition of the wak'a Lloqllaywanku, and the subsequent growth of his cult, were coupled explicitly with anxieties attendant upon Inka encroachment on the area.

Miracles, or rather the excitement and cultic momentum they generate, could thus be seen as responses to crises. A miraculous theophany offers direct and immediate access to a divine personage—in a sense, to a new one each time—in order to cope with a specific contingency. Miraculous shrines are called forth by—or, as it would appear to the people themselves, confront—the vicissitudes of nature and the injustices of history. A divine apparition, or the florescence of its cult, anchors a crisis in space: a transient event is committed to topographic memory, and ethnohistory is transformed into a temporal landscape of sacred chronotopes (cf. Bakhtin 1981, 84).

Such a view, however, can never stand alone. Miraculous shrines do not emerge onto religious tabulae rasae but into a historically configured ritual topography, a preexisting pattern of sacred sites from which they must draw their significance. It is precisely in their determinate relatedness, in time and space, with local ritual centers, with earlier sacred locales, and with one another, that their contingent quality becomes significant.

In their respective local settings important regional shrines, at least, tend to emerge and develop distinct and apart from the patron saints of villages and towns. A regional shrine is likely to be in a sanctuary separate from the village church, sometimes situated on the outskirts of a settlement, or some distance away. Indeed, its marginal location may have been the cause—or perhaps the consequence?—of competition between adjacent villages. Where the shrine does occupy the central church, as Temblores does, it occupies a side chapel rather than the high altar. It will have its own iconological identity, and its titular fiesta and pilgrimage will accordingly be staged at a different time from the local patronal festival. Or, as in Pampak'ucho (Paruro), the two events may be timed so as to coincide, the better to dramatize the rigid ritual demarcation between them. This opposition might be more than merely symbolic. In the histories of certain shrines there is evidence of a struggle between the custodians of the shrine and the parish clergy, as the latter attempt either to suppress or to control the dangerously popular miracle site.

Interlocal shrines, too, exhibit this essentially marginal quality. It is frequently symbolized, far more conspicuously than for their regional counterparts, in their extreme physical isolation and difficulty of access. Even where interlocal shrines come to serve simultaneously as patron saints of communities and hamlets, these settlements are themselves already marginal to local parish centers. The miraculous shrine sets the seal on the community's politico-ecclesiastical peripherality.[9]

The contingent character of a miraculous theophany derives from the fact that it bypasses dramatically the existing structure of intercessionary patron saints with its parochially controlled ritual technology. From the outset, this contingent character can be seen as being institutionalized and codified, both spatially and liturgically. The shrine is typically displaced physically from the local center and is screened off ritually from its cult. At the local, parochial level, a miraculous shrine is necessarily marginal. It becomes, so to speak, a perpetual parvenu.

Regionally, however, the picture is completely transformed. Now miraculous shrines emerge as centers in their own right, each the focus of a supralocal cult. At this level, contingency begins to recede in the face of determinacy: shrines appear as patterned across the landscape, according to past and present political, economic, and religious geographies of the region.

In the first place, the shrines reveal a palimpsest of pre-Hispanic sacred space. Surveying the distribution of the principal miraculous shrines of the region, what emerges most strikingly is the symmetry of their arrangement in relation to Cusco city. Almost all lie on or near either the east-west or southeast-northwest axis, taking the city as origin. Further, four of the five Marian shrines lie on the latter, southeast-northwest axis.

As already observed, these directions provided the framework for the politico-religious geography of the Inka empire. The ceques that ran east and west from the capital not only demarcated the northern from the southern quarters, or suyus, but were also the extended sightlines for sunrise and sunset at the equinoxes, from which the state calendar was constructed. The ceque that ran southeastward, meanwhile, passed over the continental divide at Willkanuta (La Raya) and terminated in the site of Tiwanaku 300 kilometers away; it was extended beyond Cusco to the northwest, traversing the Inka dominions as far as Ecuador and thereby linking the mythical birthplace of the Sun with the northernmost reaches of the empire.

At a general level, there is perhaps nothing particularly surprising about this congruence, for the cultural geographies of both Inka and Spanish colonial Peru responded to the same natural habitat and were conditioned by the same environmental features of rivers, valleys, and mountains. The Spanish colonists, like the Inkas, used the Vilcanota valley as a vertebral communications route and also used the western exit from Cusco across the Pampa de Anta to link the region with the central coast.

But the congruence is more than merely directional. On the southeast axis, nearly all the Christian sanctuaries are situated close to the sites of wak'as that were used on the day of the June solstice as ritual stations by a group of Inka priests on the long-distance pilgrimage from Cusco to Willkanuta.[10] These wak'as were themselves pre-Inkaic shrines annexed by the Inkas and incorporated into their centralized religious geography. It is significant that four of the Marian shrines lie along this southeast-northwest axis—that is, the ceque that had been associated with Tiwanaku-Titicaca. The latter site, as already noted, was early prey to Marian colonization, and though no direct mythical connections are predicated between the Copacabana Virgins and the four shrines here, there are circumstantial links with Urcos at least.

There are analogous correspondences on the eastern axis. Señor de Wank'a is linked with Mount Pachatusan, whose summit lay on the easterly ceque itself. Señor de Qoyllur Rit'i, meanwhile, is explicitly associated with Mount Ausankati, tallest mountain in the region, which lies a few degrees south. Both mountains were important pre-Inkaic and Inkaic wak'as.

Some at least of these older Christian shrines, then, are direct successors to especially revered pagan sites, wak'as that were co-opted by the Inkas to punctuate their axial cosmology centered on Cusco and which in turn were Christianized during the succeeding centuries through the convenient medium of miraculous theophany. Thus, through the apparently haphazard emergence of these prodigious Christs and Virgins, the imperial matrix of a suppressed pagan landscape gradually reasserted itself. While the church had already established its formal administrative structure of parishes and chapelries, each vested with its own patronal icon, miracles provided the vehicle—through a combination of native predilection and clerical shrewdness—for the acceptable resacralization of those ancient pre-Hispanic wak'as raised by the Inkas to the status of imperial shrines and preserved as natural monuments in the topographic memory of succeeding generations. As a precedent for the Christological reconsecration of many of these sites, the former imperial capital itself became host to a miraculous Christ—ironically, one which in its very substance betokens the mummified effigies of the Inkas.

Temblores, in fact, while marking the locus of Inka—and colonial Spanish—power in the region, can be seen as standing in a special relation with one shrine in particular: that of Qoyllur Rit'i. These two shrines, while sharing the same crucifixion advocation, are in stark contrast to each other. Temblores resides in Cusco cathedral, at the heart of ecclesiastical and political power. Qoyllur Rit'i is sited far away from any settlement in the desolate mountain heights north of Ausankati, the most powerful hill spirit in the region. The fiesta of Temblores is not really a pilgrimage at all but a civic cult, presided over by representatives of the political, military, and church élites and attended by overwhelming numbers of townspeople. Qoyllur Rit'i's, meanwhile, has the reputation of being the most authentically Indian of all the important pilgrimages in the region. The ecological-cum-ethnic contrasts between capital city and holiest peak, between civic cult and autochthonous tradition, define polarized extremes between which all other important shrines of the region fall.

These two miraculous Christs have their titular fiestas before Easter and Corpus, respectively. Easter and Corpus are movable feasts, separated by an invariant span of sixty days (see appendix 5). Zuidema (n.d.) has argued that these two feasts are in fact the Christianized fixtures of two key paired dates in the pre-Hispanic Andean calendar, the heliacal set of the Pleiades (24 April) and their heliacal rise (8 June). The former marked the death of the earth; the latter marked its revival and heralded the rebirth of the sun at the June solstice. As noted, the two great pilgrimages of Pariaqaqa and Chaupiñamka in pre-Hispanic Huarochirí were affixed to these two astronomical observations.

By what historical process has this calendrical opposition been reinvented in the cults of Temblores and Qoyllur Rit'i? The feasts of both Easter and Corpus were instituted in Cusco city in the early years of Spanish colonialism, when parallels and fusions between pagan and Christian cults and calendars were actively sought and encouraged. Following the earthquake of 1650 and the emergence of Señor de los Temblores, Easter was calendrically enshrined by the celebration of his cult on the Monday of Holy Week. In Cusco city, meanwhile, Corpus declined from being a great international pageant to become by the end of the seventeenth century a mere civic parade.

Much later, during the internecine revolt of Tupac Amaru II, Señor de Qoyllur Rit'i emerged in a remote but sacred sector of the hinterland of the city. Now Corpus, too, was calendrically enshrined, and the fiesta became a new focus for the assembly of "nations." Thus the calendrical opposition between Easter and Corpus was now reencoded and amplified through the medium of these two miraculous Christ shrines. Temblores's fiesta on Holy Monday was a cult of the Spanish-controlled state center. Qoyllur Rit'i's in the mountains during the Corpus novena was a cult of an external center—for Indians, *the* external center, allied with the most powerful mountain apu in the region.

The miraculous taytachas of Temblores and Qoyllur Rit'i have thus come to define two polar regional centers. One is the city of Cusco, the locus of politico-religious power in successive hierarchical state systems—Inka, colonial, and republican. The other is the sacred domain of Ausankati, the peak in which the autochthonous sacred power of the regional landscape has always been focused and concentrated. In this polarity, framing all other important miracle cults of the area, the enduring counterpoint between state control and provincial autonomy is regionally recapitulated and enshrined.

To turn, then, to another pattern that emerges from the Cusco shrine map, there is the conspicuous link between pilgrimage and commerce. The distribution of shrine fiestas in time and space is intimately bound up with regional trade, though some—those of Temblores and Qoyllur Rit'i, for example—just as obviously are wholly detached from commerce. In order to elucidate these connections, it is necessary to sketch briefly the marketing system of the region.

Markets and fairs in the Andes variously serve two broad functions: a horizontal, circulatory function and a vertical, extractive one. On the one hand they distribute products between the various specialist villages and ecological zones of the region. On the other, they siphon agropastoral produce from the countryside to the urban centers and in turn funnel factorymade goods to rural consumers.[11]

Cusco's regional marketing system has two principal nodes, Cusco city itself and the town of Sicuani, which respectively command two overlapping trading spheres (cf. La Lone 1978, 289). Both centers have daily vegetable markets for the provisioning of their urban populations; Sicuani also has a bigger, weekly market. Excepting a few of the larger settlements that also have permanent markets, albeit much smaller ones, village markets are always held weekly, with neighboring markets scheduled on different days—or, in some instances, on the same day—with a view to attracting not only local buyers and sellers but, more important, the traders who operate out of the regional centers of Cusco and Sicuani. It is these weekly market wheels that cater to the short-term and medium-term needs of both the urban and rural populace.

Annual regional fairs complement and transcend these cycles of local weekly markets. They are larger and more diversified events, not only providing for short-term needs but also geared to long-term capital and investment requirements in food, livestock, tools, and utensils. Their timing is coordinated with the annual rhythms of the various production cycles. The spate of regional fairs in August and September reflects the abundance of agricultural products at that time, enabling them to be purchased in bulk for storage, processing, and perhaps later resale. Fairs held earlier in the year, in January and February, tend to specialize in livestock, with animals changing hands in quantity both among peasants themselves, as they are passed from the higher to the lower altitudes for fattening, and between peasants and merchants (Poole 1982, 101–4). In addition, all the fairs have large sections devoted to artisanry—pots, tools, rubber sandals, and so on—as well as a wide range of industrial consumer items. For both peasants and regional middlemen, an annual fair provides goods in much greater variety and volume than a weekly market, not to mention the recreational diversions that are invariably offered as well.

The partial congruence between the cycles of the large pilgrimage fiestas on the one hand and regional exchange on the other follows a precedent established in the Andes 3,000 years ago with the cult of Chavín. Involved here are both cultural and practical factors. Pilgrimage provides merchants a religious guarantee of safe passage through strange lands, while the neutral location of the marketplace alongside a universally revered shrine maintains the peace between groups that may be mutually suspicious or hostile (cf. Wrigley 1919). In addition, though, the popularity of a pilgrimage shrine and the effectiveness of a regional fair depend in part on the same geographical factor: good communications. These have to do with timing as well as location. The siting of shrines and fairs on or near main roads, especially along the arterial route through the Vilcanota valley, is clearly advantageous for drawing good crowds, while the clustering of the events in the months from June to September reflects the much greater ease of travel during the dry season. Nonetheless, some fairs in the region are graced not by renowned shrines credited with miraculous powers but instead by mere titular or local patron saints, such as those at San Pablo on 6 January (Los Reyes), Calca on 15 August (Virgin of the Assumption) and Tinta on 24 August (San Bartolomé).

The evidence suggests strongly that these pilgrimage fairs started as purely religious occasions, acquiring commercial adjuncts later—in some instances much later. Fairs tend to be deliberately established so as to coincide with extant or perhaps revived religious celebrations, and if pilgrimage shrines are appropriately sited, they are obvious candidates. This is what apparently happened in connection with Señor de Inkilpata and Sicuani's Señor de Pampak'ucho, both of them shrines of long standing, fairs associated with which were instituted quite recently in response to specific regional economic developments. New annual fairs, then, are typically fastened not to the patronal fiestas of the respective host localities but to the universalistic devotions of favorably located miraculous shrines. Fair and pilgrimage can then abet each other in popularity. In this way a miraculous shrine, already marginal in the local religious setting but central in the regional one, acquires a transient commercial centrality as well, its titular fiesta becoming a beat in the economic pulse of regional production and exchange.

A third, less conspicuous correlation that is discernible in the distribution of the principal shrines in Cusco is the location of some of them in provincial or departmental capitals. Señor de los Temblores in Cusco city is the most obvious example, of course, but there are others: Señor de Pampak'ucho in Sicuani, Señor de Torrichayoq in Urubamba, and the Virgen de Carmen in Paucartambo. The last two are not really occasions for pilgrimages so much as for civic fiestas, akin to that of Temblores in Cusco: each provides an opportunity for the provincial élite to mark itself apart from the rest of the local population, with reference to a cult that is far more prestigious and commands a much more extensive devotion than does the mere titular patron saint of the district. The stereotypical marginality of a miraculous shrine is here transformed into a kind of sociopolitical centrality, signaling the superior position of the provincial élite in relation to the local population of the district.

So far, we have considered the Cusco shrine map from various objective points of view. What, though, of the sentiments of the people themselves? What patterns emerge from the relations that *they* predicate among these sacred centers?

Miraculous shrines, no matter how many or how few their devotees, are the components of a myriad locally focused, ethnocentric religious geographies, whose span, composition, and hierarchical ordering vary from place to place. Different shrines are recognized, visited on pilgrimage, and articulated into sets by communities in different areas throughout the region. In other words, different communities are drawn to different sets of shrines, thus recuperating particularistic, localized, and flexible religious geographies from the skeletal structure of the formal, imperial system.

Typically, such a set comprises either three or five miraculous shrines, including both regional and perhaps nearby interlocal ones, the shrines being construed as a group of siblings. Whereas in other areas—the

94

Ayacucho region, for example—sororal sets of Marian shrines are encountered, in the Cusco region the emphasis is on fraternal sets of the numerically preponderant Christ shrines. Interestingly, the two personages do not usually occur together as brothers and sisters in the same sibling set. The hierarchy of shrines is represented by the order of fraternal seniority and corresponds to the supposed thaumaturgic powers of the images.

In Qamawara, San Salvador district, for example, most informants concur on a hierarchy of five taytachas that runs as follows: Señor de Wank'a, Señor de Qoyllur Rit'i, Señor de Tayankani, Señor de Aqcha, and Señor el Justo Juez. It is said that this group had journeyed from place to place and that as each brother grew tired he stopped and took up residence at the spot where his shrine is located. Señor de Wank'a's titular fiesta is not in fact attended by Qamawarans, nor do they participate in that phase of the Qoyllur Rit'i fiesta for which Señor de Tayankani is mobilized, though they are said to have done so in the past. Conversely, the list excludes a number of other shrines that are currently visited by Qamawaran pilgrims, namely the vicinal centers of Wat'a, Kisikancha, and Saqaka. From map 7, appendix 1, it can be seen that, taken together, the five ranked shrines describe a narrow lozenge of space between the two senior shrines of Wank'a and Qoyllur Rit'i.

This shrine set can be compared with those reported in the literature from elsewhere in the region. Thus, a native of Acopía in the province of Acomayo proffers a shrine pentad that runs as follows: Señor de Pampamarca, Señor de Pampak'ucho (Paruro), Señor de Wank'a, Señor de Qoyllur Rit'i, and Señor de Acllamayo (Condori Mamani 1977, 65–71). This set, headed by shrines close to the informant's homeland—Pampamarca and Pampak'ucho—encapsulates the previous one through its inclusion of Wank'a and Qoyllur Rit'i and extends beyond the Cusco region to the southeast; Acllamayo is situated in the province of Melgar, department of Puno. Señor de Acllamayo, incidentally, is otherwise known as Señor de Wank'a and has its fiesta on the octave of its senior namesake in San Salvador (Garr 1972, 47).

In a listing from Paruro, in the heartland of the Pampak'ucho shrine, some of the names recur but the rank order is changed, running thus: Señor de Pampamarca, Señor de Tungasuca, Señor de Qoyllur Rit'i, Señor de Wank'a, and Señor de Pampak'ucho (Paruro). This hierarchy also includes a sixth, most junior shrine, the other Señor de Pampak'ucho in Sicuani, which may be a later appendage (Poole 1982, 105).

In Tungasuca, meanwhile, the eponymous shrine itself is linked fraternally to Pampamarca, Pampak'ucho (Paruro), Wank'a, and also to Señor de los Temblores; the source does not give an order of rank (Contreras Berrios 1957, 2–4).

In the Pampa de Anta area west of Cusco city, Temblores features in a triad of shrines with Wank'a as his senior brother and the nearby shrine of Inkilpata as his junior (J. Núñez del Prado 1970, 100). Parenthetically, recall the myth—of uncertain provenance—cited earlier, which links Temblores and Inkilpata with Mollepata (Morote Best 1953, 89). Additionally, the informant from Acomayo states that Señor de Pampamarca originally came from Curahuasi, situated on the road from Cusco to Lima a few kilometers from Mollepata and just outside the boundary of the department (Condori Mamani 1977, 66).

This is simply a cull from the published ethnography and cannot pretend to be even nearly exhaustive of all local variations. Nevertheless, it does make it possible to offer some generalizations concerning local perceptions of Cusco's miraculous landscape. These perceptions are, of course, strongly reminiscent of those that could have been noted at the subimperial level in pre-Hispanic times. From the analysis of the Huarochirí narrative offered earlier, it was concluded that, outside the state domains, political and ethnic configurations were matched by a volatile religious culture. Shrines constituted the coordinates for conceptualizing both physical and social space, the ritual ascendancy of this cult or that being reflected in ethnocentric hierarchies of shrines frequently conforming to a pentadic kinship idiom. The multiple contours of this sacred geography were constantly changing as new shrines emerged and old ones advanced their reputations or fell into desuetude. During the Inka epoch, and also those of earlier imperial theocracies, this fluid, regional pattern of central Andean society became temporarily skewed in favor of state centers, to which provincial shrines were collectively oriented. But the counterpoint between centripetality and centrifugality could never be fully resolved.

What is to be observed in the present-day configurations of Christian shrine sets is the application of a cosmological model that is derived directly from this aboriginal one. The formal continuities are manifold: the myths of the founding of shrines by itinerant deities, the pretext of instrumental efficacy for assigning rank to a shrine, the use of kinship idioms for expressing their interrelations, a predilection for pentarchical sets, local variations in composition and order of rank, and so on. But these contemporary, locally focused shrine sets are no mere survivals. Rather, they are part of people's *current* conceptions of space, mental devices for situating local religious geographies within a wider, regional geography, using as coordinates specific shrine divinities commonly recognized or customarily visited in pilgrimage.

Each of these religious ethnogeographies plots a determinate extension of sacred space from a home base. The nearest shrine is usually ranked either highest or lowest. Those localities to the east and west of Cusco city tend to nominate other shrines within a fairly short range that are located in these same two general directions. Localities to the southeast nominate shrines through a longer range and tend to orient themselves both to those shrines in and around Cusco city and to those that lie farther south—in one instance much farther south, in the department of Puno. This is perhaps a reflection of the greater involvement in long-distance trade of the agropastoral communities in this area—since most of the shrines cited are associated with regional fairs—than that of the predominantly agricultural communities in the Cusco heartland.

While these shrine sets may have an economic dimension, however, their significance is as much religious; only one shrine in the Qamawara set is linked to a regional fair. Each set expands the vision of the sacred landscape beyond local horizons by connecting distant sources of divine power with others closer to home, through an idiom of kinship, or sameness. The wanderings of the brother Christs from site to site serve as a complement to the people's own wanderings as pilgrims to those same sites. The divine journeyings throw a loose perimeter around the human peregrinations from the community to the various shrines, enclosing them in a sacred domain particular to that community—a religious ethnoregion of which their community is the focal point, a center of sacred centers.

These locally focused domains are not discrete, however. They overlap across the landscape, interpenetrating with one another to cast a tenuous but more or less continuous cultural mantle over a fragmented, locally anchored population, a mantle based not on boundedness and exclusiveness but on a degree of consensus throughout a limited territorial range on the most important sacred centers. One shrine in particular, Señor de Wank'a, emerges as the pivot of the composite ethnogeography of the entire region, featured, as it is, in all five sets. Furthermore, it provides links through its namesake in Acllamayo with the shrines of the Puno region to the southeast. On the basis of these religious ethnogeographies alone, it can be seen that Señor de Wank'a enjoys not just regional but interregional renown. While this is in part attributable to the economic importance of its September fair, a more important factor has been the zealous promotion of the cult by the religious order that controls the shrine, as will be seen later.

In the historical and geographical survey of central Andean shrines that has been presented in this and the two preceding chapters, I have argued that the contemporary configuration of Christian miraculous shrines in Cusco must first of all be understood in relation to pre-Hispanic social and political processes in the central Andes and to the spatial dimension of those processes in particular. Power in the Andes, both dominant and subversive, was always spatial, mapped out across the variegated natural environment and thus appearing to issue from the landscape itself. Social relations became spatial relations, conceptualized through an energized landscape finely contoured in accordance with gross physical topography. Political control was extended and consolidated by gaining control of the landscape, by annexing and reenergizing sacred sites and orienting them to new politico-religious centers. By the same token such control was inherently unstable, dependent ultimately upon foreign sources of naturalized sacredness. Conversely, the sedimentation of the political power of regional and state élites around certain key locations could outlast its secular exercise, giving rise to new geographical configurations of sacredness with which successive expansionist ventures would have to contend.

Direct continuity of location between early Christian shrines and some at least of the important pagan sites was thus to be expected, and is in itself unremarkable. It is the contrasts rather than the continuities between the precontact and postcontact sacred landscapes that command attention and that betray the nature of Spanish domination in contrast to indigenous modes of political legitimation.

The religious colonization of the Andean landscape by miraculous Christian personages was in fact a secondary colonization, following after—in Cusco, many years after—the initial influx of saints and Virgins into the conquered territories. At first these imported icons were installed as emblems of native ethnic constituencies, for it was upon them that the protocolonial economy was founded. After the crisis of the Taki Onqoy, these constituencies were dismembered and the population resettled in local communities. The cults of patron saints were institutionalized accordingly. The Spanish erected their new colonial order on this entirely novel politico-religious foundation and were thereby able to entrench their power in an alien land. It was as a corollary to this localized ecclesiastical control that wider cults of miraculous figures began to emerge, and it was these that tended to be focused on former pagan sites and locales.

In pre-Hispanic times, local and regional wak'as lay as it were on an identical continuum. All were actively involved in the fortunes of their devotees, and all could be assimilated to the same shifting pantheons and theogonies. The sacred landscape was graded but continuous. The Christian cult, however, was split. On the one hand there were the neutered local divinities, the community patron saints whose cults were wedded to the enduring structures of parochial administration. On the other there were the miraculous shrines, many of them born at times of social stress, patronized for their thaumaturgic powers, fought over by different wings of the clerical establishment, their cults waxing and waning through the years, frequently joined to the cycles of regional exchange and trade, becoming the coordinates of regional ethnogeographies, and capturing the processes of ethnic and geopolitical differentiation. The Christian landscape was discontinuous, the local marked off sharply from the translocal and regional. Cults of nonmiraculous images reticulated the landscape into static, narrowly exclusive ritual domains, seemingly insulated from historical contingency, whose internal structure was congruent with the distribution and exercise of local political power. Miraculous shrines and their supralocal cults, by contrast, were directly implicated in wider processes of synchronic articulation and diachronic change.

It is this continuing broad split in contemporary Andean Catholicism, between the religion of the microcosm and the religion of the macrocosm, the one timeless and sterile, the other contingent and thaumaturgic, that I shall explore in the second part of this book.

PART TWO

PART TWO

CHAPTER 5

A Local
Profile

Heading southeast from Cusco city in the direction of Urcos and Puno, the paved highway passes first through the broad, fertile Huátanay valley, the cradle of the Inka empire. Some twenty kilometers from Cusco a dirt road branches off to the left and joins the Vilcanota valley at the railway station of Huambutío. Here the dirt road forks: to the right it crosses the river and climbs by way of a series of hairpin bends to Wankarani and on to Paucartambo, while to the left it plunges into the gorge, following the twists and turns of the river for fifteen kilometers or so, until the valley begins to broaden slightly and a huddle of red-tiled houses comes into view. Leaving the road and crossing the river by a rickety suspension bridge, we come to the village of San Salvador (see appendix 1, maps 5 and 8).

The nuclear village lies at an altitude of 3,000 meters above sea level, in the maize-producing lower *kishwa* zone. To the southwest it is dominated by the towering massif of Pachatusan—literally 'stanchion of the world'—which is mostly bare rock and sheer cliffs. On the opposite side of the river, narrow glens opening on to the valley floor give access to the eastern cordillera. Footpaths wind upward through these glens, climbing through the tuber-producing upper *kishwa* and pastoral *puna* zones to the jagged chine, whose peaks rise to 4,500 meters. In this region lie a number of isolated settlements, their farmsteads of adobe and thatch scattered across the mountain slopes—Siusa, Qamawara, Oqoruro, Umachurko, and T'irakancha (see appendix 1, map 8, and plate 1).

The village of San Salvador was one of the numerous Toledan reducciones founded in the 1570s. Throughout the colonial period the village and its surrounding locality, including the two nearby valley re-

PLATE 1   *The Territory of Qamawara. View looking southeast. The chapel of Qamawara is in the middle distance to the left; that of Oqoruro lies beyond. The apus of the mountain summits are, from left to right, Panapunku, Chillwa, and Kiwár.*

ducciones of Qosqoayllu and Pillawara, were subject both politically and ecclesiastically to the reducción of Pisac, twelve kilometers downstream. Following the municipal reorganization of 1856, San Salvador became the capital of a separate district within the province of Calca, department of Cusco, but remained a vice-parish of Pisac. As elsewhere in Peru, the municipal reorganization had the effect of concentrating political power in the district capital and of further marginalizing the other communities in the locality (cf. Fuenzalida and Matos Mar 1970, 114). This polarization, expressed as an ethnic opposition between the "mestizo" village of San Salvador and the "Indian" communities of its hinterland, is clearly apparent today.

According to the National Census of 1972 the district of San Salvador had a population of 4,000, of whom a quarter lived in the village itself (see appendix 2, table 3). The village is the seat of the municipal council and the district governor, the twin political intermediaries between the locality and the outside world. But despite its administrative status, the range of services offered by the village is extremely limited. Having no civil guard post and no resident justice of the peace, it is dependent for both on the neighboring village of Pisac. In the mid 1970s there were only three shops in the village, with restricted stocks of non-perishable goods, and there was no weekly market to speak of. The village has a telegraph post but no electricity, and until very recently had no piped water or sanitation. The village school offers the full six years of primary education, whereas the schools in the hinterland communities offer the first two years only, but pupils must go elsewhere for secondary schooling. And as a vice-parish San Salvador rarely has its own resident priest, relying most of the time on the services of the minister in Pisac.

The dearth of facilities in San Salvador is in part the result of the depressed economy of its microregion. In this respect its fate has been sealed by two principal factors. The first is physiographic. For a distance of ten kilometers on either side of San Salvador the Vilcanota valley is narrow and steep-sided, widening only slightly for a few kilometers beyond the village. The shortage of alluvial bottomland for production of cereals has set a limit on commercial agriculture in the microregion: while many valley farms and estates regularly market a portion of their crops, the subsistence orientation is more pronounced than in some neighboring localities. Valley farming in San Salvador is thus poorly capitalized, and the market in land is slow. The picture of agriculture in the microregion as a whole is a continuum ranging from subsistence peasant farming in the mountains, through a more pronounced effort at commercial production on valley smallholdings on the village outskirts, to the poorly resourced government-controlled cooperatives founded during the 1970s from the expropriated manorial estates.

The second factor that contributes to the depressed economy of San Salvador is its location in relation to the departmental capital. It can be seen from map 5, appendix 1, that Cusco city tends to draw off traffic from the Vilcanota valley in such a way as to isolate San Salvador from the arterial flows of people and goods through the region. Road and rail routes to the city from Puno and the altiplano in the southeast, and from Quillabamba and the montaña in the northwest, all contrive to branch off from the Vilcanota valley some way short of San Salvador in both directions. The peculiar, collateral location of the village in relation to the city has served to cut it off from the mainstream of commercial life in the region. During the late 1970s the Cusco bus service was pruned to one daily journey in each direction. For the rest of the time, only the occasional passing truck disturbed the peace of the village.

In the setting of the regional economy, then, the microregion of San Salvador appears as an underdeveloped enclave, a status it shares with other geographically disadvantaged localities.[1] The pattern of uneven development in the region reflects unequal access to natural, commercial, and also political resources and is sustained by complex flows of labor and goods across the landscape. Before the place of San Salvador within these wider networks of migration and trade is examined, its internal agrarian structure must be considered in greater detail.

The Organization of Production

The continuum of production régimes in the microregion is characterized by three broad types: peasant, smallholder, and estate-cooperative. The first predominates in the upper kishwa and puna zones in the mountains, the second in the lower kishwa zone in the valley, while the third spans all three ecological floors.

The principal loci of peasant production are the mountain communities of Siusa, Qamawara, Oqoruro, and Umachurko, which in 1972 together accounted for a third of the total population of the district (see appendix 2, table 3). All are situated in relatively fertile enclaves in the higher reaches of the upper kishwa zone, sheltered by mountains from the cold winds that sweep across the moorland plateau and well watered by affluents from lakes and marshes.

Arable land in these communities is of two kinds. Irrigated plots in the upper kishwa zone, from about 3,500 to 4,000 meters, are subject to intensive cultivation of potatoes (*Solanum tuberosum*), *lisas* (*Ullucus tuberosus*), *añu* (*Tropaeolum tuberosum*), *oka* (*Oxalis tuberosa*), broad beans (*Vicia fabia*), *kinowa* (*Chenopodium quinoa*) and long-eared barley (*Hordeum distichum*), the last grown entirely for sale to the brewery in Cusco. The abundant flora in this zone include various bushes that are used along with animal dung as cooking fuel and eucalyptus trees, whose tall, straight boles are used in building houses.

Seasonal land in the lower puna, from about 4,000 to 4,300 meters, is used for growing bitter, frost-resistant cultivars of potato destined for freeze-drying into an acarpous foodstuff called *ch'uñu*. Here a sectorial fallowing (*laymi*) system ensures the necessarily long fallow periods of up to seven years. Fallow land in this zone together with the high *puna* provides pasture for sheep, llamas (*Lama glama glama*), and alpacas (*Lama pacos*). The principal tools are the foot plow (*chakitajlla*) and the mattock (*raukana*), the ox-drawn plow being impracticable on the hilly terrain.

All four peasant communities conform to a pan-Andean corporate organizational model. Each is an aggregate of families with a tradition of joint tenure of a territory. Within this territory community members enjoy heritable rights to cultivation of particular plots in the lower kishwa, irrigated zone, and automatic rights to cultivation in the upper kishwa, seasonal zone. The community retains reversionary rights to all land and forbids its sale or lease to outsiders. Grazing rights both to permanent pastures and to arable land lying fallow are held in common.

To retain these rights to cultivation and pasturage a member of a community must fulfill certain formal and informal obligations. These include attending the community assemblies of heads of households to discuss matters of joint concern; joining or otherwise supporting the communal work sessions and district corvées (*faenas*) for repairs to paths, bridges, and public buildings; abiding by the rules governing sectorial fallowing and irrigation; and participating in the prestige economy of the community by sponsoring religious fiestas and occupying posts in the traditional civil hierarchy of political officials (the *varayoq*) headed by the *alcalde* 'mayor'. It was these officials who traditionally represented the community before the district authorities in the village of San Salvador.

This archetypal form of community organization, while undoubtedly rooted in the pre-Hispanic past, owes as much in its specifics to early Spanish colonial policy and legislation (cf. Fuenzalida 1970). The framework was established by the Laws of the Indies, whereby Indian communities were afforded territorial protection and limited self-government in order to ensure the flows of tribute to the civil and ecclesiastical authorities and of draft labor to the mines, textile workshops, and haciendas.

In 1824 the new republican government of Peru, in an attempt to integrate these communities into the emergent nation-state, enacted a decree that partitioned their communal holdings among their members. Though provisos were later added, the original decree was not withdrawn (Davies 1974, 20–23). The nineteenth century thus witnessed the disappearance of countless communities as their members were prevailed upon to sell their plots to outsiders or were simply defrauded of their titles as their land was absorbed into private estates. As will be seen presently, some communities were converted en bloc into haciendas. Equally, however, many survived, albeit reduced in size, for the absorption of land into private estates penetrated selectively and tended to leave the intermediate ecological zones of the quebrada largely undisturbed (cf. Guillet 1980).

In 1920, partly in response to pressure from the *indigenista* 'Indianist' lobby among Peruvian intellectuals, the new constitution of President Leguía restored legal personality to the *comunidad indígena* 'indigenous community' and rendered its lands imprescriptible. Subsequent legislation established the rules for the election of a junta to represent the community in its dealings with outside bodies. In 1969 the communities were rechristened *comunidades campesinas* 'peasant communities.' Not all communities putatively eligible have sought registration according to the constitutional provisions, however: by 1969, only 2,337 out of an estimated total of more than 6,000 had done so (Davies 1974, 90). Settlements in the district of San Salvador did not begin to register until the early 1960s; since then the varayoqs have gone into steady decline.

Kinship is reckoned bilaterally. In the upland peasant communities, a person's ayllu or familia embraces the first-cousin kindred: beyond this range kinship may be recognized but marriage is permissible (cf. B. J. Isbell 1978, 105). In theory both sons and daughters are entitled to inherit, though in practice sons are treated preferentially. The system of transmission of property encourages community endogamy, since rights in land are bound up with residence in the community. Children receive portions of their inheritance on marriage and set up independent households. Residence is patrivirilocal, with married couples tending to reside a few minutes' walk from the home of the husband's parents. It is the custom for the youngest son, however, to bring his wife to the farmstead of his parents, caring for them in their old age and eventually inheriting the family home. Most farmsteads therefore consist of either nuclear or stem families; the average size of household in the four communities in 1972 was 5.6 persons.

Community land is differentially distributed in both quantity and quality. Each of the wealthiest families in Qamawara, for example, controls up to six hectares of irrigated land, besides having access to seasonal plots; other families, particularly in Oqoruro, cultivate only seasonal plots. The distribution of livestock is similarly uneven, some families owning sixty or seventy camelids and as many sheep, others none at all. All households keep cavies (*quyi*), consumed as a delicacy, and some have a few pigs, cows, or chickens.

Division of labor is based broadly on the distinctions of gender and marital status. Married men are concerned primarily with agricultural tasks, married women with domestic tasks: the husband controls the crop in the fields, but once it enters the farmstead it passes under the control of the wife, who supervises its storage, processing, and consumption. Unmarried youths and girls, meanwhile, are deputed to look after the herds, watching over them as they graze the puna pastures by day and spending the night in huts adjoining their corrals. In keeping with this spatial division of labor, the puna is recognized as the place for lovers' trysts and illicit sexual encounters. The kishwa, the zone of settlement and intensive agriculture, is by contrast associated with domesticity and the married state.

The seasonal cycle of agricultural and pastoral tasks establishes a sequence of varying constraints in urgency and in labor requirements, and the size and composition of work teams vary accordingly (see appendix 3, figure 1). A household cooperates most frequently and intensively with chosen households within the ayllu kindreds of both spouses, the most durable relations being those between brothers and brothers-in-law. Within such sets of closely cooperating households, collaboration is generally conceptualized as *yanapa,* which connotes altruistic assistance, favor, protection, and succor (Lira 1973, 442). Beyond this sphere of supposed mutualism, cooperation in the domain of friendship, neighborship, and ritual kinship tends to be regarded as transactional, being represented as either *ayni* 'exchange labor' or *mink'a* 'festive labor' (cf. Erasmus 1956).

Ayni, in principle, involves exact reciprocity in the short term and on the same task. Where it is invoked it sets up a tacit opposition between the partners, who face each other with separate interests: the other meanings of the word include contradiction and incompatibility (Lira 1973, 27), while sixteenth-century dictionaries apparently translated it as vengeance (Mayer 1974, 47). Ayni, however, is more an ideological category than a transactional formula. Not all acts of assistance construed as ayni are repaid in the short term or even in the medium term and the debt canceled thereby; conversely, where there *is* exact, short-term reciprocity it is sometimes claimed that the cooperation is yanapa, not ayni at all. Thus is the paradox familiar in the dialectic between norm and behavior encountered: the very fact of making a commitment to reciprocate correlates with a lesser likelihood of actual reciprocation than where no such commitment needs to be made.

Mink'a carries no such undertaking to return the assistance. It denotes labor collectively rendered to an individual on an explicitly nonreciprocal basis—though again, the same people, by and large, would tend to be present at one another's mink'a work parties through the long term. A mink'a session is more or less festive in character: ceremonial food is likely to be served, and the convener might provide music from a phonograph or might even hire a band of musicians.

While ayni-yanapa cooperation is used for mundane agricultural and pastoral chores, mink'a work groups are more often convened for nonperiodic tasks such as housebuilding and reroofing.[2] A common arrangement for the strenuous first plowing of fallow fields in March and April (*barbecho*) is for large rotating teams of a dozen or more men each to be mobilized, a team working for a day on the fields of each of its members in turn. The person whose field is being worked frequently nominates a leader, known as the *arariwa*—literally 'guardian of the crops'—to allocate tasks among the workers.

Sharing labor in this way has a significance that goes far beyond any purely practical response to techno-environmental constraints and seasonal exigency. It is a symbolic act, a mechanism for the formation and maintenance of social bonds per se (cf. Long and Roberts 1978, 311). Indeed, it is difficult to see any practical advantage to large rotating work teams at all, while it might actually prove cheaper—and more efficient—to hire wage labor than to use rowdy, festive mink'as. The neat normative categories of yanapa, ayni, and mink'a, so often reified in the Andean literature but in fact frequently blurred in practice, amount to variant expressions of the same fundamental commitment to mutual sustenance through the sharing of food and labor. This is made explicit in the food-sharing that accompanies all interhousehold cooperation. Whatever the transactional mode invoked, cooperation demands that the *patrón*, the sponsor of the work group, provide a midday meal, rum, and coca for his fellow workers, and for mink'a maize beer (*chicha*) as well. Subsistence labor and its transformed product, cooked food, in effect constitute a single sphere of exchange, and the social relations through which they circulate acquire an axiomatic, moral character.[3]

Wage labor (*jornal*) does occur between community peasants; the going rate in the early 1970s was S/.20 (U.S. 50 cents) a day plus lunch and coca.[4] For the most part, however, it is regarded with antipathy. Those people, typically returned migrants, who regularly hire labor are regarded with pity, since it is an admission that they have no friends on whom to call for assistance and are in a fundamental sense outsiders.[5] Cooperation, the sharing of one's most precious asset, is in fact a key component in the fixing of the perceived ethnic frontier between "Indian" and "mestizo" in the locality.

The second type of agrarian régime, smallholder production, has its principal loci in the valley settlements of San Salvador, Qosqoayllu, and Pillawara. It differs in degree rather than in kind from the peasant farming of the uplands. All three of these villages retain vestiges of a traditional corporate community organization, and Qosqoayllu has registered formally as a comunidad campesina. In contrast to that of the upland communities, however, most valley land was privately owned before agrarian reform, holdings ranging from family farms of two or three hectares to large haciendas of more than a thousand.

Most of the valley floor is given over to maize, with wheat and pulses on the lower slopes. Most plots are irrigated from the waters that drain into the valley from the cordilleras on either side. Ox-drawn plows, tractors, and chemical fertilizers are employed as well as traditional implements and techniques. Cattle, pigs, sheep, and goats are in evidence, although on the whole the raising of stock is secondary to agriculture.

Labor for farming in the valley is recruited according to a variety of mechanisms. The smaller holdings operate much like their counterparts in the mountains, relying for the most part on domestic, kin-based, and exchange labor. These holdings provide first and foremost for the subsistence of the farming family; commercial considerations are secondary. On the larger farms, wage labor features more prominently, and a greater share of their produce is destined for the market. Sharecropping arrangements are also found. In addition, a proportion of valley labor is furnished through patron-client relations, cast in the cultural idiom of *compadrazgo*.

Compadrazgo is an institution of fundamental importance in Andean society. It refers to ties of ritual coparenthood established in the Catholic ceremonies of baptism and marriage and the indigenous ceremony of *uma rutukuy* 'first haircutting'. In the area under discussion, ritual kinship of this kind is used as a means both of reinforcing or intensifying existing relations of kinship, friendship, or neighborhood and also of extending a person's social network according to a more or less explicit calculus of choice. It operates both horizontally and vertically—that is, between people of the same and different socioeconomic status (cf. Mintz and Wolf 1950, 335).

Horizontal compadrazgo between peasants from the same community leads to greater frequency of agricultural and other cooperation, while between peasants from different ecological zones it often gives rise to regular exchanges of goods—potatoes or meat, say, for maize—according to established rates of exchange known as *unay precio* 'ancient price' (cf. Mayer 1971, 190). In other cases, however, simple complementarity with regard to agropastoral resources is compounded with differential access to others, and here the latent asymmetry of compadrazgo begins to assert itself.[6]

Mountain peasants, especially Quechua monolinguals, seek to acquire at least one compadre from the valley, ideally a literate speaker of Spanish and a resident of one of the district capitals of San Salvador or Pisac, so as to gain indirect access to the political and judicial authorities and perhaps an advocate before them, should the need arise. In turn valley dwellers, and also some of the better-acculturated mountain peasants, seek compadres among the district élites or in the provincial or departmental capitals. Lawyers and—since the restoration of democracy in 1980—politicians of Alianza Popular Revolucionaria Americana (APRA) and Acción Popular are ideal candidates. At the local level such patronage, while it may involve the exchange or sale of produce between the partners, invariably also entails informal labor service on the part of the client or members of his family. A valley farmer with several compadres in the mountain communities thus has a sizable pool of laborers who can be called upon at peak periods in the agricultural cycle, especially during the maize harvest, which occurs a few weeks earlier than the potato harvest in the mountains.

The third form of production régime in the locality was undergoing radical changes in the 1970s as a result of the national agrarian reform legislation introduced by the military government of General Velasco in 1969 (Peru 1969a). The law decreed that all estates above a certain size—thirty hectares in the Cusco region—were liable to expropriation and conversion into government-controlled cooperatives.[7]

The agrarian reform authorities identified several expropriable properties in the district of San Salvador. The three smallest, Uchumuka, Vilkar, and Wank'a, covered a few hundred hectares each, while the larger properties of Wallwa (Huallhua), Vicho, T'io, Sondor, and T'irakancha covered upward of a thousand hectares apiece. The three adjacent properties of Wank'a, Sondor, and Uchumuka were owned by the Mercedarian religious order. Vicho and Vilkar were former Jesuit estates (Mörner 1978, 43); Vilkar, along with many other properties in the Cusco region expropriated from the order in 1767, eventually passed to the Colegio Nacional de Ciencias in Cusco on its founding in 1825.

All the estates except T'irakancha were based in the valley, though their lands stretched upward toward the puna. Before the reform all were operated on the basis of some form of labor tenancy, whereby workers were allocated rights to land for dwellings, cultivation, and pasturage. Wank'a, site of the important regional shrine, had a small convent with two or three Mercedarian priests in permanent residence. The manor houses of the other haciendas were used only infrequently, for private landlords tended to spend most of their time in Cusco, leaving the day-to-day running of their estates in the hands of salaried managers.

Though sharing basic economic features, the estates varied significantly in sociocultural organization and de facto politico-ecclesiastical status.[8] T'irakancha, which with 3,200 hectares of upland pasture was the largest hacienda in the district, had a resident population of labor tenants and their families numbering five hundred and functioned in many respects like the peasant communities of Siusa, Qamawara, Oqoruro, and Umachurko. The people there were classed as Indian; they had their own varayoq, like the upland communities they were subject to collective corvée at the behest of the district authorities, and they participated along with other communities in the rituals of the parish seat.

The valley-based haciendas were rather different. Wallwa, for example, in the middle range with around 1,000 hectares, had a permanent work force of only a dozen resident labor tenants and their families, who participated neither in the district corvée nor in the parish rituals. Indeed, Wallwa displayed the familiar latifundial phenomenon of tending toward the exercise of jurisdiction in its own right (Lockhart 1969, 422). Thus, the hacienda itself customarily exacted corvée from some of the surrounding communities, including T'irakancha, while its patronal fiesta rivaled that of the parish. In addition, Wallwa relied not only on resident but also on nonresident labor tenancy. Members of neighboring peasant communities, chiefly Qamawara, Oqoruro, and Siusa, would work for a certain number of days annually on the estate, each receiving tenancy of a commensurate plot of land that supplemented the family's community holding.

These differences in hacienda organization were in part reflections of different historical processes of genesis and development. The examples just described seem to typify two broad paradigms.

Haciendas such as Wallwa were established during colonial times, when the booming mining economy of the central Andes—based largely on the silver deposits of Potosí and the mercury deposits of Huancavelica—placed demands on agricultural production that the systems of encomienda and corregimiento were unable to satisfy (cf. Keith 1971). The new haciendas, based on the private ownership of land, began to be carved out of the most fertile areas of the countryside from the late sixteenth century onward.

Labor for the new enterprises was a combination of mita or corvée labor, and *yanakonaje* 'debt peonage'. Sociologically these haciendas were novel creations, and their peculiar mode of production and their position in the rural social order had to be institutionalized and legitimated. One of the means to this end, as will be seen later, was the establishment of de facto religious jurisdiction by an hacienda over the surrounding countryside, often in the face of fierce resistance from the local clergy. Once entrenched in the local politico-religious structure, the colonial *hacendados* were able to force neighboring communities into corvée on their lands while at the same time building up a core work force of resident *yanas* 'personal debt-peons' (Mörner 1978, 56–58). Through the centuries many of these estates expanded by encroaching on the lands of adjacent communities, a process hastened by the privatization decrees of the republican era and continued to the present.

Estates such as T'irakancha had their origins in a later period of economic expansion, on the basis of the international demand for tin from northern Bolivia and wool from southern Peru during the late nineteenth and early twentieth centuries. Existing estates were now expanded and new ones formed, the old landed élite joined and at times supplanted by a new breed of hacendado, fiercely entrepreneurial and with scant regard for the feudalistic etiquette of the traditional régime. Communities were converted in their entirety into haciendas, their lands no longer enjoying legal protection as communal holdings. The heavy demand for wool made the pastoral communities of the puna especially vulnerable; those cultivating the *quebrada* of the upper kishwa zone tended to escape, though frequently with their lands depredated by encroaching haciendas. In the space of a few decades, agrarian society underwent its greatest transformation since the rise of the hacienda in colonial times, a transformation all the more drastic for the suddenness and speed of the changes (cf. Chevalier 1966).

The new estates that came into being during this period faced none of the problems of legitimation encountered by their earlier, colonial counterparts. Most were simply superimposed on existing peasant communities, which continued to function locally in many respects as nonmanorial communities. Once incorporated into haciendas, however, these communities were isolated from the various reforms, beginning with those of President Leguía during the 1920s, which successive national administrations have directed at the peasant communities. Limited though these reforms have been, they have at least brought the community sector into contact with regional and national government bureaucracies, generating a certain amount of political development and cultural change. By contrast, many of the manorial communities pertaining to the "republican" haciendas have remained politically isolated and culturally conservative.

One such community, Q'ero in the province of Paucartambo, has the reputation among Cusqueños of being the most authentically Indian in the entire region (van den Berghe and Primov 1977, 180).[9] Similarly, the people of T'irakancha were regarded by valley dwellers as quintessentially Indian, in contrast to the inhabitants of the peasant communities, who were sometimes said to be not real Indians at all but *medio mestizos* 'semimestizos'. T'irakancha's weavings were regarded as the finest, its Quechua the purest, its customs the quaintest. Conversely, in recent decades it has been workers on these republican haciendas who, deprived of institutional channels for protest and reform, have tended to turn most violently against their masters.

The Departmental Peasant Federation began to mobilize the peasantry of San Salvador soon after the promulgation of the agrarian reform law in 1969. It was not until 1972, however, that the area was declared an agrarian reform zone, and expropriation proceedings were initiated the following year. Once land had been expropriated, the former haciendas were administered by provisional committees under the guidance of the Ministry of Agriculture. Various organizational models for the new cooperatives were floated.[10] It was eventually decided to create two large Cooperatives of Agrarian Production (CAPs), one based on the puna properties of T'irakancha and Chawaytiri in the district of Pisac, the other incorporating the valley-based properties of T'io, Wallwa, Wank'a, Sondor, Vilkar, and Uchumuka together with Wandar in Pisac district. Vicho, meanwhile, was to be amalgamated with other properties to the southeast (Peru 1975, 2:97).

In the adjudication of lands to the new enterprises, T'irakancha was retained more or less intact. Wallwa, however, was completely dismembered. All the labor tenants, both resident and nonresident, were awarded their plots. In addition, in recognition of the corvée that the communities of Qamawara, Oqoruro, and Siusa had rendered to the hacienda through the years, and also of the usurpation of their lands by the estate, the communities were awarded sizable tracts of demesne land. The decision to make these awards provoked much bitterness, not only among the remaining families on the estate but also among the smallholding farmers of San Salvador, who were angry that mountain peasants should have benefited so handsomely from the reforms while they themselves received nothing. Some of them demonstrated their anger by twice invading fields granted to Qamawara, destroying crops and attempting to take possession (*Sur* 10 (1978):23–25). The agrarian reform, in other words, while it eliminated the landed élite, sustained and even exacerbated divisions and conflicts among different types of rural producer in the locality.

Commerce and Migration

The microregion of San Salvador is served by the weekly market in Pisac, a bustling affair that regularly attracts about a thousand people. The catchment of the market embraces not only the districts of Pisac and San Salvador but also those of Coya, Taray, and Lamay. It also attracts a regular contingent of tourists from Cusco, lured by the mention in every guidebook to the area of Pisac's authentic Indian market.

The convoys of trucks, buses, taxis, and private cars begin to arrive in Pisac early on Sunday morning. The market consists of two distinct sections, each with its own clientèle (cf. Castillo Ardiles 1970, 78). In the center of the plaza and overflowing into the sidestreets are the vendors of "ethnic" products and souvenirs who have followed the tourists over from Cusco for the morning. The gringos, most of them from North America but an increasing number from Europe, have little contact with the locals, but pass the time buying the same souvenirs they could purchase more cheaply in Cusco, though they do inject some cash into the local economy through the hiring of guides to the Inka ruins above the village, purchases of food, drink, and photographic film in the shops, and so on. Indeed, the dozen or so commercial establishments in the village—food stores, café-bars, souvenir shops, bakers, and a barber-cobbler—all rely heavily on the Sunday crowds for their custom.

The section of the market that caters to local needs is immediately adjacent to the tourist section but is quite separate from it commercially, socially, and even linguistically. Local vendors of fresh foodstuffs—always women—sit on the ground with their wares spread out in front of them, offering between them a comprehensive range of seasonal local produce, together with some montaña products such as fruits, peppers, and coca, as well as more exotic items such as herbal medicines and components for *despachos* 'offerings to the nature spirits'. There are also stalls at which are sold such things as hats, cheap Western-style clothes, plastic sheeting, plastic bowls and water carriers, cutlery, chemical dyes, padlocks, radio batteries, and the hundred and one other industrially manufactured items for which there is a steady local demand. Besides the business of buying and selling, people come to the market to meet friends and acquaintances, exchange news and gossip, and pursue amorous intrigues. Much of the trade accordingly goes to the chicha sellers, whose stalls are ranged along one side of the plaza. Religious affairs are attended to as well: after mass the parish priest is available for consultations and baptisms. All in all, Pisac market is the hub around which much of the social life as well as the commercial activity of the area revolves.

In distribution, Pisac market operates mainly on a horizontal level, circulating foodstuffs among local producer-consumers, although it also has a vertical dimension in the sale of industrially manufactured goods to rural consumers. The extractive economy, by which agropastoral products are withdrawn from the countryside for urban consumption and export, operates in this area largely outside the marketplace as such, and instead assumes a "networked" rather than a "nodal" form of organization.

The communities of the Cordillera Vilcanota, including those of San Salvador district, are traversed by various functionaries and itinerant traders who funnel specific products through this extractive economy. They include the representatives of the Cervecería Cusqueña, the city brewery operating under German license, who collect the harvested barley and distribute new seed; the crop merchants operating out of Cusco, who frequently intercept peasants on their way to Pisac market and who sell to the municipal market in the city; the wool merchants operating out of Sicuani, who sell to the export houses there and in Arequipa (Orlove 1977) and who may peddle such items as salt and sugar; and the dealers in weavings and handicrafts, who cater to the lucrative market in folk manufactures opened up by the burgeoning tourist trade and the demand for such items overseas. Many of these traders establish compadrazgo relations with families in the communities they ply, so as to assure themselves of lodgings on their travels and also a degree of trust on the part of their clients.

The greater part of this trade, both nodal and networked, eddies around the village of San Salvador without actually impinging on it. Not only is the village bypassed by the regular traffic of regional commerce, but it is also deprived of much of the trade that emanates from its own hinterland. Pisac market caters to local consumption needs, while merchants from elsewhere move products out of the locality to urban and export markets. But for a few brief days each year, the village ceases to be a commercial backwater and becomes the cynosure of the whole of the southern Peruvian Andes. This is in September for the fiesta and fair of Señor de Wank'a. I shall describe this important regional fair later, in conjunction with the discussion of the Wank'a cult in chapter 9.

San Salvador's economic marginality also determines its function in the regional labor market. Stagnant localities such as San Salvador are generally self-sufficient in labor. Agropastoral production and exchange within such localities tend to rest, as noted earlier, on networks of social relations and labor-tenancy arrangements that draw them to a greater or lesser degree away from the market domain. More dynamic areas are less likely to be self-sufficient in manpower; in these, wage labor is more frequent, at least during seasonal shortfalls. Depressed localities therefore export labor while dynamic ones import it; some areas both import and export manpower, according to the demands of local production. Meanwhile, urban migration, mainly to Lima, funnels some labor out of the region altogether. In one sense, the San Salvador locality and others like it serve as labor reservoirs for the unevenly developed regional agrarian economy.

There are two main forms of intraregional migration. First there is short-term migration to the more commercial, maize-producing areas downriver, chiefly Calca and Urubamba. Wages in these areas at harvesttime can be almost twice those in San Salvador, if any work is available there at all.[11] This form of seasonal migration is resorted to by men of all ages, to meet some specific expenses—sponsorship of a fiesta, the purchase of a school uniform for a child, the repayment of a loan, or whatever.

The second type of intraregional migration is to the plantations of the montaña beyond Quillabamba. Before the agrarian reform, this operated by means of a system of *enganche* 'indentured labor'. An agent known as an *enganchador* would visit peasant communities in the highlands and sign up recruits to three-month contracts, advancing immediate cash loans. This system has now been prohibited, and the paltry wages have risen somewhat. Nevertheless, the subtropical climate and the uncomfortable living conditions make montaña labor an unattractive possibility for older men. The majority of recruits have always been youths and young men, many of them saving for eventual migration to Lima.

Large-scale migration from the Peruvian highlands to the coastal urban centers, particularly Lima, is a relatively recent phenomenon that became established during the period of industrial and urban expansion during and immediately following World War II (cf. Deler 1975). It was not until the early 1960s that men from the mountain communities of the San Salvador locality joined the exodus in significant numbers, following the setting up of primary schools in several of the communities. By the 1970s, Qamawaran expatriates in Lima at any one time numbered about fifteen—about 3 percent of the population of the community.

Most urban migrants from the locality fully intend to return to their communities to resume their rural livelihoods after two or three years in the city, and many have already done so. But despite their small numbers their reentry, unlike that of seasonal or indentured migrants, is generating a cumulative disequilibrium within the political economies of the sending communities. Migrants to Lima have been able to amass funds vast in comparison with those that can be saved from local wage labor, yet they have few opportunities to invest them apart from plowing them into the prestige economy by financing fiestas and other community recreations. At the same time, having become accustomed to life in the metropolis, they tend to regard aspects of highland society as anachronistic. They thus find themselves in economic, political, and also cultural tension with their former way of life.[12] During the early 1970s, their hopes of progressive change were raised by the reform program of the Velasco government. Entrenched interests in the locality, however, proved difficult to assail.

Dependence and State Reforms

As a district capital, the village of San Salvador is a node in two parallel administrative structures: the prefecture system, represented by the district governor's office, and the municipality system, represented by the district council. The prefecture system is the formal framework of Peruvian national administration, with departments headed by prefects, provinces by subprefects, districts by unsalaried governors, and *anexos*—communities politically subordinate to a district capital—by lieutenant governors. It symbolizes the centralist tendency in the Spanish heritage of Peru. The municipality system, on the other hand, with its departmental, provincial, and district councils modeled on the *cabildo* 'town council' of medieval Spain, is the institutional expression of the converse tendency, toward local self-government and autonomy.

The governor of San Salvador, usually a middle-ranking smallholder from the village, is charged with upholding law and order in the district. His function is somewhat diffuse. Since there is neither a justice of the peace nor a civil guard post in the village, he serves in effect as a judge of first instance, dealing with cases ranging from boundary disputes to criminal assault. As an appointed official of the central government, he is resented by some villagers as representing a permanent intrusive presence in local affairs. There is some justification for this view, since as in other rural areas in Peru the district governor occasionally acts as a check on the extralegal powers of the district council (cf. Stein 1961, 198). A lieutenant governor is similarly regarded as the keeper of the peace within his anexo, but in practice he simply provides his superior with local information and relays orders to his community.

The district council (*consejo distrital*) consists of six *regidores* 'aldermen' presided over by an alcalde. Apart from brief interludes during which local democracy has held sway—in the early decades of this century, between 1964 and 1968, and again since 1980—the council has been selected rather than elected, the departmental prefect having a veto over local nominations from incumbent council members. As such it is a self-perpetuating élite, reposing upon ties of patronage and unhindered by cleavages of party or principle, supported institutionally from above but possessing considerable local autonomy. Council members, whether selected or elected, tend to be drawn from the ranks of the larger landholders in the valley, many of whom have business interests outside the area, in Cusco or elsewhere. Municipal public service is held in high regard, and the mayor and aldermen are accorded polite respect by the villagers.

The district council is the pivot in a radial administrative structure that stretches outward to the peasant communities, binding each of them in a dependent relationship to the district capital. Ever since colonial times, the control of a municipality over its hinterland has meant more than mere political hegemony and has included an element of overt economic proprietorship (cf. Portes and Walton 1976, 9). Its power is traditionally exercised through the intercalary figure of the community alcalde. Established during the colonial era, this office—sometimes referred to as *alcalde de vara* or *alcalde indígena* to distinguish it from its constitutional namesake in the municipality—has never been legally recognized by any republican administration; indeed, it was outlawed by the Leguía administration in 1921 (Davies 1974, 72). Nevertheless, it has persisted in many areas as the principal instrument whereby rural municipalities maintain their hold over the peasant communities within their ambit.

Each of the larger communities in the district has a community alcalde, as does the village of San Salvador, a vestige of its former status as an "indigenous" community subordinate to the village of Pisac. Each alcalde heads a body called the varayoq, or staff bearers, after the silver-tipped staffs (*varas*) its senior members carry. The varayoq varies from area to area, even from community to community, both in its composition and in its degree of engagement with the system of religious offices or cargos.[13] In the communities of San Salvador it generally consists of the alcalde himself, his deputy (*alcalde segundo*), one or two regidores, whose chief function is to summon members of the community to assemblies and work sessions by sounding their conch shells, and—in the past—one or two *kañaris,* who served as bodyguards. While there is no formal integration of civil and religious hierarchies as described for many Meso-american communities (Carrasco 1961; Dewalt 1975), the alcalde ideally has to have a reasonable record of fiesta sponsorship to his credit and to have been married according to the rites of the Roman Catholic Church. Each alcalde is elected annually by the community assembly, subject to the veto of the district authorities, and then appoints the rest of the varayoq. The new incumbents are collectively invested in the district capital on 1 January by the district governor.

The community alcalde traditionally performed a number of important internal community functions. He embodied what Guillet (1978) has called the suprahousehold sphere of peasant production, coordinating harvesting, irrigation, the sectorial fallowing system, and collective labor (*faenas*) on community works such as footpaths and bridges. He presided over the community assemblies of household heads and was obliged to sponsor a number of fiestas during his term of office.

In addition to these internal duties, the alcalde was the representative of his community before the district authorities. All the community alcaldes were obliged to present themselves in the district capital every Sunday morning, when instructions would be issued regarding participation of communities in the rota of the corvée on public works in the district, arrangements for the distribution of irrigation water, and so on. Not that an alcalde was expected to serve merely as a mouthpiece for district mandates; on the contrary, he was expected to negotiate to the best of his ability to minimize the impositions upon his community. A skillful alcalde, equipped with good compadrazgo connections in the village, could earn the fulsome respect of his fellows through astute bargaining of this kind. A weak one, who simply acceded to every demand of the authorities, would be execrated. But the net effect of the system was to pit the communities against one another, preventing the formation of a coalition of resistance against the district authorities.

Since the early 1960s, the traditional role of the varayoq has been weakened by the advent of alternative forms of representation following the registration of several communities according to the provisions of the 1920 constitution. The first community to register, in 1963, was the most extensive, Umachurko. During the next fifteen years Qamawara, Siusa, Qosqoayllu, and Oqoruro followed suit. While the lengthy negotiations for registration were led in the main by returned urban migrants or men who had done national service in the armed forces,[14] the teachers in the recently founded community schools, most of them outsiders from Cusco city, were frequently catalysts in the process. Each registered community elected a communal junta headed by a *personero* 'attorney', and the new representatives quickly began to usurp the functions of the varayoq.

In 1970, as part of its agrarian reform program, the Velasco government introduced a new statute to bring the peasant communities into line with the new agricultural cooperatives formed from the expropriated private estates. The statute replaced the communal junta with two parallel bodies, an administrative council and a vigilance council, elected biennially, with members eligible for reelection only once. Literacy was a formal requirement for office. The president of the administrative council was to be the community's chief executive and was directly responsible to the Bureau of Peasant Communities, now transferred from the Ministry of Labor to the Ministry of Agriculture and given a higher administrative profile (Peru 1972).

As elsewhere in the highlands, the implementation of the statute in San Salvador sparked off a power struggle in each community, as individuals and factions competed for the newly enhanced offices (cf. Long and Winder 1975; Guillet 1979). The most active in the politics of the new councils have tended to be the young returned urban migrants and army veterans, many of whom were eager to push forward the social reforms announced by the Velasco régime. The literacy requirement, however, has not been strictly observed, and acculturated Spanish speakers have by no means monopolized the offices. The administrative changes have also placed more power in the hands of the schoolteachers, since the statute makes them into a kind of local mandarinate, entrusted with vetting candidates for council office, organizing elections, and advising officials on procedural and legislative matters. They can thus exert a considerable influence in community politics (cf. Primov 1980). Meanwhile, the councils expanded their control of community affairs until by the end of the 1970s the varayoqs appeared as little more than ceremonial relics.[15]

By equipping the hinterland communities with leaders responsible directly to a government agency rather than to local power brokers, registration—especially the changes effected by the 1970 statute—in principle short-circuited their dependent relationships with the district capital. But established practices proved extremely resilient in the face of reform. Two significant issues in the early 1970s were collective corvées (faenas), and irrigation.

On the first, some limited progress was made. The collective corvée, a lineal descendant of the Toledan mita, has been used for various purposes and under various names throughout the colonial and republican eras (Wiedner 1960; Davies 1974; Oakley 1972). Whether sanctioned by the government of the day or not, rural municipalities in Peru have come to regard the labor of dependent peasant communities as a resource to be appropriated as and when required, sometimes for the private purposes of political officials, and impose fines or imprisonment on defaulters as a matter of course. External community corvées of this kind are the obverse of the community faenas of more obvious mutual benefit: the two are twin aspects of a single institution, whereby the peasant is taxed regressively (van den Berghe and Primov 1977, 169). There is evidence to indicate that labor taxation of this kind is associated with low penetration of the market (Winder 1978, 223; Long and Roberts 1978) and that the decline in municipal power to convene extracommunity corvées is matched by a decline in the authority of the community alcalde to convene *internal* community faenas (Snyder 1960, 354–57).

The Velasco government, like many of its predecessors, encouraged the controlled mobilization of collective labor, which it further turned to account as a means of political co-optation. By requiring all requests for extracommunity faenas to be channeled through SINAMOS, a paraministerial development agency,[16] the central government aimed at once to check the bona fides of the projects themselves, to lessen the power of local élites, and to bring the peasantry more firmly under its control.

Under the new regulations, the municipal authorities were more circumspect. But while they sought official approval for some faenas they continued to order others independently, and the mountain peasants were usually too timorous to disobey. On one occasion, for example, the municipal mayor sent a messenger to instruct a group of visiting peasants to clean the village plaza in preparation for a football tournament. Only the intervention of a community schoolteacher, a Cusqueño, on their behalf emboldened them to defy the command.

The irrigation issue was less clear-cut. The hydrography of the microregion means that both mountain and valley farmers rely for irrigation on the streams that rise in the cordilleras (see appendix 1, map 8). Previously, access to this crucial resource was controlled by the authorities in the village, who withheld or granted the upland communities permission to open their irrigation canals depending on the requirements of the valley farmers.

The General Water Law, introduced by the Velasco government in 1969, while ostensibly aimed at eradicating inequities in water distribution, in fact set out a number of conflicting criteria for allocation in areas of scarcity and left considerable discretion in the hands of provincial water administrations (Peru 1969b). The application of the new legislation in the Calca province in 1973 initiated a series of protracted negotiations between the provincial water officers and representatives of the mountain and valley farmers which dragged on for years, and which—given the needs of the new valley-based cooperatives—seemed unlikely to produce a more favorable arrangement for the upland communities.

The centripetal administrative structure of San Salvador and the continued dominance of the district capital over its mountainous hinterland even in the face of external pressure for change are in part the result of the local and regional geographical factors outlined earlier. It is significant, therefore, that during the early 1970s, activists in the communities of Qamawara, Oqoruro, Siusa, and Umachurko, encouraged by government propaganda promising development assistance to the peasantry, rekindled a plan to build a road along the eastern cordillera of the river Vilcanota, passing through or near the four communities and connecting with Pisac in one direction and Wankarani in the other (see appendix 1, map 8). Two communities from Pisac district, Ampay and Qotatayki, were also initially keen to see the project realized, and the coalition of six communities began to lobby the SINAMOS office in Cusco for technical and material assistance.

Supporters of the plan for the new road argued that it would bring important economic benefits, not only by making it easier to market agricultural produce but also by facilitating access to the interlocal miraculous shrine of Señor el Justo Juez in Oqoruro, thereby increasing the number of pilgrims at its September fiesta. But they also recognized that the road would have long-term political repercussions as well, since the district of San Salvador would be severely dislocated. Activists for the plan in Qamawara envisaged a gradual change from the community's dispersed pattern of residence to a nucleated settlement along the new road. Some even anticipated the day when the community would grow sufficiently in commercial importance that it might challenge the authority of San Salvador and perhaps become a district in its own right.

The hope was a vain one. In 1973 SINAMOS went into decline, and two years later Velasco was ousted in a palace coup that marked the end of the radical phase of the Peruvian "revolution." By 1980, when the military handed over power to a center-right administration and Belaúnde resumed the presidency, SINAMOS had disappeared from the political scene and government help for the road was still not forthcoming.

Nevertheless, the bid for government assistance is interesting in itself, since it illustrates the manner in which, under certain circumstances, a horizontal coalition of peripheral communities may be generated outside local politico-administrative structures. On the evidence of this and earlier examples in the area—for instance the joint participation of Pisac and San Salvador communities in the construction of a hospital at Kuyo Chico during an applied anthropology project in the 1960s (O. Núñez del Prado and Whyte 1973)—the circumstances would appear to include some form of external linkage with regional or national bodies that support, or are perceived to support, interests other than those represented by local élites. Unless assistance is sought and dispensed through these alternative avenues, the distribution of any benefits will almost certainly follow the paths of existing local political hierarchies.

Given the volatility of Peruvian national politics, however, such external liaisons are extremely fragile. Administrations, policies, and ideologies have a rapid turnover. Belaúnde in fact lost the presidency in the election of 1985 to the leftist APRA candidate Alan García. By now, however, rural development had been overshadowed by a new imperative—the defeat of Sendero Luminoso 'Shining Path', a Maoist guerrilla movement originating in the Ayacucho region which has extended its operations throughout the country. The armed forces, which only a decade earlier had been trumpeting the cause of socialist reform, were now committed to the ruthless elimination of the insurgency; in the ensuing terror and counterterror some 10,000 people have died, many of them innocent peasants. The Cusco region has so far remained on the periphery of this conflict, though there is mounting fear and suspicion.

Despite all the vagaries of national politics through the 1970s and 1980s, what is remarkable about the locality of San Salvador is how little has changed. Local smallholder élites in such economically marginal districts are on the whole stable. By accommodating minimally to change, they are able to stay in place and perhaps reassert their dominance when the political climate permits. Nevertheless, the Velasco era had set some significant changes in train. These changes soon began to acquire a semblance of institutional solidity through a determinate reshaping of local ritual practice.

CHAPTER 6

Ordering
the Microcosm

The vertical Andean landscape ordains the structure of the local cosmos. Thus at least it would appear, so well attuned is the one to the other. The passage from valley to mountain peak is a passage from civilized to wild, from order to entropy, and from Christian to pagan.

In the valley, the vice-parochial church of San Salvador, with its stone façade and carved portal, facing the municipal headquarters in the village plaza, advertises itself as the focal point of the locality. Here is housed the image of the parish patron, San Salvador del Mundo 'Christ the Savior of the World', and those of a number of secondary saints as well. The church's private benefactions have recently been well publicized: a plaque records the name of the parishioner who paid for an exterior refurbishment, another the name of the donor of the handsome wooden doors. The presbytery alongside is similarly well maintained. In 1977, after a long period of vacancy, a priest was appointed to the vice-parish and began to make his presence felt in a number of ways, reinvigorating local fiestas and encouraging donations and bequests. In addition to the vice-parochial church, the village has a small chapel on its northwestern outskirts, dedicated to the Virgin of the Assumption.

Each of the other communities in the vice-parish in turn has its own chapel, modestly proportioned and less imposing than the village church, but nevertheless standing out with its white stucco walls and red tile roof from the brown adobe and greying thatch of the peasant dwellings scattered around it. Former haciendas, too, have their own chapels, generally grander than their community counterparts, reflecting their owners' mastery over the surrounding countryside. Each community or hacienda chapel houses its own patron saints, along with batteries of other Christian images. These chapels are visited by the priest—either from San Salvador or from Pisac—on only a few occasions a year, for the more important fiestas. Otherwise, the official Catholic presence in a community consists of one or two catechists, men who have undergone a few weeks' voluntary training in Cusco and whose function amounts to leading the rosary and litanies at chapel services and intoning the correct prayers over the body at funerals.

With one exception, patron saints of the vice-parish and of its constituent communities are nonmiraculous. Their cosmological significance is unelaborated: they are regarded for the most part as simply "ours" or "theirs." It is important that their cult be observed, of course, but largely for reasons of *costumbre* 'custom'. At best, they are thought to exert a kind of quiescent tutelage over the people, animals, and crops within their territories, which the performance of their annual fiestas guarantees.

The exception is the patron saint of the mountain community of Oqoruro, Señor el Justo Juez 'Lord the Just Judge'. This is a miraculous Christ shrine, a center of cult for people not just from the San Salvador locality but from neighboring localities as well. It is one of two miraculous shrines in the vice-parish: the other is Señor de Wank'a 'Lord of the Crag', housed in a sanctuary on the valley slopes two kilometers from the district capital, the focus of an important pilgrimage devotion. These two centers, one interlocal, the other regional, stage their fiestas separately but on exactly the same day, 14 September, the feast of the Exaltation of the Cross; Justo Juez attracts some 1,000 pilgrims, Wank'a about 20,000. The sanctuary of Señor de Wank'a, as noted, is run not by secular clergy but by Mercedarian friars, and for this reason it falls technically outside the ecclesiastical jurisdiction of the vice-parish. The shrine of Señor el Justo Juez, on the other hand, is both a pilgrimage center in its own right and the patron saint of a dependent chapelry of the vice-parish. The devotions attached to these two linked shrines will be analyzed in detail in chapter 9. But an appreciation at this stage of the dual status of the Oqoruro shrine is crucial to an understanding of local ritual, for the presence of a miraculous shrine in an anexo introduces subtle inflections into the fiestas and ceremonies of the local center.

The Christian saints are not the only spiritual presence in their patronal domains. The land over which they preside pertains ultimately to Pachamama, a general power that is alleged to have a pan-Andean distribution (Mariscotti de Görlitz 1978). *Pacha* (Qu.) means 'world' or 'earth'; *mama*, while it is the word in both Quechua and Spanish for mother, is perhaps better translated in this context as 'matrix'.[1] It is Pachamama's still power that makes the seeds germinate and the crops and pasture grow, thus giving life to people and animals. She is also associated with the domestic sphere, watching over the occupants of the dwellings carved out of her domain.

There is another side to this spiritual fertility and benevolence of the earth. The cultivated landscape, with its neatly patchworked terraces, fields, and farmsteads stretched along the valley floor and draped over the hillsides, is interrupted by topographical accidents, both natural and artificial. Crags, boulders, fissures, caves, clefts, gullies, ravines, the places that can never be claimed for the purposes of human subsistence or residence, are seen as scars of barrenness and sterility on the domesticated terrain. Similarly, places where untoward events have occurred—the site of a fatal accident, for example, or a house abandoned by its owner, who was haunted there by dreams of devils—these places are likely to become taboo, closed off from human activity and left for nature to reclaim. These pockets of wildness in the midst of the predial are manifestations of Pachatira (*tira* from Sp. *tierra* 'land'), the earth in its resistant, untamable, or dangerous aspect. There exists, so to speak, a negative image of the domesticated environment, consisting of uncultivable, uninhabitable, or abandoned places that lie in the interstices of human occupation and husbandry.

These generalized spirit-forces of nature are complemented by more specific tellurian powers, localized in the desolate summits and punas. First, there are the apus, the spirits of mountains, lakes, marshes, and other natural topographical features, in the vicinity and beyond. Apus are individuated, with distinct personalities: they can be cruel and capricious, but their power and protection are critical to the livelihood of the peasants. Some apus are recognized by diverse communities across an interlocal range, others across a regional range, while a few enjoy interregional renown. The apus are personifications of the primeval landscape, predating occupation by all other living beings. The apu of the tallest mountain in the region, Ausankati, is expressly likened to Dios, God, creator of all living things.[2]

Second, there are the *ñaupa machus* (Qu.) 'the ancients from long ago', also referred to as *gentiles* (Sp.) 'pagans' or 'heathens'. The machus were the people who lived in the age before the present one, when there was only the light of the moon to see by. They lived on the puna in round houses, *chullpas,* the pre-Inkaic stone tumuli which can still be seen on the high plateaux. The machus had been proud and arrogant, and Dios, the creator, decided to destroy them by raising the sun in the sky. The heat shriveled the bodies of the machus, and they fled to the shade of the jungle. Some never made it, and their dessicated corpses are the pre-Columbian mummies, *machu tullu* 'ancient bones', that are occasionally found in holes and caves in the area to this day.

The presence of the machus is still felt and has both malign and benign aspects. The wind that blows from the puna at dusk might carry the *soq'a machu* (*soq'a* 'dangerous, malevolent'), which can cause sickness and even death to those who inhale it. On the other hand, the soq'a machu also promotes the fertility of the crops, while the machus themselves are sometimes spoken of affectionately, using the familiar endearment *machula*.[3]

The primordial apus and the ancient machus are situated not only in space but also in time. The machus belong to the first age, the age of Dios and the moon. Their demise ushered in the present age of *runa* 'people', the age of Jesucristo, the saints, and the sun. This second age began with the appearance of the first human being, Inka Manko Qhapaq, and will end on the Day of Judgment, sometimes depicted as a great flood. This in turn will herald the third and final age, that of Espíritu Santo 'Holy Ghost'. This trinitarian model of time has a general spatio-religious correlate in the triad *ukhupacha* 'the underworld or the world within', *kaypacha* 'this world', and *hanaqpacha* 'the afterworld or the world above'.[4]

The three ages or worlds, while sequential in one representation, are coexistent in another. Thus, the past world of the machus persists alongside, or beneath, that of runa. Similarly, while the living toil in this world, the dead have already reached the next. There, they plow their fields and tend their flocks just as they did in life, with the difference that they never suffer hunger or want or pain. To ensure the smooth passage of the *alma* 'soul' to hanaqpacha, the correct funerary rites must be performed, with the appropriate prayers intoned over the corpse by a catechist. Equally important is the ritual laundering of the entire wardrobe of the deceased person eight days after death; if this is not done, the soul will return to complain. This is perhaps the clearest illustration of the way in which clothes are seen as constituting a person's identity in this world.[5]

The dead do, however, revisit their living kin and descendants annually, on the feasts of All Saints and All Souls, 1 and 2 November. In preparation for the visit, each household prepares a table of cooked food, drink, sweets, and cigarettes for the spirits of the dead, and a two-day fiesta is held in their honor. Many households keep the skull of the father or grandfather of the head of the household in the storehouse of the farmstead, having exhumed it some years after burial. For the fiesta of the dead it is decorated with a floral wreath and is invited to drink with the family, chicha being poured unceremoniously through its jaws.[6]

Not all almas reach hanaqpacha, however. If a person dies having committed a grave sin, such as incest, or meets with a violent death such that the body is left badly disfigured, he or she becomes a *condenado* (Sp.) or *kukuchi* (Qu.), a being that has been denied entry to hanaqpacha and is condemned to pass a twilight existence in kaypacha, the land of the living, trapping the unwary in lonely spots and feeding off their flesh. Condenados are greatly feared, particularly by the living relatives of a dead person suspected of being one, since they have a taste for the flesh of their own kin. Stories of encounters with condenados abound and are a never-ending source of fascination. Spatially, these beings are associated with the mountain peaks and punas, because these places are closest to the hanaqpacha, which they are ever striving to reach. The cannibalistic condenados, blocked in their attempts to attain hanaqpacha, can be seen as structurally equivalent to the machus, especially the machu tullu, the dried-out remains of the machus who were stopped short in their flight to ukhupacha. Both are liminal beings, trapped in the here and now but really belonging respectively to the future above and to the past within.

This, in broad outline, is the animated, temporal landscape of the peasants of San Salvador. I shall turn now to a detailed examination of the two parallel systems of cult that mediate relations with this spiritual environment, referring throughout to the ring calendar of the local ceremonial cycle, appendix 3, figure 2.

The Cult of the Nature Spirits

Among those who bring us justice are our apus, who are many: Apu Ausankati, Pachatusan, Ch'ayñakoto, Intiwatana, Willkar; Chillkapujio, Llallakallo, Qonchaqonchayoq, Liqichuyoq, Sultín, Ichupampa, Kondorpuñuna, Rondoqaqa, Pirway, Ñaqcha Orqo, Wiswachaya, Piñiyoq, Ichara, Waqramarka, Qoyotiyana, Machu Tukuyoq, Puka Tukuyoq, Sipaswarkuna, Wayna Sosiana, Apu Ñusta, Panapunku, Kuyokimka, Haqira, Qanchis Krus, Puka Saqrayoq, Chillwa, Kiwár, Wayllapata, Tayta K'asa, Chukullusq'a, Roqamoqo, Machu Sayaqaqa, Apu Ningro, Chullunkuniyoq, Suwanakana, Lluthu Wana, Hatun Tuana, Yanaqocha, Tillupampa, Chawaqallo, Hatunpata, Allpakancha, Suyt'urumipampa.

This inventory of nature spirits was recounted to me by Teodoro Qompi, an elderly resident of Qamawara. It was the longest and most comprehensive of several such lists collected. Map 9, appendix 1, shows locations that I was able to identify in the San Salvador area (see also plate 1).

There is a hierarchical dimension to this listing. The first five names were uttered deliberately, almost formulaically. First is Apu Ausankati, at 6,384 meters the highest mountain in the Cusco region, whose snow-capped peak lies out of sight of the community seventy kilometers to the southeast. Apu Ausankati was referred to as the *hatun apu*, the great or chief apu. Second is Pachatusan (4,842 meters), 'stanchion of the world', also known as Atás, tallest mountain in the vicinity of Cusco city, whose massive profile dominates Qamawara's southwestern prospect. Third is Ch'ayñakoto, 'crop of the linnet', the glacial mountain range north of Calca thirty-five kilometers to the northwest, whose summit rises to 5,727 meters. Next comes Intiwatana, 'anchor-point of the sun', the ruins of an extensive Inka settlement and solar observatory that lie atop a steep escarpment behind the village of Pisac, ten kilometers away. Then comes Willkar, the river Vilcanota, on whose cordilleras are situated all four of these mountains, as well as Qamawara itself, and which is fed by the glacial meltwaters of Ch'ayñakoto and Ausankati.

These five apus once again illustrate the use of a shrine pentad to establish the coordinates of a regional sacred landscape. Of the five, Ausankati is recognized throughout the Cusco region as the most powerful mountain spirit of all. The apus of the twin peaks of the Ch'ayñakoto chain, Sawasiray and Pitusiray, also enjoy wide renown. The sphere of influence of Apu Pachatusan is more restricted. For the mountain peasants of San Salvador it is regarded with a certain trepidation, partly because the mountain is reputed to contain much gold—it was mined intensively by both the Inkas and the Spanish—on account of which the apu is thought to be both extremely powerful and fiercely protective of its underground treasure (cf. Sallnow n.d.). For the people of Sonqo, a peasant community twelve kilometers to the northeast, the mere utterance of its name—here rendered as Pachatujsun—is inauspicious (Allen 1978, 82). Apu Intiwatana likewise has a narrower field of recognition; it is regarded by Qamawarans as a peaceable, irenic spirit, a reputation it enjoys elsewhere in the province (cf. J. Núñez del Prado 1970, 81), which is perhaps derived from its material associations with Tawantinsuyo and the pax Inkaica. The river Vilcanota, meanwhile, is both the geographical and the cosmological axis of the region; Urton (1981) has shown that it is equated with the Milky Way, the celestial axis of orientation in modern Quechua astronomy.

The remaining apus in Teodoro Qompi's inventory constitute a more informal list. Most of them are mountains in the environs of Qamawara, though not necessarily visible from the community. Some are lakes or marshes. Apu Ningro dwells in Lake T'iraqocha, which waters the lands of Qamawara; it is said to be male, though a female consort, Apu Ningra (negro, -a 'black'), was sometimes mentioned. As a rule mountain apus are male, but some are explicitly female—Sipaswarkuna, 'the young maidens', for example, four adjacent pinnacles on the mountain which is also the dwelling place of Apu Sosiana. While other Qamawaran informants agreed on the identities and ranking of the five regional apus, they would offer different listings for these local ones. People in other neighborhoods, meanwhile, furnish different regional sets as well.[7]

The word apu means, literally, "lord" or "chief." When describing these nature spirits, Qamawarans would habitually employ two apparently contradictory images. On the one hand the apus were said to be the primordial forebears of the people of the community, since they were the earliest inhabitants of the terrain. On the other they were likened to mistis, especially the mistis of San Salvador, for they held sway over the lives and destinies of the peasants much as did mestizo compadres and political authorities in the district capital.[8] All the local apus, ranked and unranked, but especially those living in the mountains that ring the community and in Lake T'iraqocha, are thought to be directly responsible for the welfare and fertility of both the human and the animal inhabitants of the community. They also guard the subterranean hordes of precious metals; those people tempted to search for gold in the placers of the mountains risk attack by the apus in the guise of demons (Qu. *supay*, Sp. *diablo*), who could drain them of their life-force and induce death within a few days.[9]

The cult of the nature spirits—of the apus and Pachamama—takes the form of ad hoc propitiatory offerings of varying gravity. The most casual is the *t'inkay* 'aspersion' of a few drops of liquid to the ground before partaking of any alcoholic drink, something that men and women do almost automatically. In ritual settings of any kind, more elaborate aspersions are made; the names of Pachamama and the surrounding apus are invoked and drops of liquor are sprinkled with thumb and forefinger toward the respective locales. A more formal offering still is the *despacho* 'despatch'. This is a bundle of maize kernels, coca leaves, llama or alpaca fat, and other ingredients, which is burned to the names of specific spirits on certain special occasions, such as laying the foundations for a house, curing the effects of the soq'a machu, and removing other spirit afflictions.[10]

The cult of the nature spirits also has a number of calendrical fixtures. A series of livestock rites—each of them preceded by a despacho—are staged during the course of the year, one of which used to involve animal sacrifice. And in the past, the nature spirits had received the sacrifice of human blood, occasionally of a human life, in the *tinkuy*, the ritual battle that used to be held annually in the puna. It is on these calendrical fixtures that I wish to focus. The animal rites and the tinkuy are closely linked, symbolically and substantially; indeed, as will be seen, they could almost be regarded as mutually transformative.

Livestock ceremonies are held on different days of the year for different species and their young (see appendix 3, figure 2). All are celebrated on a domestic basis. Adult llamas are fêted in August, generally on the first of the month; alpacas on 25 December, the Christianized summer solstice; sheep and young camelids in separate ceremonies during the pre-Lenten Carnival season; and lambs on 24 June, the feast of the patron saint of the species, San Juan, and the Christianized winter solstice. Only llamas and alpacas, of course, are native to the Andes, though in Qamawara they too have their Christian patrons: Santiago for llamas, Santa Bárbara for alpacas.

The calendrical distribution of these livestock rites varies from community to community across the central Andes.[11] A composite picture here tells us little; what is more revealing is their local ordering. In the mountain communities of San Salvador, the rites mark four distinct junctures in the annual cycle. Two are pinned to the solar calendar, to the two solstices respectively. The three others—and the tinkuy as well—mark two critical phases in the native perceptions of natural rhythms. The period around Carnival marks the climax of the growing season, during which the earth is thought gradually to give up all its energy to the maturing crops. In August, meanwhile, when the harvest has been completed, Pachamama is said to be "angry" and the earth "open" and "alive." At both these times, the nature spirits are particularly restless, seeking payment for the benefits they have bestowed. Together, the rites evince the dual calendrical logics of both the solar cycle and the agricultural cycle, by means of an alignment with appropriately timed Christian feasts and seasons whose liturgical symbolism is in this context largely incidental.

In addition, the timing of the ceremonies for young animals meets the practical constraints of reproduction. Sheep, llamas, and alpacas rut during the rainy season; sheep have a gestation period of five months, llamas and alpacas eleven months. Both rites therefore fall in those periods when there are likely to be sucklings in the respective herds.

It is worth mentioning at this point that most livestock are given personal names, drawn from specific types of lexicon. There is an implicit distinction here between domestic and domesticated species. The former include cats, dogs, chickens, and cavies. In varying degrees, each of these species shares a farmstead with its human owners, living inside or adjacent to the dwelling house; furthermore they eat human food, scavenging the scraps dropped by their human hosts. In both residence and diet, therefore, these species participate in human society: they bear a metonymical relation to people (Lévi-Strauss 1966, 205–9). Their personal names—if they are given any at all—are epithetical, and tend to be drawn from a series akin to human nicknames and diminutives: Chico 'little one', Flaco 'lanky one', Negra 'black one', Tarzán, and so on. The epitome of these domestic species is the dog, whose flesh is never consumed and which is regarded as so strongly attached to its human owner that it should be slaughtered at the death of the latter, to give assistance on the journey to the afterworld. Conversely, to call someone a dog is one of the strongest forms of invective in Quechua.

Llamas, alpacas, and sheep, on the other hand, are domesticated rather than domestic, field rather than farm. They are all grazing animals, living in herds apart from human beings and having their own enclosures in the pasture zone in which they are corralled for the night. They follow an existence parallel to that of human beings but separate from it: following Lévi-Strauss (1966), it might be said that they constitute metaphorical human societies. Their personal names accordingly take the form of proper human forenames or titles: Antonio, José, Gregorio, Cirila, Señor, and so forth. Not everyone bothers to name his sheep in this way, but llamas are without exception named. Cattle, asses, and pigs, for their part, while more closely associated with the farmstead, are still classified as field animals, and their personal names—when they are conferred—are of the same order as those of the other domesticated species.

The livestock ceremonies all follow a similar pattern, differing in certain minor details. I shall first describe the rite performed for adult llamas at the Qamawaran farmstead of Teodoro Qompi and Julia Qoyo, before indicating the main variations.

The ceremony began at about 4:00 in the afternoon. Present were the sponsoring couple, their four married children, their three daughters-in-law (their son-in-law was absent from the locality), a younger unmarried son, and Julia's sister's son and his wife, who lived near by. The sixteen llamas that constituted the Qompi patrimonial herd had been brought down from the puna and were crowded into the farmyard, already a trifle restive. Set out on the *misa,* a small piece of cloth spread out on the ground,[12] was a bottle of wine, some long steel needles, a bundle of spun red-and-pink alpaca wool cut into fifteen-centimeter lengths, several calabashes, a bunch of Michaelmas daisies, a container of red dye, a mug, a glass, and several bottles of rum. On the floor was a large pitcher of chicha, and another of *ch'uya,* a mixture of chicha and ground maize. The atmosphere was tense and expectant; Teodoro especially was extremely agitated, issuing orders in a nervous, high-pitched voice.

When everyone had received a dram of rum, the t'inkay of the animals began. First Teodoro and one of his daughters-in-law, having removed their hats, each took in the left hand a calabash of wine and in the right a bunch of daisies. Together they dipped the flowers in the wine and sprinkled the four corners of the misa. They then knelt side by side before the llamas and, again dipping the flowers in the wine, they sprinkled the liquid in the directions of the surrounding mountains, uttering the names of the apus as they did so. Each scooped up a handful of earth and kissed it. Finally they threw the remainder of the wine in the calabashes over the llamas, who backed away in alarm. They then hurried back to the misa.

Other couples repeated the procedure in turn, care being taken to ensure that none of the couples was a conjugal pair. The entire sequence was then repeated using chicha instead of wine. Teodoro was anxious that the couples should perform the t'inkay in rapid succession so that the animals should not be left unattended, and he nervously exhorted everyone to make haste with preparations at the misa.

The next stage of the ceremony was the feeding and decorating of the animals. Each llama in turn was captured and tethered with a lasso, its mouth wrenched open, and four bottles of mulled ch'uya poured down its throat. Then, with the head still held steady, red and pink tassels were threaded through each ear. At the same time, another person stained the animal's fleece on its back with a bunch of twigs dipped in the red dye, in the pattern shown in figure 6.1.

As each llama was released after being fed and adorned it staggered away coughing and spluttering, to everyone's great amusement. The more recalcitrant beasts bucked and kicked while being treated and afterward

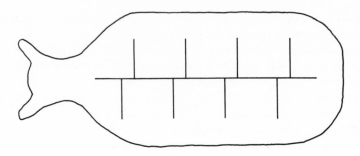

FIGURE 6.1   *Llama* t'inkay: *Pattern of Dye Marks on Animals.*

attacked and spat at the other llamas, but this merely added to the fun. It was said that they were drunk and spoiling for a fight, "just like men." When all the animals had been fed and decorated, everyone sat down in a circle around the misa and rum was served. There followed several hours of recreational *wayno* dancing to Qamawaran music I had earlier recorded on cassette.[13] When it grew too cold we moved indoors, and the party continued late into the night. Neighboring farmsteads were performing similar rites, but there was no reciprocal visiting among them. Next morning, each of the llamas was force-fed another two bottles of ch'uya before being released from the farmyard and driven up to the pastures.

Like this one, all the livestock ceremonies were staged for the patrimonial herds of extended families, with one or more guests in attendance. The rite for adult llamas, however, was the only one that customarily took place at the farmstead, most families staging the other ceremonies in their corrals in the lower puna. Though the structure of the t'inkay was the same in each instance, in the rites for adult beasts the couples performing it were nonconjugal, while in those for sucklings they were always spouses. Alpacas were not dyed, on the grounds that their fleece was too precious—most of it was sold, unlike llama fleece which was used for making homespun (*bayeta*) for the people themselves. Nor were camelid sucklings dyed, and instead of ear tassels each had a garland of tassels hung around its neck. At the lamb ceremony the lambs were garlanded with flowers, and they and the adult sheep had their faces rather than their fleeces daubed with dye. One other concession was made to the sucklings: while adult alpacas, like llamas, were obliged to consume ch'uya, young animals were not, because they were "children." Finally, at the ceremonies held during the rainy season—that is, those in December and during the Carnival period—a musical instrument called a *lawata* was sometimes played. This is a bamboo fipple flute with a deep, breathy tone, whose doleful, pentatonic melodies were heard only during this season; it was never played at other times.[14]

The ceremony for the young camelids, held during the Carnival period, has one other feature that deserves special mention. I attended this event at one of Teodoro Qompi's corrals in the puna. The atmosphere was even more tense and restrained than at the other livestock rites. When the aspersions had been completed, everyone sat down in a circle around the misa. León, Teodoro's eldest son, was served a glass of rum, and he stood up. All removed their hats and fell silent.

Clasping his hat to his chest in an oratorical pose, León then proceeded to recite a formal benediction to his parents. In it he thanked them for everything they had given him and his brothers—life, sustenance, shelter, clothing, money, land, animals, and finally wives. It was a set prayer, rendered word-perfect and lasting about three minutes, during which time all listened respectfully with their eyes lowered.

When he had finished, there was an immediate and palpable relaxing of the tension. Teodoro and Julia thanked their son fulsomely several times, after which León, by nature a quiet, reserved person, emitted a deafening yell that ripped through the night and echoed across the hills. It was obvious that he felt immensely relieved the ordeal was over. One of the guests present, a compadre from San Salvador, was an accomplished mandolinist, and one of León's brothers had brought his accordion; they both struck up with waynos. The thanksgiving prayer was later recited in a ragged fashion by two other sons, but with none of the drama that had attended León's oration.

The commonest explanation offered by the people for these rites is that they ensure the fertility of the adult beasts and the well-being of the young. The performances do indeed approximate annual rites of passage, "marriage" in the case of the mature animals and "baptism" in the case of the sucklings. Livestock rites elsewhere in the central Andes have been interpreted similarly (cf. Choqueccahua 1971, 183; Delgado Aragón 1971, 191; B. J. Isbell 1978, 161). In the instances under discussion, the statuses of human couples performing the ritual aspersion over the animals lend force to this interpretation. For the adult beasts, the couples are non-conjugal, symbolizing potential—and frequently incestuous—but as yet unrealized fertility. For the sucklings, married couples symbolize the fulfillment of this potential fertility in parenthood. The formal prayer of thanksgiving by sons to their parents during the ceremony for young camelids makes this theme of parental care explicit. Generational continuity, founded upon the procreation and nurturing of children by their parents, is thus conjoined with the natural reproduction of animals—specifically of camelids, the species of central symbolic as well as economic importance in Andean society.

In all the ceremonies, the anthropomorphism of the animals is explicit, both verbally and symbolically. They are fêted and honored like human guests, bestowed with colorful adornments, and obliged to drink to excess.[15] The adult llamas are actually brought down from their usual habitat, the wild domain of the puna, into the domain of civilization: they are invited into the farmstead for their fiesta, being temporarily incorporated into the domestic group along with their human hosts. I have already observed that the kind of personal names conferred on these field species indicates that they are each seen as constituting quasi societies, analogous to but separate from human society. In the ritual performance of the livestock ceremonies, each animal society is merged with its human counterpart, joining both human beings and animals in a single congregation and in a common destiny—a destiny that is ultimately controlled by the spirits of nature.

There is a further aspect of this anthropomorphism, one which in Qamawara is now veiled but which is fully represented elsewhere.[16] The llama rite, I was told, used to culminate in the sacrifice of one of the inebriated beasts to the apus and to Pachamama, though this now no longer takes place. People and animals, united by the ritual into a single congregation, would offer up one of their number to the spirits on whom their fecundity and welfare depended. By dissolving the boundary between the two categories, the ceremony masked the surrogate status of the sacrificial victim, a llama for a human being.

Livestock rites represent the private, domestic side of the nature-spirit cult. The tinkuy, by contrast, is a collectively organized event, though as I shall show it catches up both individual and group interests.

The tinkuy—literally, an encounter or meeting between two like persons or substances (Lira 1973)—originally took the form of a battle fought annually on the day of Comadres, the Thursday before Ash Wednesday and the beginning of Lent.[17] It thus heralds the celebration of Carnival, which in Qamawara and neighboring communities begins in earnest on the Sunday following Comadres.

The battle was fought in the puna to the northeast of San Salvador district at a place called Chuychallana, a bleak, windswept plateau some 4,400 meters above sea level (see appendix 1, map 9). The spot is close to the intersection of the boundaries between the three districts of San Salvador, Pisac, and Colquepata in the province of Paucartambo. The two armies were drawn from the communities and haciendas of the three districts and had included people from Qamawara, Oqoruro, Siusa, Umachurko, T'irakancha, Chawaytiri, Kuyo Grande, Sipaskancha, and Sonqo. Mistis from the district capitals themselves never participated. The exact composition, however, in representatives of communities and haciendas, of each of the two opposing coalitions varied from year to year: the pattern of alliances and oppositions would shift according to intercommunity rivalries and disputes, often over land. Further, all the accounts I collected stressed that, although members of the same community would always fight on the same side, the battle was not between communities as such but between individuals, pursuing private quarrels and settling outstanding debts.

The battle had in fact been the culmination of an extended series of community-based activities beginning several weeks earlier, which were still being practiced in the communities of Pisac district in the early 1960s. Each year in each community, according to this account, a dance called *wiphala* was organized.[18] A young married man would assume the cargo of *wiphala capitán,* also known as *p'asña capitán* (*wiphala* 'warlike', *p'asña* 'maiden', *capitán* 'captain'), and his wife that of *capitanaza,* and together they would recruit a number of dancers, *sargentos* 'sergeants'. The troupe consisted of both men and women, arranged in pairs. Most were young single persons, though occasionally married couples would join; the participation of a woman without her husband, however, was regarded as grounds for divorce (Casaverde Rojas, Sánchez Farfán, and Cevallos Valencia 1966, 83–84).

All sargentos, men and women, wore women's hats, the men's surmounted by two sprays of white chicken feathers and the women's with flowers hanging down to conceal their faces. Each dancer carried a crucifix. If during the dancing a male sargento dallied with one of the women, he was whipped harshly by the *wiphala capitán* and fined a bottle of rum (Casaverde Rojas, Sánchez Farfán, and Cevallos Valencia 1966, 86–88).

The group would convene for the first time on 1 January, when they accompanied the alcalde of the community to Pisac for his investiture by the district governor. Then every Sunday evening from the Sunday following the feast of San Sebastián (20 January) to Carnival Sunday, the sargentos would gather at the house of the *wiphala capitán* to dance. Music was provided by two lawatas and a tambour. As the party progressed there would be sexual joking and erotic mimicry, with the women repulsing the advances of the men by beating them with *candongas* 'carnival trick', whips decorated with colored wool, the men responding with expressions of mock ecstasy. On one occasion, when at last the women had sunk exhausted to the ground, one of those men who were still standing performed a mock t'inkay of two glasses of rum over their recumbent forms, saying, "Female alpacas, may you procreate much in the year to come" (Casaverde Rojas, Sánchez Farfán, and Cevallos Valencia 1966, 85, 93–94).

On the day of Comadres, the account continues, following a tour by the community authorities of the territorial boundaries of the settlement, the dancers, along with anyone else who wished to join in, ascended to Chuychallana for the battle (Casaverde Rojas, Sánchez Farfán, and Cevallos Valencia 1966, 95). Here my Qamawaran informants take up the story.

The people would form themselves into two camps on hillocks on opposite sides of the plain, where the women sang songs to stir the men to feats of daring and bravery. There were two encounters, the first beginning about midday and lasting for an hour or so, the second, more violent, starting in mid afternoon and continuing till dusk. The aims were to settle personal scores by injuring and possibly killing one's own enemies and in so doing to drive back the opposing army and eventually to capture their women. Weapons included slings, knives, machetes, and staves. The slingshot, a traditional Andean weapon, could be lethal if aimed at the head, but fatalities, when they occurred, were more often the result of felled or captured men being mutilated by their jubilant, intoxicated captors. Abducted women risked rape; sometimes they were taken home by their captors, whom they occasionally married.

The fighters from Qamawara customarily deployed a herd of llamas to assist them in battle. They would drive the llamas before them toward the enemy and in this way were shielded by the animals from the slingshot. The llamas would trample the enemy, and the Qamawarans would rush up behind and slaughter them all. According to the Pisac account, animals were also used as auguries. Before the battle, a herd of vicuñas would be pitted against a herd of deer. If the vicuñas drove back the deer, this presaged victory for Pisac; if the deer drove back the vicuñas, San Salvador would win (Casaverde Rojas, Sánchez Farfán, and Cevallos Valencia 1966, 96–97).

The Qamawaran dead from the battle were buried in a deep ditch near by at a place called Tallikuyoq 'the leaking vessel'. The spot is regarded with dread, for the mutilated corpses are said to be still moist and will remain so forever, perpetually oozing blood into the earth. The blood has stained the soil red—in reality, the result of deposits of hematite—and the stream that flows from the ditch is a *yawar mayu* 'river of blood'. Furthermore, some of the dead men's possessions can still be seen scattered around the grave sites—armaments that have been converted into rocks and items of clothing that have become *encantado* 'enchanted'.[19] And it is from this very spot that the red earth should be collected for concocting the dye with which to color the fleece of the livestock during the respective animal rites.

For over and above the private disputes pursued by means of the tinkuy, the event had a more general and more fundamental purpose: the offering of human blood to the apus in return for their fertility and tutelage. In the account from the communities of Pisac district, one apu in particular, Qespi Orqo, whose mountain redoubt overlooks the battlefield, is said to be especially demanding. "I am an old warrior," he says, "and I want to drink the blood of every man" (Casaverde Rojas, Sánchez Farfán, and Cevallos Valencia 1966, 96).

The tinkuy has also come to acquire other, adventitious, historical associations. It is said to commemorate an incident during the uprising of Tupac Amaru II in 1780, when a group of Indian partisans encamped at Chuychallana were supposed to have been routed and massacred by an army of mistis from San Salvador, supporters of the royalist cause. The Pisac account reports a further association with a battle supposed to have been fought in the area between partisans of Cáceres and Piérola during the civic turmoil of the late nineteenth century (Casaverde Rojas, Sánchez Farfán, and Cevallos Valencia 1966, 96).

Exactly when battle was joined at Chuychallana for the last time is difficult to determine. According to the account from Pisac it was during the 1940s, when the death of a participant from Sipaskancha was said to have provoked the intervention of the police. My older Qamawaran informants, however, claimed that the battle had ceased long before their time, though this might have been to distance themselves from what they portrayed as the era of barbarism and violence typified by the fighting. The two accounts are at one, however, in linking the abandonment of hostilities with the miraculous appearance of Señor el Justo Juez in Oqoruro. It was the miraculous Christ who brought peace to the warring communities, a peace that they—and he—have preserved ever since (cf. Casaverde Rojas, Sánchez Farfán, and Cevallos Valencia 1966, 97).

Nowadays, the event takes the form of a peaceful meeting referred to as a *parabién* 'felicitation'. Religious preparations center upon the shrine of Señor el Justo Juez. Participants from all three districts pay informal visits to the chapel on the morning of Comadres to light candles before the shrine. The alcalde and a catechist from Oqoruro greet visitors with formal embraces and invoke the taytacha to watch over them and keep them from harm.

Later, contingents of sargentos, each under the leadership of a wiphala capitán, gather at Chuychallana and greet one another with a ritual formula in which they wish one another well. They then dance for an hour or so on the site of the former battle, choosing partners from the opposite band. Afterward the contingents disperse to their communities, where each is feasted by the community alcalde on its return.

Despite the transformation of the battle into what purports to be an irenic ritual, the parabién still contains undercurrents of opposition and conflict. Before the meeting, the young men talk with bravado about how they would attack the enemy if only given the chance. "This year," they would boast, "we're going to get the youths from Sipaskancha. Why? Because they're *stupid*." Though there is no longer abduction of women, the cross-band pairing takes place in an atmosphere of latent hostility and prompts much aggressive sexual innuendo. Physical conflict has been suspended, but sexual competition and veiled antagonism remain.

Around two hundred people gathered at Chuychallana in 1974, about a quarter of them in sergeants' regalia. Most of the latter were from the district of Pisac, very few from the communities of San Salvador. Qamawara sent none, though some members of the community went in mufti; the reception at the alcalde's farmstead afterward was attended by about a dozen people. I was told that the affair had attracted more participants in the past, even since its conversion into a peaceful gathering, and that the declining attendance was because of the absence of so many young men in Lima; single youths were the traditional participants, the occasion being an opportunity to display their courage and masculine prowess. Now, however, enthusiasm for this once bloody and glorious event is slowly ebbing away.

How should the tinkuy be interpreted, in both its past and its present forms? The first thing to note is that its cultural representation sets up explicit associations between people and animals. Female sargento dancers were referred to as alpacas, and as such were appropriate objects of t'inkay, ritual aspersion, to induce their fertility. The Qamawarans deployed llamas as forward cavalry in the battle, while in the augury practised in Pisac the two sides were represented by vicuñas (*Lama vicugna*) and deer (Qu. *luychu; Hippocamelus bisulcus*) (Gilmore 1963, 383). In the Cusco region, these two native feral species are respectively held to be the "llamas" and "mules" of the apus (Cayón Armelia 1971, 157). If the livestock ceremonies betrayed a ritual anthropomorphism of the animals, the tinkuy strongly suggests the converse: the *animalism* of the human participants. Furthermore, while in the livestock rites the ruminants leave the domain of the wild and enter that of civilized, human society, for the tinkuy people move in the opposite direction, ascending from their communities to the wild, inhospitable punas.

The blood-stained soil from Talliquyoq that is used for making the dye for daubing the livestock establishes a deeper, material connection between the tinkuy and the animal rites. The beasts are consecrated with the still-fresh blood of human sacrificial victims long dead. In this crucial act, the nexus between people and animals can be seen being drawn yet tighter. The bloodied fleeces will eventually be sheared, spun, and woven into cloth, from which will be made skirts, shawls, knee breeches, and ponchos. The function of clothing in the creation of personal identity has already been noted. Cloth, whose substance passes from animals to human beings, becomes the vehicle for transferring the blood of sacrificed warriors to the bodies of their living descendants, which they then carry on their persons as a kind of voluntary stigmata. The consecration is thus extended from animals to human beings: all are marked, annointed, as potential blood offerings to the nature spirits. In the past, the llama rite was the occasion on which one of these blood-stained mortals was selected for deliberate ritual slaughter. The random sacrifice—of human beings—in the agonistic, intercommunity confrontation in the puna is transformed into controlled immolation—of llamas—by heads of families in the domestic setting of the farmstead.

The bodies of the fighters who have fallen in battle fuel this sacrificial cycle. They are suspended forever somewhere between life and death. The corpses were interred long ago, but their inner substance, their lifeblood, still magically seeps from them. Conversely, their outer tegument— the discarded clothing around the graves—is charmed and is regarded with fear. Having met their ends through violence and physical mutilation, their clothes abandoned unwashed after their deaths, these hapless cas-

ualties of the tinkuy are nothing less than a species of condenado—
enshrined condenados, whose eternal fate it is to make a kind of perpetual
blood offering to the nature spirits on behalf of the living.

This analysis makes it easier to appreciate the place of the tinkuy in
the cultural logic of sacrifice in the locality. To understand the opposi-
tional, conflictive character of the event requires locating it in a wider,
comparative setting.

Annual intergroup duels between men—and occasionally between
women—are commonplace throughout the central Andes, but there is
considerable variation.[20] The degree of ferocity varies from one instance
to another, but in many of them deaths are not unusual. Some, though
not all, are supposed to involve the capture and rape of women from the
opposing side. The span of participating groups varies from instance to
instance: they may be two moieties of a single village or town, or of an
ethnic group, or they may be coalitions of communities in a locality or
in a region. Hierarchy between the groups may or may not be created
or affected by the outcome of the encounter. Tinkuys also vary as to their
physical location, some encounters taking place squarely within human
settlements, others staged just as obviously far away from human habitation, in the high punas and cordilleras.

I would suggest that these variations can be comprehended by making a broad distinction between two types of tinkuy: internal and external.
Briefly, internal tinkuys express "within" relations, external tinkuys "between" relations. The distinction is, of course, relative, but it can be given
some substance by reference to the site of the confrontation. Internal
tinkuys generally take place in villages and towns, usually in the center,
in the plaza. They occur between groups standing in a fixed relation to
each other, a relation on which the outcome of the tinkuy in all probability
has a redundant effect. External tinkuys generally take place beyond the
domain of human settlement, in the wild. They occur between populations that stand in no such predetermined relation to each other; in a
sense, the tinkuy *is* their relationship.

Essentially, these practices manifest modalities of dual organization
(see appendix 6). I shall deal with each type of tinkuy in turn.

The former battle at Chuychallana is an example of an external
tinkuy. Perhaps the most celebrated instances of such tinkuys still fought
today are those of Chiaraje and Toqto in the province of Canas, department of Cusco (Alencastre and Dumézil 1963; Barrionuevo 1969,
183–87; Gilt Contreras 1955; Gorbak, Lischetti, and Muñoz 1962).
One of these has been located in the historical record for 1772 (Hopkins
1982). Each involves not just one but an annual series of battles between
the same bands: on 8 December (Immaculate Conception), Christmas,
1 January, 20 January (San Sebastián), 2 February (Purification), and
Thursday of Compadres, which falls one week before Thursday of Comadres. All these dates lie within the period of the maturation of the growing

crops, when the nature spirits are yielding their energy for the benefit of human beings.

The fights at Chiaraje are between communities in adjacent districts, while those at Toqto have a wider span, involving communities drawn from the neighboring provinces of Canas and Chumbivilcas. Both sets of encounters take place in desolate puna locations, far from human habitation and close to the boundaries of the districts or provinces concerned. Native exegesis and mythology in both instances correspond closely to what has been described for the tinkuy at Chuychallana. Deaths are eagerly sought, for they are deemed to be sacrifices to the local apus, who will in return make the land fertile and ensure a good harvest for the current year. If possible, so it is said, the enemy's women are abducted and sometimes wed. First-hand observation of one of the Chiaraje encounters in 1974 corroborated the accounts given me of military tactics and weaponry in the former Chuychallana conflict. On that occasion there were no fatalities, but they are by no means unusual.

External tinkuys, in sum, are agonistic confrontations, invariably ending in deaths that are construed as sacrifices to the nature spirits, staged on or near politico-territorial boundaries in the high mountains, between groupings conceived initially as equivalent, though victory—an incipient relation of superiority-inferiority—may be claimed through the idiom of bride capture. In an external tinkuy, though, there are no permanent winners or losers; in any event, the coalitions themselves may be in a constant state of flux. Dualism is just present here, but in a formative, unstable state: it has yet to be fixed in a directed relation between enduring moieties.

The literature has recently yielded an extreme example of such a conflict, a kind of super-tinkuy, reported by Harald Skar for the annual pilgrimage to Copisa, in the puna zone of the department of Apurímac (Skar 1985). Copisa does not have a Christian shrine, deriving its focal significance solely from the importance of a nearby mountain apu. The fiesta, held at Carnival, enjoys wide renown and attracts people from throughout the department. I shall briefly summarize Skar's account.

The different pilgrimage contingents from the various communities that attend place a premium en route to Copisa on internal egalitarianism and brotherhood; indeed, they comport themselves on the journey much as do pilgrim groups visiting Christian shrines in Cusco. At the ritual center itself, however, the mood changes dramatically. The entire gathering assumes the form of a violent mêlée, with men kicking and punching one another and lashing out viciously with studded whips. At one level the fighting seems to be indiscriminate, but an informant's account does suggest that the principal lines of cleavage were between communities, or between coalitions of communities (Skar 1985, 92, 95–96). The bloodletting appears to proceed unchecked, there being no visible hierarchy to maintain order as there is at the pilgrimage fiestas of Christian miraculous shrines.

In this instance, dualism has all but broken down—or rather, has not been generated. There is little evidence here of any transcendent bipartition: the pattern of conflict and coalition at any one moment is practically random. This, then, is a limiting case: something approaching total intergroup flux, embracing communities from throughout the region, centered on an apical mountain shrine, which, it is perhaps worth noting, is unashamedly pagan. As a modality of dualism it represents *non*dualism, the chaotic extreme.

Internal tinkuys signify the opposite pole, that of institutional, diametric dualism. This is the domain of human habitation, of social order, of political control, subordination, and reaction; and it is here that moieties, as constituent parts of communities, towns, regions, or ethnic groups, take on more or less fixed relational attributes in each case. Some of the more common ones can be summarized.[21]

The moieties as such are typically referred to as *hanan* 'upper' and *hurin* 'lower', though they may or may not correspond to the upper and lower halves of the village or territory in geographical terms. Where they do not, another, spatial dualism, founded upon ecological complementarity, is sometimes encountered. The hanan-hurin distinction can be further colored by reference to "foreigners," newcomers from without (upper moiety), versus "natives," the original inhabitants of the territory (lower moiety); or, more strongly, "conquerors" versus "conquered," respectively. All these distinctions signal potential or actual asymmetry and hierarchy.

There is frequently, however, a simultaneous parallelism and equivalence between the moieties, which though residentially interspersed may be conceived as spatially symmetrical, right-versus-left, and mutually self-contained. Thus each may control, at least ideally, territory in all ecological floors, and wherever a strict rule of marriage applies, it is always one of moiety endogamy. This equivalence may be further expressed in patterns of ritual complementarity. In this domain, then, dualism has become stable and institutional, the two components distinguished and differentiated to create a closed, bounded world in which relations of equivalence, symmetry, and reciprocity between the moieties coexist with difference, asymmetry, and potential hierarchy.

Where they occur, tinkuys between such groups—internal tinkuys—are as an echo of their external counterparts. They bring to the surface the essential mutability—the constructed, cultural quality—of the directed relation between the moieties, throwing up the possibility of dialectical inversion in their mutual standing. Their relationship is thus placed in temporary abeyance, and the endogamic boundary may be breached in the seizure and violation of women. But in the end, the internal tinkuy is no more than cultural play. The encounter ultimately has a redundant effect on the institutional relations between the moieties; on the contrary, it sustains them.

What I have traced here is a cultural portrayal of the passage from entropy to order (see appendix 6). As with so many Andean representations it is spatial, being variously mapped onto the vertical landscapes of different localities according to a consistent pattern. The high puna, the domain of the wild, associated with the unmarried state and with uncontrolled—that is animallike—sexual encounters, is the setting for confrontations between members of two loose, shifting, interlocal federations of communities, unstable in their internal composition and unranked in respect to each other, each successive confrontation—a pure "game" in Lévi-Strauss's sense[22]—setting up an ambiguous, temporary distinction between winners and losers which might yet be overturned in the next encounter. Here dualism is inchoate; in the extreme case of the wider, regional gathering at Copisa, it is indiscernible.

Descending to the intermontane valleys and quebradas, one enters the domain of civilization, associated with the married state, with domesticity and controlled reproduction. Here, the incipient dualism of the wild is tamed, localized, and rigidified into a fixed division between village moieties. Hierarchy between them, weakly or strongly elaborated and tempered with equivalence, is conceptually if not physically spatial in the respective statuses of high and low. Tinkuys in this domain express not so much the possibility of generating order out of chaos as the tendency countervailing in a system of vertical oppositions toward horizontal symmetry and inversion. Such encounters are Lévi-Straussian games only in a limited sense, for whatever their outcome, the relationship between the parties is preordained. Thus, dualism itself rests on a counterpoint, an existential duality, with nondualism (Hage and Harary 1983, 117).

This spatial counterpoint can be represented as one between the continuous and the discontinuous. The natural environment is unbounded, a variegated landscape whose multiple centers—mountains, lakes, crags—contour space but do not themselves enclose it. Human populations use these same centers to establish discontinuities, defining themselves by the sacred features of the landscape around them, different populations perhaps appeasing the same spirits of nature in order to guarantee their continued reproduction but in the act of such appeasement generating an incipient opposition between themselves. The unbounded field of the nature spirits is thus fragmented into a mosaic of numerous bounded communities and groups, each typically exhibiting the original, formative opposition now condensed into a rigid, diametric dualism that at once encloses, balances, and ranks its component parts.

This portrayal of the transition from disordered chaos to bisected cosmos is, however, incomplete. There is a further stage beyond that of dialectical dualism: the stage of pure concentrism (cf. Lévi-Strauss 1968). Once moieties are not merely distinguished but differentiated, the structure can transform into one of center and periphery, the moiety of higher rank constituting the dominant center, that of lower rank the dominated periphery. Power is now crystallized and focused, anchored to a point but diffusing outward in an unbounded field. It reproduces itself in new centers elsewhere, in a kind of cultural imaging of the multicentric natural environment. In a concentric system as opposed to a diametric one, hierarchy is no longer dual but linear, no longer attenuated by any countervailing equivalences but celebrated as an attribute of the cosmos itself.

Seen in this light, dialectical dualism—I have called it charged diametricality, to denote the differentiation between the moieties—appears as a mixed modality. It is a compromise between pure or neutral diametricality on the one hand and pure concentrism on the other, an attempt to reconcile symmetry with asymmetry, equality with hierarchy, fixity with change. As such, it is a system in tension, containing within itself the structural possibilities both of an enduring, perfectly balanced reciprocity and of the rise of hegemonic, centralized states.

This essential ambivalence of charged diametricality is recapitulated within the dual group itself, in the elemental dyad of the conjugal couple. The perception of the conjugal relationship in Andean culture epitomizes the dialectical ambiguity. As Platt has demonstrated, the word for couple, *yanantin*, "can designate a symmetrical pair of perfect equality; but it can also serve as an ideological mask to a relation which in fact is unequal, such as exists between a man and a woman" (1978, 1105). The concept thus merges into a single semantic field the idea of perfect mirror symmetry—right-left, male-male—and the idea of asymmetrical complementarity—high-low, male-female. Lira's definition of the word betrays both representations of conjugality: "*Yanantin:* Both lovers together, the lover (masculine) with his lover (feminine)" (1973, 442). It is here, in the cultural nucleus of the conjugal pair, that charged diametric dualism is imaged in miniature, and it is here that the potential fertility of nature is finally and completely realized.

From this, it can be seen that Andean dualism is more than a structural logic for organizing the cosmos, more than an ideology of group hierarchy and social control. It is both these things, but it could function as neither without a substantial, material foundation. Essentially, dualism is the cultural medium through which the fertility of nature is conveyed into the human realm.

I have presented a composite, generalized picture of this process. Various aspects of it are revealed, apparently piecemeal, in different localities. Thus, in San Salvador, two moments in the process are observed: the external tinkuy, as it was and as it is, between community coalitions in the high puna, and the livestock rites performed by families in their domestic enclaves.

The transformative link between these two phenomena is now consummate. I have already shown how the blood spilt in the tinkuy is transferred through the livestock rites to the bodies of the living, how the contingency of chance killings in the one gave way to the necessity of premeditated sacrifice in the other; how the warring, animalized human beings in the wild puna are replaced by unified congregations of families and their humanized herds in farmsteads and corrals. It is now possible to appreciate the way the emergent opposition between two equivalent populations in the tinkuy is inflected and condensed into the union of male and female in the livestock rites, with successive couples—symbolizing either potential or proven fecundity—invoking the blessings of the tellurian gods on themselves and their animals.

This symbolic nexus between the two expressions of the nature-spirit cult, the external tinkuy and the rites for the livestock, the former a translocal event and the latter purely domestic affairs, highlights the fact that in this particular instance the intermediate level, as it were, of the local territorial group has been completely elided. Neither Qamawara nor the other communities of San Salvador have internal tinkuys, nor indeed do they have any evident internal moiety divisions. As far as local collective identities are concerned, the dual model has in effect been displaced by another, a Christian model based on the cult of the saints.

In fact, the Christian cult has made itself felt in the translocal domain as well. The Chuychallana conflict, it was said, was suppressed as a direct result of the apparition of the miraculous Christ in Oqoruro, Señor el Justo Juez. Where the apus had presided over—indeed, had demanded—bloody confrontations between the communities, the miraculous taytacha brought peace and goodwill between them. He thus exerts his influence in precisely the same field of egalitarian, interlocal relations as do the apus, but he transforms those relations from hostility and unstable alliance into a permanent, universal accord. Yet the transformation is incomplete: bipartition and latent antagonism remain.

But if, in this locality, a miraculous Christian taytacha has only partly pacified the domain of the wild, the Christian cult has firmly secured the public domain of civilization. The power of natural fertility and the power of political control, in many cosmologies mutually reinforcing, are here disjoined, receiving quite separate and distinctive forms of religious elaboration. The power of the nature spirits is harnessed, as it must be, for the fertility, reproduction, and welfare of human beings, drawn down from the wild mountain peaks to the the heart of the domestic group. But it is the saints who signify community boundedness, solidarity, and hierarchy within the local setting. The Christian cult, not the pagan one, mediates intralocal political relations.

It is to this complementary local religious system that I shall now turn.

Community Festivals

Introverted exclusiveness characterizes these events. Qamawara customarily celebrates three: the major fiesta of the patron saint in February, a
minor fiesta of the Immaculate Conception in December, and Carnival
in March or April.

The Christian patron saint of the community is the Virgin of the
Purification, an advocation that commemorates her postnatal ritual
cleansing forty days after the birth of Christ. Her pale-skinned statuette,
about a meter high and clad in rich vestments, occupies the glass-fronted
niche behind the altar of the community chapel. She is referred to as
Mamacha 'Little Mother', though few appreciate her status in the Catholic pantheon as the mother of the adult Christ. Nor is she linked with
other Marian images or advocations, even other Candlemas Virgins; she
is exclusively the divine guardian of Qamawara, just as the identical
advocation less than ten kilometers away across the mountains is exclusively T'irakancha's.

The cosmological significance of Mamacha for the community and
its members is not consciously elaborated. Despite communitywide participation in her annual fiesta, it is an unstressed event in the ritual
calendar, observed simply as a matter of *costumbre* 'custom'. Whereas
the thaumaturgical powers of miraculous shrines are frequent topics of
discussion, the divine competence of the Mamacha could be elicited only
negatively, by asking what would happen should she withdraw her protection because of lack of attention on the part of her devotees. Then, I
was told, the whole community, but especially the negligent officials for
that year, would be liable to damage to their crops from hail, frost, or
drought. This points to a weak, implicit association between the patron
saint and the preservation of a climatic balance, particularly the regulation of rainfall. The moon, known as Killamamacha 'Mother Moon',
has similar associations, though more explicit. A partial lunar eclipse
caused consternation in the community; it was said that Killamamacha
was sick and bleeding, and women came out of their houses to wail and
to implore her to recover and send rain.

Organization of the patronal fiesta is divided between a number of
cargos. Though the titles are assumed by men, it is recognized that the
offices are in fact discharged by married couples; indeed, single men do
not as a rule take part in the cargo system.

The most important post is that of chief steward or sponsor (Sp.
prioste, Qu. *tiamisayoq*), which in 1974 involved an outlay of $25, in-
cluding a fee of $10 to the priest for saying mass. The sponsor is assisted
by the *mayor* 'major', whose cash expenses in 1974 ran to about $10.
A similar expense was incurred by the *altarero*, who is responsible for

decorating the chapel and patronal image for the fiesta. The prioste, mayor and a group of mayordomos provide the food and drink during the festival. For this, each cargo couple supplements its household resources with assistance both in kind and in labor from kin and friends. This assistance, rendered on the basis of ayni reciprocity with the expectation of return at some future fiesta, is in effect the foundation of the cargo system.

The provision of music during the fiesta is the responsibility of the *contratista* 'contractor'. In the past, music was always from a traditional Andean band of flutes and drums, but nowadays it has become customary also to hire a *disco,* a portable record player and megaphone with a stock of wayno records. The contratista in 1974 incurred an expense of $12 for the hire of this equipment, together with its owner–disc jockeys from Kuyo Grande in Pisac district, for the two-day recreational period of the fiesta.

Finally, there are two male ritual clowns, one dressed as a woman and the other—in 1974—as a Peruvian army private. They are known as Negro and Negra, though any connection with the apus of the same names who inhabit Lake T'iraqocha was denied. The pair engage in tireless burlesque throughout the fiesta, provoking much amusement among the onlookers.

The incumbents of these posts change annually. Those of prioste, altarero, mayor, and mayordomo are ranked in that order, and while there is generally no direct succession from junior to more senior posts by the same persons from year to year, the lesser offices are regarded as apprenticeships to the more prestigious ones. The traditional method of selecting officers is the San Roque dance during the fiesta itself, though prior persuasion is more often used instead. Ultimately, it is the alcalde's duty to ensure that all the posts are filled for the coming year, by whatever means. There is a certain ambivalence toward assumption of office, especially among those young men who pride themselves on their "modern" outlook. The office of contratista, however, which is to some extent outside the system of ranked cargos, is frequently assumed by urban migrants or army veterans, perhaps because it gives them an opportunity to invest in the prestige economy of the community and at the same time to demonstrate their criollo credentials by hiring a discotheque.

Despite this ambivalence toward holding cargos, there is general agreement that the fiesta should be celebrated, and there is no doubt that the prioste derives considerable prestige from the office. In the past, as noted earlier, the esteem earned from repeated participation in the fiesta system could be converted into political authority through accession to the office of alcalde. The devaluation of this office since the rise of the community councils has left largely intact the prestige attached to fiesta sponsorship in general. Ritual eminence, it seems, is the independent variable in a person's social standing, his political career—in the past—

a dependent variable. The respect accorded to the senior men of the community, the *kuraqs,* is derived in part from their records as fiesta sponsors, on which their occupancy of civil offices had rested.

The feast of the Purification falls on 2 February, but the precise date of its celebration in Qamawara depends on the availability of the priest. The hacendado of T'irakancha used to prevail upon him to say mass there on the feast-day itself, delaying the fiesta of Qamawara by a day or two. The four-day event is made up of the *víspera* 'eve'; the *día* 'the day' of the fiesta proper; the *tiyachikuy* meaning 'to make one another sit down', a reference to the mutual flattery between outgoing and incoming priostes; and finally the *kacharpariy* 'the day of farewell'. In 1974, the year in which I observed the event, most people in the community participated in one way or another, and one or two urban migrants timed their visits home so as to attend.

The activities on the eve of the fiesta concerned only the officers. They all gathered in the afternoon at the house of the prioste, whence they repaired to the chapel to make ready the statue of the Virgin. It was dressed in cream-colored robes and a golden crown, and its long hair was sprinkled with confetti. One of the community's two Christ-child dolls (*niños*) was placed in its left arm, and it was mounted on a litter decorated with masses of gladioluses. The group then returned to the sponsor's house for supper.

The next morning the priest from Pisac, accompanied by a lay sacristan from San Salvador, arrived in the community on horseback and joined the officeholders, ritual clowns, musicians, and the varayoq at the house of the prioste. The company then proceeded to the community chapel, where the congregation was already spilling out into the porch and churchyard. The officers took up positions immediately before the altar, the sponsor in the center, with the Virgin on her litter on their right, and mass was celebrated.

Immediately afterward the Virgin's litter, carried by the two clowns and two other men, was brought out into the yard and blessed the community by being made to execute three *venias.* These are ritual bows, each consisting of a movement first forward, then backward, the statue being tilted slightly forward at each extremity. It was then returned to the chapel. After a brief lunch at the prioste's farmstead, the priest and his assistant took their leave.

The rest of the day was spent in recreation, with the crowd merrily trekking from the farmstead of one officer to another in turn. Our first stop was the house of the mayor; then, after a brief visit to the house of the altarero, we moved successively to the farmsteads of two of the mayordomos, and finally to the house of the prioste.

With the exception of the visit to the altarero, at which no food was served, the procedure at each farmstead was the same. The alcalde with his deputy and regidor, the prioste, musicians, and clowns would enter the courtyard in procession, followed by the throng. Everyone in the community was entitled to join in, though in fact most of the sixty or seventy people moving from house to house were men and children, the womenfolk being occupied behind the scenes cooking.

On arrival, the deputy would take the alcalde's staff of office and would hang it, along with his own and the regidor's conch, directly above the small house cross of lashed twigs that always hangs on the outside wall of a main dwelling. The alcalde would then sit down behind a small table, flanked by the other members of the varayoq, the host, and the elders of the community. I too was obliged to sit with this group of notables; the president of the administrative council was prevailed upon to join them but was reluctant to do so, and indeed remained on the periphery of the festivities throughout. The musicians would then play a melody known as a *tiyana* (*tiyay* 'to sit down'), and the rest of the company distributed themselves around the courtyard, leaving the center free for dancing.

Meanwhile, the hired megaphone was mounted on the thatched roof, and the flutes and drums of the traditional band were soon drowned by amplified waynos blaring out across the hills. Food and drink were served, under the supervision of the male ayni assistants of the host. The meals consisted of meat-and-potato stew with no special accoutrements, accompanied by copious quantities of chicha and rum. First to be served were the alcalde and his officers, followed by the prioste, the host, me, the elders, the younger men and the women, and finally the children. All the while the two clowns performed, hardly pausing for breath or refreshment. Their antics and buffoonery set the tone for the gathering: jokes, pranks, and sexual innuendo were the order of the day. When everyone had eaten, the guests danced to the wayno music until it was time to move on to the next port of call.

The afternoon thus passed in convivial feasting and ever more energetic dancing until the prioste bade goodnight to his last guests at about nine o'clock. The festivities resumed later in the *estadio,* the assembly ground before the chapel, where a San Roque dance was held.

The original purpose of this dance was to select fiesta officers for the coming year. Participants came in disguise, and in the course of the dancing each of the incumbent officers, also disguised, would grab someone, who was then obliged to succeed him in office.[23] The dance is a feature of patronal fiestas elsewhere in the central Andes, and it is possible that in Qamawara it still serves occasionally as a selection procedure for fiesta cargos. In 1974, however, with the new prioste already chosen, it was little more than an opportunity for a nocturnal frolic. A dozen or so young men danced to the music of a flute and an accordion, wearing improvised masks and swathed in cloths and sheets. The party finally broke up around midnight. I shall return to the significance of this traditional selection procedure later.

PLATE 2 *The Purification of the Patronal Virgin of Qamawara. The statue
has been set up in the atrium of the community chapel; its gold crown has
been removed and confetti is being brushed from its hair. The community
president kneels before it.*

Next morning, the prioste's farmstead was once again the rendezvous
for the varayoq, the fiesta officers, musicians, and clowns, though on this
occasion the priest did not attend. At about ten o'clock the party moved
off to the chapel, where a large crowd was waiting to witness the Mamacha ceremony. This was really the ritual raison d'être of the entire
fiesta.

The statue of the Virgin was brought out, this time without its litter,
and was set down in front of the porch, where it was honored with
appropriate music from the trio of instrumentalists. Then, while the
discotheque played martial music, the president of the administrative
council stepped forward and knelt reverently before the statue. Two
community elders took the gold crown from its head, gently brushed the
confetti out of its hair, and gave it a silver crown instead. The Christ-
child doll was removed from its arm. Symbolically purified, it was then
restored by the president to its position behind the altar. With this act,
the religious liturgy of the fiesta was concluded (see plate 2).

Subsequent festivities followed the pattern of the preceding day, the party starting at the house of the third mayordomo and eventually moving to the prioste's farmstead. Here we were served a truly festive meal: roast cavy, potatoes, lisas, añu, carrots, cabbage, onion, goat cheese, and corn cakes, along with unlimited quantities of chicha and rum—all this at a time in the seasonal cycle when food was becoming scarce as supplies from the previous harvest were running down.

The dancing and carousing now rose to a climax. The skies darkened and the rain poured down, but no one cared. We all danced frenetically for hours on end, matching and overtaking in enthusiasm and abandon the two clowns, Negro and Negra. Men paired off with other men as well as with women; when this happened the dancers did not ask permission of the host, the prioste, as did mixed couples, and at the conclusion of each number they would thank each other with mock kisses and embraces. The burlesque seemed to have infected the entire male company at least. As the afternoon wore on there developed an effusive camaraderie, especially among the men, from which I was not exempt. I was continually being accosted, regaled with yet more alcohol, and informed that I was not any longer from "Inglatira," but from Qamawara. Taking my leave under such circumstances was a difficult and protracted process, negotiating my unsteady way home along the mountain trails even more so.

On the final day, the festive activities were restricted to the fiesta officers, clowns, musicians, and disc jockeys, who were all invited to the prioste's house in the morning for chicha. Most others in the community who were not still recovering from the excesses of the past two days, as I was, returned to their work in the fields.

The patronal fiesta is neither the most prestigious nor the most expensive religious cargo in Qamawara; the post linked to the fiesta of Señor el Justo Juez in Oqoruro is unrivaled on both counts. Indeed, the formal cargos for the patronal fiesta are spurned by some. This is not, I think, a recent phenomenon, for the tradition of the San Roque masquerade testifies to a customary reluctance to assume fiesta offices. This masquerade also reveals something about the ritual management of the contradiction between the ethos of community egalitarianism and the hierarchical nature of politico-religious organization. Hierarchy pervades the fiesta, where civil and ceremonial rank are ostentatiously displayed. But by committing the selection of fiesta officers to the random choice of anonymous maskers, it is kept free of any taint of favoritism, coercion, or self-promotion. Lack of discrimination means that the chosen persons are not revealed as candidates for office but as in the offices themselves. In this way, the dance of San Roque, the "impostor," helps to sustain the egalitarian ethos in the face of individual differentiation and rank.

Reluctance to assume politico-religious cargos is in fact characteristic of community-based prestige economies of this type (cf. W. Smith 1977).

Yet the stereotype of the unwilling cargo holder, impelled to take office and emerging with his self-esteem intact but financially ruined, represents only one aspect of traditional fiesta sponsorship. The other is the fact that, through the informal networks of festive ayni assistance generated by each cargo couple, a large number of other people are mobilized, so the organization and provisioning for the event is spread far more widely than the formal cargo allocation might suggest. Qamawara's patronal fiesta in this way touches on almost every household in the community.[24]

It is this enduring net of reciprocal obligations, as much as the cosmological connotations of the patron saint and the sustained commensality and bonhomie of the fiesta itself, which makes the occasion a potent expression of community exclusiveness and solidarity. This is not to rehearse the functionalist thesis that communal rituals mechanistically reinforce social solidarity; on the contrary, their self-conscious celebration may betray deep cleavages within a population. Such cleavages were all too evident in Qamawara during the early 1970s, but as will be seen they found religious expression not in respect of the patron saint and her fiesta, which remained above division, but of pilgrimages to external shrines.

Given the social significance of the fiesta, the parts played by the two community leaders, the alcalde and the president of the administrative council, deserve special attention.

The alcalde was in principle the overseer of the organization of the fiesta and was always accorded the seat of honor during its recreational phases. The president, however, remained on the periphery at these times, more, I think, from personal inclination than for any other reason. But for the symbolic cleansing of the Virgin—the very heart of the fiesta—it was the president who was at center stage. Here he assumed a dominant role, kneeling before the statue while the ritual adjustments were made and personally restoring it to its niche in the chapel. The participation of the incumbent of a newly introduced political office in this brief but crucial ritual is highly significant, for it indicates that the fiesta is an enduring, ineluctable institution that can rapidly assimilate the changing offices of secular community authority. As the legitimate head of the community the president was drawn inexorably into the patronal liturgy, the ritual expression par excellence of Qamawara's collective identity.

What of the ritual clowns? They too were participants in the manipulation of the icon, helping to carry it from the chapel for the blessing and purification rituals. Conversely, they established the atmosphere for the recreational phases of the fiesta, their burlesque style being eventually taken up by the (male) company at large. They comprised a male-male pair, with one member adopting a female role and the other—by appearing as a soldier—intensifying his masculinity. Their roles therefore epitomized the ambiguous male-male–male-female dyad, which, as noted earlier, is the final, most condensed expression of dialectical dualism. This image came to dominate the closing stages of the fiesta, as men paired off in the dancing and mimicked the behavior of a heterosexual couple.

The appearance of these clowns in the Candlemas fiesta in particular, both in Qamawara and elsewhere—in Qoñamuro, for example, twenty-five kilometers to the southeast in the district of Urcos (Marzal 1971, 160)—is perhaps to be explained calendrically, for the feast falls during the period when nature is at its most active and patterned dualism is being played out in many different situations. Whatever the reason, the familiar Andean motif of a differentiated and polarized unity emerges here in the midst of a Christian fiesta that celebrates a holistic unity, focused on a single, undifferentiated religious emblem and its associated hierarchical offices.

A few weeks following the patronal fiesta, Qamawara prepares for its other important community festival, the pre-Lenten Carnival. This fixture is known in Quechua as Hatun Pujllay 'the great game'.

Each community in the locality celebrates Carnival independently. The principal cargos are assumed by members of the varayoq; indeed, feasting the community at Carnival, and also on a smaller scale at Compadres and Comadres, is the main ceremonial duty of the alcalde. In addition there is the cargo of contratista, musical contractor, for the hire of a discotheque. In 1974 this office was shared by two brothers, one of whom was working in Lima and was absent from the fiesta itself, but whose generosity was fulsomely acknowledged in frequent announcements over the loudspeaker during the fiesta.

Carnival is an entirely secular, recreational affair. Youths and maidens, dressed in their finest clothes, court one another in dance and song. Older women assault men with candongas, lashing out at their legs as they dance, to which the men respond with expressions of mock ecstasy. As at all fiestas drunkenness is mandatory, but Carnival seems more prone to violence than the others, with the men determined to prove their masculine worth. There is no Christian symbolism—indeed, little public ritual of any kind. The only formal public ceremony takes place just before the festivities begin, when a young unmarried woman perfunctorily breaks the ground with a mattock to symbolize the start of first plowing after fallow, the barbecho.[25]

To convey something of the flavor of the event, I shall describe the celebrations in Qamawara in 1974 briefly. They began on Carnival Sunday, with a public reception at the alcalde's house consisting of the traditional Carnival fare of t'impu, a stew of mutton, potatoes, and white cabbage. The festivities were supposed to start the following day, but as it happened the discotheque from Cusco did not arrive until Tuesday.

Accordingly, on Tuesday morning about two hundred people gathered at the alcalde's farmstead, where the discotheque had been set up. A meal was provided for everyone. The party then moved successively to the farmsteads of the deputy alcalde and the regidor, where further meals were served. Finally, the megaphone was mounted on the roofed gate of the churchyard, and dancing continued in the stadium till dusk.

The participants on this first day of the fiesta were divided into two clearly defined groups. First there were the unmarried youths and girls of the community, dressed in their best ceremonial ponchos, skirts, and shawls, who after they had overcome their initial shyness danced continuously all day long, sometimes as separate couples, at other times performing colorful reels across the hillside. They consumed little alcohol and indeed rarely stopped for refreshment, but danced with a determined seriousness and sobriety which for all the prettiness of the performance hardly epitomized the spirit of Carnival.

The latter was more evident among the older members of the community congregated near the alcalde and the community elders, who as at the patronal fiesta were accorded places of honor at the gathering. Here, the chicha and rum flowed freely, women struck out at men with their whips, hapless revelers were smothered in flour or doused with water—both characteristic Carnival pranks—and two musicians playing tambour and lawata, the instrument proper to the season, competed valiantly with the blaring megaphone. The atmosphere among this section of the company degenerated steadily from gay abandon to inebriated hysteria, and sporadic arguments and fights punctuated the closing stages of the day's festivities.

The next day, Ash Wednesday, the dancing and revelry in the stadium continued in much the same fashion, although numbers had dropped to fewer than a hundred. The alcalde did not provide food, and each family brought its own. The pattern was repeated on Thursday and again on Friday, when money for the sound equipment ran out and the disc jockeys returned to Cusco.

The neighboring communities of Siusa and Oqoruro celebrated Carnival at the same time as Qamawara, but neither had a discotheque, relying instead on hired musicians. Some people in Qamawara noted this with pride, citing it as a mark of the community's modernity, but others disparaged their own festivities, considering the fiestas at Siusa and Oqoruro superior for adhering to custom. Indeed, the two instrumentalists in Qamawara at one point broke away from the main company along with other disenchanted men and women and established their own minifiesta some distance from the deafening megaphone.

Carnival, like the patronal fiestas, marks off each community in the area from its neighbors, although here religious symbolism is absent and the distinctiveness of a community is expressed in other ways—through the quality of the entertainment, the splendor of the young dancers, and so on. Despite its being financed by the former political leaders, in Qamawara it enjoys the support of all sections of the community. Young men are not only keen to see it survive, but also want to encourage its development in the direction of a mestizo Carnival, one that would befit Qamawara's status as a progressive modern community.[26]

General and specific factors are at work to give Carnival in the central Andes the character it has. On the one hand, it is an endemic phenomenon in Christian culture, for Carnival celebrations everywhere are typically subject to stylistic innovation and seem also to cast into relief cleavages of ethnicity, factionalism, and class (see, for example, Cohen 1980; Da Matta 1977; Gonzalez 1970; Manning 1977). Part of the reason for these shared features of Carnival in widely differing cultural settings lies in the original status of the event in the liturgical calendar. Although the etymology of the word *carnival* is obscure, a widely received explanation is that it is derived from the Latin *carne vale,* 'flesh farewell' (Rademacher 1910, 3:225–26). Pagan antecedents of the festival in the Old World were manifold, and by incorporating these into its cult the early Church sought to tame them by restricting the merrymaking to three days of tolerated license immediately before the solemn abstinence of Lent, which itself culminates in the climax of the Christian year, the three days of Easter. Carnival became the mirror image, the antithesis, of Easter, a time for throwing off the moral and liturgical constraints of the religious code and for creating in its stead a mélange of novel ritual and recreational forms—often direct inversions of normal usage—out of the cultural miscellany. For this reason, the running of a Carnival is always to some degree a matter of competition between groups or factions, and part of its very essence is that it rides close to chaos—sometimes, indeed, spilling over into riot (Le Roy Ladurie 1979).

On the other hand, Carnival in the central Andes has come to mark a turning point peculiar to the region: the transition from the rainy season to the dry. As such, it comes at the time when nature has once more exhausted itself in growth and maturation, when the fertility of the nature spirits has been given over to humankind. The libidinal character especially of Carnival, expressed in both courtship and the mock violence between the sexes, matches the tenor of ritual performances throughout this season. These performances, I have argued, may be seen at one level as establishing a conduit for directing the potential fertility of nature into the domain of human society. Located in its seasonal setting, Carnival marks the annual culmination of that cultural achievement. The Old World character of the festival, born of the seasonality of the northern hemisphere, has thus been in part appropriated in accordance with the local cultural logic.[27]

Additionally, the community banquets at the alcalde's expense during this period—not just at Carnival but also at Compadres and at Comadres following the parabién—echo the noblesse oblige of the Inka festival of Inka Raymi, held in March-April toward the end of the season of scarcity. At this time the Inka emperor offered sacrifices to the wak'as of the commoners of the realm, and regaled rich and poor alike with lavish feasts. There were also competitive games staged for the amusement of visiting chiefs and dignitaries. But what is seen to-day in the various activities of Compadres, Comadres, and Carnival in the San Salvador locality is not so much a survival of pre-Hispanic custom as a contemporary manifestation of those seasonal, local ritual observances that the Inkas appropriated and transformed into state ceremonial.

That imported feasts of the Christian temporal cycle have been sub-ject to a process of local selection and differential stress is further illus-trated by Easter, in orthodox Catholicism the climax of the entire year. In the San Salvador locality, Easter merits little interest, and there are no community fiestas or cargos of any importance associated with it. It is worth noting, though, that religious services are held at this time at the two miraculous shrines in the locality, those of Señor de Wank'a in the valley and Señor el Justo Juez in the mountains. The services at the Wank'a sanctuary, conducted by the resident Mercedarian priests, attract devotees of the shrine from throughout the region and give occasion for a minor pilgrimage. Those at the chapel of Señor el Justo Juez in Oqoruro are conducted by catechists; the congregation here has a more restricted span, but it too is composed of worshipers from a scattering of communities in the vicinity. Of interest here in these observances is the ritual parallelism between the two shrines, which becomes overt in the simultaneous cel-ebration of their titular fiestas in September. Also worthy of note is the fact that the services in Oqoruro are run on a joint, intercommunity basis by the adjacent communities of Qamawara and Oqoruro.

The fiestas of Candlemas and Carnival in Qamawara are closed and inward-looking, occasionally almost chauvinistic. From one point of view, they correspond to that intermediate level, the level of the local group, which, as noted earlier, is elided in the schematic progression from the translocal to the domestic that can be discerned in the cult of the nature spirits. In this perspective, the fiestas are interpolated into this generative process, complementing the phases of the translocal, revealed in the tinkuy, and the domestic, revealed in the livestock ceremonies, by establishing and sustaining the collective identity of the local territorial community. As it happens, both Carnival and Candlemas are in this sense appropri-ately timed, for they fall during the rainy season—Carnival in effect marking its close. The sexual oppositions and transformations that are a feature of both these fiestas likewise reflect the pervasive dualist logic of the pagan ritual process by which the fertility of nature is borne into the cultural domain.

From another point of view, however, these community festivals become part of a quite different system, one controlled by the church, in which the various local community identities are articulated into a closed pyramidal hierarchy of ecclesiastical and political authority.

Locality Festivals

Bounded centripetalism is the diagnostic feature of these performances. All involve the convergence of religious images from hinterland communities on the village of San Salvador, the seat of the vice-parish. Three are currently staged: the fiesta of the patron saint of the vice-parish; Christmas-Epiphany; and Holy Cross.

San Salvador del Mundo 'Christ the Savior of the World' is not strictly speaking a saint at all but God himself, but this theological nicety has little effect on his cult as compared to those of lesser Catholic supernaturals. Like most other village and community patrons he is a fiesta saint rather than a votive saint and is regarded as nonmiraculous. This sentiment was not lost on the local priest, who in an attempt to generate a deeper religious commitment among the villagers once proclaimed in a sermon that their patron *could* be miraculous if one were truly devoted to him.[28]

Although the patron of the vice-parish, Christ Savior is inevitably identified most closely with the village itself. The village cargos for its annual fiesta, moreover, tend to be monopolized by the wealthier stratum of the population. There is in fact a certain complementarity between Christ Savior, loosely associated with mestizoness, and another saint from the village church, San Isidro Labrador, who is clearly associated with Indianness. The two statues themselves present a remarkable contrast. That of Christ Savior displays the fair-skinned, Caucasian features which, however much at variance with historical likelihood, are the hallmarks of popular Christian iconography everywhere. The statue of San Isidro, meanwhile, not only has stereotypical Indian features but is also clad in a poncho and a community alcalde's hat.[29] As will be seen, this ethnic complementarity is also evident in the procession during the fiesta.

Christ Savior is fêted on 6 August, the feast of Christ's Transfiguration. The communities that traditionally participate are Qamawara, Siusa, Oqoruro, Umachurko, and the former hacienda of T'irakancha. All send their patron saints with the exception of Oqoruro, which instead of sending its miraculous taytacha dispatches the Virgen de Belén, a discrepancy I shall return to presently. The two other communities in the vice-parish, Pillawara and Qosqoayllu—both of them nucleated settlements situated, like San Salvador, in the river valley—traditionally abstain from the proceedings, putatively because Pillawara is too far away (it is in fact closer than T'irakancha) and because Qosqoayllu looks for its religious pastorship to the nearby sanctuary of Wank'a rather than to the village church. The participation of T'irakancha is further evidence of its comunidadlike status; none of the other former haciendas in the district take part.

In principle the fiesta is organized by the village confraternity of San Salvador del Mundo. In practice, the costs and duties devolve upon a small number of cargo holders. Sponsorship of the event in the village itself is shared between two married couples, the *alferados* 'standard-bearers'. Considerable prestige is attached to the office; in the words of one villager now in salaried employment in Cusco, having occupied it one had arrived. The cost was difficult to ascertain, but was probably not less than $250 a couple, the principal items of expenditure being food and drink. Meanwhile each participating community has its prioste, who is responsible for the transport of the community's icon to the village church and who is obliged to feast the community contingent on its return.

This was the practice that obtained until 1979. In that year, however, all but one of the communities that had traditionally participated failed to attend. The next year they were again absent, though under pressure from the priest some resumed attendance in 1981, but others—including Qamawara—continued to stay away. I observed the depleted fiesta in 1980, the only chance I had to witness the event.

The lone outside saint attending, the Virgin of Mount Carmel from Umachurko, was brought down to San Salvador on 5 August, the day of the *entrada* 'entry', accompanied by the community's fiesta prioste, its varayoq, and a band of musicians. In addition to Christ Savior, a number of other village saints were mobilized for the occasion: San Isidro from the church and the Virgin of the Assumption and San Antonio from the village chapel. The various images, mounted on their litters, were arranged in the chancel of the church as shown in figure 6.2.

The main event of the feast day itself was the benediction of the alferados. In the morning, the officers, their kin, and friends gathered at the house of one of the sponsoring couples and from there made their way to the church, accompanied by two brass bands and holding aloft the embroidered banners of the district. With the four alferados standing at the front of the congregation of two hundred, the priest celebrated a service of benediction in their honor. Immediately after the service they emerged from the church to be showered with confetti by well-wishers and to pose for official photographs. They then returned to their earlier venue for a celebratory toast, while the church services continued with the celebration of mass.

The alferados' group returned just as mass was ending, to join the procession of the Eucharist around the plaza. Leading the procession were the varayoq of the village of San Salvador itself accompanied by a band playing flutes and drums, all wearing thoroughly traditional Indian dress. Next came the alferados' party carrying the district banners, the two brass bands, and behind them a crowd of some three hundred people, mainly drawn from the village. Bringing up the rear was the priest carrying

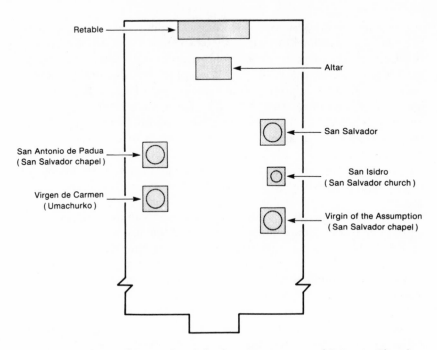

FIGURE 6.2   *Patronal Fiesta, San Salvador: Arrangement of Saints in Church.*

the Blessed Sacrament in a monstrance beneath an elaborate baldachin, with crossbearer and incense bearer in attendance. The procession moved at a slow, dignified pace counterclockwise round the plaza, stopping at three of the corners for prayers at temporary altars (*descansos* 'rests') on which the monstrance was placed and blessed with incense. The music of the three orchestras, loosely synchronized, was frequently drowned by the explosion of firecrackers and skyrockets. Several civil guards were on duty, detailed from the garrison in Pisac.

After the Eucharist had been returned to the church, the alferados' group again detached itself from the company and repaired to the house of the other sponsoring couple, where they were later joined by the priest and the civil guards. Lunch was served, followed by several rounds of bottled beer—the hallmark of a mestizo fiesta. Unlike the feasts during the patronal fiesta in Qamawara, in which most of the community took part, this was a select company consisting of the kin and friends of the alferados, together with village worthies. Though the fiesta had as its catchment the entire vice-parish—or perhaps it should be said, because of this—the boundaries of formal commensality were tightly drawn about the small village élite of alferados and their guests.

The grand parade of the saints was held the next day. Once again the alferados' group arrived in pomp in the plaza, led this time by the San Salvador varayoq with their band of flutes and drums, striving to be

PLATE 3   *The Festival of Christ Savior, San Salvador. This was the depleted procession of 1980. The order of saints is as follows: San Isidro Labrador (San Salvador); Virgen de Carmen (Umachurko); San Antonio de Padua (San Salvador); Virgin of the Assumption (San Salvador); and Christ Savior (San Salvador). The banners of the alferados are visible just in front of the litter of Christ Savior.*

heard over the alferados' brass bands. Whereas the day before the group had followed the perimeter of the plaza, this morning they marched ostentatiously through the center. Mass was celebrated, with a sermon in a mixture of Spanish and Quechua in which the congregation was urged to maintain its devotion to their patron and the alferados and others were thanked for their generosity to the church during the past year. The mass ended, the saints' litters were made ready. Eventually, the procession emerged into the sunlight.

First came the San Salvador varayoq with its musicians, followed by a brass band. Behind them was San Isidro from the village church, carried by four boys from the village. Then followed the Virgen de Carmen from Umachurko, escorted by the community prioste, varayoq, and musicians. Next came San Antonio and the Virgin of the Assumption from the village chapel. The priest, acolytes, and alferados followed, while behind them, resplendent in a white robe and with his right hand raised in blessing, came Christ Savior. The second brass band brought up the rear. Prayer chants led by the priest were taken up by the three hundred or so participants, who milled about the litters as they moved slowly round the plaza. At each corner altar the procession halted, and Christ Savior was brought before it to be blessed with incense. Even in its depleted form, the divine pageant made quite a spectacle amid the brown adobe and peeling stucco of the drowsy little village (see plate 3).

After one circuit of the plaza, Christ Savior was placed in front of the church facing the congregation, with the other saints lined up on either side. There followed a second sermon by the priest, this time amplified over a public-address system. Further benefactions to the parochial weal were acknowledged, unkept promises of donations castigated, and new commitments invited for the coming year. The loudest applause came when the priest announced the names of the new alferados, who stepped forward to be embraced by the village worthies and to receive the district banners from the outgoing officers.

The ritual closed with the saints' blessings. First, the litter of Christ Savior was made to execute a series of venias to the village, straight ahead, to the left, and to the right. Many people knelt and crossed themselves as this was done. Each of the other saints, in the reverse of their processional order, repeated this procedure after first making three venias to Christ Savior. Once having completed their blessings, the visiting saints were escorted home to their respective chapels, while San Isidro and Christ Savior were returned to the church. The alferados' party, meanwhile, had regrouped and departed with its brass bands for the home of the first alferado, there to enjoy a final celebratory meal.

The Christ Savior fiesta is a stereotypical ritual of the center. Its performance annually reconstructs a pyramidal hierarchy of local saints, which symbolizes a centripetal unity among the various territorial and status groups in the locality, an organic unity in which each group has its proper place. Thus, in the saints' parade, the Indian saint from the village itself takes the lead; the patrons of dependent communities follow; then come other saints from the village; and finally Christ Savior, the emblem of the village élite, brings up the rear. The festival serves to ordain the vice-parish as a microcosm of the universal Church, the communion of saints writ small. Since vice-parish and district here coincide, ecclesiastical and political hierarchy and dependence go hand in hand.

Clearly, however, the ritual was disintegrating. In 1980, for the second year running, four communities and their saints—Qamawara, Siusa, Oqoruro, and T'irakancha—were all absent from the fiesta. The priest had persuaded the four communities to hold substitute fiestas in each community in the days following the San Salvador festival, and a complement of officers was duly selected for each; but the events generated little enthusiasm. By 1984, however, Qamawara at least had rescheduled its own patronal festival of the Purification of the Virgin to 11 or 12 August, so that it could serve as the substitute fiesta. But the community has determinedly resisted the priest's attempts to reinstate attendance at the village fiesta.

What are the reasons for this withdrawal? The lieutenant governor of Qamawara, an army veteran who had been active in the 1960s in the movement to gain official registration of the community, was quite explicit. "We don't need to respect the district any more," he said, "we have our *own* fiesta now." He was well aware that participation spelled subordination and that withdrawal was a political statement; he despised those communities whose saints still attended, accusing them of being servile. But he added that another reason for not going was that the saints' statues could easily be dropped and damaged on the journey to and from the village, and they would be very expensive to replace.

The attitude of the villagers, meanwhile, was mostly one of resignation. They too recognized the political connotations: the action was seen as a secessionist gesture, of a piece with the growing independence of the hinterland communities from municipal control as a result of the social and economic reforms of the previous decade. But there was little that could be done to enforce attendance by the peasants of the anexos.

The liturgy of the fiesta of Christ Savior is shared by patronal festivals in other villages in the valley. In neighboring Pisac, for example, a similar festival is held on the Sunday following the feast of the de facto patron saint, the Virgin of the Assumption, on 15 August. In 1980, this festival had lost only one of the eight hinterland community saints that had been attending thirty years earlier (Paredes 1952).

Farther downstream, the provincial capital of Calca, also under the de facto patronage of the Virgin of the Assumption, celebrates her fiesta on 15 August with an accompanying fair of pottery and agricultural products, which attracts visitors from outside the parish as well. Here, however, the ritual has decayed. During the early 1940s, five of the surrounding communities used to send their saintly delegates to the celebration (Navarro del Aguila 1944, 57); according to one resident of Calca, in those days a total of eighteen images had been included in the procession. Nowadays only a few saints attend, all from the town itself, though they must still submit to the traditional *juguetes* 'jests'—tall wooden frames covered in fireworks in which processing images are trapped and released and which are then noisily exploded.

The Calca fiesta had declined, said my informant, because in 1970 the municipal authorities had tarmacked the plaza, and the market vendors, unable to drive poles into the ground, had stayed away. As noted earlier, the Calca fair competes with another, much larger one on exactly the same day only thirty kilometers away at the pilgrimage sanctuary of Tiobamba—where, incidentally, no tarmac inhibits commerce. The decline in saintly attendance, however, probably has as much to do with the weakening of local ties of political dependence between Calca and its satellites because of the effects of commercial agriculture in the area as with the declining importance of the fair in the regional economy.

The model for all these saints' parades is the Corpus Christi fiesta in Cusco city. I have already traced the early history of this event in the sixteenth and seventeenth centuries and have shown how it shrank from a diocesan pageant to a local urban festivity. Today, only three saints from outside the city attend, all from within a ten-kilometer radius: Santa

Bárbara from Poroy to the northwest and the eponymous patrons of San Jerónimo and San Sebastián to the southeast, the latter pair traditionally engaging in a race to see which will arrive first in Cusco. The remainder are all from the city churches, including La Linda, the Marian patroness of the archdiocese, from the cathedral.

Altogether, thirteen images take part. They enter the cathedral on the eve of Corpus and the next day circuit the Plaza de Armas to the accompaniment of fireworks, rockets, and pealing bells, the Eucharist following behind. Each image gives three venias to each of the three altars on the plaza, traditionally erected by various trade groups in the city. They then return to the cathedral, where they remain until the octave of the feast. During this time they are said to indulge in profane behavior, drinking, gambling, and quarreling among themselves (Morote Best 1953, 100). They return to their parishes one at a time, in a sequence of eight-day periods beginning with the octave, each being honored on its homecoming with yet another fiesta, complete with procession and juguetes. The months of June, July, and August are thus punctuated with noisy festivities that break out periodically in different parts of the city.

The most revered image in Cusco's religious pantheon, Señor de los Temblores, does not take part in the Corpus festivities. As a miraculous shrine its cult is kept quite separate from the urban locality festival of Corpus: its ritual status demands that the one be screened off, liturgically, from the other.

A similar logic dictates the absence of Señor de Wank'a and Señor el Justo Juez from the patronal festival of San Salvador. The reason these saints do not attend is not so much political, as with the boycott by the hinterland community saints, as cultural. Both Wank'a and Justo Juez are miraculous shrines, founded on the basis of apparitions, established within the precincts of the vice-parish. Señor de Wank'a does not serve as the patron saint of any community and can thus be simply disjoined from locality festivals. Señor el Justo Juez, however, does. Its ritual status is double. It is a miraculous image with a wide devotional catchment which confounds the nested hierarchy of local saints' cults that the fiesta of Christ Savior sustains. Yet the image is at the same time the religious patron of an anexo, owing ritual allegiance to the seat of the vice-parish. The dual nature of the shrine poses a cultural problem: how to establish within the local domain a dependent articulation with a ritual center that has a translocal cult.

The solution to this problem is in effect a splitting of iconic identity. Oqoruro maintains its representation at the patronal fiesta of the vice-parish by its former patron, the Virgen de Belén, to which no such ambiguities attach. Its principal shrine, the miraculous taytacha, stays away. The participation of both Christs, Justo Juez and Christ Savior, would create a tension, indeed a contradiction, for the miraculous status of the former would subvert the local hegemony of the latter. The cultural

PLATE 4 *Girls with the Niño Icon of Qamawara. This is one of two Christ-child images which the community sends to San Salvador for the Christmastide festival, being escorted in accordance with custom by virgin girls.*

compromise is in fact a triumph of localism: the pyramidal hierarchy of saints is maintained intact, and the local supremacy of the patron of the vice-parish passes unchallenged.

The second of the San Salvador locality festivals is the Christmas cycle. This begins on Christmas Eve and terminates on the feast of the Epiphany, 6 January. The first of January, the feast of the Circumcision, is the day on which the new political authorities of the subordinate communities assume office, the varayoqs changing annually and the elected committees biennially. The latter, as already noted, derive their legitimacy, in principle at least, from outside the district. But the community alcaldes gain theirs from the New Year succession ceremony, encapsulated within the Christmas cycle. The iconography of the rituals, moreover, vividly depicts the paternalistic relationship between the incoming leaders and the district authorities who vest them with office.

The icons used in the Christmastide ceremonies are figurines of the Christ child known as *niños* 'children' (see plate 4). The figurines are

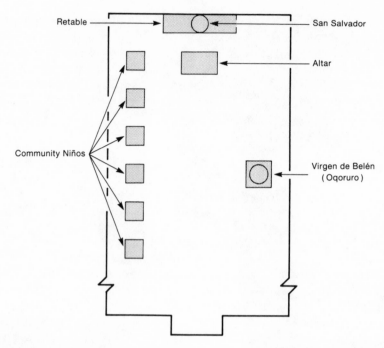

FIGURE 6.3   *Christmastide, San Salvador: Arrangement of Images in Church.*

dolls of urban manufacture, approximately life-size and dressed in fine clothes. Each is kept on the altar of the church or chapel to which it pertains, enclosed in a portable glazed case. Of the communities that traditionally participate in the Christmastide ceremonies, Siusa, Umachurko, Qosqoayllu, and T'irakancha, each has one niño, while Qamawara has two. The community of Oqoruro participates, but instead of a niño it deploys once again the Virgen de Belén, with Mary clad in maroon robes and holding the infant Jesus. This visiting image, as will be seen, is set apart from the rest. Apart from T'irakancha, which functions in many respects as a nonmanorial community, none of the other former haciendas takes part.

The Christmas liturgy conforms to the same pattern of centripetal movements as the patronal fiesta. On 24 December, the communities' niños and Oqoruro's Virgin are taken to the church in San Salvador, escorted by the respective community varayoqs. At the church the niños, mounted on litters, are lined up along the left side of the chancel. The Oqoruro Virgin, meanwhile, is placed on the right side, opposite and facing the niños, as shown in figure 6.3. They remain here for twelve days, until the Epiphany.

Meanwhile, on 1 January, the investiture ceremony for the new village and community varayoqs takes place in the village, the incoming officers receiving their insignia from the hands of the district governor.

The Epiphany begins with mass in the village church. This is followed by the veneration of the infant Jesus, the congregation filing forward to kiss another niño, from the church itself. The new community alcaldes then kneel before the priest for a blessing.

Finally, there is the procession. In the lead are the varayoqs and musicians from the village and the participating communities. Next comes the priest, then the Oqoruro Virgin, the two Qamawaran niños, and the remaining Christ children, the litters decorated with flowers and grasses that all but envelop the actual images. Afterward the Oqoruro Virgin is stationed at the entrance of the church facing the company, and each niño is made to execute three venias before it in a gesture of respect. The Virgin and niños then depart with their delegations for their home communities.

The Christmastide festival is a somewhat low-key event, with only about a hundred people present for the Epiphany procession during the early 1970s. Its primary significance seems to be not religious or recreational, but political, for it encases the investiture of the new varayoqs within a ritual sequence of uniquely apposite symbolism. The investiture, like any succession ceremony, involves a break in continuity, introducing an element of uncertainty into the established political order. The interruption is here bridged ritually, for while delegated authority is being transferred, the *niños* of the communities are cloistered in the village church—symbolic hostages whose theological meaning becomes transformed into an eloquent expression of the childlike subservience the incoming alcaldes traditionally owe to their paternalistic superiors.

Within the overall construction of village hegemony, however, Oqoruro is denoted as special. The community is represented, not by a niño, but—as at the patronal fiesta of the vice-parish—by the Virgin of Bethlehem. In the arrangement of the images in the church and in the choreography of the procession the Virgin is marked out as superior to the other visiting icons, receiving treatment similar to that accorded at the August fiesta to the vice-parochial patron himself. This all fits, of course, with the intrinsic status of the Marian image, for it is a complete representation of the nativity—the mother-and-child pair—as against the deficient ones—the niños alone—supplied by the other participating groups, and as such it commands special deference. But this does not explain why the Marian image, in preference to a niño, should have been mobilized by Oqoruro in the first place.

Again, it is the anomalous status of Oqoruro as a ritual site—simultaneously a dependent annex and a miraculous shrine—which is here producing visible perturbations into the ceremonial of the local center.

And yet, despite these perturbations, the Virgin's very presence at the fiesta can only serve to validate Oqoruro's subordinate status. The ceremonial inflections it generates merely signal Oqoruro's distinctiveness from its sister communities—if indeed they do even that, for they are masked by the theological rationale of the nativity symbolism. The net result is that Oqoruro's extraordinary standing as the site of a miraculous shrine is ritually domesticated, recast as a matter simply of symbolically necessary internal differentiation and hierarchy between the dependent communities. Once more, localism scores a ritual triumph. The primacy of the vice-parochial center passes unsullied—or rather, is preordained.

The third of the locality festivals of San Salvador is Santa Cruz, Holy Cross, on 3 May.[30] There seems little doubt that the figure of the cross—though not the Latin cross—was indigenous to the pre-Columbian Andes (cf. Palomino 1968). Urton (1980) argues that it was related to the interpretation of star clusters and that it embodied the concept of *chaka*, an axis along which a state of equilibrium is established and maintained. Today, crosses are regarded as demonifuges: small house crosses protect the occupants from harm, while community crosses protect the crops from the meteorological wraths of snow and hail.

Unfortunately I was unable to observe the fiesta and cannot speak with confidence on the details. As elsewhere in the central Andes (cf. Urbano 1974, 45; B. J. Isbell 1978, 45ff), Santa Cruz is a celebration of first fruits. The large wooden crosses from the community chapels are festooned with early harvest produce and escorted by ritual dancers to the village church, where they are blessed and carried in procession. The principal dance styles employed are wayri ch'uncho and qhapaq qolla.

Since 1980, however, this fiesta, too, has been decaying, like the patronal festival a casualty of the growing reluctance on the part of hinterland communities to submit any longer to the symbolic hegemony of the district capital. Qamawara's community cross no longer descends to San Salvador; instead, a separate celebration is staged in the community itself. Of the three locality festivals held annually in the early 1970s, then, two are gradually being eroded, a development symptomatic of the more confident mood among community peasants inspired by the social and economic reforms of the Velasco "revolution." Only Christmastide—the most overtly "political" of these three local rituals of the center—has survived intact.

Estate Festivals

There is one further class of ritual performances in the locality that remains to be examined: the patron saint fiestas of the former latifundia. To illustrate the different modalities of these fiestas, I shall focus on two lay estates in the district: the upland hacienda of T'irakancha and the valley-based holding of Wallwa. Both estates have now been expropriated. I shall deal first with the situation in the early 1970s, before documenting the consequences of agrarian reform.

T'irakancha, it will be recalled, was a "republican" hacienda, a peasant community that passed into private hands during the nineteenth century. In common with other such estates it continued to function in many respects like a nonmanorial peasant community, not only in its internal political organization but also in its articulation with the municipality. Its patron saint, the Virgin of the Purification, bore witness to this status, being fêted on her day in much the same manner as Qamawara's patronal Virgin and traditionally joining the festival of Christ Savior along with the other community patron saints of the locality.

Wallwa, on the other hand, was a "colonial" hacienda and as such stood in a fundamentally different relation to the municipality from that of T'irakancha. Its patronal cult, too, differed significantly from T'irakancha's and demands more detailed exposition.

The religious patron of Wallwa is the Virgin of the Rosary, whose statue resides in the capacious chapel adjoining the manor house on the hillside overlooking the Vilcanota valley. What makes the statue distinctive is that it is regarded locally as a miraculous image, though less so than the two miraculous Christs in the locality. The feast of the advocation falls on 7 October, the fiesta being held sometime during that month.

Before agrarian reform, the Wallwa fiesta was an event of some note in the local calendar, attracting ritual delegations from throughout the area. To use a native index of popularity, in the early 1940s a total of eight different dance styles were represented among the groups attending (Navarro del Aguila 1944, 63). In 1973, there were six; following the expropriation of the estate the fiesta declined rapidly, shrinking in size and importance until by the end of the decade it had forfeited all of its wider appeal.

When I attended the fiesta in 1973, the hacienda was in the throes of reform, with the expropriation order already before the land tribunal. It was owned by an elderly widow who lived in Cusco and was managed by a man from San Salvador. The buildings, which had been badly neglected through the years, were steadily crumbling. Nevertheless the proprietor and her manager made a brave effort to recapture the spirit of bygone days. They invited members of their families from Cusco and Lima to witness the celebrations and engaged the priest from Pisac to say masses during the three days of the fiesta. The priest and guests, who traveled out each day from Cusco, were entertained at lunch on the terrace of the manor house, and I was invited to join them. As we were dining, waited upon by one of the old family retainers, a group of dancers came in from the courtyard to entertain us. The seigniorial trappings amid the general dilapidation only heightened the feeling that these were the last rites of the old régime.

Meanwhile, the courtyard was the scene of dancing, drinking, and revelry. Three cargo holders from San Salvador fielded dance troupes that exhibited a variety of different styles: k'achampa, saqra, ukuku, and ch'uncho extranjero. These groups were composed mainly of young men from the village of San Salvador or its immediate environs, and their function was chiefly that of providing entertainment for their two hundred or so fellow villagers who had come along to watch. The three offices, each entailing outlays of several hundred dollars, were not restricted to hacienda workers but instead had become opportunities for display of status by young men from the village.

In addition to these principal dance groups, there had also in the past been sponsored dancers from each of the surrounding communities traditionally obliged to render corvée to the estate. The fiesta, said the peasants, was their mink'a "payment" for this work, though in fact it entailed an expenditure on the part of the individual community sponsors. Each of these community dance troupes, accompanied by its band of musicians, would escort a religious image from the community to the hacienda—not the patron saint of the community but a miniature icon known as a *lámina*, a painted image of the Virgin about forty centimeters in height set in a wooden frame. Similar miniature icons, also known as láminas, are used in connection with pilgrimages to many miraculous shrines, as will be seen later, in chapter 7. Indeed, the liturgy of the Wallwa fiesta was clearly redolent of that of sponsored pilgrimage to such shrines. The láminas would be kept on the altar of the hacienda chapel beneath the statue for the duration of the fiesta, each lámina being escorted during its entry and exit by the troupe of ritual dancers. The year 1972 had seen a turnout of lámina-bearing dance groups from most of the communities concerned, but in 1973 there were only two: *k'ara ch'unchos,* from T'irakancha, and *negrillos,* from Qosqoayllu. The absence of contingents from the other communities was attributed to dereliction on the part of the sponsors but was accepted with general equanimity.

The fiesta culminated on the final day in a brief procession of the Virgin. The white-robed statue, mounted on a litter covered in white draperies and escorted by the priest and dancers, was carried through the courtyard and along the path to the point where the village of San Salvador first comes into view. After it had been restored to the chapel, the láminas were removed from the altar and taken back to their home communities.

Why should the patronal cult of Wallwa hacienda have assumed the character of a pilgrimage to a miraculous shrine, while that of another estate in the same area was all but identical to the patronal devotion of a nonmanorial community?[31] There is evidently a correlation between this ritual contrast and the respective positions of the two former haciendas in the political economy of the locality. Unlike T'irakancha, whose inhabitants have always been administratively subordinate to the municipality, Wallwa was to some extent impervious to municipal jurisdiction. Indeed, in its levying of corvée from surrounding communities— including T'irakancha—it could be seen as tending toward the exercise of jurisdiction in its own right. The significance of this correlation becomes the more telling, however, if the different historical circumstances of the genesis and development of colonial and republican haciendas are recalled.

The colonial hacienda had its origins in the flourishing mining economy of sixteenth- and early seventeenth-century Peru, when the traditional structures of agrarian production preserved under the régimes of encomienda and corregimiento were no longer able to meet the commercial demands for agropastoral products. The institutionalization and legitimation of the new estates within a rural social order dominated by doctrinas and state-controlled corregimientos was achieved largely through religious means. The very recognition of a hacienda as a center of population turned on whether or not it possessed a place of worship (Mörner 1975, 354). A survey of religious centers in the diocese of Cusco in the late eighteenth century includes the chapels and oratories of the principal haciendas (Oricaín [1790] 1906), and several of the hacienda patron saints mentioned in this account were said to be miraculous. The establishment of de facto religious jurisdiction by an estate often met with fierce resistence from local clergy in the doctrinas (Mörner 1978, 56– 57). Once entrenched in the local politico-religious structure, however, the colonial hacendado was able to exert control over neighboring Indian communities, obliging them to render mita to the estate in the same fashion as to other bodies and enterprises. In time, the hacienda chapels became nuclei of new communities of *yanas* 'personal retainers'. Some haciendas even attained the status of vice-parishes, occasionally boasting more people than the rest of the parish (Bueno [1768] 1951, 49).

To return to the ethnography. In principle, the Wallwa chapelry was subordinate to the vice-parish of San Salvador, though as noted its patronal Virgin did not attend the festival of Christ Savior. But the manorial cult leaned away from the microcosmic exclusiveness of the vice-parish toward a flexible, more inclusive devotional form. The mobilization of láminas proper to a miraculous shrine meant that participation in the event, unlike participation in the festival of San Salvador, was not tied to parochial affiliation but instead constituted a field autonomous from the prevailing ecclesiastical structure. The ritual contrast neatly captures the opposition between the emergent colonial hacienda, poised to expand its dominion over the surrounding countryside, and the established, bounded doctrina in whose jurisdiction it lay and to whose authority it posed an implicit threat. It might be hypothesized, then, that certain colonial haciendas developed—or adopted—for their patronal cults a liturgical idiom which was uniquely appropriate to the strategy of political and economic aggrandizement that they pursued within the constraints of rural colonial society. In its use of community corvées—the modern mitas—alongside a core of resident and nonresident labor tenants—the latter-day yanas—the mode of production comprehended by the Wallwa estate had changed structurally but little since colonial times, and its legitimating cult had likewise persisted in its distinctive form.

This hypothesis—based, it must be admitted, on very limited evidence—can be extended from the structural-functional to the ideological plane. The establishment of the first colonial haciendas and of their patronal shrines was contemporaneous with the emergence of the first Christian miraculous pilgrimage shrines of the region, whose liturgy some of the manorial cults seem to have shared. The founding of these miraculous shrines closely paralleled that of colonial haciendas. Both emerged contingently, as it were, and both were initially extraneous to the prevailing ecclesiastical and socioeconomic structures of doctrinas and corregimientos. Common to both was an ideology of contract—between devotees and their chosen shrine in the one instance, and between yanas and their hacendado in the other—as distinct from the fixed ascriptions and obligations of community and parish.

In neither instance, however, did the contractual ideology reign supreme. It was tempered by notions of duty, bonds of commitment—what Turner (1974a, 182) has called "structural obligatoriness." Pilgrimages to extralocal shrines, Turner argues, tend to flourish in those societies that stand midway between Maine's "status" and "contract": they represent "an amplified symbol of the dilemma of choice versus obligation in the midst of a social order where status prevails" (1974a, 177). Underlying Christian pilgrimage and crystallizing this essential ambiguity is the notion of the vow, freely made but morally compelling.

The emergent hacienda system evinced this same ideological ambiguity. It set up novel contractual relations that were yet cast in the idiom of fealty to one's lord. Much of the debate over whether the Andean estate is or ever was feudal misses this crucial ambiguity—contradiction, if you will—inherent in its production relations from the outset. It is from this that the hacienda system derived its flexibility and longevity. For while under certain conditions, particularly those of economic depression, it may appear feudal, under others it may display distinctively capitalist traits—indeed, landlords attempting to dispossess their labor tenants might use an antifeudal ideology precisely to support their efforts (cf Martinez-Alier 1974, 144).

The use of the liturgy of pilgrimage and miraculousness in the patronal cults of colonial haciendas can thus be seen to be of a piece with the quasi-feudal, quasi-capitalist ideology with which they insinuated themselves into rural colonial society. In the Andes, as in medieval Europe, offerings to a miraculous shrine were regarded as tribute, by which vassals gained the saint's protection. Equally, however, they could be construed by devotees in purely commercial terms, as payment in return for favors and indulgences; indeed, it was the latter construction that prevailed in Europe by the late Middle Ages (Sumption 1975, 159, 292). The use of the liturgy of pilgrimage in the new manorial devotions thus not only marked them off from the cults of community and parish; it also provided a religious rationale that matched directly the essentially ambivalent character of the colonial estate, at once a seemingly feudal hierarchy of individuals and groups subordinate to a patrón and a capitalist enterprise based on contract labor.

Republican haciendas, for their part, date from the late nineteenth and early twentieth centuries, when in response to the regional economic resurgence based on the international demand for tin and wool, communities throughout the central Andes were annexed and transformed in their entirety into privately owned estates—a process aided by the Bolivarian decrees that partitioned the lands of Indian communities among their members. The new hacienda communities were frequently retained intact, their internal organization and external politico-religious linkages continuing much as before.

T'irakancha belongs to this class of republican haciendas. Despite its transformation into an estate, it has continued to operate in many respects as a community administratively and ecclesiastically dependent on the village of San Salvador. The configuration of its patronal cult, then, betrays T'irakancha's origins as a peasant community that was absorbed en bloc during the nineteenth century into the burgeoning commercial sector of the regional economy, while remaining structurally intact. Wallwa hacienda, on the other hand, has a patronal cult that bears the marks of its genesis and development as a novel colonial institution forced to vie with the local centers of political and ecclesiastical power. The two contrasting estates and their associated patronal festivals typify the successive processes of hacienda formation and their ritual correlates in the central Andes.

Agrarian reform amalgamated the expropriated lands of T'irakancha with those of other upland haciendas to form an extensive cooperative. Its patronal cult, for the time being at least, continues unchanged. Wallwa hacienda, however, was split up. With the demise of the estate, its patronal festival declined, becoming little more than a recreational event for the villagers of San Salvador. By the late 1970s, none of the communities that had traditionally participated was sending a ritual delegation to the shrine. The subjection of those communities to the estate having ended, the religious expression of that subordination ceased also. The ritual relations between Wallwa and its satellites, lacking as they did any formal ecclesiastical foundation, were even more vulnerable than those of the vice-parish to the vagaries of politico-economic change. As the cult of the miraculous hacienda Virgin could expand in line with the expansion of the field of production relations of the estate, so also did it contract as those relations were attenuated or ruptured. Once the latifundial power of Wallwa had been dissolved, its ritual concomitants fell away.

Two icons define the local microcosm. One is the landscape itself, an unbounded field enshrined in the spirits of the earth, mountains, and lakes. These tellurian gods alone are the sources of life and fertility, but left to themselves, their power is diffuse and uncontrolled. The other is the manufactured effigy of Christ Savior, the patron saint of the vice-parish. In the person of this image, the locality is focused and enshrined as a bounded domain and as an enduring hierarchy of individuals and groups.

The transformation from one icon to the other is accomplished by means of not one but two semiotic systems, partially overlaping, one pagan, the other Christian. The pagan system channels the fertility and power of the nature spirits into the human realm, and in doing so progressively dualizes, balances, and ranks the populations and groups to whom their fertility and power accrue. The end point of this process of division and subdivision is the conjugal couple. But in San Salvador, the intermediate level of the dualized local group is suppressed, pretermitted. It is at this level that the tangential, Christian system of social identities begins to operate. Groups now define themselves and their internal hierarchies through their collective Christian festivities, at successive levels: first, that of the local territorial group, in the introverted celebrations of community exclusiveness; then at the more inclusive level of the locality, in the centripetal totalization of the communities' religious emblems.

The local cosmos, then, is hybrid. In one sense, there is a continuity between the two systems. The Christian system is the final realization of the Andean quest for pure concentrism, or very nearly so. The ambiguities of dialectical dualism, often the consort of centripetal constructions of social space in Andean culture, have been all but eliminated in favor of a rigid pyramidal hierarchy of saints' cults, recapitulated within each dependent community in the ranked statuses of religious and civil personnel.

In another sense, the two systems are incommensurable. Between them there is some interference, but no coherence.[32] Both systems program ritual processes of differentiation and hierarchy. But whereas in the one these processes necessarily operate through cultural ideas of fertility and reproduction, in the other they operate for the most part independent of such understandings. According to Turner (1967, 28), dominant symbols derive their social efficacy by conjoining a normative or ideological pole with an affective or sensory one. In this technical sense, the pagan system is dominantly symbolic. Its concerns are as much physiological as political: through it, the processes of natural and social reproduction are fused. In the Christian system, on the other hand, such links as have been established are weak and unelaborated. At the same time, orthodox, theological meanings are scarcely evoked. For the actors, the Christian system at the local level is largely devoid of symbolism; it is a system of emblems, arbitrarily signaling division and union, equality and rank, but lacking intrinsic motivation (cf Sperber 1975, 23ff.). In Tambiah's terms (1979, 160 and passim), its meanings are indexical rather than symbolic.

The Christian cult, however, is by no means wholly comprehended by this ritual construction—and dismantling—of local hierarchy. Miraculous shrines in the neighborhood cannot easily be accommodated within the concentric structure of local saints and cults: they are potential sources of disequilibrium and dissonance. A miraculous shrine is a Christian image that has begun to forge a direct link with the landscape, in which vernacular meanings are infused into imported religious forms. Here, in the extralocal domain, Christian and pagan cosmologies converge.

CHAPTER 7

Pilgrimage

At dusk one Friday in June 1973, a little procession wove its way along the paths through Qamawara to the chapel in the center of the community. They had come from the farmstead of Juana Waraqa and Julio Qompi, and Julio was among them, cradling a small painted icon. Accompanying him, besides me, were the ten men who were to occupy the offices of dancers and musicians on the pilgrimage to the shrine of Señor de Qoyllur Rit'i, which was to leave the following day.

The chapel was locked and the sacristan who kept the key could not be found. We contented ourselves with a brief vigil in the porch. The atmosphere was solemn and subdued.

We returned through the moonlit, monochromatic landscape to Julio's house, where his wife, parents, brothers and sisters-in-law had gathered. They came out into the yard to greet us quietly, kneeling one by one before the icon to kiss it. Then it was locked away in the storehouse and we all trooped into the main dwelling.

Now a more festive atmosphere took over. The rum began to flow, a meal was served, and there was excited chatter about arrangements for the pilgrimage. We were to travel on foot to the village of Wankarani, whence we would take an overnight truck by way of Ocongate to the hamlet of Mawallani. Here, I was assured gleefully, the dawn cold would be intense. There would then be a three-hour climb to Sinakara, the site of the shrine. There was disagreement concerning the return journey, some saying we should aim to arrive back Tuesday, others Wednesday. But was there enough food and drink for five days? In any event, how many people were planning to come?

While these discussions were going on, Julio hovered nervously by the door. He was the patrón or sponsor of the pilgrimage for that year. I knew him well, for I lived near by at the farm of his parents, Teodoro Qompi and Julia Qoyo, who were respected senior residents of the community. Julio was in his mid twenties with a young family—the typical age and stage for assuming the sponsorship of this event, the most prestigious of the five pilgrimages in the Qamawaran calendar. Much was at stake for him during the next few days. If everything went according to plan and there was plenty of food and drink, people would credit him with the success of the pilgrimage and his personal stock would rise. But if there was a serious hitch or if supplies ran short, people would grumble and his reputation would plummet. Julio was by nature reticent in company, but tonight it was obvious that he was tense and anxious.

The dominant figure at the party, meanwhile, was one Manuel Mamani, a tall dignified man of Julio's age, whom the sponsor had nominated pilgrimage master—*maestro* (Sp.) or *arariwa* (Qu.). Manuel was treated with deference, always being served first with food and drink; people even sought his permission to step outside to relieve themselves. He disdained involvement in arguments about arrangements for the pilgrimage, for ultimately his decision on all such matters was final. He clearly enjoyed his position and had a confident, relaxed air. He even presumed to poke fun at his host, remarking that the door of the house was hanging on only one hinge. Julio, standing by the door, shrank into the shadows.

Manuel announced that everyone present must donate a candle to burn before the icon, or *lámina*. He went round collecting them, smiling silently through the lame protestations that some people raised, and presented them to Julio, who took them to the storehouse. It was decided that we should leave at nine o'clock the next morning, so at midnight I took my leave. At three in the morning I could still hear the music from the party drifting across the hills.

In fact, it was well past midday before we set out. We spent the morning at Julio's farmstead, nursing mild hangovers, chewing coca, drinking and chatting, and making unhurried preparations for the journey. By mid morning, when an impressive meal of roast cavy and rice was served, about thirty people had gathered in the yard. Most of the men wore their best ponchos, not the brown or grey ones they used every day but their ceremonial ones in Qamawara's distinctive style of crimson, scarlet, maroon, pink, grey, and black stripes. The women wore their best *llijllas* 'shawls'. Some of the younger men, especially the returned urban migrants and army veterans, sported their best store-bought shirts and trousers. The quartet of musicians—two *pitos* 'transverse flutes', a tambour, and a bass drum—serenaded us through the morning with a liquid, pentatonic melody, the dance of the wayri ch'unchos, which was to fill the air throughout the pilgrimage.[1]

Stacked in a corner of the yard were heaps of tubers and firewood. As we made ready to depart, Manuel began distributing them among the pilgrims for transport. Some complained loudly about their allocations, but Manuel was impervious. He took his fair share, and I was given mine. Only the musicians and a mother carrying her baby were exempt.

When everyone was loaded the icon was brought out, now shrouded in a blue towel that Julio had borrowed from me for the occasion. First Julio's father, then his father-in-law, knelt before the master, who passed the icon over their heads from front to back. They and the others who were staying behind, including Julio's wife, then kissed the icon. The formalities completed, we left the yard and threaded our way along the paths through the community.

I felt intensely exhilarated. Since coming to live in Qamawara three months earlier, I had heard much about this pilgrimage and the miraculous shrine that was its goal. Apart from this I knew nothing about Señor de Qoyllur Rit'i, not even its precise location.[2] At last I was setting out for the fabled place, my welfare entrusted to the people into whose lives I had so rudely trespassed. From now on I was entirely at their disposal, and the thought of such dependence engendered a sense of oneness, of communion with them. The straggle of individuals stretching ahead of me on the path became in my eyes a wandering fellowship, a solidary band united in the face of the uncertainties that lay ahead. Was this feeling merely the self-indulgent sentiment of an anthropologist finally counting himself "one of the people"? Perhaps; but then Manuel, the master, who was walking just in front of me, turned and interrupted my musings. "Now," he said emphatically, "we're all brothers."

The Nación

Señor de Qoyllur Rit'i was one of several shrines visited annually by contingents from Qamawara. The community's pilgrimage calendar ran as follows (for locations, see appendix 1, maps 6 and 8):

Novena of Corpus Christi	Señor de Qoyllur Rit'i
6 August	Señor de Aqcha
16 August	Señor de Kisikancha
31 August	Señor de Wat'a
14 September	Señor de Justo Juez, Oqoruro
15 October	Señor de Saqaka

All these pilgrimages fell in the dry season, when work was light, food abundant, and travel easy. Qoyllur Rit'i was the only regional shrine in the listing, and its pilgrimage was the largest and most important. The visit to Señor el Justo Juez in the adjacent community of Oqoruro did not constitute for Qamawarans a pilgrimage proper, because they were closely involved in the central organization of the fiesta. The pilgrimage to Señor de Saqaka, meanwhile, was falling into desuetude, as successive sponsors defaulted on their commitment—to no great concern in the community at large.

The ostensible purpose of a pilgrimage was to escort a lámina—there was a separate one for each—from the community to the shrine sanctuary, where it would repose for a night before being returned to the community. The Qoyllur Rit'i lámina was a picture of a crucifix in front of Mount Ausankati and flanked by ch'uncho dancers, enclosed in a wooden frame surmounted by a gablet (plate 5). *Lámina* means 'print' or 'engraving.' Some pilgrimage contingents, notably those from the larger villages and district capitals rather than hinterland communities, had more elaborate portable icons, consisting of statuettes in glass-fronted wooden cases. These were referred to as *demandas,* the Spanish word for an image carried about by hermits or devotees who ask charity.

The Qamawaran Qoyllur Rit'i lámina was normally kept, like the others, on the altar of the community chapel. But for some months preceding the pilgrimage Julio had kept the icon at his farmstead, as patrones were entitled to do. It had thus passed temporarily from the public to the private domain, having been partially appropriated by a particular household. Now they were obliged to recharge it and restore it to the collectivity.

Of all the pilgrimage sponsorships, that for Qoyllur Rit'i was the most coveted and the costliest. Julio was obliged to satisfy the temporal needs of the entire party for the duration of the pilgrimage, providing potatoes, maize, meat, noodles, rice, coca, coffee, sugar, and rum. He also had to slaughter a sheep to feast the pilgrims on their return and to brew quantities of chicha. In addition, he had to hire the musicians and pay their transport costs, as well as those of the dancers; he had to purchase fireworks and other ritual paraphernalia. His cash outlay alone was in the region of $70–90.

There was no formal selection mechanism for pilgrimage offices. Julio had been nominated by the previous incumbent and had already decided to nominate his older brother León for the following year. In fact, so prestigious was the office that it was filled for three years ahead. Julio had chosen the ritual dancers from among his kin, friends, and acquaintances. Manuel Mamani had been selected as troupe leader because he was such an experienced dancer, well versed in the wayri ch'uncho choreography and also in the various rituals and formalities of this particular pilgrimage. As capitán, or second in command, Julio had chosen his first cousin Fernando Champi; these two were fast friends, frequently working together in the fields. Julio's other dancers were his younger

PLATE 5 *Pilgrimage: The Lámina. The portable icon of the Qoyllur Rit'i pilgrimage. Approximately forty centimeters in height, it depicts the Qoyllur Rit'i taytacha attended by two wayri ch'uncho dancers, with Mount Ausankati in the background.*

brother Miguel, Luis Hanq'o and Guillermo Mantupa, two of his brothers-in-law, and Fermín Mantupa, another first cousin. With respect to the last, however, the kin tie belied the actual relationship. Julio and his brothers had little time for Fermín and his immediate family, and they never shared their labor. Fermín appeared to owe his cargo of ukuku dancer to his friendship with the maestro, whose sister he had married.

Without ritual dancers, the purpose of a sponsored pilgrimage cannot be fulfilled. Apart from providing entertainment for the other pilgrims, their routines serve as rites of entry and exit at critical points in the passage of the lámina, especially at the shrine sanctuary itself. There are dozens of different ceremonial dance styles in the central Andes, each with its own costume, choreography, music, and symbolism. Very often a style carries undertones as to the social status of the performers. Styles may become defunct, but new ones, or subvariants of old ones, are being created all the time.

The wayri ch'uncho was favored by Qamawarans for all their pilgrimages. It is one of several *ch'uncho* 'savage' styles, all of which are supposed to be mimetic portrayals of the tribal Indians who dwell in the tropical lowlands to the northeast. The four wayri ch'uncho dancers were accompanied by two other characters. One was an ukuku, a figure ostensibly representing a bear, who is tricksterlike, alternately comic and threatening, and who is linked mythically and ritually to the feared condenados. The other was a *maqt'acha* 'youngster', 'youth', a role filled by a boy dancing for the first time—in this instance Julio's younger brother (plate 8).[3] All the dancers were male; there are very few female dance roles in the stylistic inventory.

Dance cargos, while prestigious, did not enhance a person's reputation as it did to be a patrón. They certainly involved expense in the hire or manufacture of costumes, but they were undertaken as much out of reciprocal obligation to the sponsor as for the honor they brought to the performer. People tended to dance for one another from year to year, in what amounted to a long-term sequence of interlaced ayni transactions. There were in fact striking parallels between agropastoral cooperation on the one hand and the organization of pilgrimage on the other. Both activities entailed the complementary roles of *patrón* 'sponsor' and *arariwa* 'leader' or 'guardian'. Furthermore, it was precisely the enduring relationships of moral cooperation in production that underlay the choices of successive pilgrimage sponsors and their respective ceremonial dancers.

The musicians, unlike the dancers, were engaged by the sponsor for cash. On this occasion, all four were from Qamawara. Musical skill rather than personal ties had dictated the choice of pito players: the leader of the quartet, Simón Champi, was acknowledged as the finest flutist in the community. The bass drummer, though, was León Qompi, Julio's older brother.

There were two formal female cargos, the crossbearers, known as *alfereces* 'ensigns'. They were filled by two relatives of Julio's wife Juana, a younger sister and a first cousin, both of them unmarried. They and the other women in the contingent shared the duties of cooking and cleaning dishes, under the general direction of the maestro. Altogether, apart from cargo holders and musicians, there were about forty nonoffice-holding pilgrims in the group, most of them friends of one or other of the principal officers. Men far outnumbered women, and the few married women were accompanied by their spouses; most pilgrims were married men traveling without their wives. Several urban migrants had scheduled their visits home so as to attend. The rigors of the journey meant that there was no one much older than forty-five. An elderly or sick person could, however, sponsor a pilgrimage if he wished, nominating a son or another close kinsman to act as his representative on the journey.[4]

Why had they all come? The responses to this question reflected a mix of religious and social motivations. A pervasive theme was the special character of the site. Here is Manuel's answer:

> We go together each year to Señor de Qoyllur Rit'i and Apu Ausankati, to visit the taytacha. We walk there and we all light candles. When the novena is over we come back home.
>
> We go there because in that faraway place, a long, long time ago, a miraculous taytacha appeared. Later, he also appeared in Tayankani, and having been seen by human beings, he returned to the spot to hide. He was discovered there by two little boys who were playing together, called Manuel and Mariano. The three of them stayed together, and the taytacha gave the two boys bread which they lived on for three whole weeks. Then suddenly, as the boys looked on, the taytacha was transformed into a body inside a rock. He had died, but he still lives on.
>
> Since then, little by little, everyone has come to know about that miraculous taytacha. All the naciones go there to light candles, because now everyone understands what happened. The number of pilgrims is increasing all the time. Nowadays all the dancers go there, and the place is filled to overflowing.

This account is closely related to the "official" version of the myth of the founding of the shrine, to be discussed later, though as will be seen there are some significant variations. Here it is enough to note that the account stresses the theophanic rather than the thaumaturgic aspect of the shrine's miraculousness. It is because those true events happened, *at that place,* that so many people now want to visit it. The presence of the taytacha, dead yet still living, at that particular spot is reason enough for going.

The exalted status of Qoyllur Rit'i as a sacred place is expressed in its position second only to Señor de Wank'a in the community's pentadic hierarchy of miraculous taytachas. These five, it will be recalled—Wank'a, Qoyllur Rit'i, Tayankani, Aqcha, and Justo Juez—were said to have been brothers who had wandered about the region, each brother stopping to rest at the spot where his shrine is now located. Señor de Wank'a is not visited in pilgrimage by Qamawarans, making Señor de Qoyllur Rit'i the most senior of those that are. Señor de Tayankani, a parallel advocation of Señor de Qoyllur Rit'i, is fêted along with Qoyllur Rit'i during the later phases of the latter's Corpus fiesta, but the Qamawaran pilgrims do not take part in these activities. Besides these ranked shrines, there

are three customarily visited by pilgrim groups from the community—
Wat'a, Kisikancha, and Saqaka—that are unranked. These shrines were
said to have originated from isolated apparitions, sui generis, and were
regarded as less important than those founded by itinerant divinities.

Group pilgrimage, then, at the very level of conscious motivation,
is a kinesthetic mapping of space. By physically traversing the landscape,
an individuated local community—Manuel used the Quechua first person
plural exclusive throughout—inserts itself into a variegated macrocosmic
domain, defined by collectively recognized sacred places, of greater or
lesser magnitude, where theophanies are known to have occurred.

This is not to say that the thaumaturgic capabilities of the shrines
were irrelevant. Many of the pilgrims were going to Qoyllur Rit'i to
supplicate the taytacha or its nearby Virgin consort with private requests
or were fulfilling a vow to make the journey in return for a petition
already granted. A few claimed to be going simply to gain grace. Individual religious motivation of this kind was entertained simultaneously
with the collective goal of merely visiting the site: it would be pointless
to attempt to specify which was primary or deeper.

Coexisting with these religious motivations were more obviously
social ones. For the patrón, there was an element of social duty: the
prestigious Qoyllur Rit'i cargo was said to be *casi obligatorio* 'almost
obligatory', although the sponsorship of other pilgrimages was less imperative. In return, the event promised to memorialize the sponsor and
to win him the approbation and acclaim of the community at large and
especially of his close associates and acquaintances—that is, those specific
persons on whose goodwill and cooperation his and his family's future
and livelihood depended. For the dancers, there was both personal honor
and a sense of obligation to the sponsor to help him pass the cargo, and
perhaps a recognition that they would be able to call on him in the future
when their turn came. Nonofficeholding pilgrims, too, were drawn in by
more diffuse social commitments to the sponsor and other officeholders.
Finally, there was the recreational aspect of the affair. For everyone it
was a holiday, an escape from everyday routine into a distant, different
world, with all the heightened sense of intimacy that such an excursion
brings.

Around this web of motives coalesced the Qoyllur Rit'i contingent—
nación—of Qamawara. The word *nación* was used to designate any
sponsored pilgrimage group, regardless of the administrative status or
official title of its home community—comunidad campesina, annex, hacienda, cooperative, district capital, or whatever. It was the word used
in early colonial times to denote the subimperial native ethnic groupings,
which began to be broken up from the late sixteenth century onward.
That the usage has persisted solely in the context of pilgrimage, as a
common denominator for diverse local groups, suggests a degree of continuity in the mode of ritual articulation at the regional level despite the

collapse of ethnic identities into narrow communal loyalties anchored to exclusive territorialities. It suggests, too, that regional ritual identities and processes are to a degree detached from local ones founded upon fixed hierarchies of communal religious icons and operate in an independent realm.

I shall pursue these conjectures later. For now, I shall return to the pilgrimage.

The Journey

We proceeded single file along the trail. At the head of the column was the captain, like all the dancers uncostumed, carrying a staff to which was attached his ch'uncho headdress—a cascade of orange and red macaw feathers. Behind him was another of the dancers, with a staff similarly decorated. Next came the musicians in full flood, followed by the two crossbearers, each with a staff surmounted by a tin cross shrouded in gaily colored rayon scarves. Then came the main body of pilgrims, which I had now joined, with our burdens slung across our shoulders. Behind us came more dancers with feathered staves, the sponsor carrying the shrouded icon, and finally the master bringing up the rear (plate 6).

On the outskirts of Qamawara the captain stopped, and the rest of us crowded behind him. The musicians played a tiyana. To our right the fields swept away steeply, and through a narrow cleft in the hills one could see the sanctuary of Señor de Wank'a as a tiny cluster of buildings a thousand meters below. We all turned to face the shrine. Taking the icon from the sponsor, the master stepped forward and intoned a short Quechua prayer invoking the protection of the taytacha of Wank'a on our journey. He then held the icon as the pilgrims came forward one by one, hats removed, to kiss its wooden base, crossing themselves as they did so. With right hands raised in a low salute the entire company then said twice over the invocation, *Tayta Mariawan p'istuy* 'God and Mary protect us'. The musicians struck up with an *alabado* 'hymn of praise', and a rocket was lit, screeching into the sky and exploding above our heads. The master returned the icon to the sponsor, and we continued on our way.

We were now in the territory of the adjacent community of Oqoruro. At the gateway of Oqoruro church we stopped again. The ritual was repeated, the master this time invoking the protection of the taytacha within, Señor el Justo Juez. Having paid homage to our two neighboring miraculous shrines, we began the steep ascent to the puna.

On the mountain ridge several people were waiting for us, residents of Oqoruro who were kin, friends, or affines of Qamawaran pilgrims. Oqoruro did not in fact send an independent contingent to Señor de

PLATE 6 *Pilgrimage: the Nación. This group of Qamawaran pilgrims, en route to the interlocal shrine of Señor de Wat'a, is led by the musicians—two flutists and two drummers. Shrouded crosses and dancers' headdresses can be seen at the rear of the column.*

Qoyllur Rit'i, and our nación in effect spanned the two communities. Once again the ceremony of veneration of the icon was performed, the master's prayer this time a formal farewell to Qamawara.

The terrain from now on was flat and marshy, devoid of dwellings, desolate save for the occasional shepherdess with her flock of sheep or llamas. The sun beat down relentlessly. Heat, alcohol, and fatigue were beginning to take their toll, and several pilgrims would invariably be lagging behind the main column. Every so often the captain and musicians would stop and wait for everyone to catch up, for it was important that we travel as far as possible in a single united body.

The musicians played continuously and flawlessly, apparently unaffected by the excess of drink and lack of breath that afflicted the rest of us. Their music was like a guide. Trudging across the rough pampa, my eyes fixed on the ground a short distance ahead and my concentration centered upon the best place for my next step, I was aware of following music rather than a path or the people in front. The familiar tune, repeated hypnotically over and over, seemed to blaze a trail across the featureless landscape, the sound of the shrill flutes and the throbbing drum rising and falling on the breeze but moving ever onward, like some ethereal vanguard.

We had been marching for about two hours when we came upon another nación, seated in a tight circle and taking refreshment. They were from Siusa. Fernando, our captain, halted and we drew up in a line opposite them. Our quartet played the standard tiyana; the Siusa musicians struck up the identical piece, but there was no attempt to synchronize the two bands, and the result was cacophony. Manuel stepped forward with our icon, his Siusa counterpart came forward with theirs, and the images were exchanged. We then filed past to kiss Siusa's icon, while the members of the Siusa contingent kissed ours. The icons were returned and the two groups uttered twice in ragged unison the invocation, "Tayta Mariawan p'istuy." Skyrockets were lit, the two bands played the alabado—again the one a few beats behind the other—and we moved off.

This ritual of icon exchange was mandatory whenever we passed another nación. Always the procedure was the same, punctuated by the same musical phrases, and always the respective bands would perversely eschew any coordination with each other.[5] We must have performed the ritual at least thirty times in the course of the pilgrimage; it would have been more but for the fact that, in the vicinity of the shrine, where contingents were constantly passing one another, our captain would occasionally make a swift diversion to another footpath to avoid the delay entailed by the ritual.

Two hundred meters beyond the Siusa circle we too stopped to rest. The icon, still wrapped in my towel, was leaned against a large boulder, and the staves with the feathers and crosses were arranged symmetrically on either side. We sat down in a circle, Manuel taking some trouble to ensure that there were no gaps between us and delivering a little homily on the importance of always sitting close together lest evil spirits (supay) intrude. Fernando proffered Manuel a dish of spiced jerked llama meat, but the master held out his hand and Fernando was obliged to select a piece for him. This he then did for everyone else, thus ensuring that all received equal amounts. Rum was served, again in strictly equal drafts; several people, however, including all the women, offered theirs to Manuel, who it seemed had no choice but to drink them down.

While we were resting the Siusa contingent came past, and we were obliged to perform the ritual of icon exchange with them all over again. It was evident that this formality was already proving irksome to a few.

After about an hour we resumed our trek. There was a gentle climb as we approached the watershed; then suddenly, a magnificent panorama of snow-covered mountains rose into view. We were at the first coign of vantage of Mount Ausankati. We lined up facing the range, and venerated our icon in the usual fashion. Beneath us was a broad valley, treeless except for a distant grove of eucalyptus. That was Wankarani, I was informed, but it was still a long way off.

Manuel was by now suffering badly from the effect of the extra drink. He was so inebriated that he was keeling over every ten paces or so, though he still made a brave effort to maintain the dignity and authority of his office. Whereas in other circumstances his condition might have provoked amusement, it now caused great concern among the other pilgrims, who relieved him of his baggage and tried to revive him with cigarette smoke and ointment rubbed on his chest. I offered him aspirin, more as a placebo than anything else, and it seemed to have the desired psychological effect, as he became more cheerful and didn't fall over quite so often.

It was now dark. We had descended into the valley and were climbing again. Most of us were all but overcome with exhaustion. The musicians played gamely on to keep up our flagging spirits as we staggered across the moonlit countryside. Feeling myself close to collapse, I suddenly found myself walking between buildings, and minutes later we were in the plaza of Wankarani.

The little village was bustling. It lies on the road from Paucartambo to Ocongate and Mawallani, and it was here that hundreds of pilgrims from a wide radius converged in order to take trucks for the remainder of the journey. The few shops and bars were all open, their interiors ablaze with kerosene lamps, and were doing a brisk business. Women plied chicha and hot punch from tables along one side of the square. Truck drivers engaged in shouted negotiations with potential customers. All the time more and more pilgrim groups poured into the plaza, their bands playing stridently.

Fernando skated around trying to arrange transport. Eventually he struck a deal with the driver of a large Volvo; it looked full already, but we bundled in.

It was 10:00 P.M. before we departed. Even by the standards of Andean truck travel, the journey was extremely uncomfortable. The vehicle was grossly overcrowded, and we were packed so tightly that if anyone shifted his or her position practically everyone else was eventually obliged to do likewise. All the passengers were en route for Qoyllur Rit'i, but as it happened ours was the only nación among them, the rest being devotees traveling singly or in informal groups. All in the truck were speaking Quechua among themselves, but an ethnic boundary was swiftly drawn. One woman, seeing that I was with the nación group, addressed me sniggeringly as *Kispi*, a stereotypical Indian surname. Another passenger, demanding that a woman from our party give him more room, spoke to her haughtily in Spanish and was immediately rebuked by our master—in Quechua—for doing so. Our doughty musicians, meanwhile, stood proudly on the platform over the cab and played away as we lurched and bumped through the night, until one of them fell asleep where he stood and plunged headlong, drum and all, onto the startled passengers below.

We reached Ocongate at about 4:00 A.M. and joined a long queue of stationary trucks that stretched from one end of the village to the other. The local police would not allow any to proceed until first light, in order to lessen the risk of accidents on the busy final section of the route. When we eventually arrived at the hamlet of Mawallani dozens of trucks were disgorging their human cargos, and despite the rigors of the journey and the searing cold the crowd had an air of excited anticipation. Manuel, now fully recovered, rented a hearth in a small roadside hut owned by a woman from Ocongate, and the women in our party prepared a breakfast of potato stew and sweet coffee. The sun came up, and we basked in the warmth. I was so tired that I dozed off where I sat and toppled over into my neighbor's lap. But there was little respite, for as soon as we had finished eating Manuel gave the order for the ascent.

The eight-kilometer climb to the sanctuary at Sinakara was studded with special sites and landmarks (see appendix 1, map 10). The first was the hillside chapel of Mawallani. Here we stood in two lines leading from the door while the band played the tiyana, and Manuel made to enter the chapel with our icon to have it blessed. But there were so many people inside that he decided not to wait, and we continued on our way.

The next landmark was an *apachita* 'cairn', at the top of a steep scree. Each pilgrim carried a stone to the summit, spat on it, and threw it on to the cairn—the purpose being, I was told, to relieve the soul of its sins before one approached the shrine. One joker amused himself by placing enormous boulders on other people's packs, much to their annoyance since they could not dispose of them but had to carry them up to the cairn.

The third site was a cluster of small, unroofed, three-sided stone shelters on a stretch of level ground known as Pujllaypampa 'the playground'. Here there was a strange interlude.

Manuel selected a vacant shelter, and we formed two lines in front of the entrance while the icon, staves, crosses, and headdresses were placed inside. We retired to a spot about ten meters away to sit down in a circle, and potatoes, jerked meat, and rum were served. Groups of people then began to leave the circle to engage in various kinds of foolery. All around, members of other naciones were doing the same. Some indulged in general horseplay, leaping and jumping around amid much shouting and laughter. Others played at games of make-believe. One of our number bought a cow from a companion, in reality a lump of quartz, for which he gave a handful of scraps of paper representing money and which he tethered with a strand of wool from his knitted cap. He then took his cow over to a group from another nación and proceeded to sell it to them in turn. The original vendor's scraps of paper, meanwhile, had become seeds, which he went off to plant with another Qamawaran. A group from another nación performed a mock ceremony to "marry" an attractive young woman from their party to our master, rather against her wishes but to everyone else's great delight. I had to act as a magistrate, and various cases were brought before me. One involved a man from our contingent jokingly accused of abandoning his wife for another woman; judgment having been passed, he was hustled away and thrown into prison behind some rocks. Others, meanwhile, occupied themselves privately in the construction of elaborate miniature houses and corrals out of rocks, with stones representing llamas, alpacas, and sheep, to indicate to the spirits of the shrine the devotee's desire. Everyone from our party without exception joined in some of these antics, though not all with equal enthusiasm. Participation seemed to be mandatory.

The games ceased as quickly as they had begun. We collected our packs, formed two lines before the shelter while the master retrieved our lámina, and resumed the climb.

This episode had served as a catharsis, for the mood was now somber and our progress more dignified. We had joined a continuous stream of pilgrims trudging single file up a footpath that ran along the side of a broad, U-shaped valley. Other pilgrims, having paid their respects to the taytacha, were already on their way down. We passed about a dozen naciones resting by the side of the path and engaged in reciprocal exchange of icons with each of them.

As we climbed higher, the patchy grass of the valley slopes gave way to steep scree. A large wooden cross came into view, marking the final approach to the sanctuary. Just beyond, there was a shallow concrete bath measuring about four meters by three, into which gushed the waters of a spring. This was the Agua del Señor 'the Lord's Water', reputed to possess miraculous healing powers. The tub was filled to capacity with men and women, trousers and skirts hitched up, splashing water over their bodies.

We did not stop, but proceeded past a second cross to a third, this one surmounting a large cairn, which marked the entrance to the shrine precincts. Here we deposited our icon in a small stone shelter and sat down. Our climb from Mawallani had been speedy and without incident—a good sign, since a slow ascent indicates that the group is weighed down by the sins of its members. Our six dancers donned their costumes for the first time; Fermín, the ukuku, would not quit his until we returned to Qamawara. When all were ready the lámina was reclaimed, and with the dancers escorting him in formation, the sponsor bore it to the sanctuary.

At the Shrine

The pilgrimage site occupied the head of the valley, with snow-capped peaks rearing up on three sides. At this altitude—4,750 meters above sea level—it was chilly even in the full glare of the sun. Thousands of people

PLATE 7   *Qoyllur Rit'i: the Sinakara Sanctuary. View looking down the valley, during the titular fiesta. The picture was taken in 1973, when the new sanctuary was still under construction.*

swarmed across the broad, grassy combe, the bright colors of their clothing contrasting with the greys and dull greens of the landscape. Several makeshift food tents had been set up, and a pall of smoke hung motionless above them. The music of countless bands ebbed and flowed—rippling flutes and harps, thudding drums, and the coarse clash of brass. Clinging to the scree was an ugly, half-finished building of breeze blocks and galvanized metal. We picked our way toward it through the throng (see plate 7).

The first sensation on entering the sanctuary was the wave of heat from the hundreds of flickering candles lining the walls. Devotees were standing or kneeling, praying, weeping, or just gazing at the illuminated image of the crucified Christ, Señor de Qoyllur Rit'i. This was painted on a rock about three meters in height, adorned with an embroidered loincloth and protected by a glass screen. To its left stood a statue of the Virgin and to its right one of San Martín de Porras, Peru's mestizo saint. The Qamawaran delegation jostled their way to the altar and presented their icon to a *celador* 'warden', who placed it along with dozens of others on a bench near the miraculous image. Our dancers and musicians then retreated backward to the entrance—not an easy maneuver in the crush—and went to rejoin their comrades.

Meanwhile, the rest of the party had been seeking out a place to camp. There were few permanent shelters in the area, and most of the pilgrims slept out in the open if they slept at all. Each nación staked out a territory for itself, using baggage and rocks as boundary markers. Our patch measured about three meters square. The women constructed a makeshift hearth of stones, and soon a potato stew was cooking. All around us, other naciones were preparing or eating their meals, but there was never any commensality, or much intercourse of any kind, among them.

I asked permission of the master and went off in search of privacy. Attending to one's natural functions at such an event is an unbeguiling experience. One instantly became aware that the pilgrimage rites were being enacted in a cesspit. This was the inescapable concomitant of massed humanity. We were all united, to the extent that we were, not only by our common devotion to the sacred shrine in our midst, but also by our own unsanitary cordon, which ringed us on all sides.

I returned to our group. A procession was wending its way slowly through the pilgrims' encampment: two long lines of dancers—wayri ch'unchos, ukukus, and others in a bewildering array of costumes and styles—were trooping sullenly before a priest shaded beneath a baldachin, with a monstrance held aloft. Celadores, the wardens of the Hermandad del Señor de Qoyllur Rit'i, easily identifiable by their dark suits and the rope whips around their necks, marched ahead of the processional route, snatching off hats and brusquely ordering people to kneel.

When we had eaten, I unfurled my sleeping bag and selfishly claimed a precious strip of ground. I slept fitfully. The music never abated, and whenever I opened my eyes a troupe of dancers was whirling past my head. All night long a floodlight glared down on us, an electric generator chugged away tirelessly, and a distorting loudspeaker went on broad-casting the cash donations of pilgrims to the shrine.

Next morning was crisp and clear, with a heavy ground frost. The sheer crush of bodies, however, had kept the cold at bay. As the first rays of the sun crept over the snowy peaks and struck the frozen valley, the musicians of each contingent scrambled to their feet, gathered round their master, and performed a joyful aubade in his honor. For several minutes, the dawn was filled with a pleasant musical jangle. Manuel sat motionless and solemn throughout the fanfare.

After breakfast, we were at liberty to do as we wished. I ascended to the grotto of the Virgin of Fátima, just beyond the sanctuary. This consisted of a large rock, on which stood a rough shelter of stone and mortar. Inside, protected by a wooden grille, was a statue of the Virgin. Written requests were posted through the grille, and at the foot of the rock supplicants planted candles surrounded by little heaps of money, which were periodically collected by a celador. The Virgin was held in special affection by young girls, to whom she was thought to impart the skills of weaving. Some presented their first efforts at the loom to her in thanksgiving.

Dotted about the slopes above the grotto were dozens of miniature stone houses and corrals, similar to those which members of our nación had made at Pujllaypampa. Some of the constructions here, however, had written labels identifying them as the desired property of this or that family. Amid this Lilliputian scene, pilgrims similarly engaged in make-believe transactions, using scraps of paper to buy and sell pebbles representing livestock, and in some instances trucks. The combination of this surreal spectacle and the rarefied mountain air was dizzying.

Some members of our party visited the sanctuary for mass, celebrated by a Spanish priest, who delivered a sermon in halting Quechua. Others wandered among the stalls and tents in which fruit, cooked food, and drinks were sold or went down to bathe in the Agua del Señor. There was very little interaction among strangers from different naciones. I attracted a lot of attention, of course, and my Qamawaran companions seemed proud to have a bumbling gringo as the mascot of their group. But it was impressed upon me that I was theirs and no one else's: Manuel advised me, for example, to decline invitations to take photographs of other contingents. About the only contact our camp had with our immediate neighbors was a glass of rum proffered to me, but to no one else, out of curiosity.

People did, however, seek out friends and acquaintances in the crowd, and bits of gossip began to drift back to our group. The previous day an infant had died at the shrine, and there had also been an accident on the Mawallani road: a truck loaded with pilgrims had overturned, and several persons had been killed. Reaction to the latter deaths was equivocal. On the one hand it was asserted that the souls of the dead would go straight to hanaqpacha, for death on a pilgrimage was believed to guarantee salvation.[6] On the other hand there was a suspicion that the deaths might have been punishment meted out by the taytacha, who was regarded as particularly vengeful. He was said, for example, to visit death upon any of his devotees who failed to record three pilgrimages to his shrine in succession—a belief that caused my companions some concern on my behalf. If the accident casualties were indeed victims of the taytacha's wrath then their deaths were bad, and they were destined to become condenados—of whom there were already legions around Sinakara.

An open-air mass was celebrated later that morning, to be followed by the principal procession through the shrine precincts of a crucifix modeled on the Qoyllur Rit'i image. The fiesta would then rise to a climax. That night the ukukus would ascend en masse to the glacier, while the next day a mass procession would leave Sinakara on a kind of pilgrimage within a pilgrimage, making its way across the mountains to the hamlet of Tayankani and thence to Ocongate.

The Qamawarans participated in none of these activities. Immediately the mass ended, Manuel gave the signal to depart. The dancers donned their outfits and retrieved our icon from the sanctuary, while the rest of us broke camp and headed down the path toward Mawallani. We stopped near the cairn cross and waited for the dancers and musicians to arrive. The costumes were removed—except for the ukuku's—and we retraced our steps to Mawallani, abstaining from food and drink for the duration of the journey.

The Return

"Now we can get drunk," said Fernando when we reached the vast truck park that now engulfed the little hamlet. We did not do so immediately, however, but took a truck back to Wankarani, arriving at about 9:00 P.M.

Lodgings had been arranged for at a farmstead on the outskirts of the village, and the owners were expecting us. They took formal reception of the icon, kneeling before it and kissing it before installing it in their house, clearly honored to give it shelter. Our party was directed to a small outbuilding. Having had two sleepless nights, people were impatient to retire. Before we were allowed to do so, however, the master supervised a stocktaking of the remaining communal provisions, and loads were reallocated.

We remained at the farmstead until the following afternoon. It was evident that the whole character of the pilgrimage had now changed. The atmosphere was more relaxed, jokes and insults were traded freely, and drinking was less inhibited. Collections were made for more liquor, and as the day wore on people became more and more inebriated. The landlord brought out an ancient phonograph, and for the first time during the pilgrimage people danced waynos, the recreational style of dance.

In the early afternoon we made ready to leave, but the landlord detained us in an ill-tempered altercation over how much he should be paid and refused to release the icon. The account was to be settled not in money but in an alpine flower, prized for its medicinal qualities, that we had gathered at Sinakara.[7] The argument had an extraordinary effect on three men in our group. One by one they came away, their faces contorted, and burst into tears, sobbing openly and uncontrollably. This behavior struck me as most unusual, particularly uncharacteristic of the individuals concerned. At last a price was agreed upon, and we departed.

We were now an extremely disheveled bunch, some of the men so drunk they were barely able to walk. Quantities of alcohol, however, had failed to impair the skill of the musicians, who continued to play with élan. We were heading for Aqcha, the site of a miraculous Christ shrine whose interlocal pilgrimage is held independent of that of Qoyllur Rit'i, on 6 August; ours was, so to speak, a courtesy visit. We halted on the outskirts of the village while the dancers changed into their costumes.

They then escorted the icon to the shrine chapel and handed it to the lay custodian there; many other Qoyllur Rit'i contingents called at the shrine on their homeward journeys, and the altar was kept permanently manned.

The dancers performed for a long time in front of the chapel, for once having sufficient space for a proper display. The usual formation was for four of the dancers to stake out a square, prancing on the spot, the ch'unchos with their staves held aloft, while the other two circled round each other in the center of the square, alternately clockwise and counter clockwise, clashing their staves against each other as they turned. The central pair would then be replaced by another. A second formation consisted of two parallel lines of dancers, the members of each pair confronting each other and exchanging positions (see appendix 4).

We made for the cottage in which we were to spend the night. The trek had had a sobering effect on most people, so they now determinedly set about getting drunk again. Intoxication, it seemed, was de rigueur. It happened that a contingent from the Paucartambo area was staying next door, but the two naciones kept apart from each other, and Manuel warned me not to fraternize with the other group. Any interaction between them was competitive. There was a "whip duel" between the respective ukukus, each lashing out at the legs of the other with his whip and shrieking in a high falsetto voice. Much to the delight of his companions, Fermín gave his opponent such a drubbing that he was forced to retire. The two bands also engaged in informal contest: whenever one struck up the other immediately took up the same piece, striving to play it louder, faster, and with more embellishments.

Men began to go off in twos and threes to visit bars in the village, returning in the evening in varying states of drunkenness. After supper we all piled into the tiny cottage and distributed ourselves alongside and on top of each other. Fermín and Gregorio, Julio's brother-in-law from Oqoruro, returned late from a drinking bout, and Gregorio clambered on to the raised bench next to where I was sleeping on the floor. Suddenly he rolled off, crashing down on top of me. It took me several seconds to recover from the shock, but everyone else dissolved in laughter. Meanwhile Gregorio, looking as if he felt very sorry for himself, proceeded to vomit on the floor. Fermín eventually persuaded him to leave.

Next morning we arose as usual at first light. The convivial drunkards of the previous night were noticeably quiet, and Gregorio in particular was the butt of some cruel jokes. We left at about midday, paying our landlord in flowers as before. The dancers—uncostumed this time— retrieved the icon from the chapel and we headed for home.

On the high puna we came to a small wayside chapel, and, depositing the icon within, we sat down in a circle nearby. There now took place the eagerly anticipated *costumbre de cargas*, the baggage search to ensure that no one had smuggled any of the communal provisions he or she had been carrying. The operation was supervised by Manuel, Fernando, and

Fermín, the ukuku. First Manuel emptied the contents of his own pack onto the ground, and the rest of us were obliged to follow suit. Any communal goods remaining were set to one side. One or two people were reluctant to allow their loads to be inspected; the goods they were harboring were then gleefully paraded around the circle, and they were made to feel thoroughly ashamed.

At one point Julio tried to take a hand in the proceedings, but he was so incapable that he was brushed aside. Smarting at this treatment, he then took the considerable risk of accusing Manuel of taking snatches of rum from the flask he had been carrying. He was immediately assailed with yells of derision and retreated in tears. Manuel stood silently by, smiling superciliously.

The communal goods were sorted into piles. Cigarettes and toasted maize were distributed there and then in equal portions, while the rum was consolidated and reserved for later. Noodles, coffee, sugar, and meat were auctioned off, the proceeds destined for the sponsor to help defray his expenses. Julio had by now regained his composure and returned fearlessly to the fray by contesting Manuel's integrity over the handling of the cash. But by now the entertainment value of the event had been exhausted and people ignored him, impatient to be off. A skyrocket was exploded, and we resumed our homeward trek.

The group was now in complete disarray, with figures dotted all over the pampa. The musicians still played occasionally, and between renderings Simón, the lead flutist, who was in high spirits, skipped playfully across the furrows. But the combination of excessive alcohol, weariness, and general license was causing quarrels to break out with increasing frequency, most confrontations ending with one or another of the parties weeping pitifully. Manuel and Fermín had an argument that rumbled on for some time, drawing several other people into its wake. The bumptious Fermín, an army veteran with a slim command of Spanish, was attempting to vaunt his mestizo credentials to Manuel in particular—who was a Quechua monolingual—and to the company in general. "*I can speak correct Spanish, I can,*" he kept shouting—in Spanish—"*I may be an Indian* [indio], *but I'm a soldier as well—I'm a Peruvian! I speak Quechua but I speak Spanish too.*" Manuel smiled condescendingly at his drunken clamor. But Gregorio, Fermín's drinking companion from the night before and also a Quechua monolingual, tried to calm him and was repaid by a wounding insult that reduced him to tears. Later, I overheard Fernando, another monolingual, discussing Fermín's outburst with a friend. "Like it or not," he was saying with resignation, "we're all indios."

Four kilometers from Qamawara we were met by an advance party, the community alcalde and two companions. They had a pile of potatoes and a pitcher of chicha to sustain us for the last leg of the journey. We ate and drank hurriedly, for the light was fading fast and the moon would not rise till well after dark. Everyone was elated. When we moved off, however, it became apparent that one of the advance party, an elderly man, had consumed so much liquor while waiting for us that he was unable to stand. "Leave him!" shouted Fermín, who was riding high and in any case wanted to have me close so that he could have the benefit of my flashlight. Fernando and I carried the poor creature down the mountain and deposited him in the first house we encountered, with a hurried explanation to the startled family within.

On other Qamawaran pilgrimages I attended, the dancers would reenter the community in full dress. On this occasion, however, the disorganization was total, and they simply made for the sponsor's house as they were. We were greeted by Julio's wife, parents, parents-in-law, and his brother who had stayed behind, each of whom kissed the icon in turn before it was locked away in the storehouse. Spiced cavy and chicha were served. There was little conversation, for everyone was by now exhausted, and all returned to their homes as soon as was decently possible.

Next day was Thursday, Corpus Christi. Most of the pilgrims gathered once again at Julio's house. The dancers gave a long and elaborate performance in the yard before escorting the icon to the church, where the sacristan was waiting. It was placed on the altar and the dancers retreated backward to the entrance, performing for a while outside. By this time the rest of the company had moved to the house of one of the crossbearers, and the dancers and musicians joined them there. Lunch was served, and the afternoon was whiled away watching more dancing and reminiscing about our experiences on the pilgrimage. The consensus was that it had been a success; Julio's reputation was safe.

At dusk we returned to Julio's house. The dancers were still in costume, but by this time they were almost too tired to move. For his part Fermín, the ukuku, was stupefied. As he entered the yard he tripped clumsily over the step and fell down in a furry heap, disdaining even his sister's aid. A little later he recovered enough to proclaim to no one in particular, "I'm a soldier! A macho soldier!" but he soon collapsed again and lay on the floor, motionless. "A dead soldier," someone said.

The other dancers were seated behind a table in the yard—a clear sign that the egalitarianism of the nación was giving way to hierarchy and privilege. A supper of rice, potatoes, salad, and roast cavy was served, and the dancers quit their costumes for the last time. There then followed the final ceremonial act of the pilgrimage, the *costumbre de cargo* 'ceremony of office'. Garlands were brought out, each made up of maize cobs, onions, carrots, and other vegetables strung on a length of rope. Each dancer in turn was served with chicha, a few drops of which he poured onto the four corners of the table before drinking it. Then two elderly female affines of the sponsor pinned a shawl around his shoulders and tied a garland of vegetables around his neck, arranging it so that it hung down his back. The master was the first to be festooned, followed by the captain, then the other dancers in order of age. Fermín, of course, was still prostrate and missed the ceremony. This, the sponsor's symbolic payment to the ritual dancers who have formally executed the pilgrimage on his behalf, was received with dignity and pride.

Finally, with the yard lit by a few spluttering candles, those who were still able danced waynos until the exhausted musicians refused to play more.

At this point it is worth adding an ethnographic postscript. The following year, not one but two separate pilgrimages departed Qamawara for Señor de Qoyllur Rit'i. Julio, it will be recalled, had already nominated his brother León as sponsor, and a team of dancers was duly mobilized and musicians were hired. The cargo that year was even more prestigious than usual, because I had arranged for the event to be recorded by a film crew from a British television company.[8] Resentment had been building up for some time against the nepotism that governed the occupancy of this coveted post. The same families who during the early 1970s were handing out the Qoyllur Rit'i offices to each other, moreover, also featured prominently in the organization of three other pilgrimages, those to the shrines of Aqcha, Kisikancha, and Saqaka. The leading positions for the other pilgrimage in the community calendar, meanwhile, that to Señor de Wat'a, were circulating through an identifiably separate set of persons. It was the latter group which decided that year to challenge the official Qoyllur Rit'i party by staging a rival pilgrimage.

This unofficial pilgrimage was a small-scale affair, and though it poached a few people who might otherwise have joined the official party it was less than half the size of the latter, numbering about twenty. The organizers had appropriated another lámina from the chapel for their pilgrimage, and as it happened their separateness from the official contingent was signaled through the adoption of contrasting ritual dance styles.

The rival party retained the customary wayri ch'uncho style. But León, a Quechua monolingual, decided to break with precedent and chose to employ the qhapaq qolla style, claiming that it was more attractive and less *atrasado* 'backward' than ch'uncho. The qhapaq qolla style is a mimetic portrayal of the Aymara (Qolla) traders from the altiplano, who in the past were a common sight in the Quechua villages of the Cusco region. Music was provided by a harp, an accordion, and a *kina* 'notched flute', the usual instrumentation for the qolla style.

So far as performance was concerned, the innovation was not a complete success. Some of the dancers were evidently unfamiliar with the choreography and appeared hesitant during the routines. The underlying message, however, was clear. As will be seen later, the qolla dance style is associated with mestizo ethnicity, the ch'uncho style with Indianness. The qolla dance troupe proclaimed the aspirations of the official contingent to superior, mestizo status; conversely, the ch'uncho dancers of the rival party advertised their fidelity to Indian custom and identity. In this instance, the two contrasting styles had become metaphors of social differentiation at the level of the microcosm, carrying all their multiple connotations and resonances into the intimate domain of interpersonal relations.

On the journey, and at the shrine itself, the two naciones kept well apart. But the two homecoming fiestas, with their respective costumbres de cargo, were held in full sight of each other, for whether by accident or design the rivals had selected as sponsor a man whose house directly overlooked León's. There was little visiting between the two groups, each maintaining a studied disregard of the other. The Qamawaran pilgrimage to Qoyllur Rit'i had on this occasion crystallized into two mutually exclusive contingents, and the divisions inherent in the mode of distribution of nación offices were cast into sharp relief.

Pilgrimage and the Local Community

Some of the general features of sponsored Andean pilgrimage which emerge from this account can now be systematized.

First, the nación and its emblem. The religious icon around which a pilgrim group coalesces is wholly distinct from those images—chief among them the statues of patron saints—that are deployed in the local rituals of community and vice-parish or parish. Patronal images and pilgrimage icons are semiologically contrasted. The former are typically drawn from a standard liturgical inventory of saints and advocations; within each locality they differentiate populations one from another, giving rise to mutually exclusive, microcosmic enclaves. Láminas, on the other hand, have no intrinsic iconological status: each is known only by the name of the shrine with which it is associated. Nominally, at least, the portable icons pertaining to a miraculous shrine are identical and in theory are susceptible to infinite replication across a macrocosmic domain. In other words, the ritual identity of a community is multifaceted, its patronal image epitomizing the facet directed inward, toward the microcosm, the pilgrimage icons those directed outward, toward the macrocosm.

This mutation of community identity at the iconic level is matched at the sociological level. Pilgrimage is grounded not in mandated representation but in personal networks. The fiestas of local saints are community concerns, discharged by a collective mandate and overseen by the community's political representatives. But apart from the alcalde's formal welcome of a returning nación, the latter do not play any official part in the organization of a pilgrimage. Pilgrimage is ultimately voluntary, and its officers are not subject to community opprobrium in the event of default. Indeed, the *lámina* is in effect appropriated by the sponsor's household just before the pilgrimage.

This autonomy from local political and ritual organization means that a nación might well have a span wider than the single community whose name it bears, catching up outsiders who are kin, affines, or friends of members of the community. It also means that devotions attaching to miraculous shrines can more easily reflect, exacerbate, or provoke divisions within the community, possibly leading to the splintering of the contingent and the duplication of naciones. In other words, pilgrimage icons, the emblems of extralocal identity, can also serve as markers of internal differentiation within the community. What is of interest here is that the immanent rivalry for the mantle, or mantles, of community identity tends to be focused not on the patronal icon, which for the most part remains above division, but on the external shrines.

In this regard, the comparison between participation in a pilgrimage and secular cooperation is instructive. Both give rise to loosely organized groups founded upon convergence or, more accurately, parallelism of interest but which may otherwise be gratuitous. Both represent settings in which interpersonal relations can be fixed and given meaning and cogency in relation to a profound common value. Sponsored pilgrimage explicitly uses the same constitution, roles, and imagery as labor sharing. Furthermore, there is a partial congruence between the two sets of activities in personnel, with joint participation in a pilgrimage building upon and amplifying the more restricted networks established in the sphere of production. Pilgrimage, indeed, emerges as the religious counterpart of spontaneous interhousehold cooperation, just as the fiesta of the patron saint and other community rituals stand as the religious counterparts of community-level faena cooperation—an activity that as was noted is inseparable from local collective political subordination.

Internally, a nación group is ostentatiously, even aggressively egalitarian. The fraternal ideology, the sharing of food and lodging, the rigorous control of pooled provisions, the congeniality, joking, and banter—all attest to a self-conscious affirmation of equality, to something akin to communitas reigning among its members. In marked contrast to the way I was fêted at community fiestas, I was, I am glad to say, accorded no special treatment on pilgrimages and was expected like the rest of the party to submit to the strict communal régime.

Set against this collectivist ethos, the office of master is necessarily paradoxical. In one sense he is simply primus inter pares, for the success of the enterprise redounds not to his credit but to that of the sponsor. Yet in another sense he exercises an autocratic authority within the group, precisely in the interest of maintaining absolute equality among its members. It was this contradiction that made Manuel the focus of anger and resentment in the closing stages of the pilgrimage, when emotional thresholds had been lowered by days of intemperance, and individual jealousies and insecurities began to surface. In particular, the inherent conflict between the roles of sponsor and master became manifest. Even here, though, the frequent and uncharacteristic outbursts of weeping seemed to serve as an institutionalized sublimation, which curtailed argument and avoided the disruptive physical violence that would surely have broken out on home ground.

As this solidary band of pilgrims traverses the landscape, it simultaneously transforms it. In its ritual passage from local refuge to distant prospect, to use Appleton's (1975) terminology, it creates a unique corridor that joins the community to the macrocosm. Each corridor incorporates a series of landmarks to guide the travelers toward their goal—chapels, crosses, rocks, springs, cairns, mountains, other miraculous shrines or their prospects—and these landmarks become the more frequent and charged with greater sanctity as the shrine is neared and the various corridors converge, funneling the pilgrims into a single stream toward the center. Now, distant prospect becomes sacred refuge, harboring all comers. Through the media of percussion, music, and dance, passive physical features and locations are culturally appropriated and transformed into a continuous sacred topography, contoured concentrically around the shrine.

The significance of this topographical code varies with directionality. Ritually, centripetal movement is stressed, centrifugal movement is muted. Behaviorally, the one is controlled, the other relaxed. Going, the atmosphere is tense and formal, with the prayers and rites associated with the various stages of the route executed in meticulous detail. Detours and delays are kept to a minimum. As far as possible the nación stays together in a compact group, marching in an orderly fashion and maintaining an unbroken circle when resting. The homeward journey, by contrast, is deliberately protracted, and the group is frequently ragged and disorganized. Alcohol is consumed in quantity, insults are bandied about, and rituals are performed perfunctorily if at all. The outward and return journeys are contrasted as ritualism to release, restraint to license, signifying the imbalance between the supercharged center and its neutral peripheries.

Dance performs a critical function in this ritual passage. Leaving aside the symbolism of particular dance styles, any dance routine is itself a formal, kinesthetic mapping of space. When dancers escort the lámina to or from its place of repose, they are enclosing it within a tightly ordered, mobile ritual frame that is synoptic of the entire pilgrimage. Though actual dance is confined to these critical junctures, dance music is practically continuous throughout the journey. The ritual passage is pervaded by melody and rhythm: the pilgrimage, in a sense, is not so much walked as danced.

The activities at Pujllaypampa and around the Virgin's grotto on the Qoyllur Rit'i pilgrimage project the pilgrims from ritual formality into sacred fantasy. The miniature stone houses and herds, of course, directly express the devotees' requests to the taytacha for material benefits, but the setting in which they are assembled makes them far more than mere Roman Catholic ex-votos. Their construction is part of a cluster of activities that vividly exemplify what the Turners, following Huizinga, call the ludic aspect of pilgrimage (Turner and Turner 1978, 35). The behavior suspends mundane experience for a few moments to throw open a realm of pure possibility. In the improvised games, series of make-believe personae are conjured up from the uniform individual identities of the pilgrim band. The sketches I observed all involved achieved, rather than ascribed, roles—of labor sharers, of buyer and seller, of husband and wife, of felon and judge. One or two tentatively transgressed the barriers of the nación to enlace individuals of different contingents in successive extemporizations. Neither the boundary nor the structure of the nación, however, was completely dissolved. The offer from our neighbors of a young woman in marriage, it will be recalled, was directed not at anyone at random but at our maestro, the figurehead of our group. And it was surely no accident that I was singled out to act as mock magistrate: the egalitarian ethos of the pilgrimage did not fully suppress my status as a high-ranking outsider.[9]

The second level of the pilgrimage process is that of relations between naciones. Just as percussion, music and dance animate the fixed landmarks of the sacred domain, so also do they mediate between itinerant groups. Indeed, mobile láminas themselves, as much as physical features of the landscape, are elements of the sacred topography. When groups meet, their icons invade each other's ritual space, its unique pilgrimage corridor, and they must be reciprocally venerated before the contingents can pass and proceed. In this ritual encounter, directly redolent of the ambivalent parabién which now replaces the violent tinkuy, there is distinction without difference. The ceremony is entirely symmetrical, but the music performed by each group to frame it is deliberately uncoordinated with that of the other. Furthermore, the fact that where possible the formality is evaded is in itself an important datum. Other naciones are hazards to be negotiated, obstacles that impede the free passage of one's own contingent to the miraculous shrine. Each separate nación regards the shrine particularistically, seeking unhindered access to its divine powers.

At the shrine itself, the congregation seems to be fractionated into its constituent naciones, joined now perhaps by individual devotees who have made the journey alone. Internación commensality is absent. Dance troupes go through their routines separately, their music unharmonized. On one occasion, during the interlocal pilgrimage to Señor de Wat'a, the ch'uncho dancers of Qamawara became involved in a brawl with another ch'uncho troupe, who claimed they were unfairly monopolizing the arena in front of the shrine sanctuary for their performance. Punches were thrown and the dancers' staves clashed in earnest until the guardian of the shrine intervened and separated the two groups. Generally the musical contests, the whip duels, and the persistent reluctance to fraternize betray a veiled antagonism between naciones—an antagonism which, as noted, can penetrate to the very heart of a community.

Intragroup collectivism, then, is offset by intergroup differentiation. External opposition goes hand in hand with internal leveling, and the boundaries of the nación seem to be drawn more tightly the farther the party ventures from its homeland. Pilgrimage contingents, regardless of provenance, stand opposed to one another as identical elements of the macrocosm. Freed from the various local systems of politico-ecclesiastical administration, relations among contingents are decontrolled, and intergroup relations are essentially unstable. Egalitarianism reigns here, too, but it is the equality of opposition rather than the equality of brotherhood. Paradoxically, microcosmic exclusiveness is not dissolved but is rather enhanced in the macrocosmic domain.

This same syndrome of local particularisms nestling within an overarching pilgrimage cult is encountered elsewhere in Latin America, and a brief comparative glance may be instructive. In the Mexican municipio of San Bernadino Contla, Tlaxcala state, for example, there are two kinds of organization concerned with religious fiestas: stewardships (mayordomías) tied to local patron saints and local brotherhoods (hermandades) that organize pilgrimages to distant shrines. Brotherhoods are sponsored on a voluntary basis; each is associated with a particular shrine and possesses a portable religious image linked to it. It is noteworthy that at the time of Nutini's fieldwork there were forty brotherhoods in the municipio that sponsored pilgrimages to only seventeen different external shrines, which means that for some shrines at least there was more than one local brotherhood (Nutini 1968, 63–75).

The village of Chinautla, in central Guatemala, exemplifies a looser modality of pilgrimage organization. While again there is an elaborate system of cofradías geared to the devotion of village saints, pilgrimages to the national shrine of Señor de Esquipulas are convened spontaneously. A person of renown, perhaps a former officer of a cofradía, announces that he has made a vow to visit the shrine, and his kin, friends, and acquaintances enroll voluntarily in his group. There may thus be a number of independent groups from the various cantones 'sections' of the village. On their return each group is met on the outskirts of the village by an advance party of friends and relatives, who escort the group back to a private homecoming fiesta. In this instance each individual pilgrim keeps a replica of Señor de Esquipulas on a household altar; no mention is made of any collective emblems (Reina 1966, 176–77).

For the enormous pilgrimage to Bom Jesus da Lapa in northeastern Brazil, there is a similar informal style of participation. A group of kin and neighbors from a single rural locality share a truck to the shrine hired by a self-appointed leader, who frequently arranges accommodation as well. No prestige economy here, though: the leader levies a charge on each member to cover his expenses, and he may even show a profit. Once at the shrine, "contact with members of groups from other areas appears to be minimal"; indeed, "it is difficult to make a case for a sense of unity among pilgrims to Bom Jesus" (Gross 1971, 137, 138, 145).

All these instances, and the Andean one show pilgrimage to be founded upon local attachments, which are carried outward into the extralocal arena. Furthermore, in all of them pilgrimage is voluntary and thus— quite literally—contingent upon specific personal relationships and networks. Where they vary is in the degree of formal organization of the pilgrim group. The Tlaxcala pattern is closest to Andean practice in this respect. In both, local allegiances are symbolized by icons hedged about with their own acolytes and rituals, which make sacred the boundaries and discontinuities between the various groups of devotees. In these instances especially, division as much as communion is evident in the pilgrimage process and demands analysis on its own terms.

There is a third dimension to nación-based pilgrimage in the central Andes, one that is only intimated in the Qamawaran account. I was identified with my Qamawaran companions in a far more thoroughgoing manner on pilgrimages than I ever was in other situations, both by them and by others; recall the snide use of a Quechua surname by a truck passenger on the Qoyllur Rit'i pilgrimage. I became acutely aware in a whole range of ways that the very act of pilgrimage, as an assertion of or acquiescence in a particular ethnic self-profile, carried a heavy emotional load. To participate in a nación group is to declare oneself, in Fernando's words, an indio, though in a manner that projects one's local ethnic status, founded upon a marginal peasant livelihood, onto a wider, translocal landscape, where it begins to acquire a more categorical meaning. But conversely, mestizo status may be claimed or asserted through the cults as well, though perhaps less unambiguously, for here it is more a matter of distancing oneself from things Indian, of exploiting or constructing differentiae—however trivial they appear to be—which will set a person apart as an ethnic superior: patronizing more orthodox shrines and avoiding stereotypical Indian ones, or merely abjuring Indian devotional practices on a pilgrimage, or on an interpersonal level ostentatiously using linguistic or other cultural markers to distinguish oneself from nación groups—even, as could be observed in Fermín's drunken bombast, from the members of one's own nación. Pilgrimage, in sum, is a potent instrument for denying, claiming, reaffirming, or temporarily recovering ethnic status—a fact that is fully appreciated by the urbane young criollos, who return home each year, sporting the latest Lima fashions, to join their rural cousins on a full-blown cargo-type pilgrimage.

I suggested earlier and have argued at length elsewhere (Sallnow 1981) that a deterministic model of pilgrimage such as Turner's, which sets up as the universal ideal of the phenomenon the achievement of a state of communitas, is likely at the very least to obscure or play down any divisive aspects or tendencies. To represent such divisiveness merely as a structural residue carried over into an activity fundamentally opposed to structure, or alternatively as a response to the organizational exigencies of a cult, is to fail to confront it as an inherent characteristic of pilgrimage itself. So far, I have shown that central Andean pilgrimage can stimulate neighborhood factionalism, foster intercommunity conflict, and serve as a vehicle of ethnic segregation. Such processes occur not as perversions of a fraternalistic ideal but rather as the concomitants of the very extralocal, universal status that the shrines proclaim.

I have pursued the discussion as far as the Qamawaran data allow. To complete the picture of Andean regional cults, I must switch my vantage point from that of a local participant community to the shrines themselves.

CHAPTER 8

The Cult of Qoyllur Rit'i

The miraculous crag of Señor de Qoyllur Rit'i has the reputation of being the preeminent Indian shrine of the region. It was frequently contrasted with the so-called mestizo shrine of Señor de Wank'a, whose titular fiesta attracts pilgrims in about the same numbers—around 20,000. Wank'a, it was said, was patronized by the *clase media* 'middle class'; Qoyllur Rit'i, on the other hand, attracted mainly *campesinos* 'peasants'. An examination of the two cults will demonstrate that this gross contrast conceals complex relativities in the cultural and social organization of each, which make them far more than mere passive reflectors of regional class-ethnic stratification.

There exist several published accounts of the Qoyllur Rit'i cult, from diverse points of view.[1] In what follows, I shall highlight in particular the spatial configuration of the composite shrine, with the aim of displaying the manner in which its double insertion into the hinterland of a local politico-ecclesiastical domain and the heartland of a regional cosmography determines the nature of the cult organization and of its cultural design. I shall begin, though, with its mythohistorical origin. Map 10, appendix 1, shows the principal locations and activities mentioned.

Mythohistory of the Shrine

The official version of the Qoyllur Rit'i legend was compiled by the priest who served in Ccatca from 1928 to 1946, though its documentary sources are unclear (Ramirez 1969, 61–68; Marzal 1971, 231–33).[2] It tells of an Indian boy named Mariano Mayta, younger son of a herd owner who lived near the settlement of Mawallani around the year 1780. Mariano and his brother used to pasture their father's animals on the slopes of Mount Sinakara, but the older boy mistreated the younger, making him flee toward the snowfields. Despairing of life, the young Mariano suddenly encountered a mestizo boy, fair and handsome, with whom he struck up a friendship. The boy comforted Mariano and shared his bread with him, and they spent a carefree day chatting and playing. In the evening, Mariano returned alone to his mountain hut.

Next day he sought out his friend, and they again passed the hours in childish amusement. So it went, day after day, for Mariano, sustained by the bread his friend shared with him, had no need to return to his father's house for provisions.

One day the two playmates were spotted by a crony of Mariano's father, who told the old man what he had seen. Suspecting that Mariano was neglecting his flock, he decided to go to investigate. To his surprise, he found that the herd had increased greatly. Mariano told his father about his new friend, and the old man instructed him to ask this mysterious boy who he was and where he was from. Well pleased with his son's shepherding the old man returned home, promising to reward Mariano with some new clothes.

Next day, Mariano again met his friend and put his father's inquiry to him. The boy replied that his name was Manuel and that he was from Tayankani.

Having been promised new clothes, Mariano suddenly realized that Manuel always wore the same garments and that they never seemed to wear out. He questioned Manuel about this, only to find that a few days later his friend appeared with his clothes in rags. Determined to help him, Mariano sought permission from his father to take a sample of the cloth to Cusco in order to buy material for a new suit of clothes for Manuel.

The tailors of Cusco were unable to help, for the sample was of fine canonical cloth. They directed him to the bishop of Cusco, who immediately suspected sacrilege. He sent Mariano away, promising to obtain some of the cloth for him, but notified the curate of Ocongate and instructed him to investigate the matter.

The priest interrogated Mariano closely on his return, and decided to accompany the young shepherd to Sinakara to see his mysterious friend for himself. On 12 June 1783 they ascended the mountain together with the sacristan and a church steward. Sure enough, in the distance next to the herd, they spotted the mestizo boy dressed in a white tunic. Mariano, full of joy, ran to greet him. The other members of the party were blinded by a brilliant light that radiated from Manuel's body and were unable to approach him. They suspected trickery, that a large mirror had been held up to dazzle them.

On his return the priest organized another expedition, comprising the local Spanish tribute collector and his successor, other vecinos and the Indian *cacique* 'chief'. They saw the silhouette of the child from afar, next to Mariano and again radiating a blinding light. On the instructions of the priest, they approached it from two directions. As the figure moved toward a rock, the priest reached out to catch him but found that he had instead caught hold of a *tayanka* bush. Believing that the person had climbed the tree, he looked up only to behold Christ's body hanging there in dying agony, bleeding from his wounds and raising his eyes to heaven.

The party fell to their knees in astonishment while Mariano, thinking that they had tortured his friend, cried out for mercy. When they recovered their senses, they found only the *tayanka* tree in the shape of a cross and the body of Mariano, who had collapsed in a fit and died. He was buried at the spot, beneath the rock alongside which Manuel had appeared for the last time.

The miraculous events at Sinakara came to the notice of the king of Spain, Carlos III, who asked that the tayanka cross be sent to him. When he failed to return it the Indians of the locality became restive, and to calm them the priest commissioned a replica. This image, known as Señor de Tayankani, is today kept on the side altar of the church in Ocongate. Five kilometers from Ocongate, at a spot that bears the name of Tayankani after a spreading tayanka bush which grows there, a chapel has been erected under the same advocation, Señor de Tayankani.

Nevertheless, it was the sepulcher of Mariano at Sinakara that commanded the principal devotion of the Indians of the area, who came to light candles at the foot of the rock. To avoid the possibility of superstitious error, the religious authorities had an image of Christ crucified painted on the rock itself. This is the image known today as Señor de Qoyllur Rit'i, 'Lord of the Snow Star'.

This official mythohistory, set down by a cleric, is built around a fairly orthodox, Ibero-Christian symbolism. The boy Christ—fair-skinned, like the Spanish—sported the cloth of priestly vestments. The breaking of bread with his friend directly recalls Christ's Last Supper and also the more general symbolism of bread in the New Testament. His name, Manuel, is the Spanish rendering of Immanuel, a Hebrew expression meaning "with us is God," which appears in the Old Testament as the name of a child to be born to a virgin as a divine sign to the people of Judah (Isaiah 7:14, 8:8; Young 1980, 685–86). And the instant metamorphosis of the innocent child into the racked body of the adult Christ accorded with the dominant devotional emphases in Spanish religiosity.

There is another, specifically Andean theme running through the official mythohistorical account. The original seer was a humble Indian boy. The devotion was initiated, however, by the priest and the local, predominantly Spanish, élite. Furthermore, almost from the outset the shrine was split between two icons, which were likewise ethnically contrasted: Señor de Tayankani, the wooden crucifix the original of which first manifested itself to the higher-status, Hispanic visionaries and which was later retained by the monarch himself, and Señor de Qoyllur Rit'i, the painting of the crucifixion on the rock beneath which the Indian seer was interred. Of the latter image there is now also a portable, three-dimensional version. As will be seen, the ritual passages of the two portable crucifixes during the titular fiesta map out two contiguous spatial domains, in a manner consistent with the ethnic associations of their respective prototypes in the official legend.

Oral traditions of Qoyllur Rit'i use the same cultural geography and sequential framework as the official tradition, but vary considerably in narrative details and emphases. A version collected in Ccatca, while following the official one closely, rings some revealing changes. Instead of Mariano taking pity on Manuel for his tattered clothes, it is Manuel who pities Mariano's *ropita de runa* 'Indian clothes'. "Don't your knees get cold?" he asks solicitously. Giving him a fragment of his own garment, he dispatches Mariano to Cusco to procure more cloth, so that he too can dress like a priest—that is, with an ankle-length robe. The priest and the other misti witnesses observe the final transfiguration, but there is no mention here of the tayanka tree. Instead, the Christ child is seen to discard his clothes and enter into the rock at Sinakara, his body suddenly becoming weak and broken. "So in this way, in this rock, our father Jesus Christ entered naked, and from that time our miraculous father was formed there, on the rock" (*Sur* 1982, 52–53).

As in the official version, it is the mistis who witness the miraculous occurrence and on whose testimony the subsequent cult rests. But in its stress on the rock as opposed to the tayanka tree as the locus of the miracle, this version begins to anchor the cult more securely to the Indian domain of Sinakara. Indeed, the tayanka tree in the official mythohistory is an incongruity, since Sinakara is situated well above the tree line. Tayanka, *Baccharis odorata,* a resinous shrub used as a combustible (Gade 1975; 218), is not encountered at this altitude.

The Ccatca account also makes play with the deep-seated association in Andean culture of clothing with personal identity, an association discussed earlier in relation to the tinkuy and the livestock rites. The same logic that was uncovered with regard to the fallen warriors in the tinkuy recurs here. A naked body is interred beneath a rock, its clothes discarded near by, and is thereafter suspended forever in a liminal state between life and death.

A chronic indeterminacy as to whether the Qoyllur Rit'i taytacha is alive or dead was also explicit in the Qamawaran version of the legend, cited earlier. The tayanka tree, moreover, is not mentioned here, only the crag that received and displays the living corpse of the Christ child. In this account the names Mariano and Manuel, which in the official legend refer to human visionary and divine manifestation, respectively, are affixed to two Indian seers. This has the effect of compounding the confusion in the official myth between the Indian saint buried beneath the rock and the crucified Christ manifested upon or within it.

Most conspicuously, however, in contrast to both the official account and that from Ccatca, the Qamawaran version makes no mention whatsoever of priests or mistis. The cult is represented here as an entirely Indian affair. The original witnesses to or participants in the miracle are a pair of Indian boys; thereafter, devotees in traditional nación groups come to dance in ever increasing numbers before the taytacha. Finally, in keeping with this stress on the autochthonous origins of the cult, the Qamawaran account establishes an overt connection between the taytacha and Apu Ausankati: a pilgrimage to the Christian shrine is deemed to be at the same time a visit to the pagan mountain deity.

Oral versions collected in Pinchimuro, an upland community not far from Ocongate and formerly within the jurisdiction of the extensive hacienda of Lauramarca, likewise lay stress on the crag as opposed to the tayanka branch. One account, however, signals the tension between the two ethnically polarized domains of Ocongate, the home of Señor de Tayankani, and Sinakara, the site of its original theophany. The crucified Christ who appeared miraculously at Sinakara is said to have been carried down to Ocongate by the mestizo witnesses, but he escaped and returned to the scene of the miracle. The mestizos took him back to Ocongate, but once again he escaped and returned to Sinakara. After his third escape, he appeared in a dream to the Ocongate priest and told him he would remain in the village only if the wayri ch'uncho dancers of Paucartambo came to perform for him. This they did, and he stayed (D. Gow 1976, 217–18, 227). Not only is ritual dancing the devotional style associated with runa, but the wayri ch'uncho dancers in particular are identified with the poor and underprivileged. By making the Indians' rendering cult to it a condition of the Ocongate mestizos' custody of the Tayankani image, this myth attempts to resolve the ethnic conflict that surrounds the miraculous taytacha.

The Pinchimuro narratives, like the Qamawaran legend, also link Señor de Qoyllur Rit'i with Mount Ausankati, which lies within the territory of the former hacienda of Lauramarca. Both the taytacha and Apu Ausankati are believed to bestow health, fertility, and abundance on their devotees and to be sympathetic to their demands for social justice. Furthermore, Apu Ausankati is sometimes said to have appeared to the people in the guise of a fair-skinned mestizo child, dressed in white. Yet the association between the two powers is in no sense an identification; indeed, they are sometimes seen to be in competition for the attention of the people. The former peons of Lauramarca hacienda claim that while both Apu Ausankati and Taytacha Qoyllur Rit'i have been responsive to their pleas for help in the past, in particular with regard to their campaign of resistance against the rapacious hacendados, the powers of the mountain spirit are waning in proportion to the increasing popularity of the Christian shrine and to the number and size of chapels erected on its slopes (D. Gow 1980).

It is worth recounting here another myth in which Mount Ausankati is featured, one which places the apu within the temporal framework of the three ages mentioned earlier. It comes from the community of Paqchanta, also a part of the former Lauramarca hacienda.

In the time of darkness, Inkariy ["King Inka"] created Apu Ausankati, so that he would grow in competition with other peaks: Aqhanaku, Kallankati, Pachatusan and other smaller ones. Apu Ausankati wanted to grow to the sky, and to stop him growing further, Inkariy placed an enormous heavy silver cross on his head.

Then, light dawned. So if Apu Ausankati had not won the competition, today we would be living in darkness; and thus Españariy ["King Spaniard"], when he arrived, would not have seen us, nor would Inkariy have died.

When light dawned, the moon fell sick and the sun was born. Then the ñaupa machus, ancient inhabitants of Lauramarca, with their eyes burned by the sun, fled to the caves in the hills, and there they remained forever. . . .

One day, in ancient times, so my grandfather told me, Inkariy said to Apu Ausankati:

If you are no longer revered and respected in the heart of the runa, on that day will come the final judgment. . . . For the arrival of the final judgment, you, Apu Ausankati, little by little will become grey until you have turned completely black. And when you have changed into a mountain of black cinder, on that day will come the final judgment.

When the final judgment arrives, we will return to ancient times, and the bitter black heart of the misti will be sweetened; then, all of us will be with one clean heart, just as in the time of the Inkas (Valderrama Fernández and Escalante Gutiérrez 1975, 175–77, my translation).

Thus, the successive mutations of Mount Ausankati—its initial appearance as the tallest peak in the region and the eventual melting of its snows—respectively mark the transitions from the epoch of the ñaupa machus to the present age of runas and mistis, and from the present to the future, postjudgment era of nondifferentiation and brotherhood. A remarkable feature of this millenarian myth is the ethnosociological insight that the present situation of runa-misti differentiation and antagonism is sustained by the continuing devotion of the runas to their pagan god and that it will be superseded only when that devotion dies.

Given the importance of Mount Ausankati in Andean cosmology from pre-Hispanic times to the present, it is perhaps surprising that the Christian shrine of Qoyllur Rit'i was not founded until 1783, 250 years after the Spanish conquest. It will be recalled that most of the principal miraculous shrines established in rural areas during the colonial period lay on or near principal transport routes and became the venues for annual regional fairs. If poor communications explain the late arrival of Ausankati's Christian counterpart, political factors perhaps help to explain why it arrived when it did.

In 1780, the Cusco region was torn apart by the most severe rebellion of the colonial epoch. Led by José Gabriel Kondorkanki, alias Tupac Amaru II, the Spanish-educated kuraka of Surimana, Pampamarca, and Tungasuca and a wealthy muleteer, the rebellion drew upon and channeled resentments among the Indian population that had been accumulating for decades and that had already caused a series of minor uprisings. The chief grievance was the *repartimiento de efectos,* the forced sale of goods to Indians by corregidores; draft labor in the mines and textile workshops might also have been a factor. The rebel leaders professed loyalty to church and crown, directing their aggression at the corregidores and other officials who operated the oppressive apparatus of colonial administration.

The revolt began on 10 November 1780, when Tupac Amaru had a hated corregidor executed. From January to April 1781 the rebels laid siege to the city of Cusco, but they were eventually routed. On 18 May 1781 Tupac Amaru was executed in the plaza in Cusco, along with his wife and lieutenants. The uprising was not finally crushed until 1783, when on 19 July the last of the leaders were put to death in Cusco (Fisher 1966; C. Valcárcel 1973; Vega 1969).

The revolt was in large measure a conflict between Indians, mobilized for one side or the other by their kurakas (Vega 1969, 32–33). Partly as a consequence of this, the geographical distribution of the rebellion was highly uneven. In the diocese of Cusco, the provinces in which support was strongest were Canas and Canchis, Quispicanchis, and Chumbivilcas—all predominantly pastoral. Fierce resistance to the rebels was encountered in the agricultural provinces of Urubamba, Calca, and Lares, and especially Paucartambo, where all the maize haciendas around the town were laid waste. In the grisly distribution throughout the region of the dismembered bodies of the executed leaders, the allotment to the village of Paucartambo was probably in the way of a trophy for never having submitted to the rebels. By contrast, the village of Ccatca in the same province stood out as strongly supportive of the rebel cause. The remaining provinces were not seriously affected (Mörner 1978, 109–29).

Here, then, is the local political setting for the events at Sinakara: a wretched local Indian population at the sociogeographic interface of two warring factions, divided among themselves in perhaps the most extreme polarization between the rebel and royalist causes of any locality in the region. And on 23 June 1783—if for the moment the official legend is accepted as testimonially true—just as the last members of this internecine revolt are being stamped out, a party of Ocongate notables descends from Sinakara and announces a miracle: the suffering Christ has appeared before them, on the mountain all Indians consider the most sacred. Instantly there is created a shrine uniquely capable of transcending the divided loyalties of a distressed people and extending its grace to all comers. Conscious strategy on the part of the priest, seeking a spiritual unguent for his troubled flock, perhaps played its part in this scenario, much as Kurtz (1982) has argued for the miracle of the Virgin of Guadalupe in Mexico. At the very least, the documentary sources would seem to indicate that the miracle was based almost entirely on the priest's testimony, backed up by the local worthies.

Yet the miracle evidently satisfied a religious craving among the local Indians—witness their restlessness when the original tayanka cross failed to return from Spain. That it was apparently brought to the notice of Carlos III, who died in 1788, indicates that it was rapidly and widely publicized.

In 1783 Corpus Christi fell on 19 June.[3] The commemorative fiesta of the miracle at Sinakara was therefore tied to a feast which from the earliest years of Spanish colonialism had been a key fixture in Cusco's ceremonial calendar. At first, as I have pointed out, it took the form of an enormous gathering in the city of all the nations of the diocese; already by the seventeenth century it was much less grand, though still an important civic event. Following the cosmic convulsion of 1650, which threatened to reduce the city to rubble, Cusco acquired a new regional focus of devotion, a miraculous civic patron in the shape of a novel advocation of Christ crucified, fêted at Eastertime. Now, following an even greater regional catastrophe, the same advocation became the focus for an alternative Corpus, at a location that was politically and economically marginal but was close to the orographic dead center of the region: the peak of Ausankati.

The latest surge in the fortunes of the cult dates from the retouching of the fading image on the crag at Sinakara in 1935, made possible by a donation from a cloth merchant from Pirque, province of Acomayo. The task was duly accomplished in just one day (Marzal 1971, 244). In 1944, the restored image was blessed by the archbishop of Cusco; indeed, Qoyllur Rit'i was one of the first pilgrimage centers to be consecrated by the prelate following the elevation of Cusco to the status of archdiocese in 1943. Thereafter, the number of pilgrims swelled considerably. The growth in the popularity of the cult, however, clearly owed much to the improvement in communications in the area at that time, the road from Cusco to Ocongate having been completed in 1938.

As the number of pilgrims increased in the years that followed, an organizational hierarchy took shape. In 1948 a group of devotees founded the Asociación del Señor de Tayankani, which set itself the task of keeping order at the fiesta, improving facilities, and promoting the cult. Two years later, the grotto of the Virgin of Fátima was established at Sinakara, just beyond the Qoyllur Rit'i shrine.

In 1960 the group was reorganized as a lay brotherhood, known as La Hermandad del Señor de Qoyllur Rit'i. Significantly, the body now switched its nominal association from the Ocongate crucifix to the Sinakara image. The brotherhood consisted of a president, twenty or so celadores charged with the upkeep and improvement of the shrine and the spiritual welfare of the pilgrims, a group of *socios protectores* 'conservators,' and the local priest as advisor (Ramirez 1969, 86–88). Members of the brotherhood have always been drawn from the larger district and provincial capitals of the region, with strong representation from the village of Urcos in particular.

Meanwhile, the shrine has continued to receive the attentions of Cusco's archbishops, most recently of Monseñor Luis Vallejo Santoni, who attended the titular fiesta in 1980, and of his successor Monseñor Alcides Mendoza Castro, who attended in 1984 and again in 1985. The fiesta is now treated as a convenient occasion for the archdiocesan establishment to acknowledge and connect with popular religiosity in the region, its principal observances during the novena of Corpus neatly dovetailing with the city festival on the feast day itself. But the participation of these eminent devotees provokes ambivalent feelings among the pilgrims, some of whom see them as ill-starred, foreign intruders. During the visit of Monseñor Luis Vallejo, as he was being carried through the shrine precincts on a litter, a huge rock toppled down on a young boy, killing him. The misfortune was attributed directly to the archbishop's presence at the shrine (Valencia Espinoza 1983, 56).

Organization of the Cult

The Qoyllur Rit'i brotherhood exercises its control over the cult in a number of ways. First, it manages the income of the shrine, part of which comes from fund-raising activities such as dinner dances—regularly reported in the society columns of the Cusco press—and part from the donations of pilgrims. In 1969, cash ex-votos during the Corpus fiesta amounted to $1,300 (Marzal 1971, 237); in 1984 the amount collected was $2,300, despite the appalling economic situation in Peru at the time. The money is ostensibly committed to the upkeep of the shrine and to the provision of facilities for visitors. The present sanctuary, erected by the brotherhood during the 1960s, boasts its own electric generator for lighting and for sound amplification. The brotherhood has its own *celda* 'cell' at Sinakara for its members to sleep in. During the late 1970s, in a thoroughly unhygienic attempt to educate the pilgrims in civilized habits, a rudimentary latrine was installed over the stream that runs down from the glaciers. Recently, a plan was broached to build a road to the shrine from Mawallani, but this has been shelved for the time being.

Second, the brotherhood organizes the titular fiesta itself. It arranges for priests to celebrate masses and hear confessions at the sanctuary and meets their fees and expenses. It sets up the rendezvous for the various processions between Mawallani, Sinakara, Tayankani, and Ocongate. It licenses the vendors of drinks and cooked food who set up makeshift *cantinas* 'restaurant tents' at Sinakara for the duration of the fiesta. During the early 1970s there were no more than half a dozen of these, but by 1984 their number had swelled to around forty, run by people from the locality. In addition, the folkloric reputation of Qoyllur Rit'i having become well established in Andeanist circles, the brotherhood usually has to contend with at least one film crew, sometimes Peruvian but more often from North America, Europe, or—with growing frequency—Japan. Indeed, gringos of one kind or another—filmmakers, photographers, anthropologists, and the better-informed backpackers—now constitute a regular and conspicuous presence at the fiesta, prompting the archbishop in 1984 to plead in his sermon that they refrain from interfering in the religious activities and distracting the pilgrims from their devotions.

Third, the celadores of the brotherhood are on hand at most stages of the fiesta and its associated processions to police the congregation and to ensure that matters proceed smoothly and with dignity. They are easily recognizable by their dark lounge suits and the rope whips around their necks, which are far from merely decorative. They tend to be brusque, not to say officious, when dealing with devotees. Throughout the fiesta proper they man the altar continuously, receiving and returning the láminas and demandas of the various naciones, assisting the priests at mass, and administering on request three lashes of the whip—in the names of the three persons of the Trinity—to penitential pilgrims. During the processions of the Blessed Sacrament and the shrine images through the sanctuary precincts, they patrol the crowds, silencing musicians, knocking hats off heads, and forcing people to kneel. Finally, a group of them accompanies the images on the long overnight trek from Sinakara to Tayankani and Ocongate, marshaling the pilgrims and captiously flaunting their authority at every opportunity.

Encased within the rigid hierarchy of a church-sanctioned lay brotherhood, the Qoyllur Rit'i cult nonetheless gives occasion for the most elaborate display of Indian religious devotion of any shrine in the region. Not only do naciones of Quechua-speaking peasants mass in their hundreds for the titular fiesta in a great pageant of Andean ceremonial dance, but the fiesta itself unfolds according to a grand dualistic design, giving expression thereby to a fundamental tenet of native Andean cosmology.

This dualist design casts the entire congeries of pilgrims as two great moieties, labeled "Paucartambo" and "Quispicanchis," respectively. These are the names of the adjacent provinces whose mutual boundary passes through the Sinakara mountain range. In fact, the labels are synechdochic. "Paucartambo" in this context also includes the provinces of Cusco, Calca, Urubamba, and beyond—that is, the predominantly agricultural zone to the northwest of the shrine, the zone stretching toward the trop-ical forest; "Quispicanchis" also includes the provinces of Acomayo, Canas, Canchis, and beyond—that is, the mainly pastoral zone to the southeast of the shrine, the zone stretching toward the tundra. This sociogeographic division is amplified still further to connote the ecological contrasts of valley versus mountain, lowland versus highland, and—polarized to the extreme—jungle versus puna. Ethnically, it comes to stand for the linguistic and cultural divide between Quechua and Qolla (Aymara), which in turn becomes transformed into the critical cleavage of Indian (native) versus mestizo (Spanish).[4]

But in certain of the ritual contexts, the extensive, categorical division is condensed into a polarity between just two villages: Paucartambo, capital of the province of the same name, and Ocongate, in the province of Quispicanchis. Indeed, I shall argue that a ritual fixture that is tech-nically extraneous to the Qoyllur Rit'i ritual cycle but that can be regarded as an appendage to it takes this process of condensation a stage further, compressing the opposition into an internal polarity within a single vil-lage, that of Paucartambo itself.

The Quechua-Qolla opposition is one that receives frequent elabo-ration in the mythology, both of the Cusco region and of the altiplano. The stories typically involve competitive confrontations and affinal al-liances between representatives of the two sociogeographic categories. In a myth from Pinchimuro (Quispicanchis), one of the daughters of Apu Ausankati was betrothed to a Qolla called Mariano Inkilli. The sons of the apu, without informing their father, plotted to ensure that their new brother-in-law would take only the livestock, not the agricultural pro-duce, back to Qollao with him. But at the wedding, Apu Ausankati gave Mariano Inkilli both livestock and maize seed. As Mariano was per-forming t'inkay over them at La Raya, a bird came and stole the maize, letting it drop on the Cusco side of La Raya. From that time on, maize has grown only on this side, while in Qollao there have always been plenty of animals (Valderrama Fernández and Escalante Gutiérrez 1975, 178–180).

In a story from the community of Ch'eqa Pupuja, province of Azán-garo, department of Puno, the protagonists are Inkariy, 'King Inka', and

Qollariy, 'King Qolla'. The two met at La Raya, to decide who would have dominion over whom, and to determine on which side of the watershed maize should grow and on which side wheat. They decided to have a competition: Inkariy must eat a sack of wheat flour, Qollariy a sack of toasted beans. Qollariy seduced Inkariy's daughter, a distraction that contributed to his defeat. Inkariy's victory meant that thenceforth beans and maize would grow only on the Cusco side of La Raya. In another version from the same community, Inkariy violates Qollariy's wife in the snow and makes her bleed. The blood is still issuing from a ditch there (Flores Ochoa 1973, 306–9, 322–23). Four kilometers northwest of La Raya, there are in fact hot springs containing reddish-brown deposits of hematite, natural ferric oxide.[5]

The moiety division in the Qoyllur Rit'i cult between Paucartambo and Quispicanchis recapitulates this macrocosmic, ethnic-ecological dualism, variously expanding and reducing it in the course of the ritual performance. The ritual effects a seamless transition, through the binary logic, through a succession of geographical levels, from the interregional to the intraregional, to the interlocal, to the intralocal, at the same time transforming the relation between the elements from an emergent opposition to a dialectical duality.

It is primarily through the medium of dance and dance styles that this transcendent bipartition and its multiple connotations are signaled. The Qoyllur Rit'i fiesta permits the plethora of Andean ceremonial dance styles to be seen as an open set, making manifest the way in which the intrinsic characteristics and associations of the different styles come to acquire relational meanings when juxtaposed with one another. I shall here describe the five principal ceremonial dance styles on display: ukuku, machula, qhapaq qolla, ch'uncho extranjero, and wayri ch'uncho. Others will be mentioned in passing. All are danced by men, with the occasional exception of a single role in the qhapaq qolla formation.

First, the ukuku, also known as *paulucha* (plate 8). *Ukuku* means 'bear'. The role, seen as demanding energy and strength, should properly be danced by a young unmarried man, well able to withstand the physical—and also the mystical—dangers it entails. The ukuku dancer wears a woollen mask and a long black or brown shaggy smock; he carries a rope whip, a whistle or gourd or some other improvised wind instrument, and a small doll on whose behalf he begs money from strangers. While in costume he speaks in a high falsetto voice and is much given to pranks and japes, gringos being favorite targets. Yet ukukus are powerful: they discharge a peace-keeping role during the pilgrimage and fiesta and in many ways are impervious to the jurisdiction of the celadores. The ukuku is an ambivalent, tricksterlike figure, who both preserves order through his constabulary role and is at liberty to subvert it through his jokes and burlesque.

PLATE 8 *Wayri Ch'uncho and Ukuku Dancers. The performance is being staged in the farmstead of the patrón following a pilgrimage. The ukuku is on the left.*

Whence does the ukuku figure originate? The family Ursidae is represented in the region by one relict species, the spectacled bear, *Tremarctos ornatus,* which inhabits the jungle of the eastern foothills (Gilmore 1963, 376). The entry of the ukuku figure into ritual and myth, however, seems to have been a postcontact development stimulated by the Spanish folktale of Juanito el Oso 'Johnny the Bear' (Allen 1983, 38). Versions of this story are widespread throughout the Andes (Morote Best 1958). They all involve one or more *ukumari,* the wild and uncontrollable offspring of a peasant woman and a bear. A priest frequently features as *padrino* 'godfather' to the ukumari and plots to kill him by pitting him against a condenado who is terrorizing the people. But the ukumari overcomes the condenado and thereby wins him salvation. In some versions the condenado is identified as a hacendado, the ukumari himself becoming the owner of the hacienda. In others, the priest contrives to have him buried alive.[6]

The ukuku dancers at Qoyllur Rit'i are likewise intimately associated with condenados. It is widely believed that the glaciers in the vicinity of Mount Ausankati are infested with condenados, for by climbing the mountain, naked and in chains, to reach the silver cross near the summit, they can obtain forgiveness from the apu and release from their tortured state of living death. But they invariably fail to reach their goal, slipping backward on the snow and ice. Some also seek forgiveness from the taytacha at Sinakara, but he forbids them to enter the sanctuary, and they are obliged to worship him from the glacier (cf. Casaverde Rojas 1970, 206). The ukukus at Qoyllur Rit'i are in one sense the protectors of their fellow pilgrims against the dangerous condenados, but they also directly enact the penance of the condenados and are sometimes said to be condenados themselves.[7]

Second, there are the machula dancers. The machula is a ridiculous old man. He sports a grotesque mask, often with a long nose and white beard, a humpback, and a long coat, and he hobbles about with the aid of a stick. He is manifestly a figure of fun, but he too exercises a constabulary role at the fiesta, a function more evident in the past when dancers in this style were more numerous (cf. Ramirez 1969, 86; D. Gow 1974, 79).

As mentioned earlier, the ñaupa machus are believed to have been the first race of people in the Andes, the ancestors of the present inhabitants, who lived in the high puna. When the sun rose, they either fled to the jungle or were shriveled up in the heat. They can bring harm to the living in the guise of the soq'a machu, but they also bring fertility and are talked of with affection. The machula dancer embodies the harmless, comical aspect of the machu figure, but like the ukuku he is ambivalent, for he too can be a defender of order and sobriety.

Just as condenados and machus both occupy liminal positions in relation to kaypacha, so also do the ukuku and machula dancers who represent them. They are both preterhuman beings on the margins of sociogeographic space. The ukukus, the wild bears of the jungle, become the malevolent spirits of the restless dead roaming the glaciers. The machulas are the distant ancestors who dwelt in the puna but fled to the montaña. Furthermore, the dancers are also marginal in relation to their fellow pilgrims. At the level of the nación, neither ukukus nor machulas constitute dance groups in themselves. Instead they are adjuncts to a formation of some other dance style, lacking musicians or choreographies of their own. Thus a troupe might consist of as many as a dozen dancers in the principal style, together with one or two ukukus and a machula; in the dance routines the ukukus and the machula might participate formally, but they would be just as likely to engage in foolery among themselves, or they might taunt, mimic, or beat the other dancers. A few naciones do have larger contingents of these clowns, organized beneath the authority of a capitán for ukukus or a *caporal* 'corporal' for machulas, but these are the exceptions. At the shrine, however, both ukukus—and in the past machulas—are the only dancers to leave their naciones and to coalesce into wider, stylistically homogeneous groups. Thus, while they are for the most part peripheral to the dance troupes of their own naciones, they unite at the shrine, where the massed ukukus at least play a central role.

Until 1978, the Qoyllur Rit'i ukukus were organized into the two moiety groupings of Paucartambo and Quispicanchis. These were not merely ad hoc coalitions but were formally constituted bodies, having their own hierarchies of presidents, secretaries, and treasurers based on the provincial capitals of Paucartambo and Urcos, respectively. In 1979 a splinter group from Acomayo province broke away from the Quispicanchis grouping (Randall 1982a, 38) but seems not to have survived as an independent entity. There has since been another secession from the Quispicanchis moiety, by ukukus from the province of Canchis. The latter faction has been institutionalized, with its center in Sicuani, the capital of Canchis. There are therefore now three ukuku bodies: Paucartambo, Quispicanchis, and Canchis. The larger nación contingents of ukukus tend to come from the three provincial capitals of Paucartambo, Urcos, and Sicuani, respectively.

Third, there are the qhapaq qollas. *Qhapaq* here means 'rich', 'noble'; *Qolla* is the word applied to the inhabitants of the altiplano to the southeast, whose livelihood is seen by the Quechua as revolving around herding, commerce, and medicine. In the past, Qolla traders were frequent visitors to the villages and towns of the Cusco region, and the qhapaq qollas are a mimetic portrayal of these traders.

The qhapaq qolla costume includes a white woollen mask; a flat embroidered hat decorated with beads, spangles, and gold coins and having short trailing ribbons on either side; a woollen *llijlla;* a vicuña or alpaca skin slung across the shoulders; and a rope sling. The head of a troupe is known as the capitán; the style might also include a female role, the *imilla* (Aymara) 'woman', which may be danced either by a woman or by a man in drag. Qolla music is generally played on a kina, harp or violin, accordion, and drums. There are several musical variants, but the one most often heard at Qoyllur Rit'i is set out in appendix 4, example 1. It is in simple time and uses a pentatonic scale, though there are other qolla tunes in the diatonic. The accompanying choreography is energetic, but nevertheless has a graceful, courtly air. Many villages from both moieties send qhapaq qolla dancers, but it is the qhapaq qolla troupe from Ocongate village, capital of the moiety, who are the principal representatives of the Quispicanchis moiety and who play an important ritual role in the titular fiesta.[8]

Finally, two styles of ch'uncho dancers are on display at Qoyllur Rit'i. *Ch'uncho* is a derogatory term in both Quechua and Aymara for the tribal inhabitants, said to be uncivilized, of the lowland jungle to the north. Dances incorporating the savage motif became fashionable during the last decades of the Inka empire, as the colonization of the montaña was intensified (L. Valcárcel 1951, 19). The style was rapidly incorporated into Christian ritual. One of Poma de Ayala's illustrations ([1620] 1966, 3:41) shows two sons of an Indian chief, masked and sporting feathered ch'uncho headdresses, dancing in front of the Eucharist displayed on an altar. The style is now widely diffused throughout the central and southern Andes. On the altiplano it is encountered in the villages of the provinces of Sandia and Carabaya—that is, those on the northeastern side of the watershed (Portugal Catacora 1981, 93). It also features in the devotional dances at the sanctuary of the Virgin of Mount Carmel at Tirana in Tarapacá province, northern Chile (Kessel 1981, 158ff.; see also Kessel 1980).

Today in the Cusco region, ch'uncho dancers, representing as they do the inhabitants of the jungle into which the ñaupa machus fled to escape the heat of the sun, are associated with the ancestral forebears of present-day highlanders, especially of the agriculturalists on the eastern Andean slopes. There are now several distinct ch'uncho dance styles, some of them explicitly associated with particular highland villages or areas, though they have been adopted by naciones elsewhere. The two that concern us here are ch'uncho extranjero and wayri ch'uncho.[9]

The style of ch'uncho extranjero—literally, 'foreign savage' (extranjero 'strange, foreign, alien')—is associated with the village of Paucartambo. Its costume includes a headdress of pink heron feathers with a long decorated plait, a gauze mask, a brightly colored skirt with matching sashes across the shoulders, and a staff of chonta wood.[10] The leader of a troupe, the rey 'king' has a crown and a long cape.

The costume of the wayri ch'unchos is subtly contrasted (plate 8). They wear a headdress and plait of orange and red macaw feathers, a brightly colored waistcoat, and black trousers with rayon scarves trailing from the waistband, and they also carry chonta staves. They are not masked, though they may choose to wear dark glasses. Their leader is known as the arariwa, the Quechua word for field guardian or work organizer. Wayri is not in fact a Quechua word at all, but means 'chief' in the language of the tribal Machiguenga to the northwest (Camino 1978, 92).[11] Thus, while both ch'uncho styles are mimetic portrayals of jungle Indians, they are contrasted to each other as "native chiefs" to "aliens," as indigenous savages to foreign savages.

The two ch'uncho styles share a "traditional" instrumentation of two pitos, tambour, and bass drum. Ch'uncho extranjero troupes, however, frequently employ the more Hispanic instrumentation of violin, harp, and accordion, or—a mark of real modernity—a brass band. The choreographies of both styles are gymnastic and warlike, with pairs of dancers clashing their staves against each other. Many of the formations exhibit the basic Andean designs of diametric and concentric dualism (see appendix 6). Ch'unchos extranjeros have a fairly wide musical and choreographic repertoire (cf Roel Pineda 1950). The tune favored at Qoyllur Rit'i is set out in appendix 4, example 2; it is in the pentatonic, though there are others in the diatonic, and is played at a brisk tempo.

The wayri ch'unchos, however, use just one tune, which is set out in example 3. It too is in the pentatonic, but alone of the examples considered here it is in compound time. Played as it is with a pounding drumbeat, it is this distinctive rhythm that sets the music obviously apart from most of the other music at the fiesta. Indeed, this tune is in many ways the leitmotif of the entire pilgrimage. When dance troupes of what-ever style dance from point to point, rather than perform in an arena, their musicians frequently adopt this piece and the dancers imitate the basic wayri ch'uncho step.

As far as ritual duties are concerned, the principal dance troupe of the Paucartambo moiety is the team of wayri ch'unchos from Paucar-tambo village, though there are ch'unchos extranjeros and qhapaq qollas from the village as well. Ocongate, too, has a troupe of wayri ch'unchos, who also have a particular role to play in the ritual performance alongside the village's principal dance troupe of qhapaq qollas.

Some dance styles have come to acquire an association with one or another of the two pervasive ethnic categories of Andean society, mestizo or misti and Indian or runa. The qhapaq qolla style is regarded as having a distinctly misti connotation, one that it shares with certain other styles on view at Qoyllur Rit'i—the *chilenos* from the village of Urcos, for instance, who represent the invading Chilean soldiers in the nineteenth-century War of the Pacific, and the *tontunas* from Juliaca in the depart-ment of Puno to the southeast, a thoroughly criollo formation that has recently made its appearance at the fiesta. Against these misti dance styles, the ch'uncho forms are associated with Indian ethnic status.

There is perhaps a dimension here of newcomers or outsiders versus natives or autochthons. Misti styles commonly represent either foreigners who have trespassed into the Cusco region for one reason or another—Qolla traders, Chilean soldiers—or are clearly Hispanic in inspiration, as are the Juliaca tontunas. Ch'uncho dancers, on the other hand, tend to be identified with the native Quechua highlanders.

Yet ch'uncho styles, in their turn, are differentiated among them-selves along ethnic lines. That of ch'uncho extranjero connotes misti status when counterposed to that of wayri ch'uncho, which is associated with an unqualified Indian ethnic identity. This contrast, too, fits the newcomer-native dichotomy. I should stress that I am here talking of associations with ethnic categories rather than monopolization by ethnic groups, however the latter might be defined. It is relevant to note that the styles of ukuku and machula to a large extent stand outside this pattern of ethnic discriminations, apparently immune to either Indian or mestizo stereotyping.

Finally, mention should be made of those pilgrims who are outside the formal cultural and social organization of the cult altogether. These are the devotees who attend, not as dancers, not even as members of naciones, but privately, in small groups of kin, neighbors, or friends, or alone. Such unattached devotees tend to be drawn from the ranks of the so-called clase media—merchants and commercial farmers in the countryside and teachers, clerks, and service workers in the towns. Between 1973 and 1984 there was a marked increase in the number of these private pilgrims. There was evidence, too, of a pattern of staggered attendance developing. In 1984, several busloads of them visited Sinakara just off peak, over the weekend before Corpus, thus avoiding the later influx of naciones on the Sunday evening and Monday. Given the intense pressure on space and facilities at the shrine, the self-segregation of unattached devotees from the nación pilgrimage proper might be expected to become even sharper in the future.

The Ritual Cycle

The titular fiesta of Señor de Qoyllur Rit'i unfolds during the three-week period between the movable feasts of the Ascension and Corpus Christi (see appendix 5). It is a complex affair, involving several sites that are united into a single ritual system through a combination of mass pilgrimage and organized processions. The most important site, of course, is the Sinakara combe containing the main sanctuary and the Virgin's grotto, the entrance to which is marked by three crosses—the third surmounting an apachita—and which is backed by the towering glaciers of Mount Sinakara (plates 7 and 9). The others are the chapel of Señor de Tayankani in the hamlet of the same name, the parish church of Ocongate, and finally the chapel at Mawallani, the home of the seer Mariano Mayta and today the point of disembarcation for the truckloads of pilgrims who visit the shrine during the fiesta season (see appendix 1, map 10).

Two levels of ritual activity can be distinguished. There is, first, the pilgrimage itself, the convergence of human traffic on the miraculous crag at Sinakara. The majority of pilgrims arrive during the weekend preceding Corpus, most, though not all, in community-based nación groups. I have already followed such a group on their journey to the shrine and back. This devotional style is not unique to Qoyllur Rit'i, but is characteristic of the fiestas of some other regional shrines and of all interlocal ones. The Sinakara gathering, however, is undoubtedly the largest of its kind.

What gives the Qoyllur Rit'i fiesta its distinctiveness is the second level of ritual activity: a complex sequence of rites, processions and minipilgrimages focused on the Sinakara shrine and embracing all its associated sacred sites and religious images. This second set of ritual activities is superimposed on the first, though by no means all the visiting pilgrims participate in it in its entirety. Some naciones—that of Qamawara for one—shun it altogether.[12] It is also disdained by most private pilgrims, those who attend not as members of nación groups but on their own behalves. One of the questions that must be posed, then, alongside those

PLATE 9 *Qoyllur Rit'i: Ukukus on the Glacier. A group from the Quispicanchis moiety retrieving their cross. One ukuku has a block of ice strapped to his back.*

that address the significance of the actual events, is, Why do some people who visit the shrine choose not to participate in them at all?

For the earlier stages of the ritual sequence, I have relied chiefly on the account of Ramirez (1969, 69–70). It begins on the feast of the Ascension, with two parallel processions that serve to stake out the cardinal points of the local religious landscape for the activities in the weeks to come. First, the crucifix of Señor de Tayankani is removed from the side altar of Ocongate parish church and is carried in procession to its eponymous chapel ten kilometers away, accompanied by a group of villagers and their political authorities (appendix 1, map 10, procession 1). Having installed the image in its chapel, the group returns to Ocongate.

In the afternoon of the same day, another group of devotees carries the statue of Señor de Qoyllur Rit'i from the chapel at Mawallani, where it normally resides, to the sanctuary at Sinakara, where vigil is kept before the shrine (procession 2). Most of those in this second procession are peasants, and the group includes a band of flutists and drummers who play through the night.

Two weeks later, on the Wednesday after Pentecost, a third procession, organized by devotees from the village of Urcos, leaves the Sinakara sanctuary with the statue of the Virgin of Fátima. Reciting the rosary, they walk up to the grotto above the sanctuary and install the statue in her niche (procession 3).

For the central phases of the ritual cycle, I have drawn on my own observation of the fiesta in 1984.

By Trinity Sunday, about 15,000 pilgrims had gathered at Sinakara. In the evening, there was the customary procession of the Blessed Sacrament through the shrine precincts. The following morning, with a priest from Urcos officiating, there was an open-air mass, the traditional requiem for the souls of all deceased celadores and benefactors to the shrine.

Most ukukus now segregated themselves from the rest of the congregation and gathered on the hillside opposite the sanctuary. They divided into assemblies based on their three groupings—Paucartambo, Quispicanchis, and Canchis—and each laid its own plans for the visit to the glaciers that night.

Later in the day, a detailed recitation over the public address system of the official foundation myth announced the main procession of Señor de Qoyllur Rit'i (procession 4). The procession departed from the sanctuary and made its way slowly to the Virgin's grotto, whence it descended in a wide arc to the cairn cross before returning to the balcony of the sanctuary. It was formed of two parallel lines of walking dancers, with all the ukukus grouped toward the front, followed by a random mix of other styles, each dancer holding the whip, staff, or scarf of the one behind. Toward the end of the procession, between the two lines, was the captain of the Ocongate qhapaq qollas, followed by two celadores, who were followed in turn by the archbishop, flanked by his auxiliary and the officiating priest. Behind him came the statue of Señor de Qoyllur Rit'i, enclosed in a glass-fronted cruciform wooden case surmounted by three sprays of wayri ch'uncho headdress feathers—a clear sign that this was an Indian Christ, a Christ of the peasants.

The procession halted at the grotto, and the archbishop gave an address in Quechua, urging people to maintain their devotion to the Señor and affirming that he would indeed grant them whatever favor they asked. On returning to the sanctuary the archbishop celebrated benediction, after which there was another sermon, by the auxiliary bishop. Both prelates then knelt before the image of the Señor, and the archbishop blessed it. Finally, the crucifix gave three venias to the congregation before being backed into the sanctuary.

The special function discharged in this procession by the qolla captain of Ocongate stems from the status of the village as the "capital" of the Quispicanchis moiety. Ocongate in fact regularly sent three dance troupes to the fiesta: qhapaq qollas, *contradanzas* 'country dance', and wayri ch'unchos. The qollas were the village's chief dancer delegates. The qolla and contradanza troupes were composed of Spanish speakers in wage employment, who as individuals projected an obviously mestizo status. It was noticeable, however, that during the fiesta they frequently chose to speak Quechua to one another, especially in their joking and banter, and in various other ways collectively affected an Indian identity. The wayri ch'unchos, on the other hand, were Quechua-speaking peasants from the village and its environs. While the qollas and contradanzas traveled together as the nación of Ocongate, and by 1984 had built adjacent celdas for themselves at Sinakara—one of the few naciones to enjoy such facilities—the tiny band of wayri ch'unchos kept themselves apart from their fellow villagers throughout the fiesta. There was practically no interaction between the two contingents.[13]

That night, the fiesta reached its climax. The sanctuary was filled to capacity with pilgrims. One dance troupe after another came to take leave of the taytacha, dancing before the altar as best they could in the crush, while the celadores and some ukukus endeavored to maintain order.

In the early hours of the morning, the ukukus started to call to one another by blowing on their whistles and gourds. Gathering in their groups, they began to ascend the steep hogbacks to the glaciers. Four separate snowfields overhang the Sinakara valley. Formerly, only the two central ones were occupied by ukukus, the one on the left by those from the Paucartambo moiety and the one on the right by those from Quispicanchis, but since 1980 the Canchis group has taken over one of the vacant glaciers.

Each group followed a separate route to its snowfield. As they stepped off the moraine onto the glacier, the ukukus linked themselves into long chains with their whips to prevent their slipping backward on the treacherous, icy slopes. By dawn there were about a thousand of them, possibly more, dotted across the three great tongues of snow that swept down from the mountain peaks. Some were kneeling singly or in groups of two or three, facing the summit, lighted candles planted before them in the snow, their lips moving in silent prayer. Others engaged in horseplay, throwing snowballs at one another and sliding down snow chutes with yells and shouts. Where a single nación included several ukukus, as, for example, did that from Urcos, they tended to gather in nación groups with other, uncostumed companions who had come up with them, displaying the banner of their community or village. Among such groups an ukuku visiting the glacier for the first time was obliged to receive a *bautismo* 'baptism' in the form of three strokes of the whip on the rump administered by the ukuku captain of his nación. An ukuku who had "sinned" received similar treatment. After such a whipping, the victim kissed the whip and embraced the whipper.

Originally, the ostensible purpose of the ukukus' ascent to the glacier was to reclaim a cross that had been planted there a few days before. For this, the two ukuku armies of Paucartambo and Quispicanchis would engage in a battle, pelting each other with snowballs in the darkness. Machula dancers from each moiety would assist the ukukus in this confrontation. The victors would then bear the cross in triumph back to the sanctuary (Ramirez 1969, 86).

Although deaths were not actively sought in this encounter, it was nevertheless apparently not uncommon for ukukus to be killed by falling into crevasses as they chased each other across the glacier. Nowadays there is no battle. Instead, each group—including, since 1980, that from Canchis—has its own cross erected beforehand on its particular section of the glacier, which it merely retrieves and returns to the sanctuary (plate 9).

In preparation for the descent, ukukus set about carving out chunks of ice from the glacier, sawing away laboriously with their rope whips; a few had brought picks for the purpose. The blocks of ice were then tied to their backs with their whips and carried down to the sanctuary as a penance. Many were simply dumped, but some people collected their meltwater in bottles and conserved it for medicinal use. A few ukukus even tied little blocks of ice to their dolls.

Around 8:00 A.M. the ukuku bands came down from the glaciers in formation, each with its cross, banner, and Peruvian flag proudly held aloft (procession 5). Several dance groups were waiting just above the Virgin's grotto and each fell in with its ukuku band as it passed. Each procession marched through the pilgrims' encampment to the cairn cross, then returned to the sanctuary to deposit its cross. The ukukus and dancers then dispersed to their local nación groups.[14]

A final mass was celebrated on the balcony by the officiating priest from Urcos. As soon as it was over, there was an exodus. The majority of pilgrims began to stream down the path toward Mawallani, whence they would board trucks for home. A substantial contingent, however—more than a thousand—set off up the trail on the opposite side of the valley. This was the beginning of the minipilgrimage to Tayankani and thence to Ocongate, a twenty-five-kilometer trek across the hills retracing the steps of Mariano and Manuel in the legend of the founding of the shrine (processions 6 and 8).

On this pilgrimage within a pilgrimage, besides the many láminas and demandas of the various naciones taking part, there were two images to which the entire company served as a collective escort. One was the portable statue of Señor de Qoyllur Rit'i, enclosed within its wooden case decorated with the macaw feathers of the wayri ch'unchos. The other was the Virgen Dolorosa, the 'Virgin of Sorrows', which had been donated some years earlier by a pious devotee from Ocongate. The Virgin would be taken all the way to Ocongate. The crucifix, though, would be exchanged at Tayankani for another, that of Señor de Tayankani, which would proceed to Ocongate, while Señor de Qoyllur Rit'i would be escorted back across the hills to Mawallani.

For this central, collective pilgrimage of the shrine statues themselves across their sacred territory, the ritual escort at once coalesced and divided along moiety lines into two great regional naciones. It is a convention strictly observed on this march that the task of carrying the images alternates between the Paucartambo and Quispicanchis group for successive sections of the journey, and within each group between its constituent local naciones. Ritual labor is also divided by sex: men carry the Señor, women the Virgin.

The trail reached the rim of the valley at a place called Machu Cruz. Here there was a small shrine-shelter, and the Qoyllur Rit'i crucifix and the Virgin were placed inside, along with the láminas and demandas of the various local naciones. The ragged column of pilgrims now grouped themselves into their local naciones, and apart from the ceremonial descents at Yanakancha and Tayankani were to remain thus for the entire pilgrimage.

The president of the brotherhood then began to address the assembly, in a manner that set the tone for these ritual stops for the rest of the journey. After introducing himself, he immediately launched into an ill-tempered harangue, castigating first of all the Paucartambo group, who had been responsible for carrying the images on this initial leg of the journey, for their late arrival at the spot. The person who bore the brunt of this rebuke was the arariwa of the wayri ch'uncho dancers from Paucartambo village, for it was his duty to lead the principal images and to arrange the succession of their bearers on the Paucartambo sections of the procession. He was dragged forward and stood in silence with his head bowed while the president continued his tirade. A few of the onlookers demanded that the arariwa be whipped there and then for his dereliction, but the president demurred, saying he did not want to commit an abuse. He then turned his attention to the musicians, or rather to those of them who had arrived inebriated, and chided them for their disrespect.

This outburst was delivered in Spanish. When he had finished, the president, who was bilingual, asked his audience disdainfully whether they had understood, for the Quechua monolinguals among them obviously had not. The intention seems to have been deliberately to humiliate the monolingual members of the congregation. Two of his colleagues then repeated the general message concerning punctuality and discipline in Quechua, in more moderate tones. Referring to alcohol, one of them pointed out that it was permissible to drink a little, to combat the cold, but that drunkenness would not be tolerated.

For the next section of the journey, it was the turn of the Quispicanchis group to carry the principal images. Now that the moiety and its constituent naciones had been consolidated, matters proceeded in a better organized fashion. The aim was to allow everyone in each nación to carry one of the images for a short distance, men the crucifix and women the Virgin. Men far outnumbered women, so the crucifix changed hands more frequently—every dozen paces or so. In order to facilitate smooth transfers from one bearer to the next, the members of the different naciones went ahead and spaced themselves along the path; when the crucifix arrived each would carry it on his back, holding it in place by means of a rope, until he came to the next volunteer.

The successive bearers were referred to by their naciones. First came the nacion of the district capital of Ocongate, "capital" of the moiety, followed by that from the provincial capital of Urcos. Naciones from other district capitals and hinterland communities, including Lucre, Huaro, Surimana, and Ccapana, fell in behind.

It was for supervision of the intermittent passage of the crucifix that the Ocongate wayri ch'unchos, or at least the arariwa, took charge. He walked immediately before the image and directed its loading and unloading in a confident, almost imperious manner, frequently issuing peremptory orders to the volunteers at the side of the path to position themselves still farther ahead. He wore his dance costume, minus the headdress; all the other dancers except the ukukus were in mufti. Immediately behind the crucifix the musicians were playing the wayri ch'uncho tune continuously, and those pilgrims waiting to assume the holy burden did not stand still but performed a vestigial dance on the spot, executing rhythmic ch'uncho foot movements in time to the music. The entire journey, then, like the nación pilgrimage on which it was modeled, was in effect a dance.

This dancelike character of the march became explicit on two occasions. The first was the descent into the broad valley of Yanakancha, the site of the next ritual halt. Here, dancers donned their costumes and formed into three groups. On the left were the ukukus and other dancers from the Paucartambo moiety, on the right the same from the Quispicanchis moiety, and in the center, women crossbearers from both. The three groups ran down the slope in parallel lines with Christ and the Virgin following, the Virgin now being carried by a man, and the images were installed in the chapel of the little hamlet.

People now segregated themselves into their nación groups to eat and rest, each occupying a customary location on the pampa. Naciones continued to arrive for several hours, dancing before the chapel before depositing their demandas. All the while, fireworks exploded into the sky.

The pilgrimage did not officially resume until the moon had risen. The Quispicanchis moiety departed early, however, at about 11:00 P.M., so as to arrive at Markoskunka, the next stopping place, well ahead of Paucartambo, whose turn it now was to carry the principal images. The members of the Paucartambo moiety shared their sacred burdens exactly as had those of Quispicanchis, the arariwa of the wayri ch'unchos of Paucartambo village supervising. The president of the brotherhood always stayed with the crucifix but took no direct part in arrangements for its conveyance.

At Markoskunka, as the images were being installed in the shrine-shelter for the halt, there was another vigorous remonstrance. This time, the president accused the arariwa of another troupe of wayri ch'unchos of not showing proper respect for the group's lámina during its formal placing in the shelter. On this occasion, though, the president's strictures met with defiant rejoinders not just from the arariwa but from other members of the nación. All to no avail: the president insisted he must be whipped. The punishment was administered, not by the president, but by one of his colleagues from the brotherhood. The victim received the usual three strokes, afterward kissing the whip and embracing his scourger. The episode was greeted with schadenfreude, members of other naciones evidently relishing the fact that someone had been arraigned and punished.

The Quispicanchis moiety resumed responsibility for the images for the next leg of the journey to the shrine-shelter at Wak'a Ocongate, arriving at about 4:00 A.M. From here Paucartambo carried them to the shrine-shelter at Araskancha, where there was a final changeover.

As the sky was beginning to lighten with the gathering dawn, the company arrived at a narrow plateau, Tabla-Cruz. One ridge commanded an extensive view of the eastern horizon. From the other, the ground swept down toward the hamlet of Tayankani, nestling in the valley far below. Here was to take place the *inti alabado*, the hymn of praise to the sun.

The group broke up into naciones, and dancers changed into costume. They then formed a single line strung out across the eastern ridge facing the direction of the rising sun, Paucartambo to the left and Quispicanchis to the right. The leader of each troupe inspected his dancers to ensure that they were properly positioned. The celadores who were accompanying the pilgrimage, joined by several others who had come up from Tayankani, stood in a line in front. The principal images, meanwhile, had been dumped unceremoniously on the ground, rather than installed in a shrine-shelter as they had been at every other ritual halt. The focus of attention now was not the images, but the sun.

For some minutes, the dancers hopped from one foot to the other in time to the various bands. Seconds before the sun rose, the musicians fell silent and everyone knelt. As it came up they all scrambled to their feet and gave an exultant cry of ¡Alabado!, "Hail!"

Various formalities followed. First, there were the ritual whippings. Most were bautismos, administered by the leader of a dance troupe to those dancers who were serving for the first time and confined to the Paucartambo moiety. All this was treated as good sport, and an excited crowd pressed close to watch. At one point, the president intervened and drew aside the rey of a troupe of ch'uncho extranjero dancers who had just finished enthusiastically initiating his neophytes. After the two had conferred briefly, the president announced that the rey had admitted a delict—he did not specify what—and would have to be disciplined. Begging the crowd to excuse him, he then proceeded to administer the flogging himself. While all this was going on, the officiating priest from Urcos, who was accompanying the procession, looked on inscrutably.

Next came the formal *abrazos* 'embraces'. First, all the celadores and the priest embraced one another. Then they all stood in a line while the dancers filed past, embracing each person in turn. This was all done quickly and cursorily, for the dancers were impatient to be off.

The abrazos over, all ran across to the opposite ridge, where they reformed into moiety lines. First, they faced the sun, kneeling in silence for a few seconds. Then they stood, turned round, and knelt facing the escarpment. Suddenly they arose as a single body and proceeded to filter down the hillside at a trot in two columns, led respectively by the ukukus of each moiety with Peruvian flags streaming in the wind. All the musicians were playing the same tune, the alabado, with an obvious attempt at synchronization. The two lines of dancers wheeled, wove, and zigzagged across the landscape, successively converging, crossing, and separating in a serpentine choreography that was entirely symmetrical across a vertical axis. This was the climax of the procession. For the participants, it must have been a brief experience of submersion in a vast, coordinated, moving design, one that transcended the boundaries of naciones and linked the two moieties together in perfectly symmetrical complementarity. For the observer, it was a stunning, unforgettable spectacle.

The two principal images joined the ends of the lines and wound up in a small whitewashed chapel on a hillock overlooking Tayankani. Within minutes, the fleeting, Terpsichorean unity had given way to exclusiveness and localism, as naciones reformed into separate groups, dotted about the hillside, to take breakfast.

The actual entry into Tayankani later in the morning was much less dramatic: a conventional procession of two lines of dancers, with the principal images in their midst. The little hamlet was a flurry of activity, with dozens of vendors of food and drink all ready to cater to the hungry pilgrims. At the chapel, the image of Señor de Tayankani had been set up on a table in the atrium. When the traveling icons arrived they were taken inside, and mass was celebrated. Later that day, a small escort bore the image of Señor de Qoyllur Rit'i across the hills to the chapel at Mawallani (procession 7).

For the final stage of the main pilgrimage to Ocongate, Señor de Tayankani, unboxed, was carried to a small chapel on the outskirts of the hamlet. Here, it was carefully placed inside its case. The celador who had until then had custody of the image formally handed it over to the president with an affected tearfulness. For his part, the president took the opportunity of delivering another harangue, directed this time at the arariwa of the wayri ch'unchos of Paucartambo, who was alleged to have committed another ritual infraction.

The walk to Ocongate involved a punishing climb to the summit chapel of Calvario, followed by an equally punishing descent to the Mapacho valley. The images of Christ and the Virgin again passed from bearer to bearer, though there seemed to be no rigid demarcation now between the moieties. Just outside Ocongate the procession was met by the village alcalde, who took Señor de Tayankani onto his shoulders and carried it the last few hundred meters to the chapel of San Antonio on the edge of the village.

The images were given new clothes and mounted on litters, each with an *achiwa*, a parasol of feathers, in the style of the Inka kings. Later in the afternoon they were carried to the central plaza, Señor de Tayankani by four dancers from Ocongate—two qhapaq qollas and two contradanzas—and the Virgin by four women from Paucartambo. Each image was made to execute three venias to the crowd, before being taken inside the church.

The plaza was bustling, with stalls selling clothes and trinkets set up alongside the cantinas. For the rest of the day, one dance troupe after another performed outside the church, surrounded by spectators. Some members of the audience held up cassette machines to record the music of the various bands. My impression was that the religious aspect of the dancing had now largely given way to its entertainment value; the religious piety that had pervaded the activities at Sinakara had all but dissipated.

The following day was Thursday, Corpus Christi. Señor de Tayankani having been inducted back into the village, activities in Ocongate now took on a more local, civic aspect. In the morning, mass was followed by a procession of the Blessed Sacrament, with the three village dance groups—qhapaq qollas, contradanzas, and wayri ch'unchos—in attendance. Afterward the dancers retired for private celebrations, returning later to perform once more in the plaza.

In the afternoon of Corpus Christi, there is supposed to take place in the plaza a mock battle between the qhapaq qollas of Ocongate and the wayri ch'unchos of Paucartambo. This piece of comic theater is eagerly anticipated by the spectators. Unfortunately, in 1984, because of a dispute among the dance groups, it was not staged. I therefore rely on the account of Ramirez from the 1960s.

The qollas, grouped into one corner of the plaza, come under attack from the ch'unchos. They consult coca leaves to divine who will win the fight and invoke Ausankati and the other apus to turn back the ch'unchos' arrows. But eventually one of the ch'unchos breaks through and slaughters the bodyguard of the imilla, the qolla woman. When the ch'unchos have left with their prize, the qollas return to collect their dead. The bodyguard is carried in the cortège by a group of ukukus. Suddenly, from one corner of the plaza emerges a group of *k'achampa* dancers from the village, driving mules laden with gifts for the festive farewells; at the same time the qollas enter from the opposite side, with loaded llamas.[15] The two groups then invite the village authorities to celebrate the conclusion of the fight. The result of the battle does not vary from year to year: the qollas are always defeated (Ramirez 1969, 80–82; see also D. Gow 1976; 232–33).[16]

The Corpus fiesta in Ocongate continues on Friday with a procession of Señor de Tayankani around the plaza (procession 9). It concludes on the Saturday, when Señor de Tayankani, carried now by the Paucartambo wayri ch'unchos, and the Virgin, carried by Paucartambo women, are taken to the edge of the village toward Paucartambo. Here the taytacha bestows its blessing on the distant population of Paucartambo. The two images are then returned to the church (procession 10).

So ends the extended ceremonial cycle of the titular fiesta of Señor de Qoyllur Rit'i. There are two other ritual fixtures later in the year, however, that should be mentioned here. One is the festival of the patron saint of Paucartambo, the Virgin of Mount Carmel, on 16 July, an event which in some ways serves as a coda to the Corpus cycle at Sinakara and Ocongate.

There are various versions of the legend of the Paucartambo Virgin. In one account she was originally the patroness of the chapel at Asunción, some distance from Paucartambo, where she was taken every year at Corpus Christi in common with the other saints of the locality. In an uprising of wild jungle Indians (ch'unchos), the extensive haciendas in the area were destroyed, the resident Spaniards killed, and the chapel at Asunción burned. The wooden statue of the Virgin was thrown into the river but was beached on an island, where it was later discovered. The river was named Madre de Dios, 'Mother of God', and has given its name to the jungle department through which it flows. The statue was taken to Paucartambo; it still bears the marks of the ch'unchos' arrows in the eye and breast (Roel Pineda 1950, 61). In another version, the statue was being brought to Paucartambo for Corpus Christi by Qollas from the altiplano when they were attacked by ch'unchos and the Virgin was cast into the river. Despite this, the Virgin prefers the ch'uncho dancers to all others; if they did not attend her fiesta, her face would turn pale, signifying imminent disaster (Barrionuevo 1969, 276).

The village of Paucartambo does traditionally hold the parade of the saints from its local hinterland communities at Corpus, as these legends indicate. The Virgen de Carmen, as a quasi-miraculous image, has its fiesta apart from this locality festival. Like the festivities surrounding Señor de Tayankani at Ocongate, however, the Carmen fiesta has little of the atmosphere of a pilgrimage but is very much a civic occasion, participation in which reflects the social stratification of the village. Traditionally, there were three tables at the banquet: one for whites—*decentes* 'respectable ones', one for mestizos, and one for Indians (cf. Navarro del Aguila 1944, 52, 79). Today, it is also an important tourist attraction.

There are many different dance styles on display at the fiesta, prominent among them being the *negrillos* 'young blacks', a memorialization of the African slaves who once labored in the plantations of the area. Of interest here is that the fiesta includes as a central event a ritual battle between qhapaq qollas and ch'unchos—on this occasion ch'unchos extranjeros. Both dance troupes are drawn from the village itself. The battle follows the same pattern as that enacted at Ocongate: the ch'unchos again emerge victorious (Roel Pineda 1950, 63–64; Barrionuevo 1969, 276).

The other event that must be mentioned here is the fiesta at the Sinakara sanctuary on 14 September, the feast of the Exaltation of the Cross. This affair is in sharp contrast to the regional pilgrimage that precedes Corpus. It is attended almost exclusively by dancers and devotees from Ocongate, along with members of the Qoyllur Rit'i brotherhood. The miraculous taytacha of the crag, fêted by all and sundry a few months before, is now reclaimed by the villagers: the regional shrine is ritually reinserted into the local domain.

Dualism and Hierarchy

Around the petrified Christ of Sinakara has grown up a thicket of cultural uses, organizational controls, and social conventions. What registers first is the sheer, exuberant nativism of the cult. In it, through the media of music and dance, traditional Indian culture seems to achieve its apotheosis. It is this exotic character of the annual festival, staged in such an isolated, awesome setting, that seems to make it such an authentic cultural spectacle.

The seductive artistry of the fiesta does indeed dramatize an endemic theme of Andean culture. The dualism that pervades Andean cosmology and social organization is here mapped out on an epic scale, its successive mutations enacted at appropriate points on the landscape within the sacred domain of the shrine. The performance is focused on a nominally Christian shrine, the crag at Sinakara with its lithic image of the crucifixion. But this seems only to be the epicenter of the cult; the center is surely the Ausankati mountain range, home of the preeminent pagan deity of the region.

There is, however, another dimension to this apparently quintessentially Indian cult. It is presided over by priests and prelates; indeed, it owes the recent surge in its popularity largely to archiepiscopal patronage. It has its own church-sanctioned hierarchical organization, whose officers project an élite, mestizo status. As for the devotees themselves, they defy any simplistic characterization as Indian. At the principal fiesta, the traditional devotional style of cargo-type pilgrimage predominates. But this masks a wide span of meanings and motives—Indianness unambiguously proclaimed, or resentfully acquiesced in, or purposely recovered, or even temporarily affected by people who would otherwise consider themselves to be thoroughly mestizo. Finally, there is a growing number of private, individual pilgrims, many from urban areas, some of whom have begun to schedule their visits to take place just before the main influx of nación groups.

In this final section of the case study I shall examine these two indissociable dimensions of the Qoyllur Rit'i cult, its sociological dynamics and its cultural design, beginning with a summary and glossary of the ritual sequence of the titular fiesta. The cycle consists of a number of distinct phases (see appendix 1, map 10).

Phase one consists of a preliminary series of transfers of ritual objects from their normal resting places to their ceremonial stations, in readiness for the prolonged denouement: Señor de Tayankani is taken from Ocongate to Tayankani, Señor de Qoyllur Rit'i from Mawallani to Sinakara, the Virgin of Fátima from the sanctuary to her grotto, and the ukukus' crosses to their respective glaciers.

Phase two consists of the masses, benedictions, blessings, and local processions of the Blessed Sacrament and Señor de Qoyllur Rit'i at Sinakara, circumscribing and sanctifying the rock shrine, the sanctuary, and its immediate precincts. Priests and occasionally archbishops are the chief officiants in these activities.

Phase three shifts the focus from the Sinakara sanctuary to the encircling mountains. Now the dual organization of the fiesta begins to make itself manifest. The ukukus ascend to the glaciers to pay private homage to the apus. Then—in the past—there was a fight for the possession of a cross between the massed ukukus of the two moieties of Paucartambo and Quispicanchis, assisted by the machulas. This was a contest, a genuine competition, in which either side might emerge as victor. The suppression of this battle in favor of the present practice of the recovery of a separate cross by each ukuku band freezes this essential indeterminacy in the relation between them and has led, moreover, to the fissioning of the bands themselves.

Phase four, the long-distance pilgrimage procession from Sinakara to Ocongate, is transitional in both time and space. It is intermediate between two centers: Sinakara, the regional mountain center of the rock shrine and the apus, where the main rites of the fiesta have been enacted, and Ocongate, the local valley center of the district and parish, where the feast of Corpus Christi will be celebrated. The hamlet of Tayankani, the provenance of the divine child in the myth, is the boundary between these two spheres of influence. The contrast between them is rendered explicit in the pilgrimage procession through the use of two ethnically charged images, iconographically identical but nominally distinguished, to map the respective spheres from their centers.

The two crucifixes, Señor de Qoyllur Rit'i and Señor de Tayankani, along with their Marian consort, now become successively the pilgrimage icons of two great naciones, the Paucartambo and Quispicanchis moieties. Just as local nación groups on pilgrimage related to one another according to a rigid, ritual symmetry, so also do the moieties observe a strictly symmetrical complementarity. Ceremonial labor—the transport of the images—is divided equally between them. Each provides the crucifixes with an identical dancer-escort of wayri ch'unchos, from the moiety capitals of Paucartambo and Ocongate, respectively, whose music choreographs the procession and whose arariwas police and pace the passage of the icons.

The two descent sequences interrupt this alternating division of ceremonial labor. The sequences punctuate the midpoint and conclusion of the journey from Sinakara to Tayankani. The first is a kind of rehearsal for the second, which follows a collective hymn of praise to the rising sun. In these sequences, boundaries of local nación groups are temporarily suspended, and the overarching binary division is granted the perfect visual depiction: two lines moving across the landscape, successively parallel, converging, crossing, and recrossing, but always exact mirror images of each other.

For the journey from Tayankani to Ocongate, the Tayankani crucifix replaces the one from Sinakara, which is taken back to its resting place at Mawallani. The regional shrine has been exchanged for a local one, for while Señor de Qoyllur Rit'i commands universal devotion, Señor de Tayankani has been in effect appropriated by the parish of Ocongate. The alcalde himself therefore comes out to carry it symbolically into the village.

Phase five sees the regional completely superseded by the local. Its twin fixtures are the Corpus fiesta in Ocongate, centered on Señor de Tayankani, and the patronal fiesta in the village of Paucartambo, centered on the Virgin of Mount Carmel, an event that I have argued may be considered part of the Qoyllur Rit'i cycle. Apart from the usual trappings of a village fiesta—masses, processions and so on—both events entail a determinate reconstruction of the moiety division.

At Ocongate, bordering the puna, on the upper reaches of the Mapacho river, the qhapaq qollas of Ocongate fight and lose a ritual battle with the wayri ch'unchos of the village of Paucartambo. Here the two great moieties are metonymically condensed into their head villages; they are also symbolically contrasted in the juxtaposition of the two dance styles. At Paucartambo, bordering the subtropical montaña forty kilometers downriver, the process of condensation is taken a stage further. Here the bipartition between the warring dance groups is contained within the village itself. In both ritual settings, the symmetrical relation between the moieties in the transitional stage of phase four has given way in the local setting to a dialectical one: qollas, senior as ritual officiants, are defeated by ch'unchos, favorites of the Christ and the Virgin.

This synoptic account shows how the cultural design of the Qoyllur Rit'i festival is spatialized across the landscape. The shrine territory is ritually demarcated into two mutually exclusive spheres. One is centered on Sinakara, the regional pilgrimage site in the mountains, situated on the territorial boundary between the two moieties of Paucartambo and Quispicanchis. The other is centered on the village of Ocongate, the seat of local political and parochial control. The latter sphere has its own internal polarity of local centers, between Ocongate, capital of Quispicanchis moiety and straddling the ecological divide between the puna and kishwa zones, and Paucartambo, capital of the eponymous moiety and straddling the divide between kishwa and montaña.

The heart of this extensive geographical system, the Sinakara center, is itself partitioned into two sectors: the valley with its miraculous, Christianized crag, and the encircling glaciated peaks, northern outposts of the Ausankati range. To understand why Qoyllur Rit'i, of all the regional shrines in Cusco, has become the focus for such an elaborate cultural drama, it is necessary to unpack the symbolism of this sacred core.

I have already remarked that Christ's enclavement in the rock recapitulates the theme of the fallen warrior's interment after the tinkuy. In both instances, clothes are discarded—a crucial detail, since the ritual laundering of the clothes of a dead person is essential for a smooth passage to the other world—and in both the corpses live, emanating a constant power from their graves, a power given substance in the leaking blood of the warrior and the ichorous waters of the taytacha. Having met untimely ends, their bodies violently mutilated, they are in effect enshrined condenados, though positively rather than negatively charged.

The snow-covered slopes of Ausankati, as noted, are peopled with condenados vainly attempting to scale the peak and attain salvation. The taytacha, too, ascends the glacier in the shape of a cross—or, nowadays, crosses—but he is reclaimed and returned to the sanctuary by the ukukus, themselves condenados and hence the only beings capable of performing such a feat. Imprisoned in his rock abode just beneath the peaks, permanently denied the possibility of release from his condition, his living corpse radiates a power that can be tapped by human beings to alter their private or collective destinies.

Señor de Qoyllur Rit'i, then, is a petrified Christ situated in the very heartlands of his kindred spirits, the condenados. It is this unique concatenation that has caused the cult to assume such a distinctive character. While its current mass popularity stems from its relaunching and promotion by the Church authorities, assisted by the improvement in communications in the region, the particular and intricate liturgy of its titular fiesta is a consequence of the direct, material insertion of the miraculous shrine into the regional cosmography of the living dead.

It can now be seen why this liturgy should be pervaded by dualism. In chapter 6 I pointed out that dualism is the cultural mechanism by which the random power of the wild is channeled into the domain of human society. Drawing on material from various localities, I traced the successive stages in the construction of a dual cosmos, from the external tinkuy, an agonistic, intercommunity encounter in the wild puna, where dualism is merely incipient, to the internal tinkuy, an intracommunity confrontation within a settlement that expresses the dialectical nature of dual organization.

The fiesta of Qoyllur Rit'i, focused upon the syncretized powers of Sinakara, reproduces this process in its entirety. Inscribed within the cult is a ritual cycle that reveals itself as a paradigm of Andean dualism, an inventory of its progressively more highly organized forms, displaying the passage from entropy to society (see appendix 6). The cycle reads as an extended dramatization on a regional scale, deploying the landscape itself as its mise-en-scène, of the process whereby the harnessing of extrasocial power ipso facto organizes human society into a dual system.

A rapid replay of the cycle will make this clear. First, there is—or was—the battle on the glacier, an external tinkuy between the massed ukukus of the respective moieties, aided by the machulas. Both characters are permanently marginal to civilized society. The goal is to capture the taytacha himself, to sacrifice him once more to the apus so that his power may continue to flow. Here dualism is fluid and inchoate. There are competition, fission, and fusion; hierarchy between the moieties, indeed the boundary between them, is indeterminate.

Next comes the intermediate stage of the pilgrimage procession, as the portable image of the miraculous taytacha is borne on its extended passage to the domain of civilization. Intermoiety relations now take the form of neutral diametricality, with rigid equivalence and mirrored symmetry between them. Identical escorts—wayri ch'unchos, whose style is regarded as the most autochthonous—are here deployed by both moieties, in imitation of the typical regional style of nación pilgrimage, the dancers now signaling the capitals of the respective moieties.

Finally, in the valley, the moieties crystallize and differentiate into contrasting groups of qollas and ch'unchos, who engage in ritual battles in the village plazas. First, with the miraculous taytacha from the mountains now transformed into a domesticated one from the parish church, Ocongate hosts a confrontation between its own qhapaq qollas and Paucartambo's wayri ch'unchos. Later, Paucartambo's patronal Virgin presides over the concluding stage of the internal tinkuy, a ritual battle between the village's qhapaq qollas and ch'unchos extranjeros, the latter being the foreign, "civilized" variant of the savage autochthons. Dualism is finally manifested in the local setting in dialectical opposition and inversion.

But if the ceremonial cycle of the Qoyllur Rit'i fiesta reveals the fundamental principles of a native Andean cosmology, the social organization within which it unfolds—indeed, with which it is inextricably bound up—betrays the endemic tensions and contradictions of a society that sustains a dualism of a different kind: a double cultural identity.

Ethnic polarization and hierarchy are most clearly evident in the relation between cult staff and devotees. The projection of misti status enables the members of the brotherhood to mark themselves apart from and superior to the masses. Through a contrived superciliousness, through their ostentatious use of Spanish, through their ultimate sanction of the use of physical violence, they are able to define their position in relation to the broad mass of devotees as an ineluctable ethnic superiority. Lest this be seen as a mere carryover of an intrinsic ethnic status from outside the cult, it is worth mentioning again that ethnic superordination in a weak form is similarly deployed by the peasant staffs of some interlocal shrines, people who in other relations are scarcely distinguishable from the devotees over whom they preside.

Inasmuch as these shrine cults are suffused with paganism, it obviously befits their official hierarchies to align themselves with the Hispanic, Western culture from which their Christian meanings derive. The captiousness of the brotherhood, it will be recalled, had to do mostly with what they saw as a lack of piety and punctilio with respect to the Christian icons and identified them unequivocally as the guardians of the Christian tradition of the cult. It is significant that the ukukus of Qoyllur Rit'i, and to a lesser extent the machulas, share the brotherhood's jurisdiction over the congregation during the fiesta and, moreover, possess durable hierarchies of their own.

The equation of misti status with a supposedly orthodox Christian religiosity, albeit an orthodoxy centered upon an Indian shrine, also manifests itself in the participation of private pilgrims alongside, or in advance of, the naciones of dancers and musicians. Here a partial appropriation of the exotic by sophisticated town dwellers—perhaps even an element of voyeurism— might be perceived. More important, though, the presence of such pilgrims typifies a syndrome whereby members of an urban élite seek recourse to what they see as a primitive, indigenous source of sacredness for directly instrumental ends, for such a shrine is considered especially appropriate for worldly purposes. Parenthetically it may be noted that Redfield's contrast between the instrumental religiosity of the rural little tradition and the contemplative religiosity of the urban-based great tradition here receives a subtle twist, for it is precisely the urban and school-educated pilgrims for whom the miracle-working capabilities of Christ and the Virgin are paramount. Devotees who attend as members of naciones are motivated as much by social considerations and obligations as by hopes of any personal divine favor.

Naciones, for their part, are all based in rural communities and villages. All share a public image of Quechua-speaking, Indian identity, and all are at one level equivalent components of a single, macrocosmic field. Yet here, too, entrenched or emergent distinctions are expressed through or acquire an ethnic coding. The overarching moiety division between Quispicanchis and Paucartambo, between Qolla and Quechua, comes to possess an ethnic flavor, signaled by the contrast between their respective leading dance styles, the qolla of Ocongate and the ch'uncho of Paucartambo. The ch'uncho of Cusco, in turn reflects the ethnic heterogeneity of the population of the region in its fractionation into substyles, which recapitulate the ethnic cleavage.

In practice, the styles of both qhapaq qolla and ch'uncho extranjero, along with certain others, tend now to be assumed by people who lay claim to mestizo status and who might make no secret of their disdain for those pilgrims whom they regarded as Indian. The wayri ch'uncho style, meanwhile, signifies an unequivocal commitment to Indian, peasant identity. This ethnic-stylistic opposition is institutionalized in the internal configuration of dance groups from the respective moiety capitals. Thus, the nación of Ocongate consists of the principal teams of qollas and contradanzas, counterbalanced by wayri ch'unchos from the village. The nación of Paucartambo village comprises the principal team of wayri ch'unchos counterbalanced by ch'unchos extranjeros and other misti styles from the village. In this way, mimetic dance styles inspired by peoples lying on the horizons of the Quechua universe signify the permanent cultural divide that sunders central Andean society. As was shown in the last chapter, the strategic use of dance styles can even inject this opposition into a single, factional, peasant nación.

Finally the question of nonparticipation must be addressed. The diacritical rites described and analyzed here, which have earned Qoyllur Rit'i the status of the principal Indian shrine of the Cusco region, are shunned by not a few of the nación groups, who, like Qamawara, merely stay overnight, their láminas sojourning briefly in the holy presence of the taytacha, and depart to celebrate Corpus in their own communities. Why this should be so now becomes clear.

The central ceremonial sequence of the fiesta, in particular the main pilgrimage procession from Sinakara to Ocongate, makes blatant the cultural and social contradictions that pervade the cult. It transports the pilgrim from the loose congeries of devotees in the mountain fastness of Señor de Qoyllur Rit'i to the hierarchical, misti-controlled world of Señor de Tayankani. Latent oppositions between the ethnic dance styles and between the groups performing them suddenly become all too explicit. To participate in the cycle in any capacity, moreover, is inevitably to submit directly to an overweening mestizo officialdom. The choice of many naciones, particularly those from peasant communities of the uplands, is to segregate themselves as much as possible from these activities, to pay their respects to the shrine and leave, with their self-esteem intact.[17]

CHAPTER 9

The Cults
of Wank'a
and Justo Juez

A miraculous shrine has two aspects. It is a center of supralocal cult, the focus of a more a less extensive pilgrimage catchment that cross-cuts district, departmental, or even international boundaries. At the same time, it must necessarily be inserted into the ritual space and politico-ecclesiastical organization of a specific locality. The configuration of its cult can be seen in part as the outcome of a process whereby the extralocal shrine is institutionalized, ritually and organizationally, in its local setting.

For my second case study, I return to a familiar locality, the district of San Salvador. Now, though, the locality is not seen as a bounded microcosm, focused ultimately on the vice-parochial patron of Christ Savior, but rather as a neighborhood in which happen to be situated two miraculous shrines, one regional, the other interlocal, which are historically and mythically linked. But their relationship is quite different from the systematic articulation between Señor de Qoyllur Rit'i and Señor de Tayankani, described in the preceding chapter. In the present instance, the two cults are entirely separate. Indeed, the priestly custodians of the regional shrine profess total ignorance of the very existence of the interlocal one, which is not ten kilometers away.

The regional shrine, Señor de Wank'a, 'Lord of the Crag', is situated in the lower kishwa zone some two kilometers northwest of the village of San Salvador, on the eastern slopes of Mount Pachatusan (see appendix 1, map 8). It consists of a large rock outcrop jutting from the mountainside, on which has been painted a mural of Christ tied to a column, being whipped by torturers (plate 10). Around the crag has been built a large temple, wherein the mural forms part of a massive gold reredos in the baroque style.

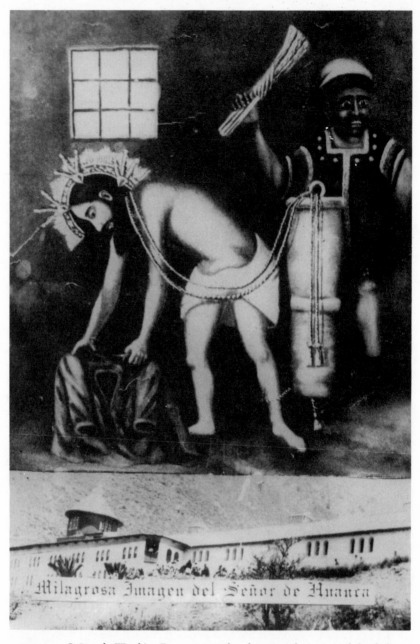

PLATE 10   *Señor de Wank'a. From a popular devotional picture of the fading rock painting; the features are more distinct but more stylized than in the original. The lower portion shows part of the Mercedarian monastery.*

Clustered around the temple are sleeping quarters for pilgrims and a small monastery for the Mercedarian Fathers who manage the shrine. Behind the shrine complex, in a wooded area called the Park of Siloam, there are three rivulets known as the waters, respectively, of Christ, of the Virgin, and of the Devil, the first two of which are reputed to possess miraculous healing powers. The shrine is easily accessible by motor vehicle, by way of a spur that branches off from the valley road opposite San Salvador. Two or three Mercedarian priests are in permanent residence, while for the titular fiesta of the shrine in September several others come across from the monastery of the order in Cusco. Because the shrine is run by a religious order, it is technically outside parochial jurisdiction, a source of much contention through the years between the guardians of the shrine and the priests of the parish.

The interlocal shrine, Señor el Justo Juez, 'Lord the Just Judge,' is situated on the borders of the upper kishwa and puna zones in the chapel of the hinterland community of Oqoruro, of which it is the de facto religious patron. It consists of a boulder about a meter high, with a sculptured face, dark-skinned and bearded, and draped with a maroon cloak trimmed in gold (plate 11). It sits in a glass-fronted niche above the modest altar, hung about with electric lights and wires. The shrine is managed by local peasants, the parish priest visiting only to celebrate mass during the titular fiesta. This is held in September, on exactly the same day as that of Señor de Wank'a. The development of the cult of Señor el Justo Juez came about in large measure as a consequence of the devotional strictures imposed by the Mercedarians at Wank'a, which had the effect of disenfranchising local peasant devotees of the shrine.

I shall begin with the mythohistory of Señor de Wank'a and the ethnography of its fiesta and fair.[1]

Wank'a: The Mythohistory

The official mythohistory of Señor de Wank'a, compiled by one of the shrine chaplains during the 1930s, tells of three separate apparitions (Márquez Eyzaguirre 1937, 1:40ff.).[2] The first is said to have taken place in May 1674. Diego Kispi, an Indian laborer in the gold mine of Yanantin on the summit of Pachatusan, was due to be punished for some misdemeanor, and he decided to run to freedom. He took refuge in a small cave on the mountainside, intending to travel to his home village of Chinchero under cover of darkness.

As night fell the cave was suddenly suffused with a glow, and on a rock at the back of the cave Diego saw the figure of a man, stripped and bleeding from the blows of a whip. The Indian was overcome and lost consciousness. The figure appeared to him in his sleep, saying that he

PLATE 11 *Señor el Justo Juez. The shrine image, housed in a niche above the altar of the chapel in Oqoruro, consists of a boulder, clothed and with a sculptured face. It is bedecked with electric lights of various kinds.*

wanted the spot to become a fount of salvation and love. He instructed Diego to return, after first telling his parish priest about the incident and making his first communion.

A few weeks later Diego, his family, and the priest from Chinchero visited the spot, where they witnessed the second vision of the flagellated Christ. The priest informed the Mercedarian Fathers, to whose hacienda the land pertained, and they in turn notified the bishop of Cusco. A commission visited the site and interrogated the witnesses, and the Mercedarians were subsequently given permission to paint a mural of Christ on the rock, recording all the details of the original visions. A modest thatched chapel was built around it and the cult was launched. At first, though, pilgrims were few in number and came only from the immediate locality.

The third apparition took place in 1717 in Alto-Perú, present-day Bolivia. Pedro Valero, a wealthy mineowner living in Cochabamba, fell ill of a terrible disease that was resistant to all known cures. But a strange doctor arrived in the city and healed him simply by giving him water. He told Pedro that his name was Immanuel and that, as payment, he should visit his home in Wank'a, Cusco.

A year later, during a pause in his business commitments, Pedro set out to find his curer, loaded with gifts of gold and silver. Eventually, after several months of searching in vain, he overheard some Indians in Cusco talking of Wank'a. He made his way there and discovered the chapel, now abandoned and ruined. Hidden behind a tangle of weeds was the rock mural, the features of the tortured Christ corresponding exactly to those of his mysterious doctor. The date was 14 September 1718.

Once again the bishop of Cusco was notified, and a new commission of investigation was formed to inquire into the alleged miracle. It was pronounced authentic, and the devotion received full diocesan sanction. Its popularity has been growing ever since.

Local tradition in the district of San Salvador reiterates the main themes of this official myth but has it that the image of the flagellated Christ appeared miraculously on the rock and that no artist's hand was involved. It also makes a significant addendum, which has to do with the converse of miraculous theophany—miraculous disappearance. A woman pasturing her flocks in the vicinity is said to have been visited by angels, who told her that the image of Christ and his torturers would eventually vanish and that when this happened, the Day of Judgment would have arrived. In popular tradition, the cult thus acquires a millenial flavor by means of a symbolism analogous to that of Mount Ausankati. Many observers have testified to the fact that the lithic image is indeed fading away (cf Barrionuevo 1969, 211–12).

An account of the origin of Wank'a by an informant from farther afield, a native of the province of Acomayo, differs significantly from the official one, for it is strongly redolent of the myth of Qoyllur Rit'i, though with local place names accurately rendered.

This version tells of a group of Indian boys from Waqoto, a property on the western side of Pachatusan, who were pasturing their sheep and llamas on the mountainside. They came upon a misti boy from Atás, the name given to the summit of Pachatusan. The boy had descended to Wank'a to escape the cold. He shared his bread with the young shepherds, and his presence miraculously augmented the herd, as the father of one of the boys discovered when he came to find out what was happening.

Following his encounter with the Indian boys, the misti child cured a wealthy, ailing mineowner by the name of Pedro Arias. Pedro was a sinner, a bigamist. He sought out his curer at Wank'a but when he eventually found him there he saw that he was sweating blood. He went to inform the priest at San Salvador. Together with the sacristans from the church there, they returned to the spot, but the figure ran away. They gave chase, and the priest was on the point of catching him when the figure was suddenly enclaved within a crag in the form in which he is now seen.

Pedro Arias built a chapel at the site, and a chaplain, who has been there ever since, arrived from Chile to administer the cult. Later, however, the taytacha appeared to Pedro again and commanded him to renounce one of his wives. This Pedro agreed to do, but he never fulfilled his promise. As punishment, the taytacha sent him a fever and he died (Condori Mamani 1977, 68–71). Given the similarity of this account to the Qoyllur Rit'i legend, it is worth noting that the informant professed ignorance of the latter.

Further variations are introduced in versions of the story from elsewhere. In one, for example, the sick Spaniard is from the northern Peruvian department of Ancash; he is given drugs, not water; he takes cheese and cured mutton as gifts, not gold and silver; and the element of the Last Judgment is included (Morote Best 1953, 87–88).

All the myths are alike in drawing a strong contrast between the two visionaries of Señor de Wank'a. In the official version, the first visionary was a poor Indian mineworker—Kispi, as will have been observed, is a stereotypical Indian name—while the second was a wealthy mineowner, whose surname denotes Spanish descent. The transformation of social status correlates with parallel transformations in other domains, those of religious meaning and cult organization.

First, there are shifts in Christology and in theodicy. Diego Kispi, fleeing an unjust punishment, saw a tortured divinity who delivered a general promise of salvation and love. Indeed, the advocation of the shrine, Cristo de la Columna, unusual in the Andes, permits an indirect corroboration of the official mythohistory. According to contemporary records, the village of Chinchero actually had a confraternity of Cristo de la Columna at that time, the iconography of whose titular image could well have inspired Diego's vision.[3] Pedro Valero's apparition, by contrast, was of Christ as divine healer, and his devotion was more overtly instrumental: votive offerings in return for a miraculous cure, albeit a cure portrayed as a symbolic rebaptism.

Second, the transformation in the social status of the seers is correlated with a change in the ecclesiastical standing of the cult. The first apparitions, though they were brought to the attention of the religious authorities, did not attract widespread devotion. Indeed, the story suggests that by 1718, the cult had all but collapsed. It required a visionary of more exalted social status than Diego Kispi to secure full ecclesiastical recognition of the devotion and thence to relaunch it in its present form. The myth states, in other words, that while the cult originated from the vision of an Indian, it owes its present popularity to a seer who nowadays would be classed as mestizo and who, moreover, made a pilgrimage of some 900 kilometers, bearing gifts of gold and silver for his benefactor.

What of the pagan antecedents of the cult? It is possible that the monolith itself was originally venerated as an eponymous wanq'a. What is certain is that Pachatusan, the mountain on whose slopes the shrine is located, was and is a renowned pagan deity. At 4,842 meters it is the tallest mountain in the vicinity of Cusco city, and its summit lies on the eastern ceque that was the Inkas' sight line for observing the sunrise at the equinoxes (Zuidema 1977, 233). It may be significant, therefore, that the titular fiesta of Señor de Wank'a is celebrated in September and that its octave, the day on which the rites are formally concluded, falls on the vernal equinox itself.[4]

Pachatusan recurs several times in Inka mythology, often in connection with hidden gold. The mountain was in fact mined in Inka times at Waqoto, the provenance of the Indian seers in the Acomayo version of the Wank'a myth. Diego Kispi, for his part, was from a local mine, while the offerings of Pedro Valero or Arias were the fruits of mining. Today, locals will confide that the interior of Pachatusan is an enormous gold mine, guarded by the apu of the mountain—the most powerful, by some the most feared, in the locality. The Christian shrine was evidently able to feed on the renown and mythological associations of this powerful pagan deity.

During the decades immediately following the first apparitions, however, it seems that the Wank'a shrine did attract only local interest. A diocesan letter indicates that it was not until 1693 that the bishop of Cusco granted permission for mass to be celebrated in the chapel, stipulating that it must be low, not sung, and expressly prohibiting Easter services so as not to encroach upon parochial rights (Márquez Eyzaguirre 1937, 2:160).

Following its alleged rediscovery in 1718, the shrine is said to have begun to attract wider attention. Its fortunes were almost certainly assisted in this regard by a virulent epidemic that was afflicting Cusco and other parts of highland Peru at that time. Other shrines near Cusco also benefited from the tribulations caused by this pestilence, among them the Virgin of Tiobamba.

The epidemic was horrifying. It spread to Cusco from Buenos Aires and ravaged the population for several years. A letter of 1720 estimates 60,000 dead in Cusco city alone. In a report on the plague by a Cusco doctor it is attributed to the conjunction of Mars and Saturn two years earlier, coupled with a solar eclipse at León, and the doctor goes on to recommend herbal cures involving viper's grass, burnet, chicory, pomegranate, and pared deer-horn. But the author adds with circumspection that it is useless to apply such remedies unless the patients have first begged the mercy of God, for it is he who makes them efficacious (Colin 1966, 35, 37–38).

The distraught populace sought whatever spiritual succor it could:

There remained not one image that they did not shower with promises, nor saint to whom they did not pay special cult, imploring their protection; in particular to the patronal assistants of the plagues: San Sebastián, San Antonio the Martyr, San Roque, San Juan de Sahagún and others, with sung masses, devout novenas and respectful reverence (Esquivel y Navia [1749] 1980, 2:222, my translation).

But "superstitious" beliefs and practices were rife as well:

The Indians practised their abuses, claiming to have seen various apparitions and dreams; in particular, they said that an old blind pilgrim came from the province of Collao to Cusco in the name of the plague, threatening each village. . . . In a neighborhood of the parish of San Gerónimo . . . they rendered cult to the common enemy [Devil], whose effigy they had painted on some paper, and just as they were celebrating their diabolical rites, the friar José de Aspilcueta of the Order of Preachers found them in this abominable exercise (Esquivel y Navia [1749] 1980, 2:224, my translation).

The unpredictable pathogeny of the disease inspired both fear and hope:

They observed various occurrences, such as how many of those infected recovered through some chance incident: some, by bathing in cold water, by which they rid themselves of the heat of the fever; others, for having drunk it; some already placed in the cemetery recovered and remained healthy (Esquivel y Navia [1749] 1980, 2:224, my translation).

Conditions were clearly propitious at this time for the reemergence of a shrine boasting the miraculous cure of a wealthy Spaniard. Indeed, it is tempting to see in Pedro Valero's vision and cure a strategic repackaging of the myth and cult of an obscure, interlocal shrine by its priestly staff so as to capitalize on the panic that was sweeping the region. The remarkable coincidences and parallels—the time and place of Pedro's affliction, which fitted the trajectory of the plague exactly, and the water cure administered to him—are otherwise hard to explain.

Now that the cult had acquired a miracle-working momentum—the occasional chance recovery was as likely among pilgrims as among any others—Señor de Wank'a's popularity continued to increase. From 1760 onward the Mercedarians maintained a chaplain in continuous residence at the shrine (Márquez Eyzaguirre 1937, 1:269). Cosme Bueno, writing in 1768, refers to the "great gatherings of devotees" at Wank'a (Bueno [1768] 1951, 108). The Mercedarians were determined to maintain the purely religious character of the titular fiesta, which was "without a fair of any kind, because the priests of the said order prevent even the sale of liquor" (Oricaín [1790] 1906, 352). But apparently the merchants of Cusco did attempt to stage fairs during the pilgrimage, just outside the sanctuary gates, and the chaplains had to make strenuous efforts to suppress them. Commerce, it seems, was attempting to follow in the wake of pilgrimage. Quechua was apparently the main language of preaching in those days, suggesting that the majority of pilgrims were of Indian descent rather than Spanish (Márquez Eyzaguirre 1937, 2:20–21).

To consolidate its position as a pilgrimage center, the custodians of Wank'a—like those of shrines of medieval Europe—sought to obtain papal indulgences to offer its devotees. Ironically, their appeals to the Vatican to this end were stimulated in part by the persistent hostility of the secular priests of the parish of Pisac, in which the shrine was situated, toward the regular custodians of Wank'a. The Mercedarian order had a direct line of communication to the pope through their general in Rome, and in 1801 they were able to obtain from Pius VII a plenary indulgence for attendance during the fiesta and novena (Márquez Eyzaguirre 1937, 2:202–3).

Despite papal support, however, Wank'a was still subjected to interference by the Pisac clergy. They prevented the Mercedarian friars from receiving fees for masses at the sanctuary and attempted to bring them under parochial jurisdiction (Márquez Eyzaguirre 1937, 2:205). Faced with this continuing opposition, and apparently receiving little support from the bishop of Cusco in defense of rights conferred on the shrine by his own office, the Mercedarians again appealed to Rome. Pius VIII gave them his full backing, stating in a brief of 1829 that it was "his will to segregate and make independent Señor de Guanca where without the intervention of the parish priests they might freely summon the dues of sung masses and perform all the offices of Holy Week and of the other feasts of the year." In 1842 Gregory XVI bestowed further indulgences on the sanctuary, while in 1930 Pius XI united Wank'a to the Lateran Basilica in Rome, thereby instantly granting it all the indulgences and spiritual benefits conceded to the Basilica (Márquez Eyzaguirre 1937, 2:207, 217–19).

This bitter conflict between the regular clergy of Wank'a and the secular clergy of the parish of Pisac was a local resonance of a persistent structural contradiction in the colonial church, between a diocesan establishment controlled by the Spanish crown and a regular clergy lying partly outside its jurisdiction and responsible ultimately to Rome. Miraculous shrines in the Andes have frequently been the foci of struggle between different ecclesiastical interests: witness the early histories of Copacabana and Tiobamaba. Wank'a presents an especially stark illustration of this phenomenon, opening up at the local level the principal split in Church organization. In this instance the burgeoning pilgrimage cult on the local periphery was controlled from the outset by regulars, who could not easily be dislodged. Furthermore, their credentials as custodians were impeccable, for they had done their utmost to preserve the sanctity of the shrine. The more the parochial clergy tried to circumscribe and regulate the cult, the more the Mercedarians lobbied the Vatican, thereby validating the orthodox, official status of the cult, which in turn made it even more difficult for its local opponents to assail.

The Mercedarian Fathers have recently been even more assiduous in their propagation of the Wank'a cult. During the 1930s, under an energetic Chilean chaplain, Luis G. Márquez Eyzaguirre, the Hermandad del Señor de Wank'a was founded. This brotherhood is quite different from that of Señor de Qoyllur Rit'i. The latter is a central organization, managing the shrine's finances and orchestrating its fiesta; it has little to do with the operation of the pilgrimage at the local level, which is in the hands of naciones. Wank'a already had a central hierarchy in the Mercedarian staff, and it seems that until the early years of the present century the pilgrimage was similarly organized along nación lines, with community contingents attending with their musicians and dancers. But around that time, music and dancing in the precincts of the sanctuary were banned.[5]

The effect of the prohibition was to rule the fiesta out of bounds to nación contingents from peasant communities, for whom this was the standard devotional style. The brotherhood seems to have been instituted as a replacement at the local level for the nación system. Branches *(coros)* of the brotherhood were established in towns and villages throughout the Cusco region and beyond, with separate sections for men and women. The title *celador* here refers to the head of a men's or women's branch. Members of the brotherhood pledge themselves to an annual payment to the shrine and are promised masses there when they die—provided their subscriptions are up to date (Márquez Eyzaguirre 1937, 2:228–29). Márquez Eyzaguirre himself undertook several missions throughout the region, touring towns and villages with a copy of the shrine image and founding numerous coros en route.

The ban on ceremonial music and dancing during the titular fiesta was presumably intended to nudge the cult in the direction of what was perceived as a more orthodox style of religiosity, emptied of the more profane folk forms of ritual expression. It accordingly enabled the staff to promote the shrine not only among the rural masses, but also among the more Hispanic sectors of regional society, those with a preference for a more Catholic, less indigenous devotional apparatus, and of course who were more reliable as benefactors.

The building program initiated at the shrine during the 1930s also indicates that the cult was now courting a more sophisticated clientèle. Sleeping quarters were erected for the use of the various branches of the brotherhood. A motor road was built to the sanctuary from the village of San Salvador, the express purpose being to encourage the attendance of townspeople deterred by the taxing climb. In fact there are now two roads up to the shrine from the valley, one for incoming and one for outgoing motor traffic, to ease the heavy congestion during the September fiesta. This, coupled with the convenience of the railhead at Huambutío, which had opened thirty years earlier, made Wank'a a highly accessible pilgrimage venue. Electric illumination, first installed during the 1920s when it was still a novelty in urban areas, was improved and extended (Márquez Eyzaguirre 1937, 2:304, 117). San Salvador still has no electricity. Building at the shrine complex continued apace, and in 1965 a new temple to house the sacred crag was finally completed.

Meanwhile, the annual fair in the environs of the sanctuary was moved to the valley, to a site opposite the village of San Salvador. It is now one of the largest such events in the region.

Wank'a: The Cult and the Fair

The sanctuary of Señor de Wank'a receives a trickle of visitors all year round, and there is a sizable congregation for the services during Holy Week. The main influx, though, is for the titular fiesta held during the novena and octave of the feast of the Exaltation of the Cross on 14 September. I attended this event in 1980.

The fiesta followed a program that has remained unchanged in its essentials for more than half a century (cf. Márquez Eyzaguirre 1937, 2:119–21). During the novena, as pilgrims began to arrive in numbers, daily masses and rosary services were held in the basilica. There were, of course, no láminas or demandas as at Qoyllur Rit'i, but a Mercedarian priest was always on duty between services to receive the monetary offerings of pilgrims, which he would then place at the foot of the sacred crag at the base of the reredos. Sick or disabled pilgrims who managed to gain the ear of one of the priests would occasionally be escorted to the altar to touch the image itself.

Outside the basilica, there were two main centers of activity. One was an awning on the esplanade in front of the sanctuary, beneath which two statues had been set up: a copy of the shrine image, depicting Christ stooping forward, clad in a maroon girdle but with the torso naked, and bearing a crown of thorns, and the Virgin of Sorrows, wearing a maroon cape. A cloth chute had been attached to the hands of the Christ-statue to direct the cash offerings into a collection box. A male celador supervised the donations to Christ, a female celador those to the Virgin.

The other focus of activity was the Park of Siloam. Here, at the two main springs of Christ and the Virgin, orderly queues would form each day as pilgrims took their turns to splash themselves in the holy water, collecting it in bottles and receptacles to take home. In the sanctuary, piles of ex-votos—crude models of arms, legs, and other parts of the body for which pilgrims were seeking cures—testified to the continuing belief in the healing powers of the divine doctor.

Each evening during the novena, after dark, the lights in the shrine complex would be turned out for a while, and those devotees who wished to do so engaged in self-flagellation. It is worth noting that, whereas at Qoyllur Rit'i, penitential discipline was applied to pilgrims by the celadores, here it is self-administered—although the celadores at Wank'a, women as well as men, are authorized to whip people into line during the public ceremonies.

On the 14th, the number of pilgrims reached its peak. At times the convoy of trucks, buses, taxis, and private cars crawling up to the sanctuary was immobilized in a jam that extended back for several kilometers. The archbishop of Cusco sometimes visits the shrine on this day to conduct a service of confirmation, but none was held on this occasion. The climax of the fiesta comes in the late afternoon, when two solemn processions pass along different routes through the shrine complex and converge in front of the sanctuary. The two processions do not, however, signal any moiety division, as at Qoyllur Rit'i; they merely represent a sexual division of ritual labor, reflecting the organization of the hermandad and its local coros.

The women's procession was led by a boy carrying a crucifix, followed by female members of various coros, each group with its embroidered banner. In their midst was a statue of San Juan on a litter. Then came six women dressed in black, intoning a Quechua chant:

Haku mamay puririsun	Come, mother, let us set off
Wawaykita maskharisun	Let us search for your child.

Finally came the statue of the Virgin of Sorrows. The procession was marshaled by female celadores, who lashed out with their whips at anyone who attempted to take water from the springs as they passed by. Many of the women wore crowns of thorns made out of a spiny shrub that grows in the area, in imitation of the one placed on Christ's head before his crucifixion.

Participants in the men's procession likewise wore crowns of thorns. Besides the local coros with their banners held aloft, this procession also included a group of costumed devotees representing various characters

PLATE 12 *The Calvary Tableau at Wank'a. The boy with the hammer, nails, and crown of thorns leads; next to the Mercedarian priest is the bearer of the vinegar sponge; behind come Christ and the thieves with their crosses and the soldier with a lance; bringing up the rear are Simon of Cyrene and the bearers of the holy shroud and the cock and brazier.*

from the biblical story of the crucifixion (plate 12). In the center was Christ himself, wearing a white robe, staggering under the weight of an enormous cross. Flanking him were the two thieves, clad in mauve robes and dragging along smaller crosses. Behind came Simon of Cyrene, the bearer of the holy shroud with Christ's visage printed on it, and a man carrying the cock whose crow announced Peter's third denial of Jesus, together with the brazier at which the disciple was warming himself at the time. Ahead marched a Roman soldier with the lance that opened Christ's side, another soldier with the vinegar sponge on a long pole, and a boy bearing a platter on which were prominently displayed the instruments of execution: the crown of thorns, a hammer, some nails, and a pair of severed, pierced hands.

Some way behind this little tableau, led by a group of Mercedarian priests, came the stooping figure of Señor de Wank'a standing high on a litter-mounted pedestal. The priests led refrains in Spanish and Quechua, while celadores sternly patrolled the procession and the audience.

As the two processions converged in front of the basilica, the statues of Christ and the Virgin were brought together side by side. Then, with darkness closing in around the sacred aerie, there was a long, emotional address by one of the Mercedarian priests. Most of it was in Quechua, with occasional lapses into Spanish. The theme was the grace that Señor de Wank'a could bestow on his devotees to help each of them lead a truly Christian life, a life based on the values of the family, with love between spouses and respect between children and their parents, their godparents, and their teachers, a life that was under threat from the corruption and evils of the modern world, of which two specific examples were television and the atomic bomb. The miraculous healing powers of the image were scarcely mentioned, nor did the sermon dwell on the idea of penitential punishment that the shrine obviously symbolized.

It was a virtuoso performance, lasting about an hour, beginning as a grandiloquent exhortation but later becoming an impassioned prayer. At this point the assembled pilgrims fell to their knees, many of them weeping uncontrollably. With waves of piteous sobbing and wailing sweeping across the congregation, the effusion rose to a crescendo, the preacher's voice faltering and cracking with emotion.

The oration was followed by a hymn of praise to Señor de Wank'a, sung solo by a female celador from Juliaca. Then to more mundane matters: an announcement about arrangements for breakfast for the Juliaca contingent. The congregation began to disperse. Some devotees left later that night, others the next day. A dwindling number stayed on for the octave, when daily masses and rosary services were repeated.

The banners of the coros and the dress of the pilgrims at the fiesta gave some idea of the geographical and socioeconomic catchment of the cult. Within the Cusco region, the more traditional female attire indicated pilgrims from the localities of Pisac, Ollantaytambo, Chinchero, Paucartambo, Ocongate, Quiquijana, and Tinta, while there were banners of branches of the brotherhood from Calca, Coya, San Sebastián, and Anta. There was also a strong and evidently wealthy branch from Cusco city, who at the time were building a new celda and private chapel for themselves at the shrine. From farther afield, there were banners from towns and villages in the neighboring Andean departments of Apurímac, Arequipa, and Puno; from the coastal cities of Tacna and Lima; and from La Paz in Bolivia.[6] I was told that pilgrims from Argentina and Chile were not uncommon. But there was no coro from the village of San Salvador. The chaplain admitted his puzzlement to me that, while pilgrims traveled great distances to visit the shrine, the people who lived on its doorstep, so to speak, hardly ever bothered to come.

Socioeconomically devotees tended to be drawn from the ranks of the lower middle and working classes in the towns and from those of small farmers and petty traders in the countryside. Visitors from farther afield tended to be wealthier and more cosmopolitan than those from near by. From their banners, it was apparent that all the coros were from district, departmental, or national capitals; there was none from hinterland peasant communities.

The chaplain of Wank'a was slightly embarrassed by the theatrical nature of the cult, by its overt iconolatry, and especially by the conspicuous forms of public penance in which some of the votaries engage. He stressed to me that the clergy did nothing to encourage these practices, which, he said, stemmed from the naiveté of certain pilgrims, particularly the peasants (campesinos). These people, he claimed, had two conceptions of God, the God who loves and the God who punishes, and it is the latter that for them takes precedence. But he pointed to the absence of drinking, dancing, and music as a feature that distinguished Wank'a from other, less sublimated devotions.

The Wank'a fair runs contemporaneously with the activities at the sanctuary but is entirely separate from it. The fair is overseen by the municipality of San Salvador, and the Mercedarian priests have no part in its organization. Some visitors, including most of those from the immediate locality, attended only the fair and never went to the sanctuary.

The first stalls were set up along the valley road near the bridge around 8 September, later spreading out onto the plain beyond. Trading reached a peak on the 13th and 14th. Produce on sale included tubers and ch'uñu from the upper kishwa and puna zones in the immediate area, maize from Calca and Urubamba, tropical fruits and peppers from Quillabamba, kinowa and kañiwa from the cold lands beyond La Raya pass, and fish from Lake Titicaca brought by merchants from Juliaca.

Occupying as much space as foodstuffs were the earthenware pots and other utensils, whose sellers grouped their pitches according to their places of origin. The biggest groups were those from Tinta, San Pedro, Pucará, and Puno. Transactions with these pottery merchants frequently assumed the form of barter, the container being traded for the amount of produce it would hold. There was also a group of artisans from Sicuani, who specialized in the conversion of old automobile tires into the ubiquitous rubber sandals (ojotas), as well as several vendors of metal tools and plowshares from the same area.

Snappily dressed traders from Cusco city, meanwhile, had set up a row of stalls dealing in factory-made clothes, radios, record players, and records, while other Cusqueños were running a number of cantinas at which they offered drinks and cooked food. There were tombolas and other amusements, photographers with monkeys and parrots for props, despacho sellers, soothsayers, and stands at which devotional literature and medallions of Señor de Wank'a were sold.

On the hillside behind the fair, livestock were being traded under the supervision of the district governor. Horses and burros were the principal merchandise here, though there was some small-scale trading of llamas and alpacas.

As in other years, the event also had its share of beggars, thieves, and confidence tricksters. Poor peasants were as vulnerable as wealthier visitors to the attentions of the last, perhaps more so: my Qamawaran informants had a fund of stories about how they or their friends had been robbed or defrauded of cash or goods at the fair.

For transport, hundreds of bus and truck operators assigned their fleets exclusively to the task of ferrying visitors, while the Southern Peruvian Railway laid on extra trains to the nearest station of Huambutío for visitors from the southeast and Arequipa. Lodgings for those not eligible to sleep in one of the celdas at the shrine were more haphazard. There are no hotels in San Salvador, though some households took in a few visitors as paying guests. The rest spent the nights in the open.

The Wank'a fair is the principal event in the village calendar, eagerly anticipated by all, and the municipality realizes several hundred dollars in tariffs from stallholders. But the flurry of commercial activity in the district is short-lived. The majority of visitors prepare to leave following the procession and sermon at the shrine on the 14th. By the 18th or 19th the last stalls are being dismantled, and a languorous quiet descends once more upon the village. It is the fate of San Salvador to lie in the commercial doldrums of the regional economy. Yet for a few days each year the village plays host to an event which—thanks to the religious renown of Señor de Wank'a—is one of the most celebrated of its kind in Peru.

Justo Juez

The fiesta of Señor el Justo Juez in the hinterland community of Oqoruro coincides exactly with that of Señor de Wank'a, but few visitors to the valley shrine from outside the locality are even aware of the existence of the mountain shrine. While the reputation of Wank'a is international, Justo Juez has only a narrow, interlocal catchment restricted mainly to the districts of San Salvador, Pisac, and Colquepata. Furthermore, its congregation consists exclusively of peasants from upland communities and haciendas or cooperatives.

There is no official version of the origin myth, and local oral versions vary. In one representation, as noted earlier, the shrines of Wank'a and Justo Juez, along with those of Qoyllur Rit'i, Tayankani, and Aqcha, were said to be the resting places of five brother taytachas who wandered through the region. In another representation, the two shrines are linked to another, interlocal center, Señor de Sani near Wankarani (see appendix 1, map 8).

These three brother Christs, it was said, were walking together in the area. Señor de Wank'a, the oldest, was the first to tire; he stopped to rest and immediately became enclaved in a crag at the spot. Señor el Justo Juez continued on his way, headed for the mountain peaks. He was passing through the Qewar gorge when he met a woman. He asked her the way to Roqa Moqo 'Hill of Rocks', a location within the territory of Qamawara, but she did not reply. For this reason, although he had originally intended to come to Qamawara, he never reached it. Exhausted by his climb, he stopped to rest at a spot called Tayta Qora 'God's Thicket', where he miraculously entered a rock. His cloak was found near by.

Meanwhile, the woman ran to tell her family in Oqoruro. They discovered the taytacha in the rock, and took him back to their community. But the people of Qamawara were the first to come and celebrate mass for him; the people of Oqoruro arrived at the service later, so they came simply as a nación. It was thus the Qamawarans who attended upon the children of the Señor at his first mass.

Señor de Sani, for his part, walked on toward Wankarani. But he too failed to reach his destination. Stopping to rest, he also miraculously entered a rock, at the place where his shrine is now located.

In this myth the theme of a living being shedding its clothes before passing into a rock, to become a petrified body imbued with miraculous powers, is encountered once more. People were emphatic that Taytacha Justo Juez was still alive, although he now no longer speaks—"just stares."

This particular story of brother taytachas stopped short in their tracks situates the Oqoruro image within a wider system of "Exaltation" shrines. Señor de Sani, a vicinal shrine fifteen kilometers to the southeast, is also a Just Judge advocation and has its fiesta on exactly the same day as Wank'a and Oqoruro, 14 September. Its catchment in fact complements that of the Oqoruro shrine, embracing peasant communities in the neighboring districts of Caicay and Ccatca. Thus, while Wank'a caters to a heterogeneous clientèle from farther afield, the shrines of Oqoruro and Sani between them capture the pilgrimage custom of the mountain peasants who live in its heartlands.

Turning from myth to history, even the approximate date of the founding of Señor el Justo Juez is difficult to gauge. Some claimed that it was 300 years old, others a century, while the Pisac priest said it was *fresco* 'recent'. All my informants agreed, however, that its appearance had put an end to the tinkuy, the annual bloodletting to the apus. A published source cited earlier places the cessation of hostilities in the 1940s (Casaverde Rojas, Sánchez Farfán, and Cevallos Valencia 1966, 97). I doubt that the founding of the shrine was quite so recent, for it was beyond the living memory of my oldest informants in Qamawara.[7] This would suggest that it occurred no later than the 1920s and possibly earlier.

As it happens, the area immediately surrounding the Oqoruro chapel contains a high concentration of sites pertaining to the Killki culture, which preceded that of the Inkas in the region. Recent archaeological research by the Instituto Nacional de Cultura in Cusco has revealed dozens of graves, corrals, and terraces, all clustered within a hundred meters or so of the present shrine sanctuary, indicating that this was a pre-Inka settlement of some importance. At the very least, this would suggest that the Christ shrine was anchored to a place which was by no means neutral in the indigenous perception of the sacred terrain. The minutely variegated sacred contours of the local landscape could well have preserved the special status of this zone through the ages, thereby making it a ready receptacle for the new miraculous taytacha.[8]

Today, the titular fiesta of Señor el Justo Juez is attended by as many as a thousand pilgrims, divided among twenty or so naciones. Each contingent comes with its lámina, its troupe of ceremonial dancers, and its band of musicians. Most of the dancers are wayri ch'unchos, with one or two ukukus and machulas in each troupe, though a few naciones attend as qhapaq qollas. There are no private devotees; all visitors come as members of community-based naciones.

The competitive relationship between Qamawara and Oqoruro in the founding myth is translated into a cooperative one in the central organization of the fiesta. Until 1972 each community had a principal sponsor, the prioste (Sp.) or tiamisayoq (Qu). Oqoruro also has a number of mayordomos, while Qamawara has two dance-group convenors known as contadores 'accountant', 'auditor', each responsible for a ch'uncho troupe. These dancers escort, not a lámina, but a large wooden cross from Qamawara to the shrine, signifiying the special status of the community in relation to those communities that come as visiting naciones. In addition to these local cargos, the sacristan from the church in San Salvador supervises activities in Oqoruro chapel throughout the three days of the fiesta and attends the priest when he visits to celebrate mass.

Qamawara's prioste was the most expensive and the most prestigious cargo in the community inventory. The main items of expenditure were food and drink for feasting all the visiting dance troupes, and in the early 1970s the total cost was estimated to be $275. In 1973, the cargo lapsed, since no one was prepared to shoulder this considerable burden. It was subsequently revived but was split into two posts so as to spread the expense, an arrangement that has continued to date.

The most important fruit of the cooperation between Qamawara and Oqoruro in the running of the fiesta has been a Honda electric generator, purchased jointly in the 1960s for the illumination of the shrine image and chapel and the operation of a public-address system. The purchase price of $500 was met partly from the communities' coffers and partly from the donations of devotees; the communities similarly share the costs of fuel and maintenance. The generator is a source of enormous pride to the people of both communities, who delight in pointing out that while they have their own source of power, the village of San Salvador still has no electricity.[9]

In 1973, when I observed the fiesta, attendance was said to be *regular* 'average'. Around 12 September, locals began to set up the *mercado* 'market'—makeshift tents and stalls outside the Oqoruro churchyard for the sale of liquor, soft drinks, cooked food, popcorn, and candy to the visitors. Most of the vendors were from Qamawara, where there is more capital for this kind of activity than in Oqoruro.

Naciones began arriving at the chapel on the 13th. Dancers would enter the churchyard in formation and would kiss the stone cross in front of the chapel. Inside, they handed their láminas and their cash donations to the Oqoruro steward on duty, who broadcast the names of donors and the amounts received over the public-address system. As darkness fell the prized electric lights were switched on, and a somewhat inebriated vigil ensued. Throughout the fiesta, Oqoruro stewards prowled among the congregation in the chapel, brusquely knocking off hats, poking people who had failed to remove their sandals, and pushing people aside to keep the aisle clear.

Next day the parish priest arrived to celebrate mass. Since Qamawara's office of prioste was in abeyance, the lieutenant governor of the community had agreed to serve as proxy sponsor for ritual purposes only, though he had convened a small group of his friends—most of them young returned migrants and army veterans—each of whom had made a small cash contribution to buy chicha for the visiting dancers. The cross was carried in procession from the lieutenant governor's house to the Oqoruro chapel, and he stood with it immediately in front of the altar during the service. The mass and litany were in Quechua, with music provided by one of the bands. There was no sermon, nor were there any communicants.

The rest of the day, and the following night as well, were passed in informal socializing, drinking, and dancing. Conspicuous among the mainly traditionally dressed crowd was a knot of migrants from Lima on home visits to Qamawara. They were dressed in ostentatious store-bought clothes, danced to the latest hit songs on a battery record player, and drank their way rowdily through several crates of bottled beer. Some of the visiting pilgrims, amazed at this spectacle, stood around gaping in astonishment.

The priest spent the night in lodgings prepared for him by the Oqoruro prioste, and celebrated mass again the following morning. Afterward many of the naciones retrieved their láminas from the chapel and left for their home communities. Each group would retire from the chapel backward on their knees, out of respect for the Señor. On the 16th there were more masses, this time in the chapel of Qamawara as well as in that of Oqoruro, but by now most of the visitors had departed, and all the stalls at Oqoruro had been dismantled.

On the 17th, meanwhile, the priest officiated at three weddings in the Oqoruro chapel. It was customary, for the few couples in both communities who chose to do so, to solemnize marriages at this time of the year. All the visitors had now left, and the public fiesta gave way to several more days of private celebrations on the part of the families and guests of the married couples.

In the course of the fiesta of Señor el Justo Juez many of the participants, both locals and visitors, descended to San Salvador to visit the fair there. In ritual participation, however, I gained the impression that Wank'a and Justo Juez were mutually exclusive fiestas; at least I met no one who attended both. The two events were continually being contrasted. The people of Qamawara and Oqoruro claimed that their fiesta, with its music and dancing, though as yet a minor pilgrimage compared with that of Wank'a, was nevertheless a far more splendid affair. Their shrine, like that of Wank'a, was equipped with electricity, and its popularity was growing all the time. Their enthusiasm in the 1970s for the project to drive a road through the area was prompted in no small part by a desire to make the shrine more easily accessible, so that it might begin to compete with its counterpart in the valley. Road access, as the Wank'a custodians had realized earlier, is crucial to devotional expansion. Indeed, the locals regularly petitioned Justo Juez itself for help with the road project—"for the benefit," as they said, "of all the taytacha's children."

Disengagement and Resistance

Two rock shrines passively confront each other across the valley, mythically linked but ritually dissociated. In this simultaneous joining and disjunction, the cultural and social contradictions inherent in Andean religious practice are pushed yet further toward a breach.

The cult of Wank'a has always been under direct hieratic control. Supposedly having originated from the distressed imaginings of an Indian fugitive, it idled for some years as a local pilgrimage on the parish periphery. Its takeoff was achieved, it seems, as a result of shrewd promotion during a serious epidemic, when miraculous cures were at a premium. As its popularity spread, feeding on the pagan associations of the site, so its threat to parochial hegemony grew.

The measures pursued by the religious order of the shrine to counter the opposition from the secular parish clergy further served the cause of wider proselytizing. Links with Rome were cultivated, thereby not only securing the ecclesiastical foundation of the shrine but also bringing indulgences and other spiritual benefits that gave the cult both added impetus in its geographical expansion and an enhanced standing in the eyes of the more Hispanic sector of the population and those who aspired to it. At the same time, recreational and festive diversions were discouraged, and ceremonial music and dancing, the hallmarks of a disparaged folk religiosity but also the devotional mode of peasant pilgrimage, were eventually forbidden. Instead, a local brotherhood was instituted, its chapters ramifying through the larger villages and towns of the region and beyond, in order to maintain the cult's momentum and to secure its economic survival.[10]

The career of Wank'a, then, is that of a peripheral miraculous shrine promoted by a religious order and transmuted into an important center of pilgrimage. As the Mercedarians expanded its catchment geographically across the landscape and socially across the different classes, so they inclined the cult further toward what they saw as a more universal, orthodox devotional style. The shrine was still a living rock, grounded in the sacred geography of a peasant livelihood, but it was also a vehicle for the propagation by an ecclesiastical élite of a quite different set of religious meanings and values, aimed not just at peasants but at a broad socioeconomic spectrum of the population.[11]

The tensions were irreconcilable. The cult, it seems, split apart at the core. New centers, their observances synchronized exactly with Wank'a's, became the foci for the community-based nación groups of the locality, with their concomitant folk rituals that were proscribed by the dominant cult. These centers, Señor el Justo Juez close by and Señor de Sani a few kilometers away, functioned once more on the ecclesiastical margins. The cult of Justo Juez is served by the priest and sacristan from the parish but is otherwise not subject to clerical interference. The active involvement of a clerical élite in the Wank'a cult has led to the sloughing off of peasant devotees from the immediate neighborhood, though, to the evident chagrin of the priests there, elements of a disdained, popular religiosity—largely, in this instance, the orthodox practices of an earlier era—persist.[12]

This polarization of pilgrimage between the regional shrine of Wank'a and the vicinal shrines of Justo Juez and Sani is encoded iconologically. The Wank'a shrine represents the punished Christ submitting to his torturers, Justo Juez and Sani the punishing Christ sitting in judgment upon mankind—twin images of Christ, suffering mortal versus omnipotent judge, that are juxtaposed time and again in Christian theology and in the Middle Ages were the dominant conceptions of God. All three shrines are miraculous theophanies, but Wank'a is fading while the others are permanent: the eventual disappearance of the tortured Lord of Wank'a will herald the dies irae of Lord the Just Judge. The complementary advocations thus mark the transition from the present age to the next in the ternary model of epochal time in the Andes. Their iconographies display the contrast bodily: the bowed, compliant Christ of the Mercedarian monastery becomes the erect, defiant Christ of the peasant countercults. Two countervailing tendencies in Andean Catholicism, a mestizo-favored lugubrious piety, fostered by a religious order, versus an Indian-favored festive religiosity, served by a secular curate, are here, quite literally, enshrined.

A comparison with Qoyllur Rit'i is instructive. The local and historical settings, of course, are quite different. From the outset, Qoyllur Rit'i fell within the ambit of parochial control; also, its managerial hierarchy is lay, not clerical, and is a fairly recent development. It is perhaps these very factors that explain why the opposition and contradictions reflected and generated by the cult have so far been wholly contained within a single ritual frame, processed through the dualist logic of the fiesta liturgy and encoded internally by means of icons, dance styles, and the division of ritual space. Even here, though, segregation and differential participation mark the beginnings of a retreat by some peasant pilgrims from those phases of the fiesta where the strains of ethnic superordination and élite control are at their most blatant.

In the instance under discussion, the course pursued by the regular custodians of Wank'a had a different outcome: not containment, but schism. The cult is now in effect partitioned into two sectors, the one regional and socially heterogeneous, the other vicinal and socially homogeneous, whose respective shrines are opposed categorically as "mestizo" to "Indian." The inevitable irony, of course, is that the structures of the regional cult are already reproducing themselves in the interlocal ones. The expansion of their devotional catchments at the periphery is matched by the development at the center of incipient hierarchies for organizing the cults and policing the congregations. The peasant guardians of the Oqoruro shrine are joined by the mestizo sacristan from the parish; they themselves flex their pietistic authority over the visiting pilgrims, assuming an aggressive superiority—just as can be observed at other interlocal shrines.

Within the San Salvador locality, the two rock shrines of Wank'a and Justo Juez, while at one level dialectically polar, at another level stand jointly opposed to the manufactured effigy of the patron of the vice-parish, San Salvador del Mundo. This offers a third, soteriologically central advocation of Christ: that of the loving redeemer, extending salvation to all mankind. But the ritual relations entertained by the two miraculous Christs on the periphery with their nonmiraculous counterpart in the local center are quite different. Wank'a, following the long struggle between the Mercedarians and the parish clergy, now enjoys complete autonomy from parochial jurisdiction and is not articulated in any way with local ceremonial. Justo Juez, by contrast, is permanently compromised. It is Janus-faced, being at once the patron of a dependent community and a focus of extralocal pilgrimage. The singular status of Oqoruro, as I have already observed, receives oblique ritual recognition in the locality festivals of Christ Savior and Christmastide through liturgical nuances which nonetheless ensure that local ecclesiastical hierarchy prevails.

The challenge presented by the Oqoruro shrine to the local center is more than merely ritual, more than purely figurative. The shrine actively foments and consolidates links between hinterland communities that cross-cut and confound local patterns of politico-religious dependency. It has come to assume a central, peacemaking role in the parabién, the inter-district gathering of communities that has replaced the bloody tinkuy fought in the names of the mountain gods. The titular fiesta in September mobilizes peasant naciones from a still wider radius and furthermore generates capital that is being invested in equipping and improving the shrine. Perhaps most important of all, the shrine is managed as a joint asset by the communities of Qamawara and Oqoruro and is seen as a symbol of their other common interests. In 1974, at a meeting of the respective community leaders on the sanctuary steps, there was even talk of the two hamlets merging to form a single comunidad campesina, so as to provide a more effective lobby before the district and governmental authorities. For these two communities, too, the shrine was an important incentive for the road project, which would of course severely dislocate the geopolitical structure of the district. The importance of the new road in generating mass pilgrimage and hence more funds for community development was expressly mentioned by Qamawaran delegates in their discussions with government officials.

Scott (1977, 31) claims that, for peripheral peoples in agararian societies, religion can act as a cradle for countervailing social links and dissentient moral values. In a religious culture as diversified and as mul-tiform as that of Andean Catholicism, that potential is unevenly distrib-uted. In some areas of religious practice it is all but stifled by the claustrophobic machinery of hierarchical control and by the relentless drive toward orthodox ritual expression. In others, it might gain space to develop and grow and to serve as a catalyst for a social movement of resistance or revolt. Most empirical instances lie somewhere between these two extremes. Under certain circumstances, local ceremonial can provide opportunities for making political statements: in San Salvador locality festivals, after probably centuries of stability, have recently begun to decay as hinterland communities withdraw from the centripetal rituals of Christ Savior and Holy Cross. In the social and symbolic domains of miraculous shrines, however, there is frequently room for wider maneu-vers, greater scope for experiment and innovation, than is offered in the setting of local ceremonial. Not inevitably: by the same token these shrines can fall prey to the strictest and most rigid hieratic régimes. Furthermore, the greater the numbers of people who are drawn into their ambits, the more they assume the trappings of superordination and hi-erarchy, displayed now in a regional forum rather than a merely local one. Nevertheless, their extralocal situation, coupled with their status in Leach's terminology (1972) as "icons of subversion," offering direct and unmediated access to the sacred, makes their cults potentially more supple, more flexible, more responsive to shifts in the wider political and economic environment, than those of the "icons of orthodoxy," the established patron saints of communities and parishes, within whose ritual routine hierarchy is encysted. Most important, miraculous shrines—unlike arbitrarily assigned local saints—have forged a bond with the rural landscape, encapsulating a tellurian power recognized beyond the confines of mere community and parochial affiliations.

The shrines considered in this chapter illustrate two extremes in the characters of miracle cults—polarities that are determinately related, for the peasant patronage of one shrine was spurred on by the tightening grip of an officializing élite on the other. The new theophany has in its turn come to provide a religious arena for the tentative, exploratory redefinition of social relations, largely untrammelled by formal allegiance to the local politico-religious center and in tacit counterpoint to it. Justo Juez stands as a mute challenge to the center, a virtual catalyst of novel, even subversive alliances and coalitions.

In its specifics, the analysis presented in this chapter has no pretensions to generality. The particular configuration of miraculous shrines elicited in this instance is unlikely to be replicated elsewhere. Local and regional settings make for a degree of historical contingency in the origin and development of such cults: this at least the widely differing examples in this chapter and the last serve to illustrate.

From these examples, though, have emerged some of the parameters of these diverse and unrepeatable processes: the kinds of social force that are vented in the cults and the logics and liturgies through which they acquire cultural form. It remains to set forth these parameters in the abstract.

CHAPTER 10

Conclusion

Regional shrines in the Andes have always been essential elements in the modeling of social space. Sacred landscapes provide the conceptual idioms for social relations, and transform along with those relations under the impact of conquest and colonization. But in time they come to possess a unique cultural geology, a layering of meanings that affects the disposition of subsequent cultural strata and exerts a restraining force on attempts to subjugate and annex the peoples who dwell within them. Sacred landscapes, in other words, are at once a means to legitimate domination and a means to resist it.

I noted in the first part of this study how very different were the strategies of the Inkas and the Spanish in their consolidation of empire. Inka hegemony was founded ultimately on loyalties and conflicts centered upon preexisting local and provincial shrines, which were assimilated into a central political geography focused on the imperial capital. To be sure, the power of the Inkas themselves was celestial, solar, transcending the place-specific deities of their subject peoples. Yet the solar cult itself became localized, most conspicuously in the sites of Titicaca, Pachakamaq, and of course the temple of Qorikancha in Cusco, and it stood, in effect, for the politico-religious center against its subordinate peripheries. Inka ritual and ideology portrayed imperial power as diffusing radially and uniformly through the artificially unified system of state, provincial, and local shrines from the center to the margins. The Inka universe was a vast, concentric macrocosm, periodically manifested in the sacrifices of the Qhapaq Hucha. This was the great achievement of the empire, but it was also its permanent weakness. For with the focal shrines of the ethnic polities left in place, secession was an ever present possibility.

The Spanish at first took over this religious and administrative design. Christian saints were installed alongside the pagan wak'as, but the old ethnic constituencies remained largely intact, serving as the templates for protocolonial agrarian organization. In southern Peru, the former Inka capital continued to be the focus of regional religious ceremonial. But after the crisis of the 1560s, all this changed. Now ethnic constituencies were chopped up, natives were resettled, administration was localized, and religious devotions came to be centered on patron saints of villages and parishes. Corporate communities busily cultivated their new, arbitrarily allocated divine tutelars, which became the indexes of local prestige and rank. State power now rested on the *lack* of translocal ritual articulation: even Cusco's great pageants declined to the status of mere civic parades.

Miraculous Christian shrines began to emerge contemporaneously with the development of this checkered politico-religious geography. Many of them were pagan sites transformed and were heavily interlaced with non-Christian religious meanings. But the relations between local and extralocal religious domains had now decisively changed from the pre-Hispanic pattern. With the cults of local saints wedded to the new, state-imposed politico-administrative structures, there was now a relatively sharp discontinuity between these neutered local divinities and the active, historically engaged spirits of the extralocal miraculous shrines. The latter came to constitute pantheons quite separate from the pyramidal hierarchies of local saints. So far from upholding an unchanging political order, such shrines are historical, not just in the sense of having originated in some prodigious event—in many instances at a time of social stress—and being subject to waxing and waning popularity through the years, but also in the sense of being able to affect radically, for better or for worse, the individual and collective fortunes of their devotees.

It is the extralocal status of miraculous shrines that makes their cults characteristically prone to conflict. Precisely because these cults are not load-bearing, in the sense of legitimating fixed spatial structures of domination and control, they can become arenas for competition and struggle between different groups and interests. Many became weapons in internal rivalries between different wings of the Church, commonly between the regular clergy, eager to exploit the potentialities of a popular pilgrimage site, and the secular episcopal establishment. A few have been taken over by lay élites, to stand as civic symbols of the transcendence of their interests over purely parochial concerns. And time and again, the cults are observed begetting an antagonistic, ethnic division and hierarchy among devotees, or between devotees and shrine staff. To identify the spirit of communitas in such phenomena would be sanguine, to say the least.

But underlying all these conflicts and oppositions and cleavages is a more fundamental contradiction, which miraculous shrines embody and materialize in a peculiarly vivid fashion. They are Christian, specifically Catholic holy sites. Their iconographies, certain of their religious meanings, and the clerical involvement in their cults all proclaim them to be so, to be the special properties of a universal church and the vehicles—particularly effective ones—for the propagation of the faith. But at the same time they are Andean, the key locations in a unique, historically configured sacred landscape, in some instances physically rooted in the bedrock of the terrain, pertaining to a wider cult of general and place-specific tellurian divinities and powers that underpins the cosmological processes of natural and social reproduction. When peasant informants speak of pentarchical systems of miraculous taytachas, they are using Christian shrines to reconstruct space according to an image which since pre-Inka times has served as the means for modeling regional, subimperial relations. When peasant pilgrims make their way as a nación across the mountain trails to a miraculous shrine, they are not merely paying obeisance to a crucifix or a Virgin, but are kinesthetically recovering a sacred space which to a degree is independent of state-controlled, politico-ecclesiastical space and in which they can redefine themselves, through union and opposition, in relation to one another and to other naciones. Andean pilgrimage, for the peasantry, is an attempt to domesticate a sector of the Christian cult, to appropriate it, and to insert it into the sociogeographic matrix of their environment, thereby recreating with Christian icons a nonimperial, translocal domain of social relations.

These two facets of miraculous shrines, Christian and Andean, are locked in a perpetual embrace. Christian icons become Andean, entrenched in the symbolic landscape of the peasantry and imbued with vernacular meanings and significance; yet it is precisely this deep-rooted and pervasive symbolism that makes them such valuable trophies for religious and social élites. Regional cults in the Andes provide a window on the process whereby a peasant consciousness of ethnic identity and resistance is continually being explored through and constructed from the mosaic of fragmented local commitments and allegiances, a consciousness that is constantly being transmuted into an ideology of superordination and hierarchy but is nonetheless susceptible to recovery and reconstruction, using the landscape itself as a perennial symbolic resource. The cults betray this permanent contradiction, swaying, changing, and splitting as different interests strive to gain the ascendant or challenge those that have. There can be no ultimate compromise or accommodation here: only a persistent split in religious belief and practice, a manifestation of the relentless cultural antagonism that history has visited upon the Andean peoples.

Notes

CHAPTER ONE Introduction

1. A cogent summary of the different treatments of pilgrimage in the wider anthropological literature appears in Morinis (1984), chapter 8.

2. Studies of pilgrimage elsewhere in which an approach similar to that of Dobyns is adopted include Spiro's study of Burmese Buddhists (1970), Rabinow on Moroccan Muslims (1975), Boyce on Persian Zoroastrians (1977) and Emmanuel Marx on Sinai Bedouin (1977). Cámara Barbachano and Reyes Couturier (1972) approach Mexican pilgrimage in this vein.

3. Studies of non-Christian pilgrimage in which specific issue is taken with Turner's dichotomized model include Pfaffenberger (1979) (Sri Lanka), Messerschmidt and Sharma (1981) (Nepal), Morinis (1984) (West Bengal), and Veer (1984) (Uttar Pradesh).

4. I shall want to distinguish later between regional and interlocal cults, the latter being formally identical to regional cults but of more restricted territorial range. For the time being, regional cult will serve as a generic category.

5. For a discussion of Simmel's dialectical sociology and its relevance to social anthropology, see Murphy (1971, 129–47).

6. The distinction, which in any case under analytical scrutiny is difficult to sustain, is ignored in the approach taken here.

7. These two modes of relatedness between human beings and the divine approximate, though do not exactly correspond, to Skorupski's cosmocentric and anthropocentric aspects of religion respectively: "I shall call religious teaching which concerns itself with the relation between God (or gods) and the world of nature (including man considered as a part of that nature) *cosmocentric* religion, and that which concerns itself with the relation between God (or gods) and the world of man *anthropocentric* religion" (Skorupski 1976, 25).

8. Cosgrove (1984) goes on to argue for the historical specificity of the landscape concept, portraying it as a product of people's alienation from the land attendant upon the transition from feudalism to capitalism. His analysis, confined within an exclusively Western frame of reference, is convincing as a historical situation of a particular European aesthetic genre, but it has little to say on the wider cross-cultural issues of environmental symbolization and perception.

9. All population figures in this study are derived from the census that was taken in 1972, at the time of my original fieldwork (Peru 1974).

10. A similar cosmetic was applied a century and a half earlier, when José de San Martín prohibited the use in the new republic of Peru of the words *indios* and *naturales* 'natives', ruling that thenceforth such people be called *ciudadanos* 'citizens' or 'freemen' (Davies 1974, 20). The Bolivian revolution of 1952 also adopted the word *campesino* in place of *indígena*.

11. Some of the problems encountered in writing about ethnicity in the Andean setting are discussed in van den Berghe (1974). The fact that, despite van den Berghe's methodological strictures, his own subsequent work on Andean ethnicity (van den Berghe and Primov 1977) does not escape similar criticism (see Gross 1979) is an indication of the difficulties involved in describing and analyzing the phenomenon.

12. Prelatures and apostolic vicariates are forms of ecclesiastical organization adapted for peripheral, quasi-missionary areas with scattered populations. Prelatures are headed by suffragan bishops and fall within the ecclesiastical province of an archbishop. Vicars-apostolic, on the other hand, are responsible directly to Rome.

13. Diocesan or secular clergy are those who do not belong to a religious order; regular clergy are those who do.

CHAPTER TWO A Pre-Columbian Panorama

1. See appendix 7 for details of orthographies employed and a guide to pronunciation.

2. The frequent conjunction of pilgrimage and extralocal trade comes about ultimately through the necessity for mediating values and equivalencies between disparate local systems, which a supralocal religious arena can provide. "In effect, economic transactions became possible when they could be made gainless. . . . This was achieved through the declaration of equivalencies in the name of the representative of the godhead itself" (Polanyi 1977, 61).

3. For early sources that have been published in later editions, a double reference system is used. The first entry, in square brackets, refers to the original manuscript or publication, giving book or chapter location when it is possible. The second entry refers to the later edition or translation that has been consulted.

4. "It was in a good house, well painted, in a very dark chamber with a close fetid smell. Here there was a very dirty idol made of wood, and they say that this is their god who created them and sustains them, and gives them their food. At the foot of the idol there were some offerings of gold, and it was held in such veneration that only the attendants and servants, who, as they say, were appointed by it, were allowed to officiate before it. . . . [It] is believed among the Indians that this idol is their god, that he can destroy them if they offend

him and do not serve him well, and that all the things in the world are in his hands. The people were so shocked and terrified at the Captain having merely gone in to see it, that they thought the idol would destroy all the Christians" (Estete [1534] 1872, 82−83).

5. While Arguedas proposes the date 1598 for the composition of the manuscript, Taylor has recently put the case for a later compilation, around 1608−9 (Taylor 1980a, 5−9).

6. *Wak'a* is a general Quechua word for any localized source of sacredness with pre-Christian connotations.

7. All translations from the Huarochirí narrative are my own.

8. According to Taylor (1980b, 234), *ñamka* or *ñamoq* refers not to a particular god but to the multiplicity of its manifestations in various shrines and sacred sites.

9. Poma de Ayala credits Topa Inka with the following ordinance: "We command that there be other populations like Cusco in Quito, Tumi, Guanoco, Hatun Colla and Charcas; and that the head of these cities be Cusco" (Poma de Ayala [1620] 1966, 1:131).

10. The points of transition from one month to the next were established by the equinoxes, such that the months ran approximately as follows: 21 March (equinox)−20 April; 21 April−19 May; 20 May−24 July (including the solstice); 25 July−22 August; 23 August−22 September (equinox); 23 September−22 October; 23 October−21 November; 22 November−20 January (including the solstice); 21 January−18 February; 19 February−20 March (Zuidema 1977, 246−47).

11. Mount Wanakauri is, in fact, about 1° off the Cusco-Tiwanaku axis. Zuidema suggests that the ceque actually ran from Wanakauri rather than Cusco, which was "hooked on" to it by one of its local ceques (Zuidema 1982, 443).

12. For the general political and ecclesiastical history of late fifteenth- and early sixteenth-century Spain I rely mainly on Elliott (1963) and Lynch (1981).

13. Peru, however, eventually began to produce its own crop of saints, who gave rise to both shrine-centered and general devotions, as will be mentioned later.

CHAPTER THREE The Andes Reconsecrated

1. *Konopas* were known in Cusco as *chankas*.

2. The authentication process has been steadily tightening. Since 1947, an alleged miraculous cure has had to be verified by three independent bodies: the Medical Bureau at Lourdes, the International Medical Commission in Paris, and an ad hoc canonical commission set up in the ecclesiastical province in which the person to whom the miracle happened resides (Neame 1968, 138).

3. Corpus Christi is a movable feast; for its timing and that of other important movable and fixed feasts in the Roman calendar, see appendix 5. A novena is the nine-day period immediately preceding a feast, an octave the eight-day period immediately following it.

4. The mental torment of Indian converts to Christianity was acute. Many were haunted for years by dreams and visions of the wak'as, who assumed the form of attractive sexual partners enticing them back to the old religion (Stern 1982, 182).

5. Diocesan ruling of 1685, Legajo 306, Audiencia de Lima, Archivo General de Indias.

6. The shrine of the Virgin of Guadalupe at Pacasmayo, founded by an encomendero around the year 1560 (Vargas Ugarte 1956, 2:99—106), lies beyond the purview of the present study. It is worth noting, however, that it too is situated close to an important pre-Columbian coastal shrine, that of Pakatnamú, which flourished during the Wari and Chimú eras.

7. The devotion to Santa Rosa is the best-known example of another syndrome in Peruvian Catholicism alongside the cult of miraculous images, namely, the cult of local female saints. These tend to occur in the coastal zone rather than in the highlands. Crumrine (1978) describes two such pilgrimage shrines in the department of Ica, both of women who were reported to have led exemplary Christian lives; one died in 1869, the other as recently as 1951.

8. Pressing the analysis further, MacCormack goes on to argue that the upper moiety favored the Virgin as confraternity patron because she had miraculously intervened to save the lives of the beleaguered Spaniards during Manko Inka's siege of Cusco. The choice of patron thus reflected their common interests with the Spaniards, and was a ploy to integrate themselves into the new ruling class. The evidence for a specific connection here is shaky. As mentioned earlier, the story of the miraculous deliverance in Cusco was recorded only in 1600, suggesting that the entire story was fabricated by later chroniclers. While Poma de Ayala, writing in the early 1600s, places the Virgen de la Descensión (identified with his own favorite Marian devotion, the Virgen de la Peña de Francia) on a par with the Virgen de Copacabana ([1620] 1966, 2:298), this in no sense confirms that the former inspired the latter. In any event, the Spaniards with whom the Inkas of Copacabana were allied were not the Pizarrist defenders of Cusco during the siege of 1536 but the enemy faction led by Almagro (Hemming 1972, 223—28). The upper moiety's choice of the Virgin as patron, and its subsequent popularity, typified a much more general leaning toward Mariolatry among Indians at the time, as I shall discuss later.

9. This elemental opposition in protocolonial Andean religion was later to give way to more complex syncretic patternings, as will be shown presently.

10. The Council of Trent, whose decrees were received in Peru in 1567, set out new regulations concerning the appearance of holy images and probably influenced the reaction of the clergy to Tito Yupanki's efforts (MacCormack 1985, 456).

CHAPTER FOUR Cusco's Miraculous Landscape

1. This incident was used as the basis for a scene in the novel *El padre Horán* by the *indigenista* precursor Narciso Aréstegui. Here there is a rumor that the retouched version was a fake and that the original had been carried off by Bolivian agents, this being a period of Bolivian hegemony in southern Peru. The citizens took to the streets but were calmed by a priest, who told them: "It is the people who lose in revolutions. We want only peace" (cited in Klaiber 1977, 73—74).

2. C-VI, 1, 13; C-L, 1, 24; C-XXXII, 1, 32; C-XLIII, 1, 13; C-XCII, 1, 5, Archivo Arzobispal del Cusco.

3. See the glossary for summary descriptions of dance styles mentioned in the text.

4. XXXVIII, 1, 7, Archivo Arzobispal del Cusco.

5. Diocesan visit of 1674, Legajo 306, Audiencia de Lima, Archivo General de Indias.

6. Urcos was originally placed under the protection of Santiago, but its de facto patron saint is the Virgin of the Immaculate Conception (Marzal 1971, 153). There is a detectable tendency for villages and parishes to adopt a Marian advocation as a patron when a lesser saint has been officially designated. Thus, Pisac, Calca, and Urubamba all originally had San Pedro; now Pisac and Calca fête the Virgin of the Assumption, Urubamba the Virgin of the Rosary (cf. "Relación de las parroquias de la Diócesis del Cusco con designación de los santos patronos respectivos" [1929], C-XII, 2, 22, Archivo Arzobispal del Cusco).

7. People from Kuyo Grande, for example, in the adjacent district of Pisac, visit Amaru, Oqoruro, Paruparu, Saqaka, Taray, and T'oqra (Casaverde Rojas 1970, 133). People from Sonqo, in the district of Colquepata, visit Aqcha, Oqoruro, Sipaskancha Baja, and T'oqra (Allen 1978).

8. C-III, 1, 18, Archivo Arzobispal del Cusco. Other reports and petitions concerning miraculous phenomena to be found in these archives include C-L, 1, 12 and C-LXVI, 1, 12.

9. This point will be documented later with respect to an interlocal shrine in the district of San Salvador, Señor el Justo Juez.

10. Another group of priests celebrated the sunset at a place northwest of the city, in the precise direction of Tiobamba. This station is not identified in the chronicles, however (Zuidema 1982, 443).

11. Not all trade takes place in marketplaces, of course. A considerable amount of agropastoral produce is sold to local or itinerant merchants who visit peasants in their homes and who pass it along in turn to wholesalers in the urban entrepôts of Cusco or Sicuani, as will be described presently.

CHAPTER FIVE A Local Profile

1. Caicay, for example, farther upstream, situated on a cul-de-sac on the "wrong" side of the river (cf. Flores Ochoa 1974).

2. The adobe farmstead, consisting of a dwelling and a storehouse, lasts for about twenty to twenty-five years but requires rethatching every four years or so.

3. The transactional aspect of Andean reciprocity is well documented in the literature—see, for example, Alberti and Mayer 1974—its ideological dimension less so.

4. The unit of Peruvian currency at the time was the *sol*, written S/. During the early 1970s, the sol was pegged to the U.S. dollar at S/.43.38 = $1.00, but by 1980 it was running at ten times that level. By the end of 1985 continuing devaluation had brought the exchange rate to more than S/.10,000, and a new currency unit was introduced, the *inti*, written I/., with S/.1000 = I/.1.00. To avoid confusion, I shall give dollar equivalents throughout.

5. Wage labor between peasants need not always spell inequality or alienation. In the community of Matapuquio, department of Apurímac, a cash payment for labor between peasants is regarded more as a security than a wage, to

be returned at a later date—often as the very same notes and coins—when the master-peon relation is reversed (Skar 1982, 215).

6. This latent asymmetry is derived from the fact that the relations between partners, once established, can never be reversed.

7. The agrarian reform program was hailed enthusiastically by radicals both inside and outside Peru. Field studies of its implementation, however, show that the expectations it raised were rarely borne out in practice. They indicate a lack of communication between planners and peasants, the emergence of unreliable informal brokers to "interpret" the dense legislation to illiterate beneficiaries, the inappropriateness of the organizational models for the new cooperatives in the Andean environment, the restricted access to decisionmaking as a result of the structure and size of the enterprises, and the emergence of cooperative members as a class distinguished by privilege from seasonal day laborers and community peasants (Conlin 1974; Guillet 1979; Harding 1975; McClintock 1981; Skar 1982). The elimination of the old landowning class under the reform could be seen as the latest phase in the long struggle between the industrial and commercial bourgeoisie on the one hand and the traditional agrarian élite on the other (Zaldívar 1974).

8. What follows is a summary of part of an argument developed at length in Sallnow (1983).

9. The isolated community of Q'ero was first described by Oscar Núñez del Prado (1969). It has since been studied by Steven Webster, who in a recent paper (1981) presents a subtle characterization of the manorial status of such communities.

10. A full discussion of the organizational models proposed and implemented by the agrarian reform legislation appears in Bourque and Palmer 1975.

11. In 1973–74, daily wages during the harvest in these areas were about $1.20.

12. Guillet (1974) describes a similar situation in the Pampa de Anta area during the early 1970s.

13. One of the earliest Andean ethnographies, of the community of Kauri, province of Quispicanchis, department of Cusco, has what is still the best description of a functioning varayoq system (Mishkin 1946, 443–48).

14. All single men over the age of nineteen are liable for the military draft, exemption applying only to men married according to civil law, which few peasants are. In principle the draft is voluntary, but volunteers never satisfy Cusco's departmental quota of 1,500 men, and to make up the deficit annual lotteries of draft-card numbers are held at provincial and district levels. Press gangs are also not unknown. The methods of recruitment, and the way they are administered by the police and civilian authorities, ensure that the majority of those drafted are peasants from hinterland communities. Most learn Spanish during their period of service, and a few lucky ones acquire marketable skills.

15. The varayoq is not always so lightly discarded. The community of T'oqra, in the nearby district of Colquepata, for example, petitioned the government to be allowed to retain the varayoq structure for internal community administration only. The petition was unsuccessful (Primov 1980, 163).

16. SINAMOS is a punning acronym for Sistema Nacional de Apoyo a la Movilización Social, National System of Support for Social Mobilization; *sin amos* means 'without masters'.

CHAPTER SIX Ordering the Microcosm

1. During the Inka period, the spirit-owners of state mines assumed material form as *mamas,* pieces of ore selected for their singular appearance, which were supplicated through sacrifice to give up their subterranean riches (Berthelot 1978, 961–62).

2. Beliefs in local nature spirits are found throughout the central Andes, but titles and functions of the deities vary from place to place. See Bastien (1978) for a detailed local study, and Favre (1967), Martínez (1983), and Morissette and Racine (1973) for more theoretical treatments.

3. Beliefs in *machus* are also general throughout the area. For an early study, see Loayza (1953).

4. For contrasting interpretations of this Andean reworking of the idea of the Christian Trinity, found throughout the area, see Fuenzalida (1979), who argues that it is a collapsed version of the pre-Columbian pentadic schema, and Urbano (1980), who claims it is an expanded, linear modification of the indigenous dual cycle. For a finely detailed mythohistorical sequence, see R. Gow and Condori (1976).

5. For further evidence on this point, see O. Núñez del Prado (1952, 9) for contemporary Andeans, Murra (1962, 712–13) for pre-Columbian culture.

6. The practice of keeping skulls is widespread; see, for example, Mishkin (1946, 465); Allen (1978, 66).

7. For Qotobamba, Pisac district, see J. Núñez del Prado (1970, 76–82); for Kuyo Grande, Pisac district, see Casaverde Rojas (1970, 140–49); for Sonqo, Colquepata district, see Allen (1978, 53–54).

8. The notion that the mountain spirits constitute a political hierarchy analogous to the secular one is elaborated elsewhere in the central Andes; see, for example, Earls (1969, 69–70), B. J. Isbell (1978, 151).

9. Martínez (1983, 95) notes a general tendency toward a specialization of certain nature spirits in the twin domains of animals and minerals.

10. The ingredients for despachos can be bought in Pisac market; complete despachos can also be purchased assembled ready for use. For detailed descriptions of the *despachos* used for different purposes in the area, see Casaverde Rojas (1970, 225–36).

11. See, for example, the collection of brief studies of these rites in volume 3 of *Allpanchis* (Cusco).

12. Since Quechua *i* is intermediate between Spanish *i* and *e,* the word *misa* spans the meanings 'mass' (Sp. *misa*) and 'table' (Sp. *mesa*) (Gose 1986, 299); see also Sharon (1976).

13. The *wayno* is the main Andean genre of recreational dance music, frequently with vocal accompaniment. Melodies are typically pentatonic, and of the form *A A' B B'.*

14. The Laymi of Bolivia also play mournful music on special flutes during the rainy season, which they claim attracts rain (Harris 1982, 57).

15. In Sonqo, district of Colquepata, sheep are made to chew coca at their ceremony (Allen 1978, 204).

16. See for example Favre (1967, 127); Nachtigall (1975).

17. Compadres and Comadres are movable feasts falling on the two Thursdays immediately preceding Lent. They are linked historically to the rit-

ual coparenthood complex, but in the San Salvador locality this aspect is not stressed.

18. Wiphala dances during the Carnival season are reported from elsewhere in the region—from Sicuani (Canchis), for instance, and Livitaca (Chumbivilcas) (Navarro del Aguila 1944, 73); Portugal Catacora (1981, 98–105) describes the altiplano variant.

19. Casaverde Rojas defines *encantarse* in this context as "to remain prisoner of supernatural beings in places considered taboo" (1970, 147).

20. Tinkuys are described in Alencastre and Dumézil (1953), Barrionuevo (1969), Gilt Contreras (1955), Gorbak, Lischetti, and Muñoz (1962), Hartman (1972), Platt (1978), and elsewhere. For an attempt at synthesis, see Mariscotti de Görlitz (1978, 159–63).

21. Instances of dual organization of local groups are described in Arguedas (1956), Barette (1972), Brush (1977), Harris (1978), B. J. Isbell (1978), Mitchell (1976), Platt (1978), Skar (1982), Stein (1961), and elsewhere. Theoretical syntheses include Fuenzalida (1970) and Skar (1982, 93–102).

22. "Games . . . have a *disjunctive* effect: they end in the establishment of a difference between individual players or teams where originally there was no indication of inequality. . . . Ritual, on the other hand, is the exact inverse: it *conjoins*, for it brings about a union . . . or in any case an organic relation between two initially separate groups" (Lévi-Strauss 1966, 32).

23. San Roque, St Rock, was a fourteenth-century healer who was himself struck down by the plague while on a pilgrimage to Rome. When he returned to his native Languedoc, his relatives failed to recognize him and he was thrown into prison, where he ended his days. Another version of the legend says that he was jailed in Lombardy, where he was taken for a spy (Attwater 1965, 299).

24. This feature of fiesta celebration has been documented by, among others, B. J. Isbell (1978) for the Ayacucho Quechua and Buechler (1980) for the Bolivian Aymara.

25. Similar symbolic plowing is reported for Carnival fiestas in Spain (Foster 1960, 176).

26. The fiesta of Carnival in Andean peasant communities is often used as an arena for innovation on the part of emergent status groups. Adams notes, for example, that a criollo ceremony known as the *yunsa*, in which a tree is symbolically felled by dancing couples, made its appearance in the Carnival fiesta in Muquiyauyo, Junín department, at the beginning of this century, when the community was starting to modernize under the economic and cultural influences of the coast (Adams 1959, 57). More recently, Guillet has documented the introduction of the same ceremony, together with a mestizo practice known as the *comparso*, into the Carnival celebrations of a community in the Pampa de Anta, Cusco department, as part of a new fiesta being promoted by returned migrants (Guillet 1974, 152–53).

27. Harris (1982) pursues a similar argument concerning Carnival among the Bolivian Laymi, though the cultural elaboration differs. Lira (1953) made much the same point.

28. Compare this clerical interpretation with the view of lay devotees of the patronal Virgin of Santa Fe, New Mexico. Their Virgin, they claimed emphatically, was *non*miraculous, the only miracle being their devotion to her: "Our faith is her miracle" (Grimes 1976, 78).

29. San Isidro Labrador, St Isidore the Farm-Servant, was an eleventh-century Spanish farm laborer, supposed to have been a model worker and a kind neighbor. He became the patron saint of Madrid, and this probably accounts for his popularity in Spanish America (Attwater 1965, 180–81; Foster 1960, 190–91). He was at the same time a convenient embodiment of the values of fealty and subservience which Indians were meant to owe to their Spanish masters.

30. Santa Cruz, the feast of the Finding of the Cross, commemorates the alleged discovery by St Helen of the cross of the crucifixion at Christ's tomb in A.D. 326.

31. Here I shall develop my earlier argument concerning hacienda organization, which is set out at length in Sallnow (1983).

32. Bastien (1978, 58) makes a similar point in reference to mountain spirits and local Christian saints among the Bolivian Qollahuaya: "They never mix the two classes of shrines and their specific rituals."

CHAPTER SEVEN Pilgrimage

1. The music is set out in appendix 4, example 3.

2. The only proper account of the fiesta that had been published was that of Ramirez (1969), which was out of print at the time.

3. The wayri ch'uncho and ukuku figures will be described in detail in the next chapter.

4. A similar practice of vicarious pilgrimage was common during the Middle Ages (Sumption 1975, 298–99).

5. Competitiveness between musicians of different naciones has been noted by other observers, among them Allen (1978, 227).

6. In the Middle Ages death on a pilgrimage was welcomed, since the deceased would be near the saint's body and would have his or her advocacy at the Last Judgment (Sumption 1975, 129).

7. The flower was used to make a medicine for the treatment of coughs. It was referred to as *sisa* 'pollen', but I have been unable to make a botanical identification.

8. The resultant footage formed part of Pasini and Sallnow (1974).

9. I am grateful to Debbie Wilson for the last observation.

CHAPTER EIGHT The Cult of Qoyllur Rit'i

1. The best general account of both the mythohistory and the fiesta is still that by Juan Ramirez (1969), who served as priest in Ccatca for six years and who had charge of the Sinakara sanctuary. David Gow (1974) aims to depict the cult within the setting of colonial Christianity in general and offers good treatments of the ceremonial dancers, with interpretations based on his fieldwork in Pinchimuro, not far from the shrine. David Gow (1976) has a fuller discussion of the cult with reference to this community, while Rosalind Gow and Bernabé Condori (1976) present detailed myths relating to the shrine. David Gow (1980) explores the relation between Qoyllur Rit'i and Ausankati. Robert Randall (1982a)

attempts to locate the cult within a general Andean cosmological framework. Accounts of pilgrimage to Qoyllur Rit'i include those of Thomas Muller (1980) (from Q'eros, Paucartambo province), Michael J. Sallnow (1974, 110-17) (from Qamawara, Calca province), and Catherine J. Allen (1978, 224-31) (from Sonqo, Paucartambo province). José María García (1983, 52-67) gives an account by a Jesuit priest working in communities in Quispicanchis province of visits to the shrine during the late 1970s, on one of which the author served as a ritual dancer. *Sur* (1982, 51-53) sets out a local legend (from Ccatca, Quispicanchis province) of the origin of the shrine. Manuel Marzal (1971, 231-43) gives a general description of the cult, together with the results of a questionnaire submitted to people in the Urcos area concerning their visits to the shrine and motives for going. Rodrigo Sánchez-Arjona Halcón (1981, 151-56) offers a similar account, together with a Jesuit's theological reflections on the cult, while Ana Gisbert-Sauch (1979) interprets the fiesta as part of a "cult for the poor." Popular illustrated reports include those of Alfonsina Barrionuevo (1969, 199-201), Robert Randall (1982b), and Peter Cloudsley (1985). The fiesta is also the subject of several recent documentary films, among them that of Carlos Pasini and Michael J. Sallnow (1974), that by Peter Getzels and Harriet Gordon (1985), and that of Alain Dumas (1986).

2. This version, entitled "Origen tradicional de la aparición del Señor que se rinde culto en Sinakara y Tayankani," by P. Adrián Mujica, is kept in the parish archives of Ccatca. The original testimony of the priest who witnessed the vision is alleged to have been lost during the wars of emancipation. There is, though, a document in the parish archives of Ocongate, dated 1785, which refers to the "altar of Señor de Tayankani" in the church there (Ramirez 1969, 63). See also David Gow (1974, 89).

3. Information kindly supplied by the Royal Astronomical Society, London.

4. This ethnic-ecological opposition and complementarity between puna dwellers and kishwa dwellers, pastoralists and agriculturalists, respectively, is general throughout the central Andes. Cf Duviols (1973).

5. At the time of the founding of the shrine Ocongate was in the anomalous position of lying within the political jurisdiction of Quispicanchis province, or *partido*, as it was then called, while it was an ecclesiastical annex of the parish (*curato*) of Ccatca, which was then in the partido of Paucartambo (Mörner 1978, plates 10 and 11). Ocongate is now a parish in its own right. Ccatca was transferred to the province of Quispicanchis in 1920, but it still pertains to the Paucartambo moiety as far as the fiesta alignments are concerned (D. Gow 1974, 89).

6. Allen (1983) offers a perceptive analysis of the ukuku story, in the light of the affirmations of her male Sonqo informants that they were simultaneously ukukus and Inkas. The ukuku figure, she argues, encapsulates the contradictions and ambiguities of runa identity: "*Runa* are caught in a dilemma, for to be civilized relative to the Inkas is to be wild in terms of national society, and vice versa. The *ukuku* story is about that dilemma and what it means to be caught in it. The [story] takes the *runa*'s wildness and turns it upside down" (pp. 46-49).

7. There is also a reported association between ukukus and alpacas. The people of Pinchimuro claim that the first alpaca was born of an ukuku or an ukumari, and that ukukus dance at Qoyllur Rit'i in order to have lots of animals. David and Rosalind Gow point to the references in the official mythohistory of the shrine to the miraculous multiplication of animals (Gow and Gow 1975,

143–46). Elsewhere, David Gow (1974, 77) suggests that an original alpaca symbolism was transformed into its present ursine form because of Spanish cultural influence, but there is no direct evidence for this.

8. There is another qolla dance style in the Cusco region, not usually represented at Qoyllur Rit'i, known as the *waqcha qolla* (*waqcha* 'poor or orphaned').

9. Another substyle is the *k'ara ch'uncho* (*k'ara* 'naked' or 'peeled'), which has a quite distinctive headdress (Verger 1951, plates 84 and 85). Ramirez (1969, 84) and Barrionuevo (1969, 201) refer to the ch'unchos at Qoyllur Rit'i as k'ara. I did not, however, observe this style at the fiesta in the 1970s and 1980s.

10. *Chonta, Bactris ciliata,* is a small palm tree with a hard, black, elastic, ebonylike wood, growing in the montaña below 1,200 meters. In Inka times it was used for making spears and other weapons, and it was an important trade item from the tropical forest peoples to the highlands (Gade 1975, 144).

11. The Machiguenga, an Arawakan-speaking group who inhabit the lower Urubamba and its mountainous tributaries, are the immediate northwesterly neighbors of the Quechua. Their traditional mode of subsistence is a mixed economy of horticulture, hunting, and fishing. In response to the pressure of raids from the Piro-Chontakiros farther downriver, some Machiguenga shamans emerged as local polygynous bigmen, *itinkame* or *wayri,* who dealt with the intruders by using tactical diplomacy and trade. During the rubber boom earlier in this century, these bigmen became intermediaries, supplying native labor to the planters; some acquired guns and terrorized their own people. By the time the rubber boom collapsed, the Machiguenga had been decimated and had become disorganized (Camino 1978, 91–95). Today, the role of bigman tends to be assumed by native Machiguenga schoolteachers (Johnson and Johnson 1975, 637).

12. The nación of Q'eros, a community that enjoys the reputation in the region of being the most traditional in its customs, in fact visits Sinakara just *after* the main fiesta, immediately before Corpus. This nación also segregates itself spatially from the mass of devotees, occupying a site on the hillside opposite the sanctuary. See Muller (1980).

13. For the opportunity to gather the information in this paragraph I am indebted to Penny Harvey, then a doctoral student at the London School of Economics, who carried out research on bilingualism and social differentiation in Ocongate between 1983 and 1985.

14. In the past, another confrontation is reported to have taken place at this point. In 1974, Rosalind Gow obtained this account from an informant: "First the ukukus went up to get plants and ice which they took to El Señor. Then the machulas did exercises on the pampa opposite the chapel. When the ukukus returned they played leap-frog and rolled in the wet snow together. They played for a long time and then they had a 'revolution.' First the machulas killed one of the ukukus and bore him to the chapel on their sticks, but the ukuku came to life again, beat back the machulas, and finally rounded them up with his whip. It was only a game but two years ago some ukukus were swallowed up by the snow and disappeared. Now we don't do it any more" (cited in D. Gow 1978, 205–6).

15. Ocongate does not at present have a k'achampa troupe.

16. In Aymara villages of the altiplano, there used to be mock battles at Candlemas fiestas between dance troupes known respectively as inkas and qollas.

The dancers would lob peaches at one another with slings. The qolla style is now defunct; only the dance of the inkas remains (Portugal Catacora 1981, 106–12).

17. A film of the Qoyllur Rit'i festival by Alain Dumas (1986) shows that a number of changes have recently been made. The games of fantasy around the grotto have been invaded by traders from the altiplano selling model trucks and houses—even toy money—a feature well established at the festival of the Virgin of Copacabana. Meanwhile, the procession of the shrine image through the sanctuary precincts is now complemented by a simultaneous procession of the Virgen Dolorosa, the two images meeting in front of the sanctuary. In this respect the liturgy is coming to resemble more closely the liturgies of more orthodox cults, such as that of Señor de Wank'a.

CHAPTER NINE The Cults of Wank'a and Justo Juez

1. The cult of Señor de Wank'a is scarcely documented. There is an official history written by a chaplain of the sanctuary in the 1930s (Márquez Eyzaguirre 1937), while Marzal (1971, 225–31) gives a brief account of the founding legend and the modern fiesta. A slightly different version of the legend appears in Barrionuevo (1969, 211–13). Some of the data and analysis in this chapter were published in a different form in Sallnow (1982).

2. The documents on which Márquez Eyzaguirre bases his account, and presumably other documents relating to the history of the shrine, are kept in the archives of the Mercedarian monastery of La Merced in Cusco. Despite strenuous efforts, I was unable to obtain permission to consult these archives. Marzal (1971, 226–27) makes use of a source that has the third apparition occurring in 1775. Since Márquez Eyzaguirre's account purports to be the official history of the shrine, I here follow his chronology, which also accords better with independent contemporary sources. Even so, it has been necessary to iron out a number of inconsistencies in his account.

3. Diocesan visit of 1687, Legajo 306, Archivo General de Indias. The cofradía would undoubtedly have inspired the Wank'a cult rather than vice versa, else the former would have been dedicated to Señor de Wank'a rather than to Cristo de la Columna.

4. The ritual significance of 14 September throughout the Andes might, however, be derived from its having been set aside by the sixteenth-century extirpators of idolatry as the day on which a special Christian festival was to be held in a town following the destruction of its *wak'as* (Arriaga [1621, chap. 16] 1968, 255).

5. The precise date of the ban cannot be determined without recourse to the Mercedarian archives, but from informants' comments it would seem to have been during the first decades of this century. The present chaplain stressed to me that the ban was in effect only for the titular fiesta, to preserve the sanctity of the event; during the rest of the year, folkloric presentations are often staged at the sanctuary.

6. I am indebted to Debbie Poole for assistance in collecting the information on the provenance of pilgrims and also of traders in the fair in San Salvador.

7. Miraculous apparitions are not inevitably consigned to a distant past; some, like that of Señor de Wat'a, are remembered as having happened within informants' lifetimes.

8. I am grateful to Rubén Orellana of the Instituto Nacional de Cultura for information on this archaeological research as of 1984. Unfortunately, I did not have the opportunity to pursue these speculations with local informants.

9. Electric light is a powerful symbol of modernity and progress in the Andes, as the studies of community development by Adams (1959) and Doughty (1968) clearly illustrate.

10. The career of Lourdes was similar. At first, as a minor shrine, it drew pilgrims from local peasants and tradesmen. Later, as its powers were disseminated through the printed word, it attracted the middle classes from farther afield. The regional and national catchments drew from a broader social base as well as from a wider geographic area than the traditional local catchment, for the literate middle classes felt more comfortable with an officially sanctioned miracle cult (Kselman 1978, 84−88). For case studies of the clerical promotion of miraculous shrines elsewhere in Latin America, see Cava 1970 (Brazil) and Kagan 1973 (Colombia).

11. A classic study by Hertz (1983) of the ecclesiastical appropriation and officialization of an Alpine rock cult reveals close parallels with the present case.

12. Much of what appears as unofficial belief and practice in contemporary Catholicism derives from this phenomenon of cultural hysteresis. Cf Foster (1953).

APPENDIX I

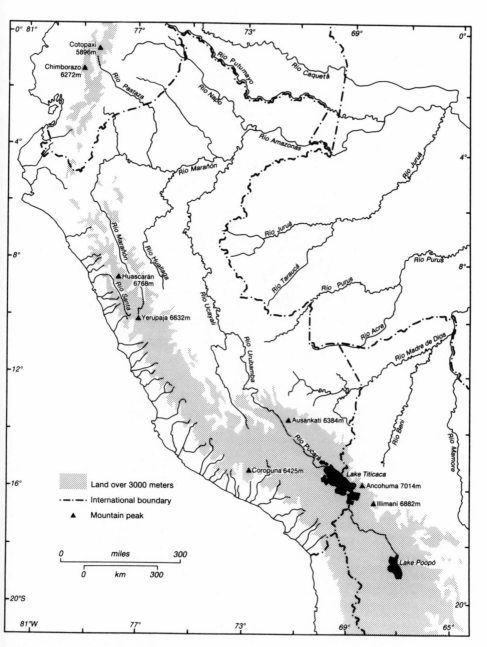

MAP 1   *Peru: Physical*

MAP 2   *Modern Peru*

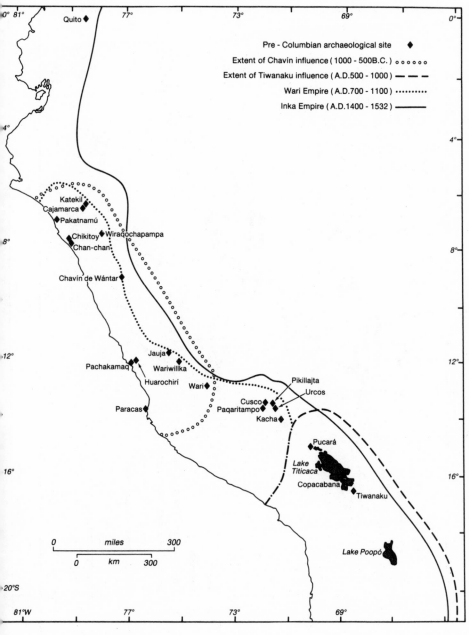

Legend:

Pre - Columbian archaeological site ◆
Extent of Chavín influence (1000 - 500B.C.) ○○○○○○
Extent of Tiwanaku influence (A.D.500 - 1000) ― ― ―
Wari Empire (A.D.700 - 1100) ··········
Inka Empire (A.D.1400 - 1532) ―――――

Quito
Katekil
Cajamarca
Pakatnamú
Chikitoy
Wiraqochapampa
Chan-chan
Chavín de Wántar
Jauja
Pachakamaq
Wariwillka
Huarochirí
Wari
Pikillajta
Urcos
Cusco
Paqaritampo
Paracas
Kacha
Pucará
Lake Titicaca
Copacabana
Tiwanaku
Lake Poopó

0   miles   300
0   km   300

MAP 3   *Ancient Peru*

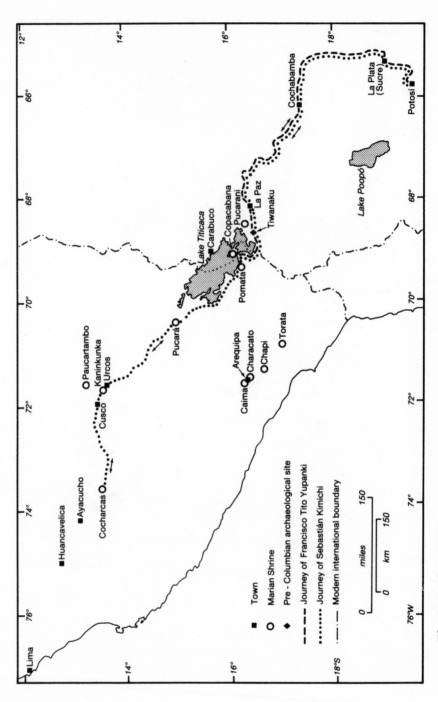

MAP 4   *The Copacabana Shrine System*

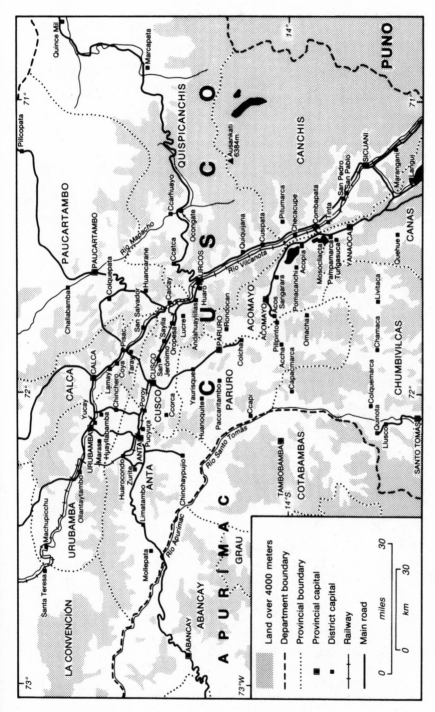

MAP 5 *The Cusco Region*

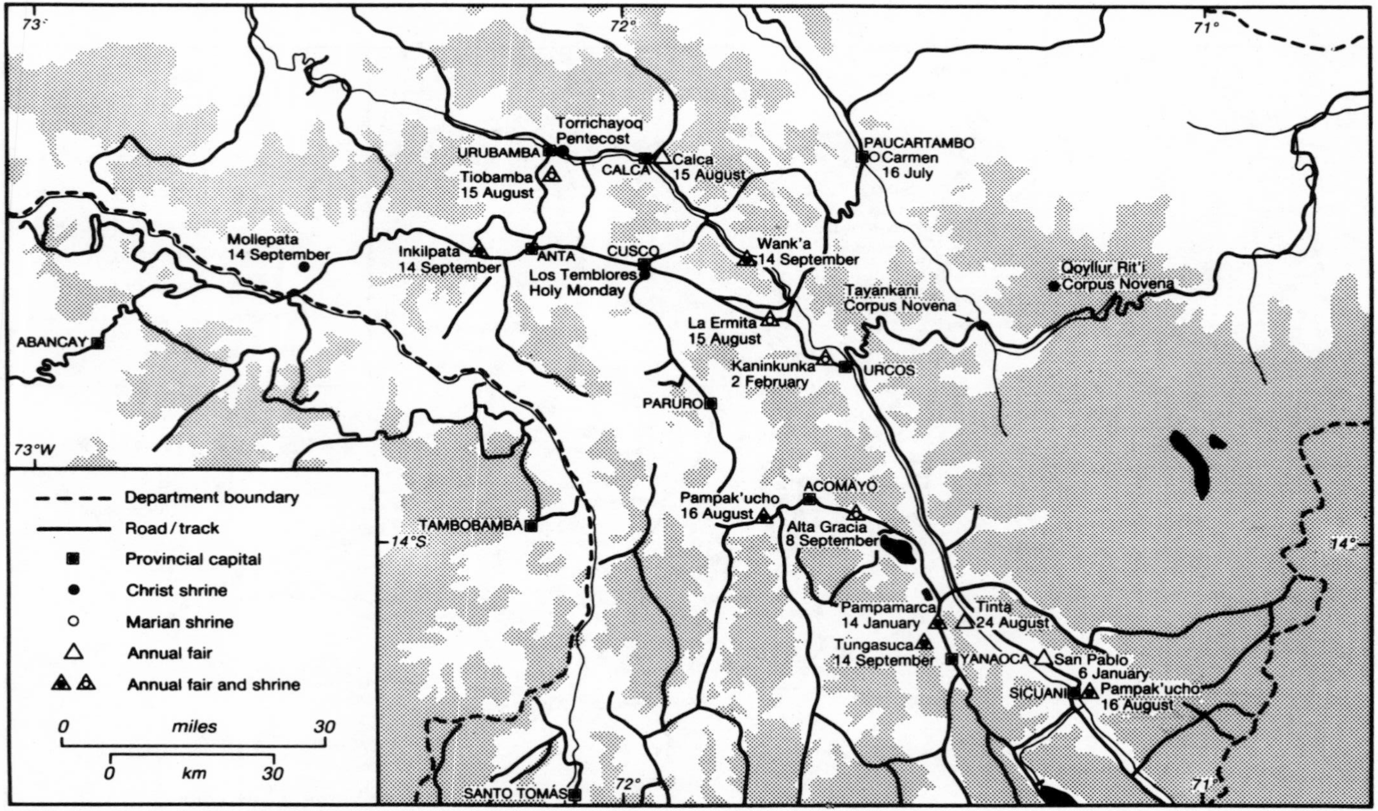

MAP 6 *Regional Shrines and Fairs in Cusco*

Qoyllur Rit'i
Corpus Novena

PAUCARTAMBO
O Carmen
16 July

San Pablo
6 January
SICUANI ▲ Pampak'ucho
16 August

YANAOCA △ San Pablo

Tinta
24 August

Pampamarca
14 January
Tungasuca
14 September

Tayankani
Corpus Novena

Wank'a
14 September

URCOS

ACOMAYO
Alta Gracia
8 September

Calca
15 August

Kaninkunka
2 February

La Ermita
15 August

Pampak'ucho
16 August

CALCA

Torrichayoq
Pentecost

Los Temblores
Holy Monday

CUSCO

PARURO

ANTA

Tiobamba
15 August

URUBAMBA

Inkilpata
14 September

TAMBOBAMBA

14°S

Mollepata
14 September

ABANCAY

SANTO TOMAS

73°W

Department boundary
Road / track
■ Provincial capital
● Christ shrine
○ Marian shrine
△ Annual fair
▲ △ Annual fair and shrine

0   miles   30
0   km   30

290

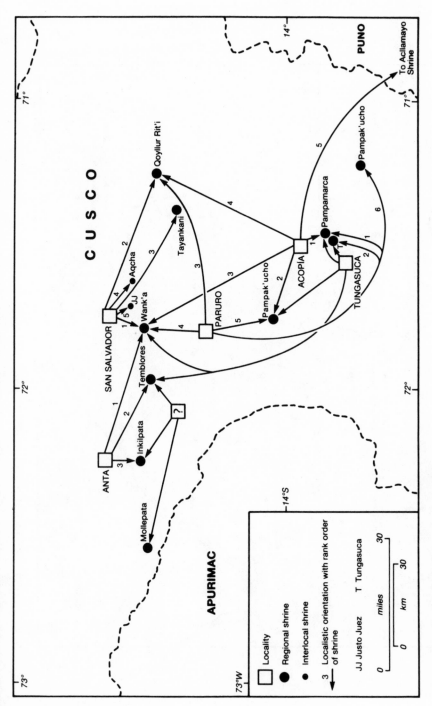

MAP 7 *Locally Focused Shrine Sets in Cusco*

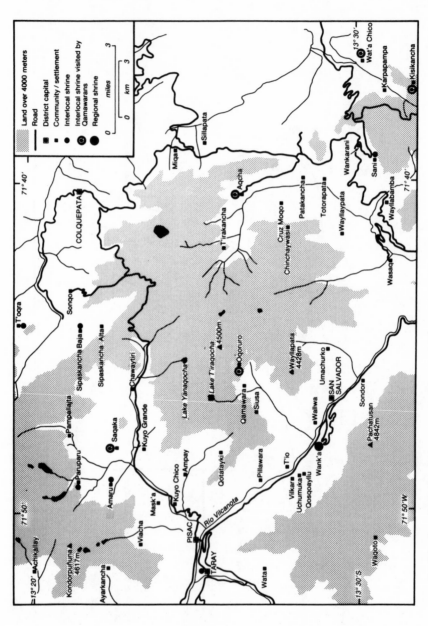

MAP 8   *The San Salvador Microregion and Its Setting: Interlocal Shrines*

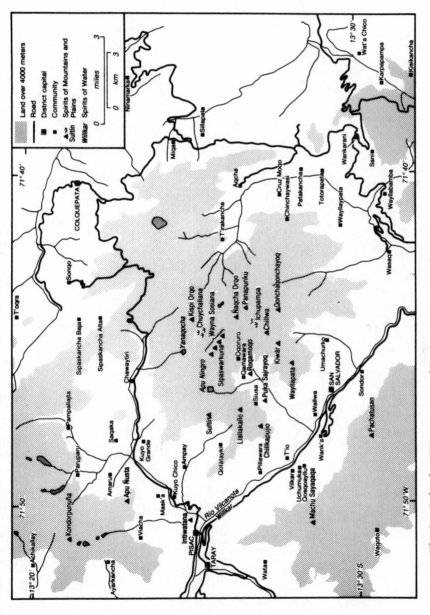

MAP 9   *The San Salvador Microregion and Its Setting: Spirits of Nature*

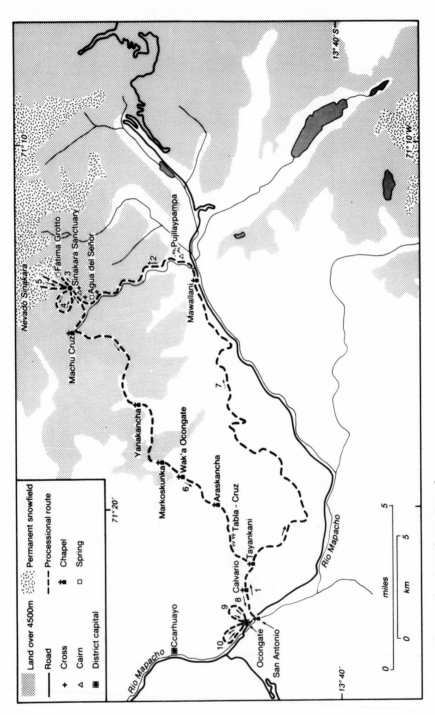

Legend:

Land over 4500m

░░░ Permanent snowfield

— Road
--- Processional route
+ Cross
△ Cairn
▣ District capital
♁ Chapel
□ Spring

MAP 10   *The Qoyllur Rit'i Shrine Complex*

294

Principal Processions of Titular Fiesta

Phase	Map reference and date	Icon	Route
I	1. Ascension Thursday	Señor de Tayankani	Ocongate → Tayankani
	2. Ascension Thursday	Señor de Qoyllur Rir'i	Mawallani → Sinakara Sanctuary
	3. Wednesday after Pentecost	Virgen de Fátima	Sinakara Sanctuary → Fátima Grotto
II	4. Monday after Trinity	Señor de Qoyllur Rir'i	Sinakara Sanctuary precincts
III	5. Tuesday after Trinity	Glacier crosses	Sinakara glacier → Sinakara Sanctuary
	6. Tuesday after Trinity	Señor de Qoyllur Rir'i and Virgen Dolorosa	Sinakara Sanctuary → Tayankani
IV	7. Wednesday after Trinity	Señor de Qoyllur Rir'i	Tayankani → Mawallani
	8. Wednesday after Trinity	Señor de Tayankani and Virgen Dolorosa	Tayankani → Ocongate
V	9. Friday after Corpus	Señor de Tayankani	Ocongate plaza
	10. Saturday after Corpus	Señor de Tayankani and Virgen Dolorosa	Ocongate plaza ↔ village boundary

APPENDIX 2

TABLE 1 *Department of Cusco: Population, by Province, 1972*

Department of Cusco	715,237
Provinces	
Cusco	143,343
Acomayo	29,980
Anta	46,330
Calca	46,191
Canas	31,546
Canchis	75,616
Chumbivilcas	58,312
Espinar	41,461
La Convención	84,161
Paruro	31,536
Paucartambo	29,983
Quispicanchis	62,155
Urubamba	34,623

Source: Peru 1974, 1:table 2.

TABLE 2 *Province of Calca: Population, by District, 1972*

Province of Calca	46,191
Districts	
Calca	9,392
Coya	2,898
Lamay	3,587
Lares	16,694
Pisac	6,579
San Salvador	4,093
Taray	2,948

Source: Peru 1974, 1:table 2.

TABLE 3   District of San Salvador: Centers of Population, 1972

District or center of population	Dwellings	Inhabitants
District of San Salvador	1,048	4,093
Centers of population		
San Salvador	331	1,129
Qamawara	118	474
Qosqoayllu	98	423
Korkopata	21	106
Llachoq	29	126
Oqoruro	48	149
Pillawara	37	119
Siusa	62	254
T'irakancha	102	499
Umachurko	111	472
Others	91	343

Source: Peru 1974, 2:table 1.

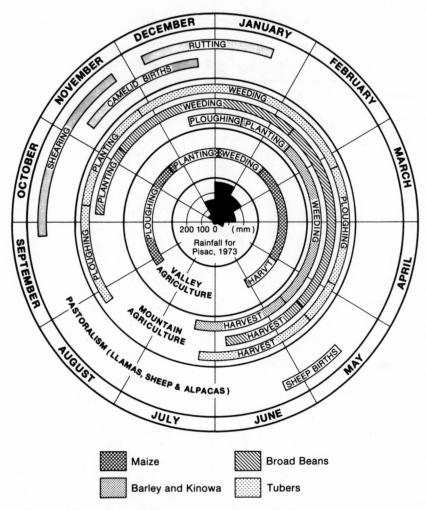

FIGURE I   *San Salvador Microregion: Production Cycle*

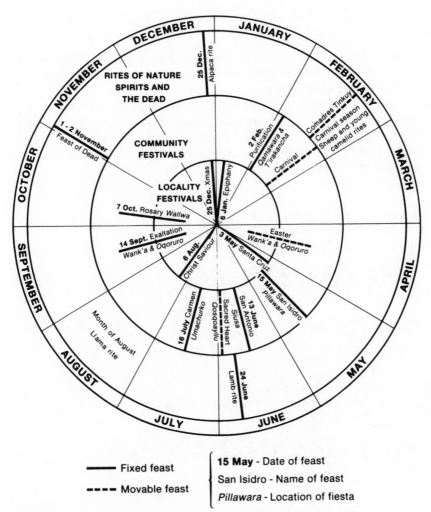

———— Fixed feast

‑ ‑ ‑ ‑ Movable feast

{
15 May - Date of feast

San Isidro - Name of feast

Pillawara - Location of fiesta
}

FIGURE 2　*San Salvador Microregion: Ceremonial Cycle*

299

APPENDIX 4

Ceremonial Dance Music

Quechua music is anhemitonic pentatonic, using all five modes (Aretz 1980, 563; according to Harcourt and Harcourt (1925, 134), only four modes were traditionally used), though the diffusion of European scales has led to extra notes being added to the closed pentatonic system. The three examples given here are of the music characteristically employed for the three main dance styles at the pilgrimage of Señor de Qoyllur Rit'i. All have been transcribed from recordings made during the fiesta in 1973 and 1974.

EXAMPLE 1 Qhapaq qolla
Two kinas *(notched flutes)*, *harp, and accordion.*

EXAMPLE 2 Ch'uncho extranjero
Two pitos *(transverse flutes), tambour, and bass drum.*

EXAMPLE 3 Wayri ch'uncho
Two pitos *(transverse flutes), tambour, and bass-drum.*

Wayri Ch'uncho Dance Formations

Andean dance choreography, as the epitome of the cultural ordering of space, manifests a number of variants on the pervasive dualist theme (see appendix 6). Formation A, with a pair of dancers defining the center and four others defining the periphery, represents the pentadic summation of concentric and diametric dualisms—a quadratic system of double dichotomies focused on a center which is itself dual. Formation B, with its perfect mirror symmetry between two rows of dancers, represents neutral diametricality.

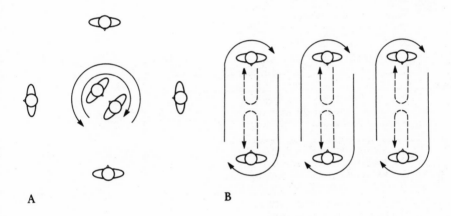

A   B

APPENDIX 5

Roman Liturgical Calendar

This composite calendar, based on the Peruvian sanctoral cycle, shows principal feasts mentioned in the text and others of importance. Movable feasts are fixed in relation to Easter, which is the first Sunday after the first full moon on or after the March equinox.

January

1	Circumcision of Christ
2	Holy Name of Jesus
6	Epiphany (Los Reyes)
14	San Hilario (St Hilary)
20	Virgin of Bethlehem (Belén)
	San Sebastián

February

2	Purification of the Virgin
11	Virgin of Lourdes

March

25	Annunciation to the Virgin

April

May

3	Finding of the Cross (Santa Cruz)
15	San Isidro (St Isidore the Farm-servant
23	Virgin of the Descent (Descensión)

June

13	San Antonio (St Anthony of Padua)
24	San Juan (St John the Baptist)
29	San Pedro y San Paulo (Ss Peter and Paul, Apostles)

July

16	Virgin of Mount Carmel (Carmen)
25	Santiago (St James the Greater)

August

6	Transfiguration of Christ
15	Assumption of the Virgin
16	San Roque (St Rock)
24	San Bartolomé
30	Santa Rosa de Lima
31	San Ramón (St Raymond Nonnatus)

September

8	Nativity of the Virgin
14	Exaltation of the Cross

October

7	Virgin of the Rosary
28	Christ the King

November

1	All Saints
2	All Souls
3	San Martín de Porras

December

8	Immaculate Conception of Virgin
12	Virgin of Guadalupe
25	Nativity of Christ

Sources: Addis and Arnold (1955), Attwater (1965), Callapiña (1974).

Movable Feasts

Sunday

Compadres Thursday

Sunday

Comadres Thursday

Carnival Sunday

Ash Wednesday

Sunday

Sunday

Sunday

Sunday

Sunday

Sunday
Holy Monday
Good Friday
EASTER SUNDAY

Sunday

Sunday

Sunday

Sunday

Sunday

(Thursday) Ascension
Sunday

Pentecost Sunday

Trinity Sunday

(Thursday) Corpus Christi
Sunday

(Friday) Sacred Heart of Jesus
Sunday

APPENDIX 6

Andean Duality:
The Entropy-Concentrism Sequence

Andean dualism, as a cultural device for ordering relations between and within human populations, can be seen as a passage from pure entropy, through a loose opposition between equivalent elements (incipient diametricality), a symmetrical opposition between equivalent elements (neutral diametricality), a dialectical opposition between nonequivalent elements (charged diametricality), to an opposition between center and peripheries (concentrism). See chapters 6 and 8 for substantive discussion.

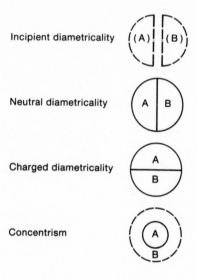

APPENDIX 7

Orthography

Two orthographies have been used in this study, in an attempt to strike a compromise between academic rectitude and conventional usage. Names of people and places that have well-established Hispanicized transcriptions—"Cusco," for example—are rendered in that style. Other native names of people and places and all Quechua and Aymara words are rendered according to an orthography following that established by the Third Interamerican Conference at La Paz in 1954. Pronunciations are as follows:

/a/	as in "h*a*t"	/o/	between "h*o*p" and "h*o*pe"
/ch/	as in "*ch*op"	/p/	as in "*p*at"
/h/	as in "*h*at"	/q/	guttural /k/
/i/	between "h*i*t" and "h*a*te"	/r/	as in "*r*at"
/j/	as in Scottish "lo*ch*"	/s/	as in "*s*at"
/k/	as in "*c*at"	/sh/	as in "*sh*ut"
/l/	as in "*l*et"	/t/	as in "*t*op"
/ll/	as in Spanish, "*ly*-"	/u/	as in "h*oo*p"
/m/	as in "*m*at"	/w/	as in "*w*et"
/n/	as in "*n*et"	/y/	as in "*y*et"
/ñ/	as in Spanish, "*ny*-"	/'/	voiceless glottal stop

Plurals in Quechua are formed by adding the suffix *-kuna* to singular nouns. To avoid confusion, however, I have used the English plural form, *-s*, throughout.

Glossary

abrazo (Sp.) embrace

Acción Popular (Sp.) Popular Action, right-of-center Peruvian political party

achiwa (Qu.) parasol

Agua del Señor (Sp.) the Lord's water

alabado (Sp.) hymn of praise

alcalde (Sp.) mayor; head of *consejo distrital;* head of *varayoq*

alcalde de vara (Sp.) mayor of the staff, *alcalde indígena*

alcalde indígena (Sp.) mayor of *comunidad indígena*, head of *varayoq*

alferado (Sp.) standard-bearer; fiesta *cargo*

alférez (Sp.) ensign; fiesta *cargo*

alma (Sp.) soul

altarero (Sp.) one who adorns altars; fiesta *cargo*

altiplano (Sp.) tableland, the high plateau around Lake Titicaca

anexo (Sp.) annex, administrative unit subordinate to district capital

añu (Qu.) *Tropaeolum tuberosum,* Andean tuber

apachita (Qu.) sacred cairn

APRA (Alianza Popular Revolucionaria Americana) (Sp.) Popular Revolutionary American Alliance, left-of-center Peruvian political party

apu (Qu.) lord, chief; nature spirit, usually of mountain

arariwa (Qu.) guardian of the crops; leader of *wayri ch'uncho* dance troupe

atrasado (Sp.) backward

auki (Qu.) grandfather, ancestor

ayllu (Qu.) local community or kin group

ayni (Qu.) exchange labor; recompense in equal measure; contradiction, incompatibility

barbecho (Sp.) first plowing of fallow land

bautismo (Sp.) baptism

bayeta (Sp.) homespun cloth

blanco (Sp.) white; person of putatively pure Spanish ancestry

cabildo (Sp.) town council

cacique (Sp.) Indian chief or headman

campesino (Sp.) countryman, peasant

candonga (Sp.) Carnival trick, Carnival whip

cantina (Sp.) canteen, restaurant tent

cantón (Sp.) village section (Guatemala)

CAP (Cooperativa Agraria de Producción) (Sp.) agrarian production cooperative established under 1969 agrarian reform

capitán (Sp.) captain

capitanaza (Sp.) female warrior

caporal (Sp.) corporal

carga (Sp.) load, burden

cargo (Sp.) office, honor

celador (Sp.) warden

celda (Sp.) cell for monks or pilgrims

ceque See *siqi*

chaka (Qu.) cross-bar, transom

chakitajlla (Qu.) foot plow

chanka (Qu.) in sixteenth century, household shrine

chicha (Sp.) fermented drink, usually made from maize

chileno (Sp.) Chilean; ceremonial dance style representing Chilean soldiers in War of the Pacific, 1879–84

cholo (Sp.) derogatory term for supposed intermediate status between Indian and *mestizo*

chonta (Sp.) *Bactris ciliata*, small palm tree with black ebonylike wood

chullpa (Ay.) pre-Inka towerlike structure of stone or adobe which served as tomb, usually located on hilltop

ch'uncho (Qu.) savage, tribal inhabitant of lowland jungle; ceremonial dance style with several variants

ch'uncho extranjero (Qu. and Sp.) foreign savage, ceremonial dance style

ch'uñu (Qu.) freeze-dried potato

ch'uya (Qu.) mixture of *chicha* and ground maize

ciudadano (Sp.) citizen, freeman

clase media (Sp.) middle class

cofradía (Sp.) religious confraternity

comadre (Sp.) reciprocal term of address between parent and godmother of child

compadrazgo (Sp.) spiritual coparenthood established through baptism, marriage, or *uma rutukuy*

compadre (Sp.) reciprocal term of address between parent and godfather of child

comparso (Sp.) Carnival processional dance

comunidad (Sp.) community

comunidad campesina (Sp.) peasant community; since 1969 agrarian reform, official title of *comunidad indígena*

comunidad indígena (Sp.) Indian community

condenado (Sp.) condemned one, soul of sinner who has died a bad death and is denied access to *hanaqpacha*

consejo distrital (Sp.) district council

contador (Sp.) accountant, auditor; fiesta *cargo*

contradanza (Sp.) country-dance; ceremonial dance style deriving from Spanish guild dances

contratista (Sp.) contractor; fiesta *cargo* responsible for musicians *cordillera* (Sp.) chain of mountains

coro (Sp.) choir; local chapter of religious brotherhood

corregimiento (Sp.) administrative unit in colonial Peru

corregidor (Sp.) crown official in charge of *corregimiento*

costumbre (Sp.) custom

criollo (Sp.) creole, person born in Americas of European parents; pertaining to coastal as opposed to highland culture

curato (Sp.) parish

decente (Sp.) respectable one, white or *mestizo* as opposed to Indian

demanda (Sp.) charity box; portable religious image carried by pilgrims

desaguadero (Sp.) outlet, channel

descanso (Sp.) rest; altar where procession pauses

despacho (Sp.) despatch; offering to nature spirits

día (Sp.) day; principal day of fiesta

diablo (Sp.) devil, demon

Dios (Sp.) God

disco (Sp.) record-player, phonograph

doctrina (Sp.) Indian parish in colonial Peru

doloroso (Sp.) sorrowful

encantado (Sp.) enchanted, haunted

encomendero (Sp.) holder of *encomienda*

encomienda (Sp.) grant by crown to Spanish colonist of labor and produce of specific Indian communities

enganche (Sp.) enlistment, indentured labor

enganchador (Sp.) recruiting agent for *enganche*

entrada (Sp.) entry

Espíritu Santo (Sp.) Holy Ghost

estadio (Sp.) stadium, assembly ground

extranjero (Sp.) foreign, alien

faena (Sp.) communal labor; collective corvée

familia (Sp.) family

forastero (Sp.) stranger, person from another community

fresco (Sp.) fresh, recent

gentil (Sp.) pagan, heathen; *ñaupa machu*

hacendado (Sp.) owner of *hacienda*

hacienda (Sp.) privately owned rural estate

hanan (Qu.) upper, superior

hanaqpacha (Qu.) afterworld, world above

hatun (Qu.) great, grand

Hatun Pujllay (Qu.) great game, Carnival

haukay (Qu.) recreation, amusement

Haukaypata (Qu.) stage for recreation, ceremonial forum in Inka Cusco

hermandad (Sp.) lay religious brotherhood

hucha (Qu.) sin, fault; dispute, business

hurin (Qu.) lower, inferior

imilla (Ay.) woman

indígena (Sp.) indigenous person, Indian

indigenismo (Sp.) ideology glorifying Indian culture and Inka past

indigenista (Sp.) follower of *indigenismo*

indio (Sp.) pejorative for Indian

inti (Qu.) sun; unit of Peruvian currency

itinkame (Machiguenga) local bigman, chief

jornal (Sp.) wage-earning day labor

juez (Sp.) judge

juguete (Sp.) jest; wooden frame for fireworks in which religious image
   is trapped and released before fireworks are exploded

justo (Sp.) just

k'achampa (Qu.) to lean to one side; ceremonial dance style supposed
   to have originated in Inka war dances

kacharpariy (Qu.) farewell, final day of fiesta

kamay (Qu.) to create

kañari (Qu.) bodyguard, office of *varayoq*

kañiwa (Qu.) *Chenopodium pallidicaule*, high-protein grain of *altiplano*

k'ara (Qu.) naked, peeled

k'ara ch'uncho (Qu.) naked savage, ceremonial dance style

kaypacha (Qu.) this world

killa (Qu.) moon

kina (Qu.) notched vertical-blown flute

kinowa (Qu.) *Chenopodium quinoa*, high-protein Andean grain

kipu (Qu.) knotted-cord abacus used by Inkas

kipukamayoq (Qu.) specialist in using *kipu*

kishwa (Qu.) temperate ''alley zone in Andes

konopa (Qu.) in sixteenth century, household shrine

k'ucho (Qu.) edge, corner

kukuchi (Qu.) *condenado*

kuraka (Qu.) native chief of community or ethnic group

kuraq (Qu.) elder, notable

kuti (Qu.) to turn, transform

lámina (Sp.) engraving; small portable religious icon carried by pilgrims

lawata (Qu.) bamboo fipple flute

laymi (Qu.) parcel of land in sectoral fallowing system

lienzo (Sp.) painted canvas

lisa (Qu.) *Ullucus tuberosus*, Andean tuber

llijlla (Qu.) woman's shawl

luychu (Qu.) *Hippocamelus bisulcus*, native Andean deer

machu (Qu.) old man, ancient; *ñaupa machu*

machu tullu (Qu.) ancient bones, pre-Columbian mummy

machula (Qu.) little old man; ceremonial dance style associated with *ñaupa machu*

madre (Sp.) mother

maestro (Sp.) master; leader of *nación*

majestat (Sp.) in medieval Catalonia, reproduction of Christ shrine

malki (Qu.) ancestral mummy

mama (Sp.) mother (Qu.) mother, matrix

mamacha (Qu.) little mother; spirit of image of Virgin Mary

maqt'acha (Qu.) youngster, youth; ceremonial dance role

mayor (Sp.) major; fiesta *cargo*

mayordomía (Sp.) stewardship

mayordomo (Sp.) steward; fiesta *cargo*

mayu (Qu.) river

mercado (Sp.) market

mesa (Sp.) table

mestizo (Sp.) mixed race; person identifying with Hispanic rather than Indian culture

milagro (Sp.) miracle

milagroso (Sp.) miraculous

mink'a (Qu.) festive labor; recompense in different form from original aid

misa (Sp.) mass; cloth on which ritual materials are prepared

misti (Qu.) *mestizo*

mita (Qu.) labor draft under Inka and Spanish colonial régimes

mitima (Qu.) colonist moved to new territory by Inkas

montaña (Sp.) subtropical forested mountain zone on northeastern flanks of Andes

mozo (Sp.) youth; *cholo*

municipio (Sp.) municipality

nación (Sp.) tribe, nation; community pilgrimage contingent

ñamka, ñamoq (Qu.) manifestations of deity in various shrines

natural (Sp.) native

ñaupa machu (Qu.) ancient from long ago, one of first race of beings in Andes

negrillo (Sp.) young black; ceremonial dance style portraying African slaves who worked on Andean *haciendas*

negro (Sp.) black

niño (Sp.) child; image of Christ child

obligatorio (Sp.) obligatory

ojotas (Sp.) sandals made from old automobile tires

oka (Qu.) *Oxalis tuberosa*, Andean tuber

originario (Sp.) original inhabitant of area

pacha (Qu.) world, earth, age

Pachakamaq (Qu.) creator of world; pre-Columbian coastal shrine

Pachakuti (Qu.) transformer of world; ninth ruler in Inka dynastic myth

Pachamama (Qu.) earth matrix, spirit of earth in its benevolent aspect

Pachatira (Qu.) spirit of earth in its malevolent aspect

Pachatusan (Qu.) stanchion of world, mountain *apu* near Cusco

padrino (Sp.) godfather

pampa (Qu.) plain

paqarina (Qu.) mythical place of origin

parabién (Sp.) felicitation, compliment

partido (Sp.) province of colonial Peru

p'asña (Qu.) maiden

p'asña capitán (Qu. and Sp.) captain of maidens, fiesta *cargo*

pata (Qu.) stage, terrace, summit

patrón (Sp.) patron, sponsor; fiesta *cargo;* guardian saint of community or town

patronato real (Sp.) royal patronage, arrangement whereby colonial church was controlled by Spanish crown

patrón jurado (Sp.) sworn patron; guardian saint adopted for its attested power

paulocha (Qu.) *ukuku*

personero (Sp.) attorney, former legal representative of *comunidad indígena*

p'istuy (Qu.) to cover, protect, defend

pito (Sp.) transverse flute

precio (Sp.) price

prioste (Sp.) steward; fiesta *cargo*

pujllay (Qu.) to play; game

pujllaypampa (Qu.) playground

puna (Qu.) high plateau zone of Andes

qaqa (Qu.) large rock, crag

qhapaq (Qu.) rich, noble

qhapaq qolla (Qu.) rich *qolla*, ceremonial dance style representing people of Qollao *qocha* (Qu.) lake

qolla (Qu.) inhabitant of Qollao, region southeast of Cusco; ceremonial dance style with several variants

qoya (Qu.) queen

qoyllur (Qu.) star

quebrada (Sp.) rugged terrain, ravine

quyi (Qu.) *Cavia porcellus*, domesticated cavy

raukana (Qu.) mattock

raymi (Qu.) Inka feast

reducción (Sp.) village in which dispersed native population was resettled by Spanish

regidor (Sp.) alderman; office of *varayoq*

regular (Sp.) moderate, average

repartimiento de efectos (Sp.) forced sale of goods to Indians by *corregidor* in colonial Peru

rey (Sp.) king

rit'i (Qu.) snow

ropita (Sp.) short garment

runa (Qu.) people

saqra (Qu.) devil, demon; ceremonial dance style betraying Moorish influence, sometimes associated with the dead

sargento (Sp.) sergeant; ceremonial dance role

selva (Sp.) jungle

Sendero Luminoso (Sp.) Shining Path, Maoist guerrilla group active in Peru since 1980

señor (Sp.) sir, lord; Lord Jesus

serrano (Sp.) highlander

sijlla (Qu.) fine fellow, gentleman; ceremonial dance style satirizing roles of judge, notary, and other officials

SINAMOS (Sistema Nacional de Apoyo a la Movilización Social) (Sp.) National System of Support for Social Mobilization, Peruvian government agency active in 1970s

sin amos (Sp.) without masters

sipas (Qu.) young maiden

siqi (Qu.) sketch, line

sisa (Qu.) pollen

socio protector (Sp.) conservator, custodian

sol (Sp.) sun; former unit of Peruvian currency

soldadito (Sp.) little soldier

soq'a (Qu.) dangerous, malevolent

soq'a machu (Qu.) wind associated with *ñaupa machus*, blowing from *puna* at dusk, which can cause sickness or death

supay (Qu.) devil, demon, evil spirit

suyu (Qu.) region; one of four quarters of the Inka empire

Taki Onqoy (Qu.) dancing sickness, millenarian movement in sixteenth-century colonial Peru

tallikuyoq (Qu.) leaking vessel

Tawantinsuyu (Qu.) four *suyus* together, Inka empire

tayanka (Qu.) *Baccharis odorata*, resinous shrub used as combustible

tayta (Qu.) father; God

taytacha (Qu.) little father; spirit of image of Christ

temblor (Sp.) earthquake

tiamisayoq (Qu.) steward, sponsor; fiesta *cargo*

tierra (Sp.) land, earth

t'impu (Qu.) stew of mutton, potatoes and white cabbage served at Carnival

t'inkay (Qu.) ritual aspersion

tinkuy (Qu.) meeting, encounter between two parties; ritual battle

tiyachikuy (Qu.) to make one another sit down; day of fiesta when incoming and outgoing officers exchange compliments

tiyana (Qu.) seat; musical phrase to mark halt or rest

tontuna (Sp.) folly, foppery; ceremonial dance style of *criollo* inspiration, with flamboyant costume and choreography

torre (Sp.) tower

tullu (Qu.) bone

Tunupa (Ay.) spirit of thunder and lightning

tusan (Qu.) prop, stanchion

ukhupacha (Qu.) underworld, world within

ukuku (Qu.) bear; ceremonial dance style with origins in Spanish folklore, symbolically associated with *condenado*

ukumari (Qu.) mythical figure, uncontrollable offspring of peasant woman and bear

uma rutukuy (Qu.) ceremonial first haircutting

unay (Qu.) ancient, persisting

unay precio (Qu. and Sp.) ancient price, fixed rate for exchange of products

uta (Ay.) house

vara (Sp.) staff of office

varayoq (Qu.) staff bearers, traditional body of civil officers in *comunidad campesina*

vecino (Sp.) citizen, neighbor; *mestizo*

venia (Sp.) bow; maneuver by which religious image confers blessing

víspera (Sp.) eve of fiesta

wak'a (Qu.) localized source of sacredness in pre-Columbian times

wanq'a (Qu.) crag, monolith; pre-Columbian field or farmstead shrine

waqcha (Qu.) poor, orphaned

waqcha qolla (Qu.) poor *qolla*, ceremonial dance style representing people of Qollao

waqsa (Qu.) nominated devotee of *wak'a*

wayno (Qu.) principal Andean genre of recreational dance music and song

wayri (Machiguenga) local bigman, chief

wayri ch'uncho (Machiguenga and Qu.) chief savage, ceremonial dance style

willka (Ay.) sun, sacred

Willkanuta (Ay.) house of the sun, Inka name for Pacific-Atlantic watershed southeast of Cusco

wiphala (Qu.) wild, warlike

wiphala capitán (Qu. and Sp.) warrior captain, fiesta *cargo*

wira (Qu.) fat, grease

Wiraqocha (Qu.) lake of grease; creator god and culture hero in Inka mythology

yana (Qu.) lover; servant, debt peon

yanakonaje (Qu.) servitude, debt peonage

yanantin (Qu.) both lovers together, lover (masc.) with his lover (fem.)

yanapa (Qu.) favor, protection, succor

yañka (Qu.) high priest of *wak'a* cult

yawar (Qu.) blood

yawar mayu (Qu.) river of blood

yunsa (Sp.) Carnival ceremony in which tree is symbolically felled by dancing couples

References

Adams, Richard M.
1959   A Community in the Andes: Problems and Progress in Muqui-
        yauyo. Seattle: University of Washington Press.
Addis, William E., and Thomas Arnold
1955   A Catholic Dictionary. London: Virtue.
Aguilar, Luis Felipe
1922   Cuestiones Indígenas. Cusco: Tipografía El Comercio.
Aguilar Claros, Rosario
1945   "La feria de Pampacucho de la provincia de Canchis." Mono-
        grafías geografía humana del Perú 4(5). Archivo Histórico del
        Cusco. MS.
Alberti, Giorgio, and Enrique Mayer, eds.
1974   Reciprocidad e intercambio en los Andes peruanos. Perú Pro-
        blema, no. 12. Lima: Instituto de Estudios Peruanos.
Alencastre, Andrés G., and Georges Dumézil
1953   "Fêtes et usages des Indiens de Langui (province de Kanas, dé-
        partement du Cuzco)." Journal de la Société des Américanistes
        42:1–118.
Allen, Catherine J.
1978   "Coca, Chicha, and Trago: Private and Communal Rituals in a
        Quechua Community." Ph.D. dissertation, University of Illinois–
        Urbana.
1983   "Of Bear-Men and He-Men: Bear Metaphors and Male Self-
        Perceptions in a Peruvian Community." Latin American Indian
        Literatures 7(1):38–51.
Angles Vargas, Víctor
1983   Historia del Cusco (Cusco Colonial). 2 vols. Lima: Industrial-
        gráfica.
Anonymous
1651   Relación del Temblor, y Terremoto que Dios Nuestro Señor fue

servido de embiar a la Ciudad del Cuzco à 31 de Março este año passado de 1650. Madrid: Julian de Paredes.

Appleton, Jay
1975   *The Experience of Landscape.* London: John Wiley.
Aretz, Isabel
1980   "Peru: Folk Music," In *The New Grove Dictionary of Music and Musicians,* edited by Stanley Sadie. 20 vols., vol. 14, pp. 559–66. London: Macmillan; Washington, D.C.: Grove's Dictionaries of Music.
Arguedas, José María
1956   "Puquio, una cultura en proceso de cambio." *Revista del Museo Nacional de Lima* 25:184–232.
Armas Medina, Fernando de
1953   *Cristianización del Perú.* Sevilla: Escuela de Estudios Hispano-Americanos.
Arriaga, Pablo José de
[1621] 1968   *The Extirpation of Idolatry in Peru.* Translated by L. Clark Keating. Lexington: University Press of Kentucky.
Attwater, Donald
1965   *The Penguin Dictionary of Saints.* Harmondsworth, U.K.: Penguin.
Ávila, Francisco de
[1598] 1966   *Dioses y hombres de Huarochirí.* Translated by José María Arguedas. Lima: Museo Nacional de Historia/Instituto de Estudios Peruanos.
Bakhtin, M. M.
1981   "Forms of Time and of the Chronotope in the Novel." In *The Dialogic Imagination: Four Essays,* edited by Michael Holquist; translated by Caryl Emerson and Michael Holquist. Austin: University of Texas Press.
Banchero Castellano, Raúl
1976   *La verdadera historia del Señor de los Milagros.* Lima: Inti-Sol.
Bandelier, Adolph F.
1904   "The Cross of Carabuco in Bolivia." *American Anthropologist* 6:599–628.
Bandera, Damián de
[1557] 1965   "Relación general de la disposición y calidad de la provincia de Guamanga." *Biblioteca de Autores Españoles* 183:176–80. Madrid: Ediciones Atlas.
Barrette, Christian
1972   "Aspects de l'ethno-écologie d'un village andin." *Canadian Review of Sociology and Anthropology* 9:255–67.
Barrionuevo, Alfonsina
1969   *Cuzco, Magic City.* Lima: Editorial Universo.
Basso, Keith
1984   " 'Stalking with Stories': Names, Places, and Moral Narratives among the Western Apache." In *Text, Play, and Story: The Construction and Reconstruction of Self and Society.* Edited by Stuart Plattner and Edward M. Bruner. Proceedings of the American Ethnological Society 1983. Washington D.C.: American Ethnological Society.
Bastien, Joseph W.
1978   *Mountain of the Condor: Metaphor and Ritual in an Andean Ayllu.* American Ethnological Society Monographs, no. 64. St. Paul, Minnesota: West Publishing Co.

Bennett, Wendell C.
1953   *Excavations at Wari, Ayacucho, Peru*. Yale University Publica-
            tions in Anthropology, no. 49. New Haven: Yale University Press.
Berger, John
1976   *Ways of Seeing*. Harmondsworth, U.K.: Penguin.
Berndt, Ronald M., and Catherine H. Berndt
1970   *Man, Land, and Myth in North Australia: The Gunwinggu Peo-
            ple*. East Lansing: Michigan State University Press.
Berthelot, Jean
1978   "L'Exploitation des métaux précieux au temps des Incas." *An-
            nales ESC* 33:948–66.
Betanzos, Juan de
[1551] 1968 "Suma y narración de los Incas." *Biblioteca de autores españoles*
            209:1–55. Madrid: Ediciones Atlas.
Bode, Barbara Ora
1974   "Explanation of the 1970 Earthquake in the Peruvian Andes."
            Ph.D. dissertation, Tulane University.
Bourque, Susan C., and David Scott Palmer
1975   "Transforming the Rural Sector: Government Policy and Peasant
            Response." In *The Peruvian Experiment: Continuity and Change
            under Military Rule*, edited by Abraham F. Lowenthal. Princeton:
            Princeton University Press.
Boxer, C. R.
1978   *The Church Militant and Iberian Expansion, 1440–1770*. Bal-
            timore: Johns Hopkins University Press.
Boyce, Mary
1977   *A Persian Stronghold of Zoroastrianism*. Oxford: Clarendon Press.
Browman, David L.
1978   "Toward the Development of the Tiahuanaco (Tiwanaku) State."
            In *Advances in Andean Archaeology*, edited by David L. Brow-
            man. The Hague: Mouton.
Brown, Peter
1981   *The Cult of the Saints: Its Rise and Function in Latin Christianity*.
            London: SCM Press.
Brush, Stephen B.
1977   *Mountain, Field, and Family: The Ecology and Human Economy
            of an Andean Valley*. Philadelphia: University of Pennsylvania
            Press.
Buechler, Hans C.
1980   *The Masked Media: Aymara Fiestas and Social Interaction in the
            Bolivian Highlands*. Approaches to Semiotics, no. 59. The Hague:
            Mouton.
Bueno, Cosme
[1768] 1951 *Geografía del Perú Virreynal (Siglo XVIII)*. Lima: Daniel Valcárcel.
Bunzel, Ruth
1953   *Chichicastenango: A Guatemalan Village*. American Ethnolog-
            ical Society Publications, no. 22. Locust Valley, New York: J. J.
            Augustin.
Bushnell, G. H. S.
1963   *Peru*. London: Thames and Hudson.
Calancha, Antonio de la
[1639] 1972 "Chronica moralizada del Orden de San Agustin." In *Crónicas
            Agustinas del Perú*, by Antonio de la Calancha and Bernado de
            Torres; edited by Manuel Merino. 2 vols. Biblioteca Missionalia

REFERENCES

Hispánica XVII. Madrid: Consejo Superior de Investigaciones Científicas, Instituto "Enrique Flores."

Callapiña, Leoncio G.
1974   *Almanaque patriótico Chaski 1974*. Cusco: Librería "Chaski."

Cámara Barbachano, Fernando, and Teófilo Reyes Couturier
1972   "Los santuarios y las peregrinaciones, una expresión de relaciones sociales en una sociedad compleja: el caso de México." *Boletín Bibliográfico de Antropología Americana* 35/2(44):29–45.

Camino, Alejandro
1978   "Trueque, correrías e intercambios entre los quechuas andinos y los piro y machiguenga de la montaña peruana." In *Etnohistoria y Antropología Andina* 1:79–100. Lima: Museo Nacional de Historia.

Carrasco, Pedro
1961   "The Civil-Religious Hierarchy in Mesoamerican Communities: Pre-Spanish Background and Colonial Development." *American Anthropologist* 63:484–97.

Casaverde Rojas, Juvenal
1970   "El mundo sobrenatural en una comunidad." *Allpanchis* 2:121–243.

Casaverde Rojas, Juvenal, Jorge Sánchez Farfán, and Tomás Camilo Cevallos Valencia
1966   "Wifala o p'asña capitán." *Folklore* (Cusco) 1:83–102.

Castillo Ardiles, Hernán
1970   *Pisac: Estructuras y mecanismos de dominación en un región de refugio*. México: Instituto Indigenista Interamericano.

Cava, Ralph della
1970   *Miracle at Joaseiro*. New York: Columbia University Press.

Cayón Armelia, Edgardo
1971   "El hombre y los animales en la cultura quechua." *Allpanchis* 3:135–62.

Celestino, Olinda
1982   "Cofradía: continuidad y transformación de la sociedad andina." *Allpanchis* 20:147–66.

Chevalier, François
1966   "Témoignages littéraires et disparités de croissance: l'expansion de la grande propriété dans le Haut-Pérou au XXe siècle." *Annales ESC* 21:815–31.

Choqueccahua, Jorge
1971   "El señalasqa en el mundo aymara." *Allpanchis* 3:182–84.

Christian, William A., Jr.
1976   "De los santos a María: panorama de las devociones a santuarios españoles desde el principio de la Edad Media hasta nuestros días." In *Temas de Antropología Española*, edited by Carmelo Lisón Tolosana. Madrid: Akal Editor.
1981a   *Local Religion in Sixteenth-Century Spain*. Princeton: Princeton University Press.
1981b   *Apparitions in Late Medieval and Renaissance Spain*. Princeton: Princeton University Press.

Cieza de León, Pedro de
[1554] 1973   *El Señorío de los Incas*. Lima: Editorial Universo.

Cloudsley, Peter
1985   "The Living Inca Heritage." *The Geographical Magazine* 57(2):84–89.

Cobo, Bernabé
[1653] 1956 "Historia del nuevo mundo." *Biblioteca de Autores Españoles* 91–92. Madrid: Ediciones Atlas.
Cohen, Abner
1980 "Drama and Politics in the Development of a London Carnival." *Man,* n.s. 15:65–87.
Colin, Michèle
1966 *Le Cuzco à la fin du XVIIe et au début du XVIIIe siècle.* Paris: Institut des Hautes Études de l'Amérique Latine.
Condori Mamani, Gregorio
1977 *Gregorio Condori Mamani, Autobiografía,* edited by Ricardo Valderrama Fernández and Carmen Escalante Gutiérrez. Biblioteca de la tradición oral andina, no. 2. Cusco: Centro de Estudios Andinos "Bartolomé de las Casas."
Conlin, Seán
1974 "Participation versus Expertise." In *Class and Ethnicity in Peru,* edited by Pierre L. van den Berghe. Leiden: E. J. Brill.
Contreras Berrios, Oscar
1957 "Fiesta de Añaypampa." *Monografías geografía humana del Perú.* Archivo Histórico del Cusco. MS.
Cosgrove, Denis
1984 *Social Formation and Symbolic Landscape.* London and Sydney: Croom Helm.
Crumrine, N. Ross
1978 "The Peruvian Pilgrimage: A Ritual Drama." *Americas* (Washington D.C.) 30(8):28–34.
Curatola, Marco
1978 "El culto de crisis 'Moro Onqoy'." In *Etnohistoria y Antropología Andina* 1:179–92. Lima: Museo Nacional de Historia.
Da Matta, Roberto
1977 "Constraint and License: A Preliminary Study of Two Brazilian National Rituals." In *Secular Ritual,* edited by Sally Falk Moore and Barbara G. Myerhoff. Assen and Amsterdam: Van Gorcum.
Davies, Thomas M.
1974 *Indian Integration in Peru: A Half-Century of Experience, 1900– 1948.* Lincoln: University of Nebraska Press.
Deler, J. P.
1975 *Lima 1940–1970: Aspectos del crecimiento de la capital peruana.* Lima: Centro de Investigaciones Geográficas.
Delgado Aragón, Julio
1971 "El señalakuy." *Allpanchis* 3:185–97.
Demarest, Arthur A.
1981 *Viracocha: The Nature and Antiquity of the Andean High God.* Peabody Museum Monographs, no. 6. Cambridge, Mass.: Peabody Museum, Harvard University.
Descola, Jean
1968 *Daily Life in Colonial Peru, 1710–1820.* London: George Allen and Unwin.
Dewalt, Billie R.
1975 "Changes in the Cargo Systems of Mesoamerica." *Anthropological Quarterly* 48:87–105.
Dobyns, Henry F.
1960 "The Religious Festival." Ph.D. dissertation, Cornell University.

REFERENCES

Documentos sobre Chucuito
[1573] 1970   *Historia y Cultura* (Lima) 4:5−48.
Doughty, Paul L.
1968   *Huaylas: An Andean District in Search of Progress.* Ithaca: Cornell University Press.
Dumas, Alain
1986   *Qoyllur Rit'i.* Paris: Films du Mangrove. Film.
Durkheim, Émile, and Marcel Mauss
1963   *Primitive Classification.* Translated by Rodney Needham. London: Cohen and West.
Duviols, Pierre
1971   *La Lutte contre les religions autochtones dans le Pérou colonial.* Paris and Lima: Institut Français d'Études Andines.
1973   "Huari y llacuaz, pastores y agricultores: un dualismo de oposición y complementaridad." *Revista del Museo Nacional de Lima* 39:153−90.
1976a   "La Capacocha." *Allpanchis* 9:11−57.
1976b   " 'Punchao,' ídolo mayor de Coricancha, historia y tipología." *Antropología Andina* (Cusco) 1−2:156−83.
1979   "Un Symbolisme de l'occupation, de l'aménagement et de l'exploitation de l'espace: le monolithe 'huanca' et sa fonction dans les Andes préhispaniques." *L'Homme* 19:7−31.
Earls, John
1969   "The Organization of Power in Quechua Mythology." *Journal of the Steward Anthropological Society* 1(1):63−82.
1981   "Patrones de jurisdicción y organización entre los Qaracha Wankas: una reconstrucción arqueológica y etnohistórica de una época flúida." *Etnohistoria y Antropología Andina* 2:55−91. Lima: Museo Nacional de Historia.
Elliott, J. H.
1963   *Imperial Spain, 1469−1716.* London: Edward Arnold.
Erasmus, Charles J.
1956   "Culture Structure and Process: The Occurrence and Disappearance of Reciprocal Farm Labour." *Southwestern Journal of Anthropology* 12:444−69.
Escobar, Gabriel
1967   *Organización social y cultural del sur del Perú.* México: Instituto Indigenista Interamericano.
Esquivel y Navia, Diego de
[1749] 1980   *Noticias cronológicas de la gran ciudad del Cuzco.* 2 vols. Lima: Fundación Augusto N. Wiese.
Estete, Miguel de
[1534] 1872   "Report on the Expedition to Pachacamac." In *Reports on the Discovery of Peru,* edited and translated by Clements R. Markham. London: Hakluyt Society.
Evans-Pritchard, Edward E.
1937   *Witchcraft, Oracles, and Magic among the Azande.* Oxford: Clarendon Press.
Favre, Henri
1967   "Tayta wamani: le culte des montagnes dans le centre sud des Andes péruviennes." In *Colloque d'études péruviennes.* Publication des Annales de la Faculté des Lettres no. 61. Aix-en-Provence: Editions Ophrys.

Fioravanti-Molinié, Antoinette
1982   "Multi-levelled Andean Society and Market Exchange: The Case
            of Yucay (Peru)." In *Ecology and Exchange in the Andes,* edited
            by David Lehmann. Cambridge: Cambridge University Press.
Fisher, Lillian Estelle
1966   *The Last Inca Revolt, 1780–1783.* Norman: University of Okla-
            homa Press.
Flores Ochoa, Jorge
1973   "Inkariy y Qollariy en una comunidad del altiplano." In *Ideología
            Mesiánica del Mundo Andino,* edited by Juan M. Ossio. Lima:
            Ignacio Prado Pastor.
1974   "Mistis and Indians: Their Relations in a Micro-Region of Cusco."
            In *Class and Ethnicity in Peru,* edited by Pierre L. van den Berghe.
            Leiden: E. J. Brill.
Foster, George
1953   "What Is Folk Culture?" *American Anthropologist* 55:159–73.
1960   *Culture and Conquest: America's Spanish Heritage.* Viking Fund
            Publications in Anthropology, no. 27. New York: Wenner-Gren
            Foundation.
Fuenzalida, Fernando
1970   "La matriz colonial de la comunidad de indígenas peruana: una
            hipótesis de trabajo." In *La Hacienda, la Comunidad y el Cam-
            pesino en el Perú,* edited by José Matos Mar. Perú problema
            no. 3. Lima: Instituto de Estudios Peruanos.
1979   "El Cristo pagano de los Andes: una cuestión de identidad."
            Debates en Antropología (Lima) 4:1–10.
Fuenzalida, Fernando, and José Matos Mar
1970   "El proceso de la sociedad rural: una micro-región del Perú cen-
            tral." In *La hacienda, la comunidad y el campesino en el Perú,*
            edited by José Matos Mar. Perú problema no. 3. Lima: Instituto
            de Estudios Peruanos.
Gade, Daniel W.
1970   "Coping with Cosmic Terror: The Earthquake Cult in Cusco,
            Peru." *The American Benedictine Review* 21 (2): 218–23.
1975   *Plants, Man, and Land in the Vilcanota Valley of Peru.* The
            Hague: Junk.
García, José María
1983   *Con las comunidades andinas del Ausangate.* Lima: Centro de
            Proyección Cristiana.
Garcilaso de la Vega ("El Inca")
[1617] 1966 *Royal Commentaries of the Incas and General History of Peru,*
            translated by Harold V. Livermore. 2 vols. Austin: University of
            Texas Press.
Garr, Thomas M.
1972   *Cristianismo y religión Quechua en la prelatura de Ayaviri.* Cusco:
            Instituto de Pastoral Andina.
Geertz, Clifford
1960   *The Religion of Java.* New York: The Free Press of Glencoe.
Getzels, Peter, and Harriet Gordon
1985   *In the Footsteps of Taytacha.* Watertown, Mass.: Documentary
            Educational Resources. Film.
Gibson, Charles
1966   *Spain in America.* New York: Harper and Row.

Gilmore, Raymond M.
1963   "Fauna and Ethnozoology of South America." In *Handbook of South American Indians,* edited by Julian H. Steward. Vol. 6, *Physical Anthropology, Linguistics, and Cultural Geography of South American Indians.* Smithsonian Institution Bureau of American Ethnology Bulletin no. 143. New York: Cooper Square.

Gilt Contreras, Mario Alberto
1955   "Las guerrillas indígenas de Chiyaraqe y Toqto." *Archivos Peruanos de Folklore* (Cusco) 1(1):110—19.

Gisbert, Teresa
1980   *Iconografía y mitos indígenas en el arte.* La Paz: Gisbert & Cía.

Gisbert-Sauch C., Ana
1979   "La fiesta del Señor de Qoyllur Rit'i." *Páginas* (Lima) 4(24).

Gonzales H., Guillermo
1957   "Origen de la feria de Huanca." *Monografías Geografía Humana del Perú* 21 (23). Archivo Histórico del Cusco. MS.

Gonzalez, Nancy
1970   "Social Functions of Carnival in a Brazilian City." *Southwestern Journal of Anthropology* 26:328—53.

Gorbak, Celina, Mirtha Lischetti, and Carmen Paula Muñoz
1962   "Batallas rituales del Chiaraje y del Toqto de la provincia de Kanas (Cuzco-Perú)." *Revista del Museo Nacional de Lima* 31:245—304.

Gose, Peter
1986   "Sacrifice and the Commodity Form in the Andes." *Man* n.s. 21:296—310.

Gow, David
1974   "Taytacha Qoyllur Rit'i." *Allpanchis* 7:49—100.
1976   "The Gods and Social Change in the High Andes." Ph.D. dissertation, University of Wisconsin—Madison.
1978   "Verticality and Andean Cosmology: Quadripartition, Opposition and Mediation." *Actes du XLIIe Congrès International des Américanistes 1976,* vol. 4. Paris: Fondation Singer Polignac.
1980   "The Roles of Christ and Inkarrí in Andean Religion." *Journal of Latin American Lore* 6(2):279—96.

Gow, David, and Rosalind Gow
1975   "La alpaca en el mito y el ritual." *Allpanchis* 8:141—74.

Gow, Rosalind, and Bernabé Condori
1976   *Kay Pacha.* Biblioteca de la Tradición Oral Andina no. 1. Cusco: Centro de Estudios Rurales Andinos "Bartolomé de las Casas."

Grimes, Ronald D.
1976   *Symbol and Conquest: Public Ritual and Drama in Santa Fe, New Mexico.* Ithaca: Cornell University Press.

Gross, Daniel R.
1971   "Ritual and Conformity: A Religious Pilgrimage to Northeastern Brazil." *Ethnology* 10:129—48.
1979   Review of van den Berghe and Primov 1977. *American Ethnologist* 6:401—3.

Guillet, David
1974   "Transformación ritual y cambio socio-político." *Allpanchis* 6:143—59.
1978   "The Supra-Household Sphere of Production in the Andean Peas-

ant Economy." *Actes du XLIIe Congrès International des Américanistes 1976*, vol. 4. Paris: Fondation Singer Polignac.

1979   *Agrarian Reform and Peasant Economy in Southern Peru*. Columbia: University of Missouri Press.

1980   "Land Tenure, Ecological Zone, and Agricultural Regime in the Central Andes." *American Ethnologist* 8:139–56.

Hage, Robert, and Frank Harary

1983   *Structural Models in Anthropology*. Cambridge: Cambridge University Press.

Harcourt, R. d', and M. d'Harcourt

1925   *La Musique des Incas et ses survivances*. Paris: Librairie Orientaliste Paul Geuthner.

Harding, Colin

1975   "Land Reform and Social Conflict in Peru." In *The Peruvian Experiment: Continuity and Change under Military Rule*, edited by Abraham F. Lowenthal. Princeton: Princeton University Press.

Hardon, J. A.

1954   "The Concept of Miracle from St Augustine to Modern Apologetics." *Theological Studies* 15:229–57.

Haring, C. H.

1947   *The Spanish Empire in America*. New York: Oxford University Press.

Harris, Olivia

1978   "Kinship and the Vertical Economy of the Laymi Ayllu, Norte de Potosí." *Actes du XLIIe Congrès International des Américanistes 1976*, vol. 4. Paris: Fondation Singer Polignac.

1982   "The Dead and the Devils among the Bolivian Laymi." In *Death and the Regeneration of Life*, edited by Maurice Bloch and Jonathan Parry. Cambridge: Cambridge University Press.

Hartman, Roswith

1972   "Otros datos sobre las llamadas 'batallas rituales.'" *Folklore Americano* (Lima) 17:125–35.

Hegy, Pierre M.

1971   *Introducción a la sociología religiosa del Perú*. Lima: Ediciones Librería "Studium."

Hemming, John

1972   *The Conquest of the Incas*. London: Sphere.

Hertz, Robert

1983   "St Besse: A Study of an Alpine Cult." In *Saints and Their Cults: Studies in Religious Sociology, Folklore, and History*, edited by Stephen Wilson. Cambridge: Cambridge University Press.

Hopkins, Diane

1982   "Juegos de enemigos." *Allpanchis* 20:167–88.

Imbelloni, José

1946   *Pachacuti IX (El Inkario crítico)*. Buenos Aires: Editorial Nova.

Isbell, Billie Jean

1978   *To Defend Ourselves: Ecology and Ritual in an Andean Village*. Latin American Monographs, no. 47. Austin: Institute of Latin American Studies, University of Texas.

Isbell, William Harris

1977   *The Rural Foundation for Urbanism: Economic and Stylistic Interaction between Rural and Urban Communities in Eighth-*

Century Peru. Illinois Studies in Anthropology, no. 10. Urbana: University of Illinois Press.

Johnson, Orna, and Allen Johnson
1975   "Male/Female Relations and the Organization of Work in a Machiguenga Community." *American Ethnologist* 2: 634–48.

Kagan, Harold
1973   "The Virgin of Bojacá: Miracles and Change in a Colombian Peasant Community." Ph.D. dissertation, University of California—Riverside.

Keatinge, Richard W.
1981   "The Nature and Role of Religious Diffusion in the Early Stages of State Formation: An Example from Peruvian Prehistory." In *The Transition to Statehood in the New World,* edited by Grant D. Jones and Robert R. Krautz. Cambridge: Cambridge University Press.

Keith, Robert G.
1971   "Encomienda, Hacienda, and Corregimiento in Spanish America: A Structural Analysis." *Hispanic American Historical Review* 51:431–46.

Kemp, Erich Waldram
1948   *Canonization and Authority in the Western Church.* Oxford: Oxford University Press.

Kessel, Johan van
1980   *Danseurs dans le désert.* The Hague: Mouton.
1981   *Danzas y estructuras sociales de los Andes.* Cusco: Instituto de Pastoral Andino.

Klaiber, Jeffrey L.
1977   *Religion and Revolution in Peru, 1824–1976.* Notre Dame, Indiana: University of Notre Dame Press.

Kselman, Thomas
1978   "Miracles and Prophecies: Popular Religion and the Church in Nineteenth-Century France." Ph.D. dissertation, University of Michigan.

Kubler, George
1946   "The Quechua in the Colonial World." In *Handbook of South American Indians,* edited by Julian H. Steward. Vol. 2: *The Andean Civilizations.* Washington, D.C.: Bureau of American Ethnology.

Kurtz, Donald V.
1982   "The Virgin of Guadalupe and the Politics of Becoming Human." *Journal of Anthropological Research* 38(2):194–210.

La Lone, Darrel E.
1978   "Historical Contexts of Trade and Markets in the Peruvian Andes." Ph.D. dissertation, University of Michigan.

Lanning, Edward Putnam
1967   *Peru before the Incas.* Englewood Cliffs, N.J.: Prentice-Hall.

Lea, Henry Charles
1964   "The Inquisition in Colonial Peru." In *The Conflict between Church and State in Latin America,* edited by Fredrick B. Pike. New York: Alfred A. Knopf.

Leach, Edmund
1972   "Melchisedech and the Emperor: Icons of Subversion and Or-

thodoxy." *Proceedings of the Royal Anthropological Institute* 1972, pp. 5–14.

Le Roy Ladurie, Emmanuel
1979   *Carnival in Romans.* Translated by Mary Feeney. New York: George Braziller.

Lévi-Strauss, Claude
1966   *The Savage Mind.* London: Weidenfeld and Nicolson.
1968   "Do Dual Organizations Exist?" In *Structural Anthropology,* translated by Claire Jacobson and Brooke Grundfest Schoepf. Harmondsworth, U.K.: Penguin.

Lira, Jorge A.
1953   "Puhllay, fiesta india." *Perú Indígena* 4:125–34.
1973   *Breve Diccionario Kkechuwa-Español.* Cusco: Librería León.

Loayza, A. L.
1953   "El viejo o machu." *Archivos Peruanos de Folklore* (Cusco) 1:56–69.

Lockhart, James
1969   "Encomienda and Hacienda: The Evolution of the Great Estate in the Spanish Indies." *Hispanic American Historical Review* 49:411–29.

Long, Norman, and Bryan R. Roberts
1978   "Peasant Cooperation and Underdevelopment in Peru." In *Peasant Cooperation and Capitalist Expansion in Central Peru,* edited by Norman Long and Bryan R. Roberts. Latin American Monographs, no. 46. Austin: Institute of Latin American Studies, University of Texas.

Long, Norman, and David Winder
1975   "From Peasant Community to Production Cooperative: An Analysis of Recent Government Policy in Peru." *Journal of Development Studies* 12:75–94.

Lowenthal, David
1976   "The Place of the Past in the American Landscape." In *Geographies of the Mind: Essays in Historical Geography in Honour of John Kirkland Wright,* edited by David Lowenthal and Martyn J. Bowden. New York: Oxford University Press.
1985   *The Past Is a Foreign Country.* Cambridge: Cambridge University Press.

Lumbreras, Luis G.
1974   *The Peoples and Cultures of Ancient Peru.* Translated by Betty J. Meggers. Washington, D.C.: Smithsonian Institution Press.

Lynch, John
1981   *Spain under the Hapsburgs.* 2d edition. 2 vols. Oxford: Basil Blackwell.

MacCormack, Sabine
1984   "From the Sun of the Incas to the Virgin of Copacabana." *Representations* (Berkeley) 8:30–60.
1985   " 'The Heart Has Its Reasons': Predicaments of Missionary Christianity in Early Colonial Peru." *Hispanic American Historical Review* 65:443–66.

Mackay, John A.
1932   *The Other Spanish Christ: A Study in the Spiritual History of Spain and South America.* London: SCM Press.

Manning, Frank
    1977   "Cup Match and Carnival: Secular Rites of Revitalization in Decolonizing, Tourist-oriented Societies." In *Secular Ritual,* edited by Sally Falk Moore and Barbara G. Myerhoff. Assen and Amsterdam: Van Gorcum.

Mariátegui, José Carlos
    1973   *Siete ensayos de interpretación de la realidad peruana.* Lima: Editorial Amauta.

Mariscotti de Görlitz, Ana María
    1978   *Pachamama Santa Tierra: Contribución al estudio de la religión autóctona en los Andes centro-meridionales.* Berlin: Gebr. Mann Verlag.

Márquez Eyzaguirre, Luis G.
    1937   *Huanka Rumi: Historia de las apariciones del Señor de Huanka y de su célebre santuario.* 2 vols. Arequipa: Editorial La Colmena.

Marriott, McKim
    1955   "Little Communities in an Indigenous Civilization." In *Village India,* edited by McKim Marriott. Memoirs of the American Anthropological Association, no. 83. Menasha, Wis.: American Anthropological Association.

Martínez, Gabriel
    1983   "Los dioses de los cerros en los Andes." *Journal de la Société des Américanistes* 69:85–115.

Martínez-Alier, Juan
    1974   "Peasants and Labourers in Southern Spain, Cuba, and Highland Peru." *Journal of Peasant Studies* 1:133–63.

Marx, Emmanuel
    1977   "Communal and Individual Pilgrimage: The Region of Saints' Tombs in South Sinai." In *Regional Cults,* edited by Richard P. Werbner. Association of Social Anthropologists Monographs, no. 16. London: Academic Press.

Marzal, Manuel
    1971   *El mundo religioso de Urcos.* Cusco: Instituto de Pastoral Andina.
    1983   *La transformación religiosa peruana.* Lima: Pontificia Universidad Católica del Perú.

Mason, J. Alden
    1968   *The Ancient Civilizations of Peru.* Harmondsworth, U.K.: Penguin.

Mayer, Enrique
    1971   "Un carnero por un saco de maíz: aspectos de trueque en la zona de Chaupiwaranga, Pasco." *Revista del Museo Nacional de Lima* 37:184–96.
    1974   "Las reglas de juego en la reciprocidad andina." In *Reciprocidad e intercambio en los Andes peruanos,* edited by Giorgio Alberti and Enrique Mayer. Perú problema no. 12. Lima: Instituto de Estudios Peruanos.

McClintock, Cynthia
    1981   *Peasant Cooperatives and Political Change in Peru.* Princeton: Princeton University Press.

Mecham, J. Lloyd
    1934   *Church and State in Latin America: A History of Politico-Ecclesiastical Relations.* Chapel Hill: University of North Carolina Press.

Menzel, Dorothy
1964   "Style and Time in the Middle Horizon." Ñawpa Pacha 2:66–73.
Mesa, José de, and Teresa Gisbert
1982   Historia de la Pintura Cuzqueña. 2 vols. Lima: Fundación Augusto N. Wiese.
Messerschmidt, Donald A., and Jyoti Sharma
1981   "Hindu Pilgrimage in the Nepal Himalayas." Current Anthropology 22:571–72.
Millones, Luis
1973   "Un movimiento nativista del siglo XVI: el Taki Onqoy." In Ideología Mesiánica del Mundo Andino, edited by Juan M. Ossio. Lima: Ignacio Prado Pastor.
Mintz, Sidney, and Eric R. Wolf
1950   "An Analysis of Ritual Co-parenthood (compadrazgo)." Southwestern Journal of Anthropology 6:341–68.
Mishkin, Bernard
1946   "The Contemporary Quechua." In Handbook of South American Indians. Vol. 2, The Andean Civilizations, edited by Julian H. Steward. Washington, D.C.: Bureau of American Ethnology.
Mitchell, William P.
1976   "Irrigation and Community in the Central Peruvian Highlands." American Anthropologist 78:25–44.
Molina, Cristóbal de, of Cusco
[1573] 1916 "Relación de las fábulas y ritos de los Incas." In Colección de Libros y Documentos Referentes a la Historia del Perú, vol. 1, edited by Horacio H. Urteaga. Lima: Sanmarti.
Moore, Sally Falk
1958   Power and Property in Inca Peru. New York: Columbia University Press.
Morinis, E. Alan
1984   Pilgrimage in the Hindu Tradition: A Case Study of West Bengal. Oxford University South Asian Series. Delhi: Oxford University Press.
Morissette, Jacques, and Luc Racine
1973   "La Hiérarchie des Wamani: essai sur la pensée classificatoire Quechua." Recherches Amérindiennes au Québec 3:167–88.
Mörner, Magnus
1975   "En turno a las haciendas de la región del Cuzco desde el siglo XVIII." In Haciendas, Latifundios y Plantaciones en América Latina, edited by Enrique Florescano. Mexico: Siglo XXI.
1978   Perfil de la Sociedad Rural del Cuzco a fines de la Colonia. Lima: Universidad del Pacífico.
Morote Best, Efraín
1953   "Dios, la Virgen y los santos (en los relatos populares)." Tradición (Cusco) 5:76–104.
1958   "El oso raptor." Archivos Venezolanos de Folklore 5:135–78.
Muller, Thomas
1980   "El Taytacha de Qoyllur Rit'i." Pastoral Andina 32:51–66.
Murphy, Robert F.
1971   The Dialectics of Social Life. New York: Basic Books.
Murra, John V.
1962   "Cloth and Its Functions in the Inca State." American Anthropologist 64:710–28.
1975   "El control vertical de un máximo de pisos ecológicos en la

economía de las sociedades andinas." In *Formaciones económicas y políticas del mundo andino,* by John V. Murra. Historia andina no. 3. Lima: Instituto de Estudios Peruanos.

1980   *The Economic Organization of the Inka State.* Research in Economic Anthropology Supplement no. 1. Edited by George Dalton. Greenwich, Connecticut: JAI Press.

Murúa, Martín de

[1611] 1964   *Historia general del Perú. Origen y descendencia de los Incas.* Wellington MS. Edited by Manuel Ballesteros-Gabrois. 2 vols. Madrid: Instituto Gonzalo Fernández de Orviedo.

Nachtigall, Horst

1975   "Ofrendas de llamas en la vida ceremonial de los pastores." *Allpanchis* 8:133–40.

Navarro del Aguila, Víctor

1944   "Calendario de fiestas populares del departamento del Cuzco." *Revista del Instituto Interamericano del Arte* (Cusco) 1:37–80.

Neame, Alan

1968   *The Happening at Lourdes; or, the Sociology of the Grotto.* London: Hodder and Stoughton.

Núñez del Prado, Juan Víctor

1970   "El mundo sobrenatural de los quechuas del sur del Perú, a través de la comunidad de Qotobamba." *Allpanchis* 2:57–120.

Núñez del Prado, Oscar

1952   *La vida y la muerte en Chinchero.* Cusco: Talleres Gráficas "La Económica."

1969   "El hombre y la familia: su matrimonio y organización político-social en Q'ero." *Allpanchis* 1:5–27.

Núñez del Prado, Oscar, and William F. Whyte

1973   *Kuyo Chico: Applied Anthropology in an Indian Community.* Translated by Lucy Whyte Russo and Richard Russo. Chicago: University of Chicago Press.

Nutini, Hugo G.

1968   *San Bernadino Contla: Marriage and Family Structure in a Tlaxcalan Municipio.* Pittsburgh: University of Pittsburgh Press.

Oakley, Peter Alan

1972   " 'El Pueblo lo Hizo': A Study of the Communal Labour Practices in the Indigenous Communities of the Peruvian Highlands and the Programme of Cooperación Popular 1963–1968." Ph.D. dissertation. University of Liverpool.

Oricaín, Pablo José

[1790] 1906   "Compendio breve de discursos varios sobre diferentes materias y noticias geográficas comprehensivas a este Obispado del Cuzco que claman remedios espirituales." In *Juicio de límites entre Perú y Bolivia: Prueba Peruana,* vol. 11, edited by Víctor Maurtua. Barcelona.

Orlove, Benjamin S.

1977   *Alpacas, Sheep, and Men: The Wool Export Economy and Regional Society in Southern Peru.* New York: Academic Press.

Ossio, Juan M.

1973   "Guaman Poma: nueva crónica o carta al rey. Un intento de aproximación a las categorías del pensamiento del mundo andino." In *Ideología mesiánica del mundo andino,* edited by Juan M. Ossio. Lima: Ignacio Prado Pastor.

Palomino, Salvador
 1968 "La cruz en los Andes." *Amaru* (Lima) 8:63–66.
Paredes, Luis Felipe
 1952 "Un Corpus en pequeño." *Perú Indígena* 2:217–18.
 1969 *La procesión del Señor de los Temblores.* Cusco: Editorial Garcilaso.
Pasini, Carlos, and Michael J. Sallnow
 1974 *The Quechua.* Manchester, U.K.: Granada Television. Film.
Pease, Franklin
 1968 "Religión andina en Francisco de Ávila." *Revista del Museo Nacional de Lima* 35:62–76.
 1973 *El Dios Creador andino.* Lima: Mosca Azul.
 1982 "The Formation of Tawantinsuyo: Mechanisms of Colonization and Relationships with Ethnic Groups." In *The Inca and Aztec States 1400–1800: Anthropology and History,* edited by George A. Collier, Renato I. Rosaldo, and John D. Wirth. New York: Academic Press.
Pélach y Feliu, Enrique
 1972 *Nuestra Señora de Cocharcas.* Lima: Editorial Andmar.
Peru
 1969a *Ley de reforma agraria (Decreto ley 17716).* Lima: Editorial-Litográfica América.
 1969b *Ley general de aguas (Decreto ley 17752).* Lima: Editorial Litográfica América.
 1972 *Estatuto de comunidades campesinas (Decreto supremo no. 37–70–A).* Lima: Editorial Mercurio.
 1974 *Censos nacionales VII de población y II de vivienda, 4 de Junio 1972: Departamento Cuzco.* 3 vols. Lima: Oficina Nacional de Estadística y Censos.
 1975 *Diagnóstico socio-económico de la micro-región Pisac.* 2 vols. Lima: Sistema Nacional de Apoyo a la Movilización Social.
Pfaffenberger, Bryan
 1979 "The Kataragama Pilgrimage: Hindu-Buddhist Interaction and Its Significance in Sri Lanka's Polyethnic Social System." *Journal of Asian Studies* 38:253–70.
Pike, Fredrick B.
 1964 Introduction to *The Conflict between Church and State in Latin America,* edited by Fredrick B. Pike. New York: Alfred A. Knopf.
Platt, Tristan
 1978 "Symétries en miroir: le concept de *yanantin* chez les Macha de Bolivie." *Annales ESC* 33:1081–1107.
Polanyi, Karl
 1977 *The Livelihood of Man.* Edited by Harry W. Pearson. New York: Academic Press.
Poma de Ayala, Felipe Guamán
 [1620] 1966 *Nueva crónica y buen gobierno.* Edited by Luis F. Bustíos Gálvez. 3 vols. Lima: Editorial Cultura.
Poole, Deborah A.
 1981 "El Taytacha viene de afuera: la ritualización del 'forastero' en la peregrinación andina." Centro de Estudios Rurales Andinos "Bartolomé de las Casas," Cusco. MS.
 1982 "Los santuarios religiosos en la economía regional andina." *Allpanchis* 19:79–116.

References

n.d.   "Geography and Sacred Space in the Andean Pilgrimage Tra-
             dition." Centro de Estudios Rurales Andinos "Bartolomé de las
             Casas," Cusco. MS.
Portes, Alejandro, and John Walton
1976   *Urban Latin America: The Political Condition from Above and
             Below.* Austin: University of Texas Press.
Portugal Catacora, José
1981   *Danzas y bailes del altiplano.* Lima: Editorial Universo.
Primov, George
1980   "The Political Role of Mestizo Schoolteachers in Indian Com-
             munities." In *Land and Power in Latin America: Agrarian Econ-
             omies and Social Processes in the Andes,* edited by Benjamin S.
             Orlove and Glynn Custred. New York: Holmes and Meier.
Rabinow, Paul
1975   *Symbolic Domination: Cultural Form and Historical Change in
             Morocco.* Chicago: University of Chicago Press.
Rademacher, C.
1910   "Carnival." In *Encyclopaedia of Religion and Ethics,* edited by
             James Hastings. Edinburgh: T. and T. Clark.
Ramirez, Juan Andrés
1969   "La novena al Señor de Qoyllur Rit'i." *Allpanchis* 1:61–88.
Ramos Gavilán, Alonso
[1621] 1976 *Historia del Célebre Santuario de Nuestra Señora de Copacabana.*
             La Paz: Academia Boliviana de la Historia.
Randall, Robert
1982a   "Qoyllur Rit'i, an Inca Fiesta of the Pleiades: Reflections on Time
             and Space in the Andean World." *Boletín del Instituto Francés
             de Estudios Andinos* 11: 37–81.
1982b   "Peru's Pilgrimage to the Sky." *National Geographic* 162(1):
             60–69.
Redfield, Robert
1956   *Peasant Society and Culture: An Anthropological Approach to
             Civilization.* Chicago: University of Chicago Press.
Reina, Ruben E.
1966   *The Law of the Saints: A Pokomam Pueblo and Its Culture.*
             Indianapolis: Bobbs-Merrill.
Relph, Edward
1976   *Place and Placelessness.* London: Pion.
Richardson, Miles, Marta Eugenia Pardo, and Barbara Bode
1971   "The Image of Christ in Spanish America as a Model for Suf-
             fering: An Explanatory Note." *Journal of Interamerican Studies
             and World Affairs* 8:246–57.
Roca W., Demetrio
1979   "Etnografía de la fiesta del Señor de Torrechayoc en Urubamba."
             Wayka (Cusco) 6–7:115–40.
Roel Pineda, Josafat
1950   "La danza de los 'c'uncos' de Paucartambo." *Tradición* (Cusco)
             1: 59–70.
Rostworowski de Diez Canseco, María
1976   "Reflexiones sobre la reciprocidad andina." *Revista del Museo
             Nacional de Lima* 42: 341–54.
1977   "Breve ensayo sobre el señorío de Ychma." In *Etnía y Sociedad,*
             by María Rostworowski de Diez Canseco. Lima: Instituto de
             Estudios Peruanos.

1983   *Estructuras andinas del poder: ideología, religiosa y política.*
        Lima: Instituto de Estudios Peruanos.
Rowe, John H.
1944   *An Introduction to the Archaeology of Cuzco.* Papers of the
        Peabody Museum, vol. 28, no. 2. Cambridge, Mass.: Peabody
        Museum, Harvard University.
1946   "Inca Culture at the Time of the Spanish Conquest." In *Hand-
        book of South American Indians,* edited by Julian H. Steward.
        Vol. 2: *The Andean Civilizations.* Washington, D.C.: Bureau of
        American Ethnology.
1960   "The Origins of Creator Worship among the Incas." In *Culture
        and History: Essays in Honor of Paul Radin,* edited by Stanley
        Diamond. New York: Columbia University Press.
1963   "Urban Settlements in Ancient Peru." *Ñawpa Pacha* 1:1−27.
1967   "Form and Meaning in Chavín art." In *Peruvian Archaeology:
        Selected Readings,* edited by John H. Rowe and Dorothy Menzel.
        Palo Alto, Calif.: Peek Publications.
1971   "The Influence of Chavín Art on Later Styles." In *Dumbarton
        Oaks Conference on Chavín,* edited by E. P. Benson. Washington
        D.C.: Dumbarton Oaks Research Library and Collection.
1976   "Religión e imperio en el Perú antiguo." *Antropología Andina*
        (Cusco) 1−2:5−12.
1979   "An Account of the Shrines of Ancient Cuzco." *Ñawpa Pacha*
        17:1−80.
1982   "Inca Policies and Institutions Relating to the Cultural Unifica-
        tion of the Empire." In *The Inca and Aztec States 1400−1800:
        Anthropology and History,* edited by George A. Collier, Renato I.
        Rosaldo, and John D. Wirth. New York: Academic Press.
Sallnow, Michael J.
1974   "La peregrinación andina." *Allpanchis* 7:101−42.
1981   "Communitas Reconsidered: The Sociology of Andean Pilgrim-
        age." *Man,* n.s. 16:163−82.
1982   "A Trinity of Christs: Cultic Processes in Andean Catholicism."
        American Ethnologist 9:730−49.
1983   "Manorial Labour and Religious Ideology in the Central Andes:
        A Working Hypothesis." *Bulletin of Latin American Research*
        2:39−56.
n.d.   "Precious Metals in the Andean Moral Economy." MS.
Sánchez-Arjona Halcón, Rodrigo
1981   *La religiosidad popular católica en el Perú.* Lima: Seminario
        Conciliar de Santo Toribio.
Santa Cruz, Víctor
1971   *Historia de Copacabana.* 2d ed. La Paz: Ediciones Camarlinghi.
Santacruz Pachacuti Yamqui, Joan de
[1615] 1950 "Relación de antigüedades deste reyno del Pirú." In *Tres rela-
        ciones de antigüedades peruanas,* edited by Marcos Jiménez de
        la Espada. Asunción: Editorial Guaranía.
Santillán, Fernando de
[1553] 1950 "Relación del origen, descendencia política, y gobierno de los
        Incas." In *Tres relaciones de antigüedades peruanas,* edited by
        Marcos Jiménez de la Espada. Asunción: Editorial Guaranía.
Sarmiento de Gamboa, Pedro
[1572] 1960 "Historia indica." *Biblioteca de Autores Españoles* 135:189−
        279. Madrid: Ediciones Atlas.

Scott, James C.
1977 "Protest and Profanation: Agrarian Revolt and the Little Tradition." *Theory and Society* 4:1–38, 211–46.
Sharon, Douglas
1976 "Distribution of the *mesa* in Latin America." *Journal of Latin American Lore* 2(1):71–95.
Shiels, W. Eugene
1961 *King and Church: The Rise and Fall of the Patronato Real.* Chicago: Loyola University Press.
Silva Santisteban, Fernando
1978 "El tiempo de cinco días en los mitos de Huarochirí." In *Etnohistoria y antropología andina* 1:209–20. Lima: Museo Nacional de Historia.
Simmel, Georg
1955 *Conflict and the Web of Group-Affiliations.* Translated by Kurt H. Wolff and Reinhard Bendix. New York: The Free Press of Glencoe.
Skar, Harald O.
1982 *The Warm Valley People: Duality and Land Reform among the Quechua Indians of Highland Peru.* Oslo Studies in Social Anthropology, no. 2. Oslo: Universitetsforlaget.
1985 "Communitas and Schismogenesis: The Andean Pilgrimage Reconsidered." *Ethnos* 50:88–102.
Skorupski, John
1976 *Symbol and Theory: A Philosophical Study of Theories of Religion in Social Anthropology.* Cambridge: Cambridge University Press.
Smart, Ninian
1964 *Philosophers and Religious Truth.* London: SCM Press.
Smith, Carol A.
1976 "Analyzing Regional Social Systems." In *Regional Analysis.* Vol. 2: *Social Systems.* New York: Academic Press.
Smith, Waldemar
1977 *The Fiesta System and Economic Change.* New York: Columbia University Press.
Snyder, Joan
1960 "Group Relations and Social Change in an Andean Village." Ph.D. dissertation, Cornell University.
Sperber, Dan
1975 *Rethinking Symbolism.* Translated by Alice L. Morton. Cambridge: Cambridge University Press.
Spiro, Melford
1970 *Buddhism and Society: A Great Tradition and Its Burmese Vicissitudes.* New York: Harper and Row.
Stein, William W.
1961 *Hualcan: Life in the Highlands of Peru.* Ithaca: Cornell University Press.
Stern, Steve J.
1982 *Peru's Indian Peoples and the Challenge of Spanish Conquest: Huamanga to 1640.* Madison: University of Wisconsin Press.
Stirrat, R. L.
1981 "The Shrine of St Sebastian at Mirisgama: An Aspect of the Cult of the Saints in Catholic Sri Lanka." *Man,* n.s. 16:183–200.

Sumption, Jonathan
    1975   *Pilgrimage: An Image of Mediaeval Religion*. London: Faber and Faber.

Sur (Boletín informativo agrario)
        Cusco: Centro de Estudios Rurales Andinos "Bartolomé de las Casas."

Swinburne, Richard
    1970   *The Concept of Miracle*. London: Macmillan.

Tambiah, S. J.
    1970   *Buddhism and the Spirit Cults in Northeast Thailand*. Cambridge: Cambridge University Press.
    1979   "A Performative Approach to Ritual." *Proceedings of the British Academy* 15:115–69.

Taylor, Gerald
    1980a   "Avant-propos." In *Rites et traditions de Huarochirí*, edited and translated by Gerald Taylor. Paris: Éditions L'Harmattan.
    1980b   "Glossaire." In *Rites et traditions de Huarochirí*, edited and translated by Gerald Taylor. Paris: Éditions L'Harmattan.

Tejado, Mario P.
    1943   "Estudio de la comunidad de Caipe, Abancay." *Monografías Geografía Humana del Perú* 2 (25). Archivo Histórico del Cusco. MS.

Torero, Alfredo
    1972   "Lingüística e historia de los Andes del Perú y Bolivia." In *El Reto de Multilingüismo en el Perú,* edited by Alberto Escobar. Perú Problema no. 9. Lima: Instituto de Estudios Peruanos.

Tuan, Yi-Fu
    1977   *Space and Place: The Perspective of Experience*. London: Edward Arnold.

Turner, Victor W.
    1967   "Symbols in Ndembu ritual." In *The Forest of Symbols,* by Victor W. Turner. Ithaca: Cornell University Press.
    1969   *The Ritual Process: Structure and Anti-Structure*. London: Routledge & Kegan Paul.
    1974a   "Pilgrimages as Social Processes." In *Dramas, Fields and Metaphors: Symbolic Action in Human Society,* by Victor W. Turner. Ithaca: Cornell University Press.
    1974b   "Pilgrimage and Communitas." *Studia Missionalia* 23:305–27.

Turner, Victor W., and Edith Turner
    1978   *Image and Pilgrimage in Christian Culture: Anthropological Perspectives*. Oxford: Basil Blackwell.

Urbano, Henrique-Osvaldo
    1974   "La representación andina del tiempo y del espacio en la fiesta." *Allpanchis* 7:9–48.
    1980   "Dios Yaya, Dios Churi y Dios Espíritu: modelos trinitarios y arqueología mental en los Andes." *Journal of Latin American Lore* 6:111–27.
    1981   *Wiracocha y Ayar: héroes y funciones en las sociedades andinas*. Biblioteca de la Tradición Oral Andina no. 3. Cusco: Centro de Estudios Rurales Andinos "Bartolomé de las Casas."

Uriel García, José
    1973   *El Nuevo Indio*. Lima: Editorial Universo.

Urton, Gary
1980   "Celestial Crosses: The Cruciform in Quechua Astronomy."
            Journal of Latin American Lore 6:87–110.
1981   *At the Crossroads of the Earth and the Sky: An Andean Cos-
            mology.* Austin: University of Texas Press.
Valcárcel, Carlos Daniel
1973   *La rebelión de Tupac Amaru.* Lima: Ediciones Peisa.
Valcárcel, Luis E.
1946   "Indian Markets and Fairs in Peru." In *Handbook of South Amer-
            ican Indians,* edited by Julian H. Steward. Vol. 2: *The Andean
            Civilizations.* Washington D.C.: Bureau of American Ethnology.
1951   "Prólogo." In *Fiestas y danzas en el Cuzco y en los Andes,* by
            Pierre Verger. 2d ed. Buenos Aires: Editorial Sudamericana.
Valderrama Fernández, Ricardo, and Carmen Escalante Gutiérrez
1975   "El Apu Ausangate en la narrativa popular." *Allpanchis* 8:175–
            84.
Valencia Espinoza, Abraham
1979   "Los mercados de los K'anas." *Wayka* (Cusco) 6–7:175–92.
1983   *Religiosidad popular cuzqueña: El Niño compadrito.* Cusco:
            Centro de Estudios Andinos.
Valera, Blas
[1589] 1950 "Relación de las costumbres antiguas de los naturales del Perú."
            In *Tres relaciones de antigüedades peruanas,* edited by Marcos
            Jiménez de la Espada. Asunción: Editorial Guaranía.
Vallier, Ivan
1970   *Catholicism, Social Control, and Modernization in Latin Amer-
            ica.* Englewood Cliffs, N.J.: Prentice-Hall.
van den Berghe, Pierre L.
1974   "The Use of Ethnic Terms in the Peruvian Social Science Litera-
            ture." *International Journal of Comparative Sociology* 15:134–42.
van den Berghe, Pierre L., and George P. Primov
1977   *Inequality in the Peruvian Andes: Class and Ethnicity in Cuzco.*
            Columbia: University of Missouri Press.
Vargas B., Isaias
1956   *Monografía de la Santa Basílica Catedral del Cuzco.* Cuzco:
            Editorial Garcilaso.
Vargas Ugarte, Rubén
1949   *Historia del Santo Cristo de los Milagros.* Lima: Editorial Lumen.
1956   *Historia del Culto María en Iberoamérica y de sus imágenes y
            santuarios mas celebrados.* 2 vols. 3d ed. Madrid: Talleres Gráfi-
            cos Jura.
1962   *Historia de la Iglesia en el Perú.* 5 vols. Lima: Imprenta Santa
            María (vol. 1). Burgos: Imprenta de Aldecoa (vols. 2–5).
Varón, Rafael
1982   "Cofradías de indios y poder local en el Perú colonial: Huaraz,
            siglo XVII." *Allpanchis* 20:127–46.
Veer, Peter van der
1984   "Structure and Anti-Structure in Hindu Pilgrimage to Ayodhya."
            In *Changing South Asia: Religion and Society,* edited by Kenneth
            Ballhatchet and David Taylor. Hong Kong and London: Asian
            Research Service for the Centre of South Asian Studies, School
            of Oriental and African Studies, University of London.

Vega, Juan José
1969   *José Gabriel Túpac Amaru.* Lima: Editorial Universo.
Verger, Pierre
1951   *Fiestas y danzas en el Cuzco y en los Andes.* 2d ed. Editorial Sudamericana.
Vrijhof, P. H.
1979   "Official and Popular Religion in 20th Century Christianity." In *Official and Popular Religion: Analysis of a Theme for Religious Studies,* edited by P. H. Vrijhof and J. D. J. Waardenburg. The Hague: Mouton.
Wachtel, Nathan
1973   *The Vision of the Vanquished: The Spanish Conquest of Peru through Indian Eyes.* Translated by Ben and Siân Reynolds. Hassocks, U.K.: Harvester Press.
Wagner, Catherine Allen
1978   See Allen, Catherine, 1978.
Warner, Marina
1976   *Alone of All Her Sex: The Myth and Cult of the Virgin Mary.* London: Weidenfeld and Nicolson.
Weber, Max
1958   "The Social Psychology of World Religions." In *From Max Weber: Essays in Sociology,* edited and translated by H. H. Gerth and C. Wright Mills. New York: Oxford University Press.
Webster, Steven
1981   "Interpretation of an Andean Social and Economic Formation." *Man,* n.s. 16:619–33.
Werbner, Richard P.
1977   Introduction. In *Regional Cults,* edited by Richard P. Werbner. Association of Social Anthropologists Monographs, no. 16. London: Academic Press.
1979   " 'Totemism' in History: The Ritual Passage of West African Strangers." *Man,* n.s. 14:663–83.
Wiedner, Donald
1960   "Forced Labour in Colonial Peru." *Americas* (Washington, D.C.) 16:357–83.
Willey, Gordon R.
1951   "The Chavín Problem: A Review and Critique." *Southwestern Journal of Anthropology* 7:103–44.
Wilson, Stephen
1983   Introduction to *Saints and Their Cults: Studies in Religious Sociology, Folklore, and History,* edited by Stephen Wilson. Cambridge: Cambridge University Press.
Winder, David
1978   "The Impact of the *comunidad* on Local Development in the Mantaro Valley." In *Peasant Cooperation and Capitalist Expansion in Central Peru.* Latin American Monographs, no. 46. Austin: Institute of Latin American Studies, University of Texas.
Wrigley, G. M.
1919   "Fairs of the Central Andes." *The Geographical Review* 7(2): 65–80.
Young, E. J.
1980   "Immanuel," vol. 2, pp. 685–86. In *The Illustrated Bible Dic-*

tionary, edited by J. D. Douglas. 3 vols. Leicester, U.K.: Inter-Varsity Press.

Zaldívar, Ramón

1974   "Agrarian Reform and Military Reformism in Peru." In *Agrarian Reform and Agrarian Reformism,* edited by David Lehmann. London: Faber & Faber.

Zuidema, R. T.

1962   "The Relationship between Mountain and Coast in Ancient Peru." In *The Wonder of Man's Ingenuity.* Mededelingen van het Rijksmuseum voor Volkenkunde, Leiden, no. 15. Leiden: E. J. Brill.

1964   *The Ceque System of Cuzco: The Social Organization of the Capital of the Inca.* Leiden: E. J. Brill.

1976   "La imagen del sol y la huaca de Susurpuquio en el sistema astronómico de los Incas del Cuzco." *Journal de la Société des Américanistes* 63–64:199–230.

1977   "The Inca Calendar." In *Native American Astronomy,* edited by Anthony F. Aveni. Austin: University of Texas Press.

1978   "Mito, rito, calendario y geografía en el antiguo Perú." *Actes du XLIIe Congrès International des Américanistes 1976,* vol. 4. Paris: Fondation Singer Polignac.

1982   "Bureaucracy and Systematic Knowledge in Andean Civilization." In *The Inca and Aztec States 1400–1800: Anthropology and History,* edited by George A. Collier, Renato I. Rosaldo, and John D. Wirth. New York: Academic Press.

n.d.   "Las pleyades y la organización política andina." MS.

Index

haircutting, first, 111
hanaqpacha, 128–29, 132
hematite, 138, 218
hierarchy, cult: in local fiestas, 152, 159–
60; in pilgrimage, 200–2; in Qoyllur
Rit'i cult, 235–36, 240–42; in Wank'a
cult, 263–66; in interlocal cults, 86,
240, 264; hierarchy-equality dichotomy,
7–10
Holy Cross fiesta. *See* cross, cult of
house building, 106, 108, 131
Huanca, Señor de. *See* Wank'a, Señor de
Huari. *See* Wari
Huaro, 84
Huarochirí narrative, 25–31, 40, 88, 91,
96, 273
humanism, Christian: of Spanish
Renaissance, 42; of Andean
missionaries, 56
Hume, David, 54

Illuminism, 42
images, Christian: in Eastern and Western
Christianity, 45; of saints in sixteenth-
century Spain, 45; in New World, 48;
as Christian *wak'as*, 52; and native
ethnic groups in Andes, 52, 57; and
Council of Trent, 274; Andeanized and
Hispanicized, 71, 77–78, 91, 226
incest, 128, 135
Independence, War of, 66
indigenismo, 107
indulgences: in sixteenth-century Spain,
44; and Andean shrines, 82, 173, 251
inheritance in peasant communities, 108
inka (dance), 281–82
Inkariy, 212, 217–18
Inkas: and Chanka confederacy, 25, 32,
34–35; empire of, 20, 35–41, 49, 130,
221; mythology of, 22–25, 31, 33–35,
71; ritual and cosmology of, 31, 36,
38–39, 63–64, 90, 129, 267, 275;
calendar and feasts of, 38–39, 90, 249,
273; and provincial shrines, 36, 38–40,
267; and Titicaca, 22–23, 33, 37, 39,
65, 267; and Pachakamaq, 24, 30, 36–
37, 267; and Ausankati, 32; in
Huarochirí narrative, 28, 30, 88; at
colonial Corpus fiesta, 57–58; in
colonial Copacabana, 65–66, 274
Inka Raymi, 38, 156–57
Inquisition, Holy Office of the, 42, 46
interlocal shrines. *See* miraculous shrines
Inti Raymi, 38
Intiwatana. *See* Pisac
irrigation, 106–7, 110, 119, 121–22
Islam in Spain, 19, 41; Christian converts
from, 42

Jarkampata, 23
Jerusalem, 4
jornal. See labor
Jesuits, 43, 67, 112
Judaism in Spain, 41
Judgment, Last, 128, 212, 247–48, 263–
64, 279
judicial system, 14, 105, 118; mock
magistrate on pilgrimage, 190, 202
juguetes, 163–64
Justo Juez, Señor de: shrine, 245–46;
myths of origin, 258–59; history, 259–
60; management, 157, 260–61, 265;
fiesta *cargos*, 152, 260; Exaltation
fiesta, 260–62; Easter at, 157; in shrine
ethnogeographies, 95, 183, 258–59; in
local pilgrimage networks, 85, 275; and
Wank'a, 243, 245, 263–64, 266; dual
status, 264–65; and ceremonial battle
and *parabién*, 139, 146, 265; and
Christ Savior fiesta, 164–65, 265; and
Christmas cycle, 167–68, 265; and
Qamawara, 179–80, 259–60; and road
project, 122, 262, 265; revered on
Qoyllur Rit'i pilgrimage, 185

Kacha, 23, 33
k'achampa, 170, 234, 281
Kañari people, 57–58
k'ara ch'uncho, 170, 281
Katekil, 34, 36, 50
kaypacha, 128, 220
Killki culture, 32, 260
Kimichi, Sebastián, 67–68, 70, 72, 84
kinship, 108; and *condenados*, 128; and
livestock rites, 134–35
kinship, ritual, 109–11, 116, 120, 135,
276–78
konopa, 51, 273
Kuyo Chico project, 123

labor: division of, 108; cooperation, 108–
11; *jornal*, 110, 275–76; and ethnicity,
ethnicity, 110; sharecropping, 110;
intraregional migration, 116–17;
enganche, 117; *yanakonaje*, 113, 171–
73. *See also* corvée; migration, urban
lámina. See pilgrimage icon, portable
landscape: aesthetics of, 11–12, 272;
subjective and objective aspects of, 13;
temporal aspects of, 12–13, 128–129;
as totemic topography, 11
landscape, sacred. *See* sacred landscape
language and status, 15, 86, 188, 196,
204, 226–27, 229, 240
Lauramarca hacienda, 211–12
La Raya. *See* Willkanuta–La Raya
lawata, 134, 137, 155

INDEX

Paullu Topa Inka, 66
paulucha. See ukuku
Peasant Federation, Departmental, 114
penance: in pre-Hispanic religion, 28; in
sixteenth-century Spain, 47–48; in
colonial Christianity, 75; in Qoyllur
Rit'i cult, 189, 216, 220, 228; in
Wank'a cult, 254, 256–57
pentadic symbolism: and dualism, 29–30;
in pre-hispanic cosmology, 26, 28–30,
96, 277; in modern shrine
ethnogeographies, 94–96, 183, 258,
269; in nature spirit ethnogeographies,
130
Philip II of Spain, 43
Pikillajta, 23
pilgrimage: Dobyns's theory of, 4–5;
Turner's theory of, 7–9, 172, 271; and
trade, 93, 272
pilgrimage, Andean: 1–3; and pre-
Hispanic interregional exchange, 21,
50; and colonial economy, 72–73; and
modern Cusco economy, 92–94; and
secular cooperation, 182, 200;
vicarious, 183, 279; motives for, 183–
84, 240–41, 280; as kinesthetic
mapping of space, 184, 201, 269; ludic
aspect of, 201–2; as ritual corridor,
201; as dance, 201, 223, 230;
directional code of, 201; private, 223–
24, 240
pilgrimage icons, portable, 180–82, 199;
ritual passage of, 177–79, 190–91,
194–97, 201, 241; veneration of, 185–
86; exchange of, 187, 202; contrasted
with patronal images, 199–200; and
interlocal shrines, 86, 260–61; and
hacienda cults, 170; on Qoyllur Rit'i
minipilgrimage, 228–33; and
Cocharcas mythohistory, 68
pilgrimage, Latin American, 4, 7, 203–4,
271
Pillawara, 104, 110, 158
Pinchimuro, 211–12, 217, 279, 280
Pisac: pre-Inka site, 32; Inka site, 115,
129–30; as local center, 104–5, 111,
119; market, 115–16, 277; patronal
cult of, 163, 275; and Wank'a, 256
Pitusiray (mountain and spirit), 32, 130
Pizarro, Francisco, 19, 55
place, existential qualities of, 11–12
place-bound and person-bound religiosity,
9, 59
Pleiades in Andean calendar, 27, 38,
57, 91
popes: Benedict XIV, 53; Gregory XVI,
251; Innocent VIII, 251; Julius II, 42;
Pius VII, 251; Pius VIII, 251;
Pius XI, 251
Portiuncula, St Mary of the, 44

Potosí, 65, 72, 112
pottery trade, 83, 163, 257
prelature, 272. *See also* Sicuani
president, community, 120, 165; and
patronal fiesta of Qamawara, 151, 153
production, agropastoral: peasant régime,
106–10, 119; smallholder régime, 110–
11; estate-cooperative régime, 111-14.
See also corvée; labor
Protestantism: in sixteenth–century Spain,
42, 48; in modern Peru, 16
Pucará: pre-Inka culture, 22; in
Wiraqocha myth, 34; in Cocharcas
myth, 68; and Carment shrine, 70, 85;
pottery manufacture in, 83, 257

Qamawara, 1, 85, 103–4, 106, 108;
dependent status of, 130, 162–63;
registration of, 120, 162; and *hacienda*
corvée, 112; and agrarian reform, 114;
and road project, 122; nature spirit
ethnogeography, 129–130; livestock
rites in, 133–35; and ceremonial battle,
136–40; and *parabién*, 139; patronal
fiesta of, 147–54, 157, 160, 162;
Carnival in, 154—57; and Christ Savior
fiesta, 158–59, 162–63; and Christmas
cycle, 166–67; and Holy Cross fiesta,
168; and Justo Juez cult, 179–80, 259–
60; joint management of Justo Juez,
157, 260–61, 265; shrine
ethnogeography, 95, 97, 183, 258–59;
local pilgrimage network of, 85, 179–
80; pilgrimage to Qoyllur Rit'i, 177–
99, 224, 241, 280
Q'ero, 114, 276, 280–81
Qhapaq Hucha, 39–40, 57, 267
Qhapaq Inti Raymi, 38
qhapaq qolla, 221; and Qoyllur Rit'i cult,
226–27, 233–35, 237–39, 241; and
other fiestas, 83, 86, 168, 260; and
Qamawaran pilgrimage, 198–99; ethnic
associations of, 198–199, 223
qolla (dance), 280–81. *See also qhapaq
qolla; waqcha qolla*
Qolla people, 198, 217, 221, 223, 234,
241
Qollariy, 218
Qorikancha, 34, 36, 77, 267
Qosqoayllu, 104, 110, 120, 166, 170
Qoya Raymi, 38
Qoyllur Rit'i, Señor de, 79, 279–80;
official mythohistory of, 207–9, 228,
248; Qamawaran myth of, 183, 211;
Ccatca myth of, 210, 211; Pinchimuro
myths of, 211–12; and Tupac Amaru
rebellion, 79, 88, 213–14; and
Ausankati, 79, 90–91, 180–81, 183,
210–12, 214, 235, 238; Andeanization
of image, 226; Sinakara sanctuary, 191,

348

INDEX

as marketing center, 92–93, 116, 275; and Pampak'ucho shrine, 80–81, 94; miraculous theophanies in, 87–88; and Qoyllur Rit'i cult, 221
sijlla, 82
Simmel, Georg, 10, 271
Sinakara. *See* Qoyllur Rit'i, Señor de
sinamos, 121–23, 276
siqis. *See ceques*
Siusa, 103, 106; registration of, 120; and *hacienda* corvée, 112; and agrarian reform, 114; and road project, 120; and ceremonial battle, 136; Carnival in, 155; and Christ Savior fiesta, 158, 162; and Christmas cycle, 166; and Qoyllur Rit'i pilgrimage, 187
Sonqo: and Pachatusan, 130; nature spirit ethnogeography, 277; livestock rites in, 277; and ceremonial battle, 136; local pilgrimage network, 275; pilgrimage to Qoyllur Rit'i, 280
soq'a machu, 127, 131, 220
soul, 128
space: dual model of, 108, 217–18; ternary model of, 128–29, 220, 277; and entropy-concentrism sequence, 144; mapped in pilgrimage, 184, 201. *See also* dualism; landscape; sacred landscape
sun: and fire symbolism, 30–31; in Tiwanaku iconography, 22; in Huarochirí, 26; in Inka mythology, 33–34, 39, 90; Inka cult of, 36, 38–39, 63, 90, 129, 267, 275; temples at Pachakamaq and Titicaca, 37, 275; Christian syncretism of, 63–64, 70; in modern cosmology, 127–28, 212, 220, 222; and Qoyllur Rit'i cult, 192, 231–32, 237. *See also* Qorikancha
syncretism. *See* Christ, iconography of; conversion, Christian; Mary, iconography of

Taki Onqoy, 58–60, 63, 71, 73
Tayankani, Señor de: mythohistory, 207–11, 277; and Qoyllur Rit'i cult, 225, 228, 232–33, 236–37, 243; and Ocongate Corpus, 233–34, 237; in shrine ethnogeographies, 95, 183, 258; ethnic status of, 210–11, 241
taytacha, 54
Temblores, Señor de los: mythohistory, 73, 75–77, 88, 274; Hispanicized and Andeanized, 77—78; modern cult, 76–77, 89, 94; and Corpus fiesta, 164; and Qoyllur Rit'i, 91–92; in shrine ethnogeographies, 78, 95–96
thaumaturgy in Andean Christianity, 54–55
theophany in Andean Christianity, 54, 88–89

Thomas Aquinas, St, on miracles, 53–55
thunder: and fire-water opposition, 30–31; in Tiwanaku iconography, 22; in Inka religion, 39
Tiahuanaco. *See* Tiwanaku
time, ternary model of, 128–29, 212, 263–64, 277
t'inkay, 131, 133, 137, 217. *See also* livestock rites
tinkuy, 131, 136. *See also* battles, annual
Tinta, 93
Tiobamba, Virgen de: mythohistory, 82–83, 249–50, 252, 275; cult, 83; fair, 83, 163
T'irakancha, 103, 111–13, 173; and agrarian reform, 114, 173; and ceremonial battle, 136; patronal cult of, 147, 149, 169, 170–71, 173; and Christ Savior fiesta, 158, 162, 169; and Christmas cycle, 166; and Wallwa, 112, 170
T'iraqocha, Lake, 130, 148
Titicaca, Lake: symbolism of, 23, 31; pre-Inka god of, 37; in Inka mythology and cosmology, 22–23, 33, 37, 90; Inka shrines at, 37, 65, 267; as sacred coordinate with Pachakamaq, 37, 50, 59, 63; and Taki Onqoy prophecy, 59; and Copacabana shrine, 63–67, 71–73
Tito Yupanki, Francisco, 65–68, 72, 274
Titu Kusi, rebellion of, 58–59
Tiwanaku: culture, 20, 22–25, 49; iconography, 21–22, 31; in Inka mythology and cosmology, 22–23, 33–34, 39, 90, 273; as sacred coordinate with Pachakamaq, 25, 50
Toledo, Francisco de, 60
tontuna, 223
Topa Inka, 36–37, 40–41, 65, 273
tourism, 14, 115–16, 216
Trinity, Christian, 277
Tunupa, 22, 71–72
Tupac Amaru II, rebellion of, 79, 88, 92, 138, 213; and Qoyllur Rit'i cult, 214
Tutaykiri, 28

ukuku, 218–19; and Qoyllur Rit'i cult, 192–93, 221, 225–28, 232–33, 238–40; and other fiestas, 83, 86, 170, 260; and Qamawaran pilgrimage, 182, 190, 194–95; and ethnicity, 223, 280; and *condenados*, 219–20, 238; and alpacas, 280–81
ukhupacha, 128–29
ukumari, 219, 280
Umachurko, 103, 106; registration of, 120; and road project, 122; and ceremonial battle, 136; and Christ Savior fiesta, 158, 159, 161; and Christmas cycle, 166
unay precio, 111

350

INDEX

Urcos: in Wiraqocha myth, 33; in Cocharcas myth, 68, 84; patronal fiesta of, 84, 275; and Kaninkunka shrine, 70, 84, 89; and Qoyllur Rit'i cult, 215, 221, 223, 225, 227, 280
Urubamba: wage labor in, 117, 276; patronal cult of, 275; and Torrichayoq cult, 81–82, 85, 94

Vallejo Santoni, Monseñor Luis, 87, 215
Valverde, Vincente de, 19, 55–56
varayoq, 107–8, 112, 119–21, 276; and patronal fiesta of Qamawara, 149–51; and Carnival in Qamawara, 154–55; and Christ Savior fiesta, 159–61; and Christmas cycle, 165–67
Velasco Alvarado, General Juan: government and reforms of, 15, 107, 120–23, 163, 168. *See also* agrarian reform
vertical ecological control. *See* ecology
vicinal shrines. *See* miraculous shrines
Vilcanota river: in pre-Hispanic cosmology, 31; in modern cosmology, 129–30
voluntarism in pilgrimage, 7, 172, 199
vow, religious, 172; in Andean pilgrimage, 2, 184; in sixteenth-century Spain, 45

Wallallo Karwinko, 26–27, 29–30
Wallwa hacienda, 111–12; and agrarian reform, 114; patronal cult of, 169–71, 173–74
Wanakauri, 34, 39, 273
Wanka people, 23–27, 31
Wank'a hacienda, 111–12, 247; and agrarian reform, 114
Wank'a, Señor de, 79, 158, 243–45, 282; official mythohistory, 245–47, 282; San Salvador myth, 247; Acomayo myth, 247–49; other versions, 248; and Pachatusan, 79, 90, 2434, 245, 248–49; development of cult, 88, 249–53; chaplain, 256–57, 282; brotherhood, 252, 263; *celadores*, 252, 254, 256; Exaltation fiesta, 253–57; archbishop at, 254; ban on dancing, 252–53, 257, 263, 282; fair, 116, 251, 253, 257–58; Easter fiesta, 157, 253; and Justo Juez, 126, 243, 245, 262–64, 266; and Christ Savior fiesta, 164, 264; in shrine

ethnogeographies, 95–97, 183, 258–59; revered on Qoyllur Rit'i pilgrimage, 185; contrasted with Qoyllur Rit'i, 207, 264, 282
wanq'a cults, 23–24, 51, 249
waqcha qolla, 281
Wari: culture, 20, 23–25, 32, 49, 274; deity, 23–26
Wariwillka, 23–25, 29, 36, 50
Warkar, 36
Wat'a, Señor de: myth and cult of, 86, 283; dancers brawl at, 202; and Qamawaran pilgrimage, 95, 179, 184, 186
water, symbolism of: and Pachakamaq, 25; in Huarochirí narrative, 26–27, 30–31; in Inka cosmology, 37; in Taki Onqoy, 59; of Christian shrines, 66, 68–70, 82, 85, 147, 190, 228, 238, 245, 247, 250, 254. *See also* Titicaca, Lake
watershed, symbolism of, 31. *See also* Willkanuta-La Raya
wayno, 134–35, 150, 194, 277
wayri ch'uncho, 195, 219, 222–23; and Qoyllur Rit'i cult, 192, 211, 226, 229–31, 233–34, 237–39; and other fiestas, 86, 168; troupes brawl, 202; and Qamawaran pilgrimage, 182,190,195, 198–99; ethnic associations of, 198–99, 211, 223
weaving, 114, 140, 192
Weber, Max, 6, 50
Willkanuta–La Raya, 31; Inka pilgrimage to, 38–39, 81, 83–85, 90; in modern cosmology, 217–18
wiphala, 137, 278
Wiraqocha, 23–25; in Huarochirí narrative, 26; in Inka mythology, 33–34, 37, 39, 71; Inka cult of, 38–39
Wiraqocha Inka, 34–35
Wiraqochapampa, 23
wool trade, 80, 88, 113, 116, 134, 173

yanakonaje. *See* labor
Yauyo people, 26
Yucatán (Mexico), 8
Yunka people, 26–28
yunsa, 278
Yupanki. *See* Pachakuti

351